Sisters on the Bridge of Fire

Sisters on the Bridge of Fire

One Woman's Journey in Afghanistan, India and Pakistan

Debra Denker

Schaffner Press
Tucson, Arizona

For information:
Schaffner Press, Inc.
PMB 313
4725 Sunrise Drive
Tucson, AZ 85718

FIRST PRINTING

Library of Congress Cataloging-in-Publication Data

Denker, Debra
Sisters on the Bridge of Fire: One Woman's Journey in Afghanistan, India and Pakistan/
Debra Denker
ISBN: 0971059810
1. Pers.–Journeys 600 17 2. Geog.–South Asia 6517
3. AE: Anlyt. ttl–Journey in Afghanistan, India and Pakistan 740 02

Library of Congress Catalog Number: 93-72784

Table of Contents

Sisters on the Bridge of Fire

Acknowledgements

Deep and heartfelt thanks are due to my parents, Maria and Joseph Denker, for their unstinting support of me throughout all the strange perambulations of my life as a writer and a healer.

Special thanks to my dear friend, sister, and fellow writer Tara Lumpkin, for her belief in me and my writing through challenging times. Her feistiness, courage, and optimism are a continuing inspiration to me.

After two decades, I remain grateful for the presence of my Afghan sister Fatana Ishaq Gailani and her husband Syed Ishaq Gailani in my life. Their commitment to human rights, women's rights, and peaceful solutions is an awesome ideal to live up to. I would also like to thank their eldest daughter, Wana, now a young married woman, for her support and prayers.

Jan Hardy and Jennifer Heath have shared the love and heartbreak of Afghanistan as only those who have lived there can. Thanks also to Eetla Soracco, my elder healer, and to Cynthia Brumm, Gail Watanabe, Kathy Moray, Maria Rose Nevels, Susan Goseyun, Nonny Ekedal, Kathleen Dittmer, Dianne Barnes, Mary Kay Arthaud, Clare Applegate, Alan Auslander, and Daniella D'Amore for supporting me through a healing process while war raged outside.

Great gratitude is also due to the Tibetan community of Santa Fe, and to my Tibetan Buddhist and Bon-po teachers throughout the world, for showing me the way of compassion and wisdom, and a glimpse of Bodhisattvahood.

Last but not least, I would like to thank my publisher Tim Schaffner for having the wisdom and insight to see the need for reprinting this book long before events focused attention on Afghanistan.

Preface

Debra Denker follows in a line of courageous women travellers and explorers of Asia beginning in the Victorian era. Luree Miller's wonderful book, *On Top of the World: Five Women Explorers in Tibet* tells the stories of five intrepid women who followed their dream of adventure and exploration into the wilds of Central Asia. And in Debra Denker's account of the first five of her fifteen years of following her vision amidst the wild high places and teeming cities of Asia, we see themes common to those women who traveled before her.

In 1869, Nina Mazuchelli organized an Himalayan expedition that led to her realizing her childhood dream of seeing Mount Everest. She was the first Western woman to do so. Annie Taylor, a romantic missionary in China in the 1890's, risked her life when she crossed into forbidden Tibet and traveled 1,300 miles in seven months.

Isabella Byrd, an invalid in the confines of Victorian society, took on a new energy in the rarefied air of high Asia. According to Luree Miller, Byrd "laughed at fatigue, was indifferent to the terrors of danger, she was careless of what the day might bring forth in the matter of food."

"What had I dared to dream...Into what mad adventures was I about to throw myself?" Alexandra David-Neel asked herself in 1926 as she began her extraordinary 2,000-mile-long walk across the frozen Tibetan Plateau from China to Lhasa, the forbidden capitol of Tibet.

These early women traveled on their own, without benefit of sponsorship and direct support. They were equipped with unquenchable curiosity and a spirit of independence. They cheerfully withstood great danger, hardship and discomfort in pursuit of their dreams. And so too did Debra Denker. No misfortune, not the loss of friends nor the theft of many of her most valued possessions daunted her from her goals of better understanding and documenting the lives of the people of Asia.

Debra's writing and photography especially articulated the voices of women and children, so frequently overlooked by the traditional media. For her, becoming a blood sister with a woman of the shamanistic Kalash tribe in a remote valley in Northern Pakistan was one of the most significant events in her life.

The people and land of Afghanistan are a special passion of Debra's. With the dreadful invasion of Afghanistan by the Soviet Union, Debra became committed to telling the world about the country she so loved and the horror of the war that was devastating it. She hoped that her writing could help people to understand and take action so that Afghanistan could be liberated from the Soviets.

Debra Denker's documentary, *A Nation Uprooted: Afghan Refugees in Pakistan,* her writing and photography, all increased public awareness of the plight of Afghanistan. A major achievement was Debra's poignant 1985 cover story in *National Geographic* magazine about the plight of Afghanistan. Many of the 14 million subscribers of *National Geographic* were doubtless moved as I was by the issue with the Afghan refugee girl with the haunting blue-green eyes on the cover of the issue containing Debra's eloquent account of her intrepid trip into Afghanistan during the war.

We should applaud Debra Denker for her intense love of the peoples of Asia, her courage in following her dreams regardless of personal cost, and her willingness to share her knowledge and experiences. Her passion and devotion will inspire us all to achieve our own dreams.

Arlene Blum
Berkeley
May, 1993

Prologue: Quest for Thirst

THE WORLD HAS CHANGED since I took the journeys described in this book. India and Pakistan are now both avowed nuclear powers, the Soviet Union and its brand of Communism have disintegrated, and global warming and other environmental degradation have accelerated. Many of the places described as I experienced them no longer exist as they did two decades ago.

Afghanistan, one of the homes of my heart, has been decimated, but hope glimmers and shifts, as intangible and tantalizing as the northern lights. Possibly Afghanistan will arise like the phoenix I saw in a dream twenty-two years ago. Perhaps the Afghan people will at last know the life of peace, freedom, and human rights, including rights for women, that so many of my friends have envisioned in these decades of exile and war.

The most frequent questions I am asked are, "Why did you ever want to go to Afghanistan?" and "Why did you travel alone?"

I was an accidental journalist, an aspiring writer looking for a peaceful place to write poetry and novels, drawn by reincarnational memories both sweet and horrific. In 1979, the Western press had so little coverage of Afghanistan that I had no idea until I was landing that the country was under martial law and over 10,000 people were in prison. I had no concept that I would soon find myself in the middle of a war.

Like many before me and since, I fell in love with the land of Afghanistan, and had my heart broken over and over again. I found a warm, loving and passionate people, a nation of poets and builders. I found resiliency and courage, the kind of courage that enabled poorly armed villages to take on superpowers, and Afghan women to risk their lives opposing both foreign invasions and alien religious fundamentalism.

The tradition of journalism, eviscerated as it has been by an age of sound bites and banner headlines, is to ask and answer the "Five W's." Who, What, When, and Where were the easy ones, with a little bit of persistence and research. The nagging and sometimes agonizing fifth "W," "Why?" remains far more complex and elusive.

"Why?" speaks to history, to economics, to spirituality, ultimately to a holistic view of the world. One cannot begin to answer the question through the fixed lenses of culture, nation of origin, class, economic status, education, or religious upbringing. One needs the flexibility to zoom in on details, and simultaneously look at the big picture, if not the whole one.

With the aid of friends and strangers, I have endeavored to ask the right questions and truthfully communicate the synthesis of answers to as many people as possible. It is said that "truth is the first casualty of war," but I and many others who have witnessed the heinous human cost of war have labored and prayed to get our facts right, and to attempt through our words and images to at least approximate the truth of experience.

Questions, if asked sincerely and profoundly, lead to quests. The great Sufi mystic poet, Maulana Jalaludin Rumi, who was born in Balkh, now in Afghanistan, said, "Do not seek water, seek thirst." As I have thirsted for truth, thirsted to be of service in planetary healing, and thirsted for enlightenment while struggling to learn the grace of non-attachment, I have come to understand something of this paradoxical phrase. It is in seeking rather than satiation that we most find fulfillment. It is the journey rather than the destination that hones our souls in a crucible of fire at once excruciating and ecstatic. And if we get the lesson and emerge from the fire scathed or unscathed, we may at last learn to live our lives with the passion of poets and the non-attachment of spiritual masters.

Quests, by their very nature, ultimately are conducted alone. Certainly there are companions and guides upon the path, but in the end each individual soul must find his or her own way to melt into Oneness. I had not intended to travel alone through Asia for so many years, but in retrospect the temporary courage engendered in me by necessity and circumstances could only have arisen from my solitude.

Whatever faith I have learned, and tested, and lost, and learned again, comes from having forced myself into dependence on Spirit's guidance to the right people and places in the perfect timing.

This book is not only about Afghanistan. It chronicles my journeys—pilgrimages really, personal, professional, and spiritual—throughout Central and South Asia from 1979-1984. These were formative years of my youth, and crucial to the contemporary history of these parts of the world. It was a time during which many ancient and timeless cultures and their unique and varied ways of perceiving the world have become threatened by the growing specter of globalization--long before we had a word for it.

Change is inevitable. Impermanence, as the Buddhists tell us, is part and parcel of life. But in this world of samsaric illusion, we are given choices. If we choose to live our lives in a compassionate manner, then we fight the valiant fight for human rights, a healed environment for future generations, and the preservation of the cultures, languages and sacred traditions that give rise to differing perceptions of reality.

Twenty-two years ago I climbed to the head of the giant Buddha at Bamyan, an ancient image of deity that is no more, having been destroyed in spring of 2001 by Taliban fundamentalists impervious to world outcry. I stood breathlessly looking out upon the early spring valley, hearing the murmurs of monks chanting nearly two thousand years ago, and the later screams of the valley's inhabitants slaughtered by the hordes of Genghis Khan in 1220. I listened to the soft sounds of the land beingtilled, to the underlying rhythms of the seasons, to the Muslim calls and responses to prayer of the Hazara people who inhabit the land. And suddenly with a heavy heart I knew that the wars were not yet over here. A sob for what was to come wrenched my throat. Words formed, and became a poem:

> Jets screamed over Afghanistan
> And on across the five-nation region
> Needling the sky
> And embroidering the Earth with death.
> The war at the center of the world had begun.

There was an inevitability about this vision's content, but not its form. I knew then that the Soviets would invade, and that a long and bloody war would ensue. In this moment of vision I saw that this war would end one day with a Soviet withdrawal, but civil war, fueled by fundamentalist ideology and armed by great powers, would follow.

Afghanistan has been devastated, a million lost, a million orphaned, ten million land mines scattered in fields and farms, mountains and pastures. But perhaps finally the time of healing is at hand. Perhaps at last, a tad wearily, the nation and people of Afghanistan will rise like a phoenix from the ashes of human folly.

During my travels and since I have been deeply moved by the courage of Afghan and other Asian women, be they the women of Hunza, Tibet, India, or the Kalash tribe. They have been Muslim, Christian, Buddhist, Hindu, and shamanic. They have exhibited a passion for life and for the Earth. Some, like Mrs. Fatana Gailani, who has worked tirelessly for human and women's rights while running a clinic and school in the Afghan refugee camps in Pakistan, are still in my life, still my inspirations.

When I think I'm having a bad day, I think of Fatana getting up every morning under a death threat from the Taliban and going out with bodyguards to do her work. I think of the sisters of the Missionaries of Charity, the order Mother Teresa founded, joyfully working with the dying and those suffering from leprosy. I think of Tibetan nuns and laywomen, risking imprisonment and torture for their country's freedom and their Buddhist Dharma. I think of the Hindu women investigating the murders of women for dowries, and of the women in mountain villages and teeming cities struggling courageously to support their families and maintain their dignity.

I hope that the story of the Afghan women under the Taliban will not soon be a forgotten footnote in history. I hope that the story of the Afghan boys orphaned by war and raised in an environment without feminine love will move us to compassion and understanding rather than reflexive hatred of the Taliban's repressive actions.

It feels appropriate to dedicate this edition to the courageous women of Afghanistan who embody the courage of women throughout the world. In these times of accelerated change, it is the resurgence of the feminine spirit, which must occur within the hearts of both women and men, that can correct the imbalances of the past 4,000 years of patriarchal domination, and create a balanced humanity with the wisdom and compassion to heal our beautiful and fragile planet's ecosystem and human systems.

Santa Fe
November, 2001

1 Wildflowers and War

Afghanistan, Spring, 1983

The Soviet helicopter gunship hovers, a vicious metal insect blotting out the intense blue sky above this roofless stone shelter. I realize that the inside of my sleeping bag is bright yellow, and I am exposed. I panic, and wake up from this restless dream—but to my horror I hear thundering rotors splitting the early morning sky. I frantically pull on my boots, cursing and praying as I look for the Afghan freedom fighters who have brought me to this mountain stronghold.

Haji comes running, shouting urgently in Dari, the Afghan dialect of Persian. "Come on, hurry!"

He grabs my hand, but I hold back, afraid of the open space outside the stone shelter. "Where?"

"To a beautiful place, a safe place. Hurry!"

The sound of the helicopter is louder, echoing in the narrow valley as if the sky itself is being chopped to pieces. I abandon everything except my camera and journalist's notebook, and follow Haji. Skittering down the side of the rocky cliff, I try to ignore the searing pain in my right knee, which I sprained last night on our long trek across the Kunar Valley.

The roar of gunships engulfs me, but to my surprise and relief they are far away over the main valley. Around a bend we scramble up an even steeper path to a deep natural cleft in the tawny mountain rock. It is well hidden, and the Mujahedeen, the Afghan guerrillas fighting the Soviet occupation of their homeland, have strewn the floor with fresh straw. Haji gallantly spreads his camel-colored wool blanket on the ground for me, then barks at me to get some sleep while he goes to find out what is going on. I cannot sleep. Ever since I read science fiction stories about future totalitarian states as a child, helicopters have populated my nightmares. I try to control my fear by controlling my breathing. I wonder if anyone knows that there is an American woman journalist here? What if someone in the last village talked too much? What if my disguise isn't fooling anyone? The government post, manned by Afghan conscripts and Soviet officers, is just up the Kunar Valley from the place where the stream flowing down this twisting side valley meets the muddy torrent of the river we crossed last night on an inflated skin raft.

Haji finally returns, bringing my camera bag and daypack. His peaked black karakul cap is set at a jaunty angle, framing his thin young face with its wispy mustache. He is a kind man who takes seriously his responsibility of escorting me through the war zone, but his penchant for melodrama makes me nervous. I am glad that the calmer Kamal is with him. "What is happening?" I shout to them in Dari.

"The Mujahedeen are attacking a Soviet tank convoy down on the road," Haji replies. "Our guard spotted it just after you went to sleep, and everybody else went down there."

I nod soberly. There is not a single anti-tank weapon among these twenty-five men. The six who are with me are armed with two Kalashnikov AK-47 semi-automatics, two .303 rifles dating from 1942, two pistols, and an assortment of grenades.

I am ordered to stay in the cave, as my bad knee would only slow them down. Down for the count on only my second day in Afghanistan, I am furious with myself. As I listen to Haji and Kamal argue over who will take a turn fighting first, I feel a profound sense of unreality. It is as if this is a movie war, and I must pass the time waiting for the frames to go by and the dust to settle to find out who survives and who won—if there can be a winner.

Gloomily, I wonder why I am here, and whether I will be able to accomplish my fervent goals. I am a freelance writer, and though I have a few major articles to my credit, I have no assurances that I will be able to publish anything about this risky trip to Afghanistan. It is a subject rarely in the news in the early 1980's, but one about which I have come to care passionately.

No amount of mere money would make me do this, I reflect. I am not here for the challenge, or the adventure, or even for my career, but because I know that my writing ability and my knowledge of Afghan customs and the language can give the American people some insight into this lopsided war. There are three million Afghan refugees in Pakistan, the largest refugee concentration in the world, and another million or so in Iran. The death toll since the Soviet invasion of December, 1979, is edging towards half a million. On this trip I have passed through the ghostly moonlit wreckage of bombed villages, and the agricultural land left untended because the irrigation water has been cut off and small "butterfly" bombs dropped in fields and along pathways.

But the bullets and bombs look the same in Afghanistan and El Salvador, Lebanon and Nicaragua. I am far more interested in the human face of war. My aim is to be a cultural translator, a channel through which an Afghan mother, widow, fighter, or wounded child, can express words and thoughts to Americans. I want to make this war real to my readers, even though it seems unreal to me while I am in the middle of it. I owe it to Haji and Kamal and their families, and to my Afghan friends back in Pakistan and in America, to tell the story. These motivations I am aware of, but as I sit in this cave I think that there are probably other, more subtle subconscious motivations that I haven't figured out yet.

I am relieved that the quieter, more thoughtful Kamal has stayed with me while the brash Haji has rejoined the fighters. At last the circling helicopters go off in search of other prey, but now artillery shells begin to fall nearby with sharp, echoing explosions. I gasp involuntarily at each one, and in between listen intently to the sound of birdsong and the gurgling river.

The beauty of this land makes it deceptively peaceful. Only in mountains is the sky this painful, lucid blue, and the scents and sights of spring this intense. This is a place I would want to laze for hours listening to the stream and the birds. The war is a jarring presence here–soon enough, gunfire or artillery shatter the sunlit morning.

Kamal sees that I am in pain every time I shift my position in the small cave, and offers to rub my knee to reduce the muscle spasm. I refuse at first, knowing that it is improper in this traditional Muslim society for a man to touch a woman's leg. But my knee is so swollen I know I will not be able to walk, so I finally relent and roll up one leg of the loose purple trousers I borrowed from Haji's wife in Pakistan as part of my disguise, and allow Kamal to try the Afghan version of physical therapy.

Kamal's hands have a healing touch, and I soon feel the spasm unknotting. "American women have men...friends, don't they?" he asks innocently. "Some of them don't marry, but live with their friends, no?"

"Oh, very few," I assure him, as I shift slightly to make sure my arm is firmly resting on my thigh, preventing him from touching any more of my leg than necessary. "I wouldn't of course, and none of my friends do," I lie. "We all want to get married."

"Muslim men can have four wives."

I laugh. "Wives are very expensive." I thank him and quickly roll my pant leg down, taking care to tuck my long, flower-printed cotton tunic over my knees and adjust my embroidered black veil over my head and shoulders.

A particularly loud explosion startles me, but Kamal laughs, and points out the dust just across the narrow valley where the shell has hit. "They don't know where we are," he says with some bravado. "I don't think any will hit here."

I muse for a moment on fate, and stare at the palms of my hands, trying to figure out if that really is a protection line next to my lifeline. Kamal looks over my shoulder with interest.

"You know how to read hands?" he asks.

"A little. Let me see yours."

I am relieved to see a long lifeline in his hands, reasoning that if he is likely to survive then so am I. His is a simple hand—I inform him that he is straightforward, full of faith, and has a strong and happy marriage.

He is impressed. I ask him many questions about his wife, a Pakistani woman from his own Pashtun ethnic group whom he had married in the border city of Peshawar, where he now lives. He tells me that she is not beautiful, but is a good Muslim and a good wife. They often go to *ziarats*—saints' shrines—to pray together. "I will take you to meet her when we get back to Peshawar—*inshallah*—if Allah wills it," he says eagerly.

"Listen!" I hold up my hand to stop his conversation. Sure enough, the sound of helicopters can be faintly heard over the rushing brook below us. Involuntarily, I crowd further back into the cave. *"Sheitan ast!"* I say angrily—"They are devils."

Kamal laughs. "Don't worry. I can tell by the sound that these *sheitan* are far away. They go every day, up and down the valley, taking supplies to the government post at Chagaserai. But they fly high, because they are afraid of the Mujahedeen."

My inexperienced ears cannot differentiate between a near helicopter and a far helicopter. I cannot relax until the sound has faded away. To calm myself, I search my pack for a little wooden flute that I had been given in Kabul years before, in more peaceful times. I know the music will comfort me, and playing the flute will force me to control my breath, and thus my fear. I defiantly try to create some semblance of normalcy, even though my music is counterpointed by shellfire above the gentle continuo of the river's voice. I play familiar tunes, some from childhood, some of them bits of classical music or rock songs. I try some Afghan folk songs like "Mullah Mohammed Jan," much to Kamal's amusement, and then make up trills and sweet tunes like a shepherd might play.

After a while, Kamal curls up like a cat and drifts off to sleep. I sneak glances at him, and then stare out into the narrow valley and daydream. Kamal is handsome in the robust, masculine way of many Afghan men.

He has fine features, a thick black mustache, heavy, expressive eyebrows, and snapping black eyes edged with luxurious lashes. Long black curls peep out from under his camel-colored rolled woolen cap. Kamal looks like a sleeping child dressed in a toy bandoleer, proud of the golden bullets gleaming against the fine black leather.

I write for a long time in my journal. I describe last night's journey in detail, and write of this morning's battle, which I hear but cannot see. Like playing the flute, writing keeps me centered, and gives me a sense of detachment. I am no longer a scared little girl, but a professional journalist with a job to do and my parents' work ethic to live up to.

I stop writing and think of the Afghan doctor whose clinic we are going to. I know nothing about him except that he speaks a little English. Knowing nothing, I have everything to imagine, and draw on the infinite power of fantasy. I imagine him looking a lot like Kamal, but debonair and sophisticated, an Afghan Cary Grant. I visualize him as a poetic Sufi mystic, brilliantly intelligent and a great idealist willing to sacrifice anything for his convictions. Maybe he used to live in America–that could make him Westernized enough to respect women as equals. But he's rediscovered a new and tolerant, transcendent form of faith through contemplating the profound Sufi poetry of Rumi while serving people in need. He is a hero, his soul on fire, and he is waiting to fall in love with me the moment he sees me.

I want to write a novel about this man. Together we will treat sick villagers and bandage wounds. We will make love under the black tent of night filled with a billion candles of stars, and recite poetry to each other by day as we walk through valleys filled with flowering trees and lush meadows...

Haji's slim figure strides purposefully up the valley. Kamal does not wake up until the returning warrior's shadow falls on him. Kamal sits up and rubs his eyes, then starts speaking rapidly in Pashtu.

"What are you saying?" I ask in Dari. "What happened? Translate." They keep on talking and I get impatient. "Tell me. *Gu, gu!*"

From the expression on their faces, half shocked and half amused I realize that I have just used the wrong word and said, "Shit" instead of "Tell me."

"Uh, *bgu, bgu,*" I say weakly. All tension is broken as they let out their repressed guffaws.

Kamal shoulders Haji's rifle and lopes off to the ridge overlooking the line of tanks, while Haji settles in next to me in the cave. He thrusts his palm at me, demanding that I tell him his future.

I tell him of long life, good health, happiness and children, hoping that I am right and he really will survive this war. Maybe he and Kamal, best friends since their childhood in nearby villages in Kunar, will someday return to their old jobs, rebuilding the roads they had helped build before the war, and now help to destroy. Both are young and bright, in their mid-twenties, and educated by Afghan standards. They are literate and speak Dari Persian as well as their native Pashtu.

Haji falls asleep, oblivious to shellfire in a way I cannot be, despite my exhaustion from the all-night journey. Asleep, the proud bravado fades from his face, and I see him as his kind mother, whom I had met in his village the night before, must still see her son.

My thoughts drift back to my imaginary doctor. I wish he would come and rescue me. I wonder if I will ever see Peshawar again, let alone America. I think of my family and friends, and am overwhelmed by a wave of missing them, and wishing I was anywhere else but here. What drives me to do this? Will my stories really make any difference?

I think of faith and fate. I remember a friend who was randomly attacked while walking down Hollywood Boulevard with her husband and small daughter. So many times I have been afraid in Los Angeles, afraid to drive across town or go to the airport at night—but most of the time I've done it anyway. Going into the war zone is the same thing for me. Certainly I am affected by the *inshallah* attitude around me, and by speaking and thinking in this language where the future tense is always conditional, and most intentions, especially journeys, are prefaced with "if God wills it."

Yet I am not a fatalist, and neither are the Afghans. They will accept war, suffering, loss of home and family, and personal death, which they see as martyrdom guaranteeing paradise—but they won't accept foreign domination of their country. I have studied Islam, especially Sufism, its mystic aspect, for seven years. My quest for understanding has brought me to Afghanistan, which along with Iran is the source of many Sufi teaching stories and poems. Like the mystic practices of all religious traditions, Sufism holds that we are all part of God, and that there are many paths to return to the Creator—"I am neither Christian, nor Jew, nor unbeliever, nor Muslim; I am not of the East, nor of the West, nor of the land, nor of the sea..." wrote the great poet Rumi, who lived in the turbulent times of Genghis Khan, 750 years ago.

Yet Sufism does not counsel asceticism and withdrawal, but enlightenment through participation in the world—"Be in the world, but not of the world," the Sufis say. It is easy to find God in the harmony of peaceful mountains, not so easy in the overcrowded cities of the West or the Third World, and harder still in the madness of a war. But I remember, too, that the word *Islam* itself means surrender, and here in this cave I surrender to God's will, for this moment and in this place, and in this surrender am embraced by an unfamiliar peace.

Like a cat, Haji is instantly alert when he hears a strange sound. He pushes my head down and covers me with a blanket, whispering quickly, "It might be a Communist spy. Keep under the blanket and don't move. He will think you are a sleeping Mujaheed."

I am terrified to move from this ignominious position. Above the pounding of my heart, I hear Haji's feet dislodging stones below, then hear him greeting someone in Pashtu. The voices fade as they round the bend in the valley, and I am left alone and fearful, wondering when and if anyone will come back.

Time ceases to pass. It is late afternoon, a golden suspension of time, and silence has enveloped sky and valley. Suddenly I hear voices, but to my anticlimactic relief it is Haji and Kamal calling me to join the others for tea.

The men are cleaning their rifles, looking satisfied. They pinned the Russians down, and they killed five soldiers, Haji says. I wonder about the soldiers, probably young pimply-faced conscripts, but I am thankful that none of our men have been hurt. They are cheerful, and a few of them have picked yellow flowers on the way back from the fighting, tucking them in their caps or behind their ears.

We drink watery green tea and suck on sweet, sticky, hard lumps of brown sugar. The rest of our evening meal is flat bread, baked on a griddle by one of the men. Typically, the group is varied, from old "whitebeards" like Haji's father to callow boys just into their teens "who don't yet have a beard." They are all rugged men, native to the area. Most are uneducated farmers, but a few, like Haji and Kamal, can read and write a little Pashtu, even Persian, and the Holy Quran.

The men lay out their camel-colored blankets as prayer carpets. They lay their rifles next to them, as if in offering for this, their Jehad, not a "holy war" as it is usually translated, but a "struggle for what is right." In this moving moment of peace, I catch some glimpse of the faith that inspires them to fight such an unequal fight. They really believe God is on their side. And maybe He is—the Soviets certainly don't claim Him.

My knee is aching as we set off into the deepening mauve twilight. At home I am a complainer, a poor patient who likes sympathy, but here I try to be as strong as the Afghan children I've seen who don't cry when an infected wound is being cleaned. I try my best to keep up on the steep rocky hills, on the path I can't even see. I stumble often, and pull the injured muscles and ligaments even more. Always, Kamal is at my elbow, a reassuring presence who catches me each time I slip.

I see the dark shape of a farmhouse crowning this endless hill. I imagine ready Afghan hospitality, hot tea and warm, fresh-baked *nan* right out of the clay oven, and a chance for blessed rest. The chance to rest is all I get—the farmhouse is a shell, long ago bombarded by artillery shells from the road far below. I look down at the thin line of road, silvery in the moonlight, and feel an awe of machines that can accurately hurl destruction from such a distance. And if artillery is unbelievable to me, nuclear missiles are incomprehensible.

I lie on my back, looking at the half-moon above.

"Americans went there once, didn't they?" asks Kamal.

"Yes, a few times."

He looks at the unchanging surface of the moon, and I wonder if he is wondering why we went to the moon and didn't spend money on hunger and homelessness. Or maybe he is wishing America and the Soviet Union would spend more time going to the moon and less time invading other countries.

"I'm glad America went and not Russia," he says finally.

The men talk among themselves in Pashtu, and then Kamal asks me to sing a song. I immediately think of Todd Rundgren's "Just One Victory," and sing for them, translating the words into Dari afterwards. They love the chorus: "Pray for it all day, fight for it all night, give us just one victory, it will be all right..."

"It's a song for the Mujahedeen," says Haji. "Was it written for the people of Afghanistan?"

I sing again, louder, as the men clap and shout, "*Allahu akbar!*—God is great!" Across the wide black void of the valley we see a ball of bright fire arc from the mountainside down towards the Soviet fort. I falter, but they clap louder and then I sing even louder, feeling defiant and victorious.

Dr. Farid Hakim, the Afghan doctor who runs this small village clinic, is nothing like the doctor I had imagined. He is short, cheerful, and rosy-cheeked, a cherubic young man with brown eyes and fair, ruddy skin. But like the character I invented, he is a hard-working doctor who wears a bandoleer under his stethoscope and treats a steady stream of sick villagers, and wounded fighters and civilians, as many as 150 people every day.

Even before the war, there was only one doctor for every 46,000 people in Afghanistan, most of them concentrated in Kabul, the capital city. After the Soviet invasion, hundreds of doctors and other educated people fled to Pakistan and thence to Western countries. A few hundred remained, some collaborating with the Marxist regime, and others leading a dangerous double life, working in government hospitals by day and sneaking off to treat Mujahedeen by night. About a hundred Afghan doctors and other medical personnel in Pakistan have set up an organization based in Peshawar with the goal of staffing and supplying clinics in the war zone. Farid, a native of Kunar who studied medicine in Jalalabad, had volunteered to run one of these clinics. A doctor friend of mine had suggested that I visit his clinic for my story on the human cost of war.

Farid greets us warmly, even though he is still treating patients as we arrive near dusk. He apologizes for his busyness, and tries to carry on a conversation while treating a woman with a severe gastro-intestinal infection, and later keeping his medical records up to date by lantern light. Farid is hospitable and solicitous. He examines my knee, and gives me a tube of analgesic balm and some muscle relaxants. To my dismay, he has a chicken killed for our dinner. As a guest, I am given the most tender pieces. Though it is delicious and the first protein we've had in days, I can't help feeling that the scrawny children and women and the undernourished fighters need it more than I.

But hospitality is a matter of sacred honor to all Afghans. Traditionally in a village women would eat separately and after the men, but because I am a foreign journalist who wants to tell their story, my companions break many traditions for me. I sleep in the same room as they do, and I eat off the same cloth spread on the floor, though out of my own bowl rather than the communal bowl. I am neither fish nor fowl, obviously a woman and a foreigner, but one who speaks their language and is familiar with and respectful of their customs and religion. They don't know what else to do, so they talk and laugh with me, and treat me sometimes like a little sister and sometimes like a male friend. I realize that I am probably the first foreigner most of them have seen at close quarters, and certainly the first foreign woman they have ever talked to.

I am glad to be a part of their camaraderie. Despite the hardship of their lives, these men are always laughing. They've begun to call helicopters *sheitan* too, and we laugh together about our long walks through what I call *sangistan,* the land of stones. "Laughter is the salt of life," the Afghans say—but I also wonder if tears are its water.

Everyone sobers up when it's time for the BBC Persian service on the radio. Not all the men speak Persian, so those who do translate the news into Pashtu. They turn the dial and listen to news from Radio Pakistan, then Radio Kabul, even Radio Moscow. And they try to make sense of it, seriously discussing world issues. "Are there really Communists in Nicaragua?" "Why does America always support Israel and never the Palestinian people?" And always, "Why won't America send us better arms?" "Go talk to your President and tell him what you have seen, and ask him to send us anti-aircraft guns," says one elderly fighter, who overestimates the influence of a freelance journalist.

The conversation lapses into Pashtu, and I lapse into daydreams. The radio dial is turned again, and stops at a muzak version of "San Francisco," John Phillip's counterculture hymn to the Summer of Love popularized by Scott McKenzie. In this improbable place I hear the words in my head:

"If you're going to San Francisco,
Be sure to wear some flowers in your hair;
If you're going to San Francisco,
You're gonna meet some loving people there...
All across the nation,
There's a strange vibration,
People in motion, people in motion
There's a whole generation
With a new explanation
People in motion, people in motion..."

I cannot imagine a more incongruous song, but tears brim in my eyes in a wave of nostalgia for the hopes for a world free of war, a world that would be different when our generation came of age. There isn't a person in this room who would know what a love-in was, but as I look around at these rough fighters, some with long flowing locks and flowers in their hats and hair, I see that they are living their ideals in a way we could never have imagined, and the stakes are life and death.

An hour after sunrise, two groups of patients gather near the clinic. Men sit on string beds outside Farid's house, and women huddle quietly in the shade of a mulberry tree. Small children, the little girls in bright floral-printed dresses with jingling coins pinned to their bodices, run back and forth between the two groups.

I take pictures and interview Farid while he is treating patients, most of whom have respiratory or gastro-intestinal disorders. Tuberculosis is a big problem here, as it is throughout Afghanistan and in the refugee camps in Pakistan, where the rate is sometimes as high as 40%. For the first time I see tubercular abscesses, on a beautiful young mother with suffering eyes. Malaria is a problem during the hot weather, Farid tells me but if only he had prophylactics, it could be prevented. Malnutrition amongst young children is a growing threat, due to the war's disruption of the food chain. The clinic has German baby food and bottles of carrot juice, but resupply is difficult, as most supplies are carried on men's backs and cross the river in the same flimsy cowskin raft we had used.

The problems sound overwhelming, but Farid is undaunted. He takes each problem in stride, examining these orthodox Muslim women in public under the watchful eyes of their male relatives. Mostly he just asks questions, rarely touching. A severely dehydrated old woman with dangerously low blood pressure is immediately put on a glucose drip with the clinic's IV. She lies on a string bed under a mud-roofed overhang, patiently awaiting her fate.

A man arrives at mid-morning with an infected bullet wound in his hand. He has walked five days to reach the clinic. He doesn't flinch as Haji's younger brother, a trained medical assistant, cleans the nasty-looking wound, and he even mugs for my camera.

I ask Farid if he has ever fought. He answers that he has had to fight a couple of times, and will again if he has to. "But I am a physician first. The Mujahedeen fight their Jehad with a gun—I fight mine with a stethoscope."

"What would you do if we came upon a Soviet patrol?" asks Kamal softly as we rest alongside the path. "Would you fight?"

"I would probably shoot my foot," I answer, laughing nervously.

"You are an Afghan girl now. You must learn to use this." He thrusts his pistol into my hand.

I try not to recoil, though I have never touched a gun before. I point it well away from anyone, off into a gorge. Kamal's finger is on mine, forcing me to squeeze the trigger. I steady myself and close my eyes as he squeezes, but nothing happens. The pistol isn't loaded. Kamal laughs, and so do I, relieved that I didn't flinch.

My work at Dr. Farid's clinic finished, we are heading back towards Haji's village and the border at the top of the mountain wall on the other side of the Kunar Valley. My knee still aches, and I often grit my teeth against the pain, but I have no choice but to walk. Sometimes Kamal carries me on his back over a stream, and though I am embarrassed, I am grateful. Somehow I must make it to the border, and back to Peshawar.

We walk by day in this part of the country, a liberated zone which the Mujahedeen insist is safe. But I keep expecting a helicopter to come roaring over a ridge, guns blazing, and as we walk I pick out hiding places under trees and rock overhangs.

All over the ground under our feet grow wildflowers, tiny alpine flowers in shades of yellow, milk-white, young rose, violet, and blue the lapis lazuli color of Afghanistan's gems and skies. Kamal picks some flowers for me, and as I walk I clutch these precious bits of beauty amidst destruction. When we stop to rest, I press them in my journal, so I will always have a little of the color and scent of this tortured land.

From the top of the mountain ridge I can see the Kunar Valley, and the side valleys through which we have come, their emerald terraces green with weeds, not new wheat. Looking at the deep pink blossoms of a fruit tree in a grassy field, I cannot believe this land is at war. But all around is war's debris: unexploded bombs, the sinister green plastic wings of exploded "butterfly" mines, the twisted wreckage of road-building equipment blooming orange in the dust, the bomb craters, the piles of rubble that once were houses, and the flapping green pennants of the graves of the martyrs.

The only machines here now are machines of death and destruction, the work of the devil done by the hand of man. The task of rebuilding after this war will be tremendous. But with everything against the Afghans, I still don't see how they can lose this war, not after I have lived with their faith daily. For this is the same faith that the slight shepherd and future king David had when he slew the giant Goliath armed with only a slingshot, skill, cleverness, and his own belief.

2 Raw and Green

"Much travel is needed before the raw one is ripened."
–Saadi, the Persian poet

Kabul, Afghanistan,
Spring, 1979

I breathe deeply of the air of another glorious Central Asian spring, unaware that four years later I and this land will be witness to a devastating war. On April Fool's Day, 1979, I fly in innocence from London to Kabul, and fate plays a trick on me. As I browse the bazaar on this indolent spring morning, I do not yet realize that my life will never again be without Afghanistan.

"Psst! Psst! Madam! Do you speak English?"

I look around to find the source of the sound. It appears to be coming from a slim young man wearing a *grey* peaked karakul cap and a somber, worried expression.

"Yes, over here," he waves.

I cross Chicken Street, Kabul's street of antique shops, tourist junk, and hippie hotels, and look at him somewhat suspiciously. "Yes, why?"

"Please, I need help writing some export forms." His young face looks pleading and disarming, and I feel safe with him.

"Well," I begin uncertainly, "let me see what you need."

"Please, come into my shop, sit, and drink tea," he says, plumping up pillows and dusting off a carpeted bench against the wall. He says something to a small boy who scurries off, and magically appears a few minutes later with a chipped blue enamel teapot and two glasses.

"I am Feda the trader," says my new friend, handing me a card. He pours a little tea into a glass, swirls it around, and to my shock throws it on a fine Afghan carpet, red with black geometric patterns. Then he fills the glass with three or four spoons of sugar, and lastly with the delicately flavored Afghan black tea.

We sip the sweet concoction slowly, as if we have all the time in the world. Finally, I ask him what I can do for him. He searches through a pile of papers and holds up some creased forms.

"I cannot read English," he apologizes. "I speak Dari, Pashtu, English, German, some French, but I cannot read and write, only add some numbers. Every time I send a shipment, I must find some tourist to help me."

He is obviously a man who knows what he wants and how to get it. But unlike many of the other shopkeepers on Chicken Street, he does not come on like a wolf on first meeting.

I take a pen out of my purse. "Sure. Just tell me what to write and I'll fill out the forms."

"Oh no, they must be typed." He lifts a colorful embroidered cover from a carved wooden table and reveals an ancient German portable typewriter. In a twinkling, it is set up on the table, paper is produced, and carbons are laid in between each sheet.

I realize I won't get to the post office today. I decide to enjoy the experience, as Feda is one of the first Afghans with whom I have talked at length.

I type, and type, and type. There are all kinds of forms—customs forms, export forms, import forms, lists of contents and lists of prices. Feda keeps the tea flowing until I am ready to burst. Then he sends the small boy, who turns out to be his little brother who he is putting through school, to get kebab. Throwing all caution to the winds I eat the delicious, fatty pieces of spiced roast lamb, picking them up with pieces of flat wheat bread called *nan.*

By 4 p.m., six hours after I arrived, we have finally typed the last form and wrapped the last huge box properly in fabric and string. Feda's brother brings a tray of baklava, the flaky honey and nut pastry known from Greece to Afghanistan. It is the best I have ever had, distilling all the sweetness of this strange new land.

Feda asks me if there is anything in his shop I would like as a gift. The shop is small, but jammed with Western-style dresses with embroidered bodices, antique rifles with long inlaid barrels, lapis and silver jewelry, many-colored knitted socks, ballooning cotton trousers, belts and saddlebags, mirror-embroidered purses and hats, and antique musical instruments. I am overwhelmed, and too embarrassed to ask for much. The one thing I have wanted is a small wooden flute like one I had seen a boy playing in the bazaar, and I ask for this.

Feda brightens. "This I do not have, but my brother will find you one. But this is a small thing. Choose something else as well."

He sends his brother out again, and I finally choose a pair of light green baggy trousers, a Westernized version of the traditional style. Feda insists that I take a lapis and silver bracelet too.

Near the front of the shop, on a dusty glass shelf, something catches my eye. I see three bronze medallions, about the size of silver dollars, with Persian writing on them.

I look at them intently as Feda brushes off the dust. "Very old," he says, the businessman coming out in him. "Sorry it is so dusty. You know, no tourists these days because of this Communist government. That's why I must do so much export business."

"What are these?"

Feda blows on one, and polishes it with the sleeve of his long shirt. "You want this one?"

I shake my head and put the medallion back on the shelf. "No. But I once knew someone who had one. He said it was a medal the king had given him."

Feda breaks into a broad smile. "Oh no, these are not from the king. There are many of these. You can buy them anywhere in Chicken Street. And they are not so expensive."

I smile, remembering a man I had loved in Africa, in the city of Nairobi, several years before. He was American, but had lived in Afghanistan and deeply loved the country. He regaled me with stories of mountains and nomads and hospitable people. He claimed to have crossed the Soviet border disguised as an Afghan and shared vodka with Soviet soldiers. He also claimed that the bronze medallion he always wore on a piece of rawhide around his neck was a medal given to him by Zaher Shah, the former king of Afghanistan, for driving hundreds of miles through a sandstorm to repair a hydroelectric station.

At 21 I had believed all of it. I didn't know much about Afghanistan beyond the *National Geographic* articles I had read as a child, so it all seemed plausible. Though my coming of age relationship was a predictable disaster, I learned forgiveness, compassion, and that it really was possible to go to Afghanistan.

Ironically, it is partly because of those wonderful stories that I am here, to see Afghanistan for myself.

My thoughts are broken as Feda's brother returns with a wooden flute, its natural wood painted with bands of dark pink and deep purple. Feda and his brother clap as I test its sweet tone. In the gentle spring dusk, I return to my hotel and practice tunes on a flute that will make me many friends in many countries.

❁ ❁ ❁

Kabul is an enchanting city in this spring of springs. I arrive from London just in time to see the first green buds burst into leaf against a deep blue mountain sky. Most days the air is clear, and the serrated mountains are snow-cloaked and close. A glorious feeling of rebirth bursts in me, and I know that I am ready to let go of three years of agony over lost love, and empty a space for new love and new life. I am happy here, and ready to write—poems, novels, stories, adventure travel articles, anything.

Like so many of my generation, I am "on the way to India," without really knowing why. I am at the tail end of the 1970's stream of young people from West to East, seeking something they found lacking in their own cultures. But I am not on the guru and dope trail, though I do have a long-standing interest in Sufism and have read many of Idries Shah's translations of Sufi teaching stories. Generally, I avoid the orange-clad couples with undisciplined and uncleaned children in tow on their way to and from disreputable ashrams. The sight of a strung-out French couple, their bare, thin, needle-tracked arms hanging out of embroidered Afghan vests, appalls me even while it fills me with compassion.

I am a neophyte on the Asian journey, looking for a peaceful yet stimulating place to write. I can live on almost nothing in this part of the world, and plan to support my simple lifestyle by writing travel articles, and maybe some freelance feature stories.

I spend days walking the city, from the broad avenues of Shahr-i-Nau, the New City, to the twisting lanes of the Old Town climbing up the hillside between the high mud walls of courtyards and houses. In the Old Town, children call out to me and ask to have their pictures taken. Small girls shyly take my hand and lead me, while their older brothers practice their English. I surprise them all with the few words of Dari I have learned.

I began studying Persian in London, when an Iranian friend told me it was one of the languages spoken in Afghanistan. He wrote out a few basic words to start me off. A book called *Teach Yourself Modern Persian* has become a helpful companion from Heathrow Airport onwards. Each day I faithfully study my written lessons. I practice the spoken language, quite different from the Iranian Farsi in the book, with people I meet on the street.

I soon tire of Chicken Street's goods for the tourist trade, though I enjoy visiting Feda for tea, and wander farther afield in the old bazaars. I like the shops where the local people go—the grain merchants with their burlap sacks and piles of grain, and the millers with their huge stones, the bicycle repairmen, the coppersmiths and spice vendors. I see strange foods, from huge bright red carrots to strings of small dead birds, which I later find out are fried and eaten whole.

All kinds of people can be seen on the street, from persistent shoeshine boys to elegant men and women dressed in fashionable Western-style suits and dresses, and occasional designer jeans. I pay one scruffy but articulate shoeshine boy one American dollar to stay away from me forever, and we become friends. I watch the elegant men and women and wonder who they are and what they do, but they go about their business, uninterested in another foreign tourist who is probably a hippie.

More traditional men and boys wear knee-length shirts and matching baggy trousers, with vests over their shirts, and usually a huge turban around their heads. Bearded old men with lined faces sell pomegranates and oranges from baskets on the backs of donkeys, looking as if they have the answer to life and know it. These men are far too proud, or simple, or pure, to be lecherous toward a foreigner, and they genuinely enjoy my attempts at conversation. For a long time I can ask, "How much?" but can never understand the answer.

I am curious about the women in the *chadoris,* the all-enveloping pleated garment which covers them from head to toe, leaving only a crocheted grill for sight and breathing. Sometimes I see their heads inclined toward me in curiosity, and I wonder what these women think, and if they are as beautiful as their more sophisticated counterparts who work in banks and schools, style their hair, and wear Vogue fashions. One day I see a shop that sells only *chadoris,* in many colors from light blue to malachite green to chocolate brown, and even bright red. I try one on, much to the amusement of the shopkeeper, and immediately find it stifling. But I wonder if it would be a good disguise, if it would allow me to observe unobserved, and thus not affect life around me. That night I dream that I am wearing a *chadori,* and have perfect sight, but when I look in the mirror my face shows very white through the grillwork.

There are few other foreign tourists in town, partly because it is early in the season, but mostly because of the Soviet-supported Marxist coup in April, 1978. The situation is unstable. There are reports of scattered resistance groups in the mountains. Overland tours now go through Afghanistan quickly, and only on main roads, with no side trips to Bamyan in the center of the country, or Mazare Sharif in the north beyond the Hindu Kush mountains.

I miss female companionship, and long to meet families, and

Afghan women. I cannot understand this culture only by talking to men, but it is only men that I meet—hotel-owners, shop-owners, and restaurant-owners. I cannot walk up to an Afghan woman on the street, and I do not know how to meet the educated women who surely must speak English and French.

So I make the best I can of conversations with men. I am perhaps too trusting and will talk, but only talk, to anyone. I notice right away that men seem to fall into three categories—wolves, foxes, and honorable men. The wolves are the largest category, the hungry men who regard a polite hello from a foreign woman as an invitation to mayhem. Foxes are the gorgeous Afghan men I see from a distance, most of whom don't speak English. I put a mental, "Look, don't touch," sign on their flowing turbans. Honorable men are the ones who mention their families right away, and call me sister.

My first day, a youngish man in a three-piece suit approaches me, asking for travel information about America. He claims to have lived for two years in Australia, but his English vocabulary is suspiciously American—"Just feel your vibes." Caught off guard and embarrassed to distrust him, I don't follow my intuition. I have tea with him, but warning bells go off when he tells me to "leave your options open" and squeezes my hand. I stand him up for dinner the next day, and am not surprised to learn a few days later that a man answering his description had asked two Australian women for travel information about Australia.

After that I am more careful. But I am lonely. I would like to break into this society, to penetrate the veil and come to understand it. I pray for a friend, a translator, and, in the form of a young man named Khalid, my prayer is granted.

Inevitably, I meet him through a hotel. Khalid is a friend of the owner of my hotel. He comes sometimes to have tea, and one day in the office we fall into conversation. He is bright and good-looking, a trim man with a black beard and devastating blue-green cat's eyes. He used to work for Afghantour as a guide, and speaks excellent English. We play games of chess, and he always beats me, perhaps because I am so distracted by him.

And we talk politics. I have arrived knowing virtually nothing, as little has been written on Afghanistan in the world press. I only know that there was a Marxist coup the year before, and there is vague talk about Islamic socialism. Some of it even sounded good to me, until my seat mate on the plane to Kabul told me that there is martial law, curfew, and a very poor record in human rights.

When no one else is around, Khalid speaks openly. He tells me quietly what has been written in the *shabnamah,* the clandestine "night letters" that appear overnight in the city with news of the Mujahedeen, Muslim Resistance fighters in mountain strongholds. He tells me about his uncle in jail, about people disappearing, and about the thousands of Soviet "advisors" in the country who live in the newest, most modern section of town, now reserved for members of the People s Democratic Party of Afghanistan and their Soviet helpers.

Khalid becomes my key to understanding the country. He answers my questions about everything, from fruits and vegetables to social customs and political views. He is a disenchanted intellectual. Like many of his class and generation throughout the world, he had envisioned a socialist economy as a more egalitarian system. He wasn't sorry to see either King Zaher Shah's government fall in 1973, or President Daoud Khan's government fall in 1978. In fact, he had hoped that a new nationalist government might bring land reform and rights for women, without threatening the foundations of the ancient culture of Afghanistan.

It quickly became evident that the "revolution" of 1978 was nothing more than a Soviet-supported coup. Professors, intellectuals, students, and mullahs—the Muslim clergy—were subject to sudden arrest and indefinite detention without trial. There were dark rumors of terrible tortures inside Kabul's infamous Pul-i-Charkhi prison. Martial law was never lifted, the promised new constitution was never written, and during the 11 p.m. to 4 a.m. curfew, searchlights scraped the sky from mountain tops, prowling into private courtyards and public streets, looking for evidence of dissent.

"You are a writer," says Khalid one day. "You must do me one favor."

"What is that?"

"Tell the world the truth about Afghanistan."

3 On the Edge of a Hurricane

One night I awaken to the sound of dogs barking and snapping at a cat. I angrily chase the dogs out of the hotel courtyard by throwing rocks and shouting, and the cat escapes onto the roof. I fall back into restless sleep and dream: the President of Afghanistan is a ginger cat with green eyes. He is called Mr. Gorbeh, which means "cat" in Persian. The cat has been attacked by four dogs from four directions, and ripped to pieces. I am reading about it in *National Geographic,* which has the cat's picture on the cover. I throw the magazine across the room and start to cry, but later I pick it up and read on that the cat, like a Phoenix, came back to life.

As the first anniversary of the 1978 coup that brought President Noor Mohammed Taraki to power approaches, Kabul grows increasingly tense. Tanks guard Shahr-i-Nau Park, where I often go for evening walks, and most of the park is cordoned off. Triumphal arches are constructed out of wood and festooned in red bunting. Soldiers are everywhere, guarding any probable target of the disaffected, and lots of improbable ones. Most of these soldiers are young conscripts in patched, ragged uniforms. Many have sprigs of flowering trees in their rifle barrels, and friendly smiles on their faces.

People are not angry at the soldiers, who are their own sons and brothers, but at the government, Khalid tells me. People are tired of curfew, tired of the fear of midnight knocks, tired of being afraid to talk in front of their own children who might repeat something at school. And each night the predatory searchlights leap down from the mountaintop and restlessly prowl the city.

"How long can a people keep living on the edge of a hurricane?" I write in my journal. Khalid, Feda, and even people I meet in restaurants complain about the regime. Khalid is afraid to be seen with foreigners, so I never see him outside his friend's hotel. Feda and some hotel and restaurant owners are less wary, as their professions by definition deal with tourists and bring in much-needed foreign exchange. But Feda only speaks plainly when no one else is in the shop, and even then he looks nervously at the door every time a figure goes by.

By day the lilacs sweetly scent the city, mixing without prejudice with the pungent scent of sizzling kebabs, the homey smell of freshly-baked *nan,* and the foul odors of the sewers. I go often to the park, always alone, but not for long. Sometimes men try to start conversations with me, and always children call out to me. For a long time I think "Mistah, mistah," is a form of Persian greeting, until I recognize it as "Mister, mister," the only English most of the kids know.

In the park is a fallen tree which I come to think of as the archetypal Tree of Life. Like all the other trees, it too buds with intensely green leaves. In the West it would have been uprooted and hauled away, but here it is allowed to keep growing, and its branches are always filled with children. I take many pictures of turban-clad boys roughhousing, and in their faces I see the wonderful ethnic diversity of Afghanistan. There are white-skinned, often light-eyed Aryan children, beautiful olive and dark-brown-skinned boys, and the high cheekbones and slightly slanted almond eyes of Turkomans, Uzbeks, and Hazaras.

I am drawn to this country, and cannot say why. A week after I arrive, I write in my journal: "My fate is inextricably intertwined with the fate of this country." I look at the sentence the next day and wonder what I mean.

I set up my portable Olivetti manual typewriter on the wide windowsill, where I can work looking out at the grapevine which is just coming into leaf. Remembering Khalid's words, "Tell the truth about Afghanistan," I begin an article. I hide it whenever anyone comes around, and take no notes.

One night I begin writing what I think is a short story, only it goes on and on. It begins with the yap of pariah dogs on the outskirts of an abandoned city, and becomes the story of a nomadic tribe at the time of Genghis Khan, the greatest destruction that Asia has known till modern times. The main woman character is named Darya. She is the daughter of a chieftain, and a healer. Her husband is a dashing but moody hero, an orphan adopted into the tribe who won her heart not by family position or wealth, but by his strength of character and his prowess at the wild horseback game of *buz kashi,* in which a goat's body filled with sand must be dragged to a goal. I name him Khalid.

I happily fantasize over the romantic parts of the story, but the terrible background of war keeps creeping in. The tribe goes from city to city, finding most already destroyed by the mysterious army from the east.

One spring evening, the fictional Khalid is ready to "explore the corners of Darya's soul" when I hear a tap on my window. To my surprise, it is the real Khalid. "Would you like to join me for a little wine and kebab?" he asks shyly.

I try to conceal my excitement as I follow him to the office. The owner, Habib, and his other friends aren't there tonight, so it is just us. We listen to cassettes of Afghan pop music, which sounds a little like romantic French music, and I drink half a glass of the acid red wine from Kabul's Italian winery. Khalid drinks rather a lot of the red wine, and begins to talk freely as we share a pile of delicious charcoal-roasted lamb kebab on a platter of *nan* wrapped in a Persian-language newspaper.

I learn more about him than I knew before. To my disappointment, he is engaged to be married. He tells me about all the foreigners he met while working as a guide for Afghantour, and how he dreams of going to visit America some day He has never been out of the country, but reads *Time* and *Newsweek* and asks many keen questions about America and about the Soviet Union, where I have traveled several times.

When the wine is finished, Hakim, the manager, discreetly brings in pot after pot of tea. "We must leave so the servants can sleep," says Khalid finally. "They sleep here, in this room."

We walk towards my room, and I grow nervous. "Let's sit on the steps," I suggest, "by the grapevine."

Khalid gives me an indecipherable look, but sits beside me. "Are you a romantic?" he asks.

"Yes, I believe in romance, but I don't think it happens very often. I believe in waiting till you meet someone you are really in love with."

He sighs. "You are far too romantic. Life is not like this."

"Maybe not. But one has to have ideals."

I am startled by a shouted challenge on the street outside the courtyard walls. "What the hell was that?"

"Soldiers. It's a Pashtu military command."

"What does it mean?"

"Oh, there are various things they are supposed to say as patrols pass each other. I used to be in the army."

"For how long?"

"One year."

"When was that?"

We hear another shout, a rifle's click, and boots marching.

"Before," he says vaguely.

"Is everyone conscripted? At what age?"

"You ask too many questions."

"Isn't that what journalists are supposed to do? I've started working on that article..."

"What article?" he asks sharply.

"The article on the truth about Afghanistan."

"Don't mention that," he says urgently. "Don't mention my name at all, and don't ever tell anyone that I helped you, or said that you should write an article. You understand?"

"Yes, of course." I am mystified by his vehemence, and think he is a little drunk. "So tell me more about your fiancee. When is your wedding?"

"I don't know."

"Is your fiancee educated?"

"Of course! You think we are village people, peasants?"

"No, I..." I can't please him, so fall silent.

"But my fiancee, she can never understand me."

I remain silent, expecting him to add, "Not the way you do." But he gently takes the teacup out of my trembling hand and leans toward me.

I smile, delighted by the closeness, but knowing this can never work out. "This is the wrong time and place."

"What do you mean?"

I look up at the luminous spring stars and breathe the scented air. I feel a sense of longing, but it is not really for Khalid. "Look, look at everything around us," I say, angry at his lack of understanding. "You are Afghan, I am a foreigner. That wouldn't matter under normal circumstances, but look at the way things are now. You won't even be seen on the street with me. And besides, you're getting married soon."

"I'm not married yet."

"But you will be soon."

"My wife understands. She knows I have friends."

I begin to laugh. "I thought you said she didn't understand you." I feel sorry for Khalid, and wonder if I have only made him discontented with his life, and if the role of the West is simply to make the East discontented. "Let me kiss you one time," I say softly, and in spite of my intention to be strong, we embrace with desire.

"Just one night to remember all my life," he says quietly.

The words break the spell. "I think we should say goodnight," I say firmly. "I don't want to hurt anyone, and I don't want to get hurt myself."

"No one will get hurt." It is the alcohol talking, and Khalid has become a spoiled, petulant eldest son.

I fight a moment of temptation, as I have been lonely for a long time. "If we made love, I would fall in love with you, and then I would lose you when you get married. It would spoil a wonderful friendship."

"Can't we make love as friends?"

"Some people can, but I'm not one of them. I have to be in love."

"You are too romantic."

"We need a little romance in this scary world." I get up, but he remains seated on the steps. "Good night."

He looks up, and starlight sparkles in his magnificent eyes.

"Where should I go?" he asks softly.

"Home."

"It is long after curfew."

I have no choice but to let him come into my room, which luckily has twin beds. He soon falls asleep, but I remain awake, wishing he weren't going to get married soon, that I had met him in America, that the country was not in a state of siege where even friendship with a foreigner could bring harm to him. I do not sleep, but when the morning call to prayer sounds and he gets up to go, I pretend to be asleep so I do not have to say good-bye.

I don't see Khalid for several days after that. In spite of myself I pine for him. I also miss English conversation, his ready answers to my many questions, and his help with my Dari. I fall into a routine, studying Persian and an English version of the Quran in the morning, going for a walk around noon, and writing in the afternoons and evenings. I am contented, but soon begin to feel stifled

I decide it's time to see the rest of the country. I book bus tickets to Bamyan, in the central mountains, and to Mazare Sharif in the north. I am excited to be seeing new places, and Khalid recedes to the back of my mind.

Bamyan surpasses all of my expectations. It is a stunning, high valley in the Hindu Kush range, set amongst rock escarpments of every imaginable color–ferrous red, golden, *grey*, white, purple, even green. The cliffs above the village shelter two huge Buddhas, the largest 53 meters high, which were carved out of the living rock in the first through third centuries A.D. The cliffs are honeycombed with thousands of caves where monks came to meditate in this great university. This place, in the very center of Afghanistan, marks the furthest western spread of Buddhism, and is part of the melting pot history of this land at the remote nexus of Central Asia.

I am awed by the now faceless Buddhas. Muslim invaders in the eighth century used catapults to destroy their faces, as the recently converted monotheists considered them idols. I climb a hill outside the town to get a better view, and on top of the hill I spread my shawl to catch the stiff, cold breeze in cloth wings. I feel as if I can fly all through the valley, all over the world. Suddenly I know why I have come to Afghanistan. Smiling, I look down at my feet, where I see a white succulent flower in the dust. It is the only thing growing on this desert mountainside, utterly unique in its survival and its simple, unpretentious beauty.

I gaze for a long time at the cliffs, hearing the voices of monks and conquerors. I hear the screams as the Mongols of Genghis Khan invade the valley, and the tears and songs of generations of peasants milking a harsh land. I look down again at the white flower, and caress it for a moment, wanting to shelter this stark, beautiful land and this flower from the boots of endless lines of soldiers.

On my way back to the village, a ragged, bearded man accosts me. He points toward his wife, who raises her tattered *chadori* and looks at me with sunken eyes. She points toward her stomach and says something. I recognize the word "pain." It could be cancer, it could be any number of things, but it is most likely some form of diarrhea, so I give her a few Lomotil tablets and tell her to take two now and one in the morning. "*Inshallah,* if Allah wills it, tomorrow you are well," I say, not yet knowing the future tense in Persian.

The couple are thankful, as if I have done them a great favor. This troubles me. I hope I have done the right thing, hope faith will take a hand as well, but I wonder if I've given enough, or if I should be giving out medicine at all.

In the early evening, I climb a crumbling mud wall to get a good picture of the Large Buddha. A man's voice calls out in English, "Watch out! Come down this way. The wall may fall."

The man helps me down. He is taking an evening walk with his wife, a slim, beautiful young woman wearing a conservative mid-calf length dress over white pantaloons, and a thin white veil over her head. Their two children scamper behind them. We chat briefly about the Buddhas, and then he says brightly, "Please, come to my room."

I stare at him, shocked.

"Yes, come to my room and we will give you a good Afghan meal. Please be my guest."

"Oh, your house."

"Yes, yes, my room, my house."

I follow the young family through the fields behind the village bazaar, happy to be invited into a home. Karim works for the Agricultural Development Bank. He is from Bamyan Province, as is his wife, whom he had never seen before the day they were married. When he went to Kabul University, he told her to stop wearing a *chadori* as he wanted her to be more modern and free.

Karim is ingenuous, and his wife hospitable. Though he has a degree in economics, they live simply, in a spotlessly clean two-room earthen house. Karim cleans and chops carrots while he talks to me, and his wife brings me sweet tea with lots of sugar at the bottom of the glass, and nuts and raisins.

"I'm sorry we don't have any meat," he apologizes. "If I had only known we would have a guest!"

"I am happy to be here. I am happy to eat whatever you eat."

Karim's father, a dignified, gracious old man with a long white beard and a snowy white turban, brings in a kerosene lantern, then goes out to chop wood in the fading sunlight. Karim's wife is cooking rice in the next room, while the children look at me curiously, smiling shyly and whispering to each other.

We sit on thin mattresses on a woven carpet of colorful orange and red geometric design, and eat off a cloth spread on the floor. Because of the company, the atmosphere, and the hospitality, this is the most delicious meal I have ever eaten. The *pilau* of rice, blond raisins, and carrots is sweet, the fresh *nan* is sweet, everything is the sweetness of innocent kindness.

Karim walks across the fields with me toward the bazaar, but some distance away he hands me his flashlight and says, "I'm sorry, but it's better I don't come with you. Times are not good, and we are not supposed to have foreigners in our house. I will come tomorrow for the light, and I will watch you now, from here."

I am dismayed, but thank him profusely. When I reach the hotel, I am glad he didn't come, for the manager shouts at me and says, "Where were you?"

"In someone's house," I say innocently. "I ate dinner with them."

My manner disarms him. I think he is only afraid of the police, so I go to bed, my mind full of vivid images.

The next day Karim comes for his flashlight. In the daylight he is nervous, so I quickly say good-bye and go exploring. I climb through the twisting, low passages that lead to the Buddha's head, and am rewarded with a magnificent vista of the Hindu Kush, still wrapped in snow. On my way back, a violent thunderstorm hits. Three soldiers guarding the foot of the Buddha call me to join them in the cave in which they have made their home. There are two *charpoys,* beds made of thick rope woven on a wooden frame, and a gas ring on which a teapot boils cheerfully. It is a cozy cave, round and womb-like, and on its ceiling is a worn carving of a lotus.

The thunder roars and cracks outside, as sheets of rain and then hail fall. But I am in warm company. The faces of these men, probably conscripts, are youthful, naive, and open. They smile with not a hint of lechery, and their friend, a truck driver who speaks some English, translates the words I don't know. They insist on a picture, even when I explain that my camera isn't a Polaroid. Much later I find out that this one picture captured not only that afternoon, but a whole era. The men's faces are serious, and the light filters in from one side, as if they are entering a long tunnel. I will often look at their faces and wonder what became of those I left on the edge of the oncoming hurricane.

That night, I wake up in the middle of the night and look out the window to see the full moon bathing the cliffs in silver. The statues are sharply etched in high relief, and throw deep black shadows. I stare at them for a long time, feeling a breathless sense of immortality. They have seen so much, blind as they are, and their visions will forever haunt me. How much blood has been spilled in this fertile valley and these rocky hills, how much more will be spilled?

I go back to sleep and dream that I return to Bamyan to find it strip-mined. There is a huge iron radio tower on the hilltop, and my task is to capture it in order to stop the machines from further destruction.

The driver of the horse-cart is a handsome, roguish dandy with a huge bristling black mustache. He sports a black-and-white striped silk turban with one end dangling provocatively down to his shoulder, and a tweed suit jacket over his Afghan shirt and trousers. I agree to his outrageous fare and climb into the back of the cart to be paraded by him and his fine bay horse, clad in red, yellow, and orange pompoms, through the city of Mazare Sharif.

Khalid had told me that northern Afghanistan, the steppes beyond the Hindu Kush mountains, is his favorite part of the country. This is Turkistan, the land of horsemen and history, and it has a different feel from the harsh mountains sheltering fertile valleys. Here the city of Mazare Sharif grew up around a shrine where Ali, son-in-law of Mohammed the Prophet, is said to be buried. This shrine successfully drew many pilgrims and made the city more prosperous than its more stately and ancient sister city, Balkh, once known as the "Mother of Cities."

My driver lets me off by the turquoise-tiled shrine, and deigns to let me take his picture. He leans against the arm of his cart, looking for all the world like Omar Sharif playing a sophisticated playboy.

The shrine is a rather new restoration, by Asian standards, only a little over a century old. But it is still beautiful, and reminds me of Samarkand and Bukhara. The continuity of the Persian cultural, linguistic, and architectural tradition throughout the region including Iran, Afghanistan, and Central Asia, is clear. In this shrine with its domes that seem to float above mosaic patterns the color of sky and mountain lakes, I see asymmetry within symmetry, unity in diversity, a Sufi lesson in life. Each panel is an elaborate geometric puzzle; from a distance they blend, but close-up, they are subtly different.

I wander through the rose garden to where turbaned men in colorfully-striped heavy silk coats are feeding white birds. I think they are doves, but later learn that they are pigeons who turn white from lime in the soil. But nothing explains why so many are in this holy place. It doesn't matter if Ali is really buried here (he is also said to be buried in Najf, in Iraq), because so many fervent believers have come here and worshipped that the place has become holy from the energy of their prayers. And so the birds come here, and turn white, and people feed them as an act of merit and mercy.

I want to feed the birds too, but I don't know where the men in their purple and green striped coats have bought the birdseed. A shoeshine boy comes to my rescue. I point to the birds and mime throwing birdseed to them. He beckons me, and I follow him on a long trek through the park, across a main street, and into a small shop. There he solemnly speaks to a shopkeeper, who hands me a pack of cards. I look mystified, and again mime feeding birds.

The boy nods eagerly and mimes playing cards, until I finally understand. The shopkeeper speaks a few words of English and tells the boy what I want. We all laugh, and the boy leads me back to a small kiosk where I can buy birdseed. For his trouble, I let him shine my shoes and pay him more than I should.

In the rose gold sunset, I feed the birds and listen to the strange waves of their cooing. They are part of a mass, well-fed but still hungry.

Up close I can see that their bodies are covered with peck marks. But as I watch them fly in the opalescent sky, they becomes symbols of prayer.

Balkh is some distance from Mazare Sharif, so the next morning I take a ramshackle local bus. The conductor stands outside, shouting, "Balkh, Balkh," until the bus is more than full and the driver decides it's time to go. We stop at numerous houses and villages along the way, until we arrive in the unprepossessing town.

I go first to the tomb of Rabia Balkhi, a great woman poet who died for the love of a slave. Her brother the king slit her wrists and put her in a steambath to die. There she wrote her last poem in blood. It is a gruesome story, but to me it is a metaphor for the fiercely defiant independence and individualism that is such a part of the Afghan character. I admire this rebellious woman, who might have fit in had she lived in the twentieth century, and I spend some time meditating at her tomb.

Balkh, once the home of mystics, is sad and withered from its days of glory. Zoroaster, the great Iranian prophet and founder of the religion that dominated Iran till the coming of Islam, is said to have been born in Balkh. Many of the greatest minds of Islam passed through here—Afghans claim the poet Rumi was born here, and also the physician Ibn Sina, known in the West as Avicenna.

I walk toward the outskirts of the city, now really only a small town or an overgrown village. I ask a passerby where the old city is. He points, but I see nothing. At last the picture resolves. There are no walls. Genghis Khan destroyed those too, as he destroyed so many of the cities from Central Asia to the gates of Europe. Where a great citadel once stood only gentle mounds of earth ring the site.

I walk around the ruins, and watch huge ants with long prehistoric-looking legs poke at bones and bits of tile. I pick up a few broken pieces of glazed tile, turquoise, lapis, white clay hardened by fire, and I feel a wave of grief for what must have been the beauty of this place. Genghis Khan was no builder, only a destroyer. What we can do with our bombs in seconds, he did with only men and primitive weapons.

I stay a long time in the heat, listening to ancient, long-vanished voices. First, I hear happy, carefree voices, bustling bazaars, women talking, children playing. But always the screams come after. The magnitude of that time of destruction terrifies me. And then I look toward the horizon, where the beautiful, cheerful, delicate and worshipful city of Mazare Sharif stands. I look north towards the Soviet border and again feel troubled. The road leads to a checkpoint, only 25 miles away, and I want to go there. Tashkent, Bukhara, Samarkand, all the places I visited last year would be so easy to get to. But there is a border, and my soul cries out that there should be no border here. I feel a deep sense of foreboding, as if history is about to repeat itself, and no one has learned its lessons.

4 The Winds of Destiny

Darya and Khalid and their tribe find great devastation wherever they go. Bukhara is already destroyed. They try to warn the King of Samarkand, but he will not listen to the tales of nomads. Only the elderly mother of the king and a mute beggar woman agree to leave the city. They become companions to Darya, who teaches them healing and herbal medicine. One day she is inspired to heal the beggar woman by laying hands on her throat and praying. As the Mongol army approaches Samarkand, the tribe flees to Balkh but they find it in ruins, the beautiful high relief brickwork of the Mosque of the Nine Domes crumbling. The countryside is deserted, except in the ragged mountains and valleys which the armies have missed. At last the tribe reaches Bamyan, in the spring of 1220 A.D., just in time to witness from the cliff tops the massacre of the city in revenge for the death of Genghis Khan's grandson.

Finally, they head east, avoiding the Khyber Pass, into remote and wild Kafiristan, whose inhabitants are unbelievers. They are headed for a distant place called Kashmir, and no one knows for sure if it even exists.

"What are you writing all the time?" asks Hakim, the hotel manager. As usual, the sound of my typewriter has been his signal to rush to my room. He is now staring over my shoulder, squinting at the typed page.

"A story."

"A story about what?"

"About the time of Genghis Khan."

"Oh, can I read?"

"When it's finished," I snap in exasperation.

When Hakim is not around, I work on my article about the attitudes of the Afghan people toward the current regime. I have memorized conversations, changed names, and researched statistics on population, literacy, and economy. I know it's a good article, though I don't know if it will get published. First I need to get it out of the country. Since it's not complimentary to the regime, I don't dare use the post office.

One night an overland bus from Australia arrives. They had been stuck in Pakistan for several days, as the Khyber Pass was closed. This news makes me feel nervous, trapped. I have already extended my visa once, and hope to extend it another month. I can't imagine leaving Afghanistan, and feel the future in Pakistan is also untenable, as Prime Minister Zulfiqar Ali Bhutto has just been executed.

I fall into conversation with Lucy, a nurse from New Zealand who is on her way to England. She is friendly, easygoing, and open, like most New Zealanders. We talk about the situation here, and she is shocked. Casual visitors see little evidence of how bad things really are. Then, glad to have a woman to talk to at last, I tell her about Khalid, and about my heartsickness for this man who is about to be married.

In the middle of the conversation, the door opens, startling us. In walks Khalid–drunk. Lucy stares at me as if I am crazy. I introduce her, and try to carry on a normal conversation.

"Lucy has agreed to take my article and send it from Turkey," I begin brightly.

Khalid's face closes like the iris of a camera. "What article?"

"You know, the one I've been writing. I'm glad you're here, as I wanted you to look at it before I send it."

He takes the folded papers from my hand and puts them in his shirt pocket, acting silly. "I don't know what you're talking about."

"Come on. You were the one who said I should write the truth."

"About what?"

I am exasperated. He starts to sing, "Que sera, sera, whatever will be, will be...," and taking the article out of his pocket, thrusts it back into my hand. "I don't want to read anything written by foreigners," he says gruffly, and stalks out of the room.

I am stunned. Lucy looks sympathetic, but doesn't know what to say.

Holding back my tears, I tell her goodnight and give her the article, addressed to my parents' business. "If anyone at the border asks what it is, just say a tall blond girl with blue eyes gave it to you in the Istanbul Cafe," I say, describing a physical type far from my own.

I am getting ready for bed when the door bursts open again. It is Khalid, still drunk. I know it is nearly curfew, and snap, "What do you want?"

"Who are you really working for?" he asks curtly.

"What?"

"Are you trying to get me in trouble?"

"No, I just wanted you to read the article before I sent it. Now it'stoo late."

"Are you crazy? Do you know who she is?"

"She's a tourist from New Zealand."

"But how do you know? She could be KGB."

I laugh. "Don't be ridiculous."

"You don't know. You would risk my life. The Russians use everyone, even foreigners. And they can pose as anyone too. They could pose as an American tourist."

I stare at him in disbelief. Suddenly he grabs me and tries to kiss me passionately. I pull away. "Khalid, please believe me. Everything I am doing, I am doing because of you. You're the one who told me to tell the truth."

It is past curfew, and I know he will not leave. It begins to rain outside, and we sleep huddled next to each other, occasionally cuddling, then pulling back. I am heartsick. I am filled with desire, but I know that if I give in to it I will fall in love.

Khalid sleeps restlessly, and wakes up in the middle of the night. "Let me sing you an Iranian song," he says. "It is about a man who is taken away by the Shah's secret police for his beliefs, and he is going to be executed So he is singing to his daughter, 'Kiss me, kiss me for the last time, for we are blown on the winds of destiny.'"

Khalid begins to sing quietly, and I hold him, listening to the words against the counterpoint of storm and rain on the roof and windows. At this moment I feel merged with him, even though I know the winds of destiny have long since blown us in different directions

❂ ❂ ❂

I dream of rescuing cats, sometimes from the ocean, and sometimes from people who want to kill them. I dream of battles, helmets, and grenades, and being in a war I don't understand. One night I am forced to drive a car on a circular track, faster and faster, till it is all I can do to stay in control

The story of Darya and Khalid is interspersed with visits from the real Khalid. He is at times persistent, and I determine that he is suffering from ebbing bachelorhood. But I don't want to be his last fling. At times

I resent him, but at other times I sympathize with him. I fantasize, what if Khalid hadn't been engaged? I see us falling in love, making love, getting married, living in this beautiful city. I become a famous novelist, traveling occasionally to America to see family and friends and sign book contracts. And Khalid...I realize I don't really know Khalid's goals in life. There is a hedonistic part of him which likes to drink, play cards, eat, and talk. Another part of him is a philosopher, and part just plain lazy.

Fortunately, I make some other friends. The restaurant where I usually eat is closed for repairs, so I go to another. Hardly anyone is there, and the lighting is dim, so I try to read by candlelight while eating my kebab and rice. In the corner is a table full of happy, laughing people, three Afghan men and one blond woman.

To my surprise, the woman comes up to me and says, "Would you like to join us for some wine? I told my friends to invite you," she adds, "but they were too shy."

Annick is from France, and has been traveling for over a year. Parwez, who owns the restaurant, also teaches literature in high school. He is shy, somber, bearded and pale-skinned, and very hospitable. His friend Wali, also a teacher, is garrulous and laughs a lot. Wali flirts with me, but not too seriously. The other man, Aziz, speaks no English but is clean-shaven and as handsome as an actor. He is an economics student who speaks excellent Russian, and we exchange a few words in that language, agreeing that we like the language and the people, but not the government.

At the end of the evening, Parwez won t accept any money. He insists that I am his guest, and he will never again accept money from me in his restaurant. It is 10 p.m., still an hour before curfew, but the streets are deserted except for a few soldiers in their red-striped guard boxes. Wali drives me home, speeding off as soon as he drops me near the hotel.

Annick and I meet the next day to explore the old bazaars. "Bread and shit!" she exclaims. "The smells of Afghanistan."

Annick is outgoing, charming, outspoken, and defensive of her own individuality and freedom, even in this alien culture. She tells me what I suspected–she is in love with Parwez. But he is difficult, so very Afghan in so many ways. He is morose these days, worried about his country, and has migraine headaches all the time. She too feels for the country, but wants him to laugh and enjoy their love.

"Would you marry him?" I ask.

"I don't know. I think of it sometimes, but I don't know if I would be allowed to live here, and I know Parwez could never live in France.

Even I don't want to live in France!"

Annick is rebellious, a seeker fleeing from the straitjacket of Western civilization. She had spent over a year traveling with her French girlfriend. When she kept mooning about Parwez and Kabul, her friend recognized lovesickness and told Annick to go back to Kabul.

I tell Annick about my own affair of the heart. She is sympathetic, but practical: "Do what you want. But he is going to get married, so don't get too attached."

It is easy for her to say, I think. But I am glad to have a woman with whom I can discuss the agonies and joys of love.

We both decide to apply to study Dari at Kabul University. At the university the man in the admissions office looks at us as if we are crazy. He tells us nowadays only Soviet and East European students are coming, but we can apply through our embassies.

At the U.S. Embassy they can barely restrain their laughter. But one man is understanding. He tells me that he too is fond of Afghanistan, though it is usually considered a hardship post. But he cautions me not to get my hopes up.

One day Habib, the owner of the hotel, tells me that Khalid is getting married in a week. I wait anxiously each day for Khalid to visit me. He had once invited me to his wedding, but I have no idea how to reach him, and don't dare mention this to Habib.

I am angry, slighted. We had been friends, close friends. We had shared a rainy night and a Persian song. I no longer want love from him, but I do want friendship. Two nights before the wedding, I sit up all night, playing my flute and intermittently sobbing.

The next day, Annick invites me to accompany her, Parwez, and Aziz to Paghman, a charming resort village not far from Kabul. Aziz has a taxi, so if we are stopped he can say we have hired him for the day. Since Parwez owns a restaurant, he could be our guide.

My sorrows fall away in the blue, blue day, filled with greenness and brilliant flowers. We climb to the mountains outside the city, where we picnic, and Annick and I chase each other and tease. Aziz wants to buy garlands of yellow and purple flowers from one of the small boys alongside the road. Parwez stops, then speeds up the car as Aziz returns. Aziz runs after us, laughing and out of breath, as Annick and I shout at Parwez to stop.

Today Parwez has no headaches. His drawn face is relaxed, his dark eyes not pained, but full of light. I see that he loves Annick, and wonder how any love can flourish in this difficult time and place. We return to Kabul in the afternoon, to find that Parwez has ordered a big feast cooked for us. It is *ashak,* a ravioli filled with leeks in a sauce of tomato, meat, and yogurt. We finish with fresh strawberry milkshakes. We listen to Afghan music, though as usual there is no one else in the restaurant. Mischievous Annick jokingly hangs our flower garlands over the obligatory portrait of President Taraki, but Parwez gets angry. He rips the flowers down, shouting, "Annick, this is not a joke! When will you understand?"

I am reluctant to go home, as I have a long, lonely night ahead. I am resigned to Khalid's marriage, even happy for him, but deeply wounded that he has ignored me. Had he only hoped for a fling, and then got angry when he couldn't have it? I pick sweet-scented roses from the garden, and stare into the moonlit courtyard.

The next morning Hakim brings tea and tells me, "Mr. Khalid told me to tell you to be ready to go to his wedding this afternoon."

I am overjoyed, but have no idea what to wear. I have no good clothes with me, no Parisian fashions and high heels, and so must wear my blue Indian print skirt with my new purple Afghan blouse, finely embroidered in the Kandahari style that looks like satin. To dress up the outfit I tie a silk scarf around my waist and put a pink rose in my hair for courage.

Habib comes in the late afternoon to drive me to Khalid's home. Khalid is resplendent in a Western-style suit with a ruffled lace shirt, and his bride, Aiesha, is wearing a white bridal gown. The rest of the guests, family and close friends numbering well over a hundred, are dressed mostly in elegant Western fashions. I am seated at a table of women. I smile shyly, and say, *"Salaam,"* but none of them speak English.

I feel out of place till Khalid looks at me across the room. I know that he really wants me to be here. I watch as ceremonies take place that I don't understand. Someone puts henna on the little fingers of bride and groom, and ties a piece of cloth around the finger. Then they exchange grape juice and *halvah,* a sweet mixture of flour, sugar, and oil. A Quran wrapped in brocade is passed over their heads, but I can't tell if they are making vows or not.

At the reception afterwards, a young woman who speaks beautiful English is sent over to talk to me. "I thought you were Afghan," she explains. "We all thought you were a member of the opposite family. I'm sorry, I didn't realize you were Khalid's American guest, or I would have come sooner."

She is dressed in black lace. Other women are in blue silk, or fawn-colored satin. I alone wear a shirt from Afghanistan. I am suddenly struck by the thought of all the Western travelers who wear Afghan clothes, and all the Afghans wearing Western clothes, just as we take up each other's mores, manners, religions, and outlooks.

The wedding feast is scrumptious. I have never seen so much food covering such a huge table. A whole roast sheep lies in the center of the table. Around it are platters of chicken, and *qabli pilau,* the rice dish with carrots, raisins, and lamb or chicken, and *chilau,* white rice, and dishes of yogurt, fried vegetables, and sauces. A seemingly limitless supply of *nan* surrounds the rich repast.

My new friend, whose name is Naheed, guides me through the feast, then back to another room where we eat wedding cake and *halvah,* and watch guests and family members dance Afghan traditional dance. The women are graceful as they move their long-fingered hands in ancient gestures and slide their heads from side to side. But the sight of beautiful women in *haute couture* doing folk dances is strange to my eyes.

There is one final part of the ceremony. Aiesha's father ties a green ribbon around her waist and hands it to Khalid, symbolizing the gift of the daughter to a new household. The two leave, and I assume all is over. The guests begin to say good-night. Naheed tells me sadly that I should have seen weddings in the old days, which would go on all night. But now everyone is anxious, afraid of being caught by curfew.

"Did you hear the joke?" Naheed asks me. "A soldier shoots a man who is out at nine o'clock. His officer says, 'Curfew isn't until eleven. Why did you shoot him?' The soldier answers, 'I know where the man lives and he wouldn't have had time to make it home by curfew, so I shot him now.'"

Everyone is somber, and I am forgotten. Finally Khalid comes to me and says quietly, "Stay here. You are invited to the family celebration."

"What about curfew?"

"Forget about the curfew tonight. You will be here. No one will know. We are already taking a chance just having you here. We are not supposed to have foreigners in our houses."

I am led to an opulent upstairs room, whose floor is covered with a huge Persian carpet. But all the other furnishings are Western, and show the sophisticated taste of Khalid's mother and father. Two musicians sit on the floor. One plays the harmonium, an instrument rather like an accordion, and the other a *tabla,* the skin drum of Asia. They are common men, uneducated, un-Westernized, but they are artists. I look at them, wishing I could understand the singer's words, and they smile back in simple welcome.

I notice that Khalid and his brothers and male friends keep disappearing, and every time they come back they are more full of jokes. When the dancing begins, Khalid dances a solo, then insists that I dance. I hold back, but he pulls me into the middle of the floor, and together we dance, whirling and clapping. I try to follow his moves, but he sits down, laughing, and everyone encourages me to continue. I have no idea what I am doing, so I stare at the medallion design in the center of the dark red carpet as if it were a mandala, and whirl around this center of gravity. On the walls are large photographs of a waterfall at Paghman and of the turquoise lake of Band-i-Ameer. These beauties transport me out of myself, and I no longer try to follow someone else's steps or hand movements, but simply move to the music, spinning to a rhythm I intuitively understand. The rose falls from my hair, and I leave it on the carpet, to be trampled by future dancers.

When the music stops I freeze, like I have seen the dancers on television do. Everyone claps for me and shouts,

"*Afarin!*–Well done!"

In the pre-dawn hours, the musicians quietly and passionately sing songs against the Communist regime. A sadness falls heavily over the tired guests, like a rough woolen blanket. I want to comfort them, and tell them a Sufi story: "There was once a king who commanded his wise men to make him a ring that would make him happy whenever he was sad, and sad whenever he was happy. They thought and thought, and finally decided that the ring should simply be engraved with the words, 'This too shall pass.' So these terrible times for Afghanistan must pass, even as Genghis Khan's times passed. He died in 1227, seven years after he passed through Afghanistan."

"I know that story," says an old man. "We say '*In hamah bguzerad*–this too will pass.' In Ghazni they make a ring like that, even today."

At dawn, curfew is over, and we all say good-bye. My heart catches as I don't know when I will see Khalid again. I know that he is drunk, and feel sorry for Aiesha. I tell her in halting Farsi that she is beautiful and looks happy. Khalid say arrogantly "She is happy because she knows what I am." I look at his clouded blue-green eyes sadly, and from the depths of my heart wish him all happiness.

I stay up in the morning light, which is the color of rose quartz. Hakim brings me tea, and chatters in my ear, but one of the other servants, much more sensitive, simply picks a rose and puts it on my tray. He looks me deep in the eyes but doesn't say a word.

Above, in the east, the morning star is bright and poignant. I watch, in awe of the recurring miracle, as it fades into a sky which first grows whiter and whiter, until it is like a clear gem, and then deepens. I watch until it becomes a thin point of light, like the tip of a needle, and then finally I cannot see it anymore. But I know it still exists, lost in the greater light of the sun even as the flame of a candle is lost in the daylight, but still burns on—even as the love and friendship I have for Khalid lives on, though unperceived.

The small, hunchbacked silversmith gestures that I should sit down for tea, and shows me his wares. He lays out belts, chains, and lapis rings, nomad earrings and ankle bracelets. I pick out a set of ankle bracelets jingling with solid silver bells, and feign disinterest. Good-naturedly, we bargain back and forth in Dari and English until we agree on a price. I am happy, as I have exactly what I want, and he is happy, having made a sale to a rare tourist.

Ghazni has been closed to foreigners on and off, he tells me. "No tourists. Business very bad this year. Afghan people have no money to buy these things, and now no tourists come. Now only tanks, and curfew."

I nod, and sip my tea. The night before, I had stepped out of the hotel at about nine o'clock to look at the bright blooms of spring stars, but the manager had run down the street after me, shouting, "Curfew, curfew."

"I am looking for a ring," I tell the silversmith.

"Rings, I have many rings."

"But this is a ring that must say, uh, *'in hamah bguzerad.'*"

"Yes, yes." He shows me many rings of low-grade silver with dark inlays of words in calligraphy I cannot read. "Yes, you take this one."

"Does it really say *'In hamah bguzerad?'*"

"Yes, exactly."

I look at the ring, and try to puzzle out the script, but cannot. I finally take his word for it, bargain a bit, and proudly put the ring on my finger. Now I too will never forget that, "This too will pass.'"

But the ring doesn't stop me from losing my temper when I am told over and over again that the road toward the minarets of Sultan Mahmoud is closed. I stubbornly pretend that I don't understand, but always a policeman materializes.

Finally I try the main road. No one stops me, and I reach a path leading to the minarets. The grass is tall and green, and I fantasize that I am with my nomad characters, getting closer and closer to the splendid carved stone minarets. Suddenly four soldiers appear out of nowhere, shouting at me.

I am caught off guard, and stupidly try to go around them, despite their guns. They block my way, and I sit down in the dirt, overcome by heat and frustration. "I am hot and tired and I want to see the minaret," I tell them in Dari.

One of them is kinder than the others. He takes me to the barracks and phones his commanding officer. I don't really care if I see the minarets any more, but at least I feel I am fighting, however Quixotically, against petty injustice and unreason. The young soldier patiently explains, "One girl. Alone. A tourist. She wants to see the minarets."

He regretfully apologizes, and takes me to a military vehicle, which will drive me back to town and put me on the bus to Kandahar. An officer stops the jeep and speaks to me in Russian. My stomach curdles. I cannot tell if he is Afghan or Soviet, but his accent is very good. I search for words of Russian left over from studies at Berkeley five years ago, and my throat goes dry. In broken Russian, I somehow convince him that I am not a spy. The soldiers drive me along the forbidden road, and I idly count 22 tanks, thinking what a good spy I might have been.

Every way is circumscribed in a tightening circle. Every historical monument, in Ghazni and in Kandahar, where I go next, is guarded. The soldiers are kind and regretful, but firm, even though the flowers many have in their rifle barrels remind me of pictures of Berkeley's People's Park in 1969.

Kandahar is a blur of dust, heat, and dysentery. I walk through the covered bazaar and visit mausoleums, but collapse with acute intestinal cramps several times a day. Finally, I return to Kabul, a long bus ride through the vast southern desert in the middle of a vicious dust storm in a sky that won't rain.

The next few days, the roads are closed intermittently, to the north, the east, the south, the west. Overland tours pass once a week, stopping one day in Kabul, then heading quickly for Herat, and maybe even to Iran in one day.

Revolutionary Iran sounds more secure than Afghanistan. I am anxious, for my visa is soon to expire, and I wonder how I will be able to leave the country if the roads are closed.

One horrifying ordinary day at about 11 a.m. the sky cracks with gunfire. I run out into the courtyard, and see helicopters circling the city. In the street people are shouting and running, bicycle bells are jingling frantically, and cars are honking and swerving. The war, so distant and silent, has at last come to Kabul.

Hakim grabs me from behind and shouts, "Get inside! They are killing people."

For a moment I am terrified–Hakim has shaved his head and is wearing a militia uniform. I obey him and hurry to my room to pack, but for what?

Sound is eclipsed by death, and the city falls silent but for the drone of patrolling helicopters. There is no news, and no one to talk to except for the only other hotel guest, an eccentric British professor of philosophy. Hakim tells us a daytime curfew has been declared, but it will be relaxed for a couple of hours for shopping. He offers to get us food, and starts to make a list on a typed paper that looks familiar. With a start I realize that it was taken from my wastebasket.

That evening I ask to take a hot shower, and burn all possibly incriminating papers in the water heater's woodfire boiler. Hakim comes afterwards and says, "The radio said Iranis came from the border and attacked the city."

I am astonished to see that he really believes this.

The next day, Khalid and Aiesha visit me in the evening. "It has begun," mutters Khalid tersely, then adds aloud, "We've come to say good-bye. I know you are going to Pakistan in a few days."

We sit in the hotel's long-empty restaurant, while Khalid sends Hakim out for kebab. "Watch him," Khalid says. "He is a spy."

"I know." I tell him about the paper Hakim took from my wastebasket, but assure him it was nothing incriminating.

Another servant brings a bottle of clear liquid, which turns out to be local moonshine, strong and dangerous. I put a little in a Coke, and Khalid fills a glass. Aiesha looks uncomfortable, and Khalid hides his glass and a bottle when the gentle white-bearded gardener comes in to ask where the owner is.

We eat our kebabs, which are made more delicious than ever by the knowledge that I won't have them much longer. Aiesha looks at me often and smiles, but I notice her growing sadness as she watches her new husband drink more and more. Finally she begins to cry.

Khalid is drunk, but translates what she is saying. "She says we were married three weeks ago, and the first two weeks were perfect, but now I have begun to drink."

"Well, stop. Can't you see you are hurting her?" I take her hand in reassurance and look at her with compassion, willing her to understand.

"I can't stop. Not in these times. Ask anyone. I didn't drink before this fucking government got in, these fucking Communists, fucking Taraki. Now what is there for us?"

"There is your wife, your family, the children you will have."

He shakes his head sadly. "What I would do in these times if I did not have a wife and family. I am not afraid for myself, but only for them. What will happen to us if the Russians invade?"

"Do you think they might?" But I already know it is only a matter of time.

On my last day, Khalid, now sober, comes with Aiesha to see me. They stand outside in the open courtyard, and Khalid says awkwardly, "We have a small gift for you. It is Aiesha's idea, and she picked it out. We want you always to remember that you have friends in Afghanistan who will never forget you."

Aiesha takes a box out of her purse and gives it to me. Inside is a bracelet made of seven pieces of fine, dark, oval-cut lapis lazuli set in silver. Aiesha puts it on my wrist . I thank them both with all the words I know, in Persian and in English, and say finally, "*Inshallah,* if God wills it, I will come again and see you." Behind us, the winds of destiny blow, stronger, closer, colder.

5 Alone but Not Lonely

I walk alone to the bus station, struggling to carry my heavy pack in the early morning heat. All my life I have wanted to see the Khyber Pass. I should be excited, but my heart is cold and heavy, filled with tears that brim over when I sit inside the green-and-white Pakistan government bus that will take me from Kabul, a city where I now have dear friends, to Peshawar, where I know no one.

None of my friends have come to see me off—everyone is afraid to admit to friendship with a foreigner. I feel devastatingly alone, and see nothing of the city as I leave it behind. Only the breathtaking beauty of the Kabul Gorge brings me back to consciousness. I look out the window in awe as the bus winds along the high edge of the spectacular defile filled with the wild forms and colors of millennia of erosion.

By comparison, the fabled Khyber Pass is drab. I see no tribesmen, bandits, or camel caravans. The scant traffic consists of a few Japanese cars and some garishly painted local buses, which have ceased to be exotic. Still, the Pakistan Government controls only the road and an easement of 50 feet on either side of it; beyond is tribal territory controlled by Islamic law and engrained Pashtun tribal customs.

The Khyber Pass is the bottleneck of Asia, through which conquerors passed and ultimately failed, from Alexander the Great to Turks, Moghuls, and the British. I immediately feel the transition from the fresh mountains and steppes of Central Asia to the steamy plains of the Subcontinent, and an unfamiliar culture.

The July heat is unbearable. By the time we reach Peshawar, I am enervated and move very slowly. I am in a strange land, for I have lost my language. Here the languages are Pashtu and Urdu, the national language of Pakistan. English remains the legacy of colonialism, but in the stultifying heat I can't seem to find the "everybody" I had been told would speak English.

I walk a couple of endless blocks to the Green Hotel, recommended in my shoestring guidebook. My heart sinks as I realize that it is the poor cousin of the comfortable-looking New Green's Hotel, which is out of my budget. The ramshackle, mint-green building faces onto the main street of Sadar Bazaar in the cantonment, the newer section of the city built during the British Raj.

I am grateful that they have a room, though I must pay each day in advance, unlike in Kabul where there was more trust. My room is a tiny windowless cubical with a lazy ceiling fan that sways alarmingly as it pushes around somnolent air. Cockroaches skitter, and geckos cling motionless to the walls. The bathroom is down a dark corridor, and there is no washbasin or shower, only a faucet and a rusty metal bucket.

I do not try to find a better hotel, as I must make my money last as long as possible. Besides, I am too heat-exhausted to move. I lie on the bed under the fan and sweat, occasionally swigging warm water from my water bottle. I feel alone as I never did in Kabul, for I had begun to meet friendly Afghans from my first few days in the city.

I remember a similarly dingy hotel in Nairobi, in Africa. In a dorm room, American and European kids were smoking cheap marijuana, playing guitar, and philosophizing. One man asked me, "Don't you mind traveling alone?"

"I don't mind being alone," I replied, "I just mind being lonely. Most of the time I meet people quickly, so I am hardly ever lonely for long."

The man liked my answer so much that he asked my name so he could quote me in his daily journal.

Now the memory brings me a little comfort. I have made a choice; I am where I want to be, though maybe not in ideal circumstances. I will meet people, travel around the country, learn a little Urdu. The cockroaches and geckos, the rusty bucket and the dying fan, even the heat, will all disappear in a golden moment of sunset over a minaret, in a friendly exchange in a bazaar, in an act of kindness from a stranger.

But first I have work to do. I set up my typewriter and begin an article about the uprising in Kabul ten days ago. At a crucial point, the electricity goes out, but I light a candle stub left by a previous occupant and continue typing.

It gets so hot without the fan that I take off most of my clothes and keep writing.

A knock on the door startles me. "Just a minute!" I shout, throwing on proper clothes. "Who is it?"

"Special Branch."

"What?" I am mystified.

The manager and a man in plainclothes with official ID stand at my door. "We have come to investigate you," the plainclothesman says.

"For what?"

"You wrote on your visa you are a film director. Journalists need special permits."

"Oh no, I am a film editor, not a director. I just put films together. They're not even films, just commercials. I work for my father."

I fumble around for a business card while the Special Branch man looks through some papers.

"You mean you're not going to make a film about Pakistan?"

"Oh no, I wouldn't dream of making a film about Pakistan."

The two men confer in a language I don't understand, and then the Special Branch man hands back my business card. "Welcome to Pakistan."

I sleep badly in the stuffy room. I dream of war and battles, and jeeps full of soldiers, and wake up in a sweat.

The city is much more hectic than Kabul, and bustles late into the night. Three-wheeled motorized rickshaw scooters spew out noise and pollution with a distinctive sputter, and other vehicles have musical horns that play "Never on Sunday" and the "Love Theme from the Godfather." Rickshaws, buses, and trucks are painted with fanciful scenes in gaudy colors, visual noise to match audible noise. Men fight with gory swords, a fierce bearded face holds a blood-dripping dagger in his teeth, disembodied arms brandish rifles. Amongst these violent tableaux are a few mountain scenes and lakes, and a very few women's faces, drawn by artists apparently unfamiliar with the female form.

I find Peshawar too chaotic, and far more Westernized than Kabul. All I have seen so far is the worst of the West: the noise and crowds, cars and pollution, cheap consumer goods and a lust for material wealth. Perhaps there is a more gentle side to this city, but for now all I want to do is finish my article, send it to my parents in California, and escape into the mountains.

"Oh no, you don't want to go to Chitral by road," says, the thin, well-dressed man who works in the Tourist Office. "It is a very rough trip, not at all suitable for a young lady, especially one alone."

His solicitousness has pushed a button. I am determined to prove that I am as strong as anyone else. "It can't be that bad. I've just come from Afghanistan."

He politely hands me a cup of the spiced green tea called *kahwa* and tells me to sit down. "No, no, Madam, you don't understand. No one goes by road to Chitral if they can possibly avoid it. It will cost you the same to fly, and be much more pleasant."

I take his advice and go to Pakistan International Airlines. In the afternoon, when they confirm tickets, a press of tall Pashtuns and gaunt mountain men all reach out their long, grasping arms to the single man behind the ticket counter. Miraculously, probably because I am a foreigner, I get on the waiting list for two days from now.

I am more cheerful once I have sent my article off. In the twisting lanes of Qissa Khani, the Storyteller's Bazaar, I experience the magic moments that make the pains of travel worthwhile. Scents, sounds, smells, and colors assail my senses. The coppersmiths clang, the silversmiths and goldsmiths hammer with sweeter tones, and the crowd buzzes. The scent of fresh coriander leaves mixes with the pungent, spicy odors of cumin and masala. In front of a yogurt shop stands an ice-sculpture with garlands of jasmine strung over it. When I ask to take a picture, the shopkeeper presents me with a garland, and waves away my offers of payment.

I no longer feel so lonely. In this crowd are friendly faces. I follow a procession, which turns out to be a funeral. The corpse is raised high, laid on a string-bed covered with a green cloth. Leaving the procession, I turn a corner and see a newly dead man, an old man lying on a *charpoy* in the open, his face caught in a death grimace. "He dead," says a passer-by. "You take photo?"

I flee down a narrow alley, between high carved balconies, and am relieved to come upon the graceful mosque of Mahabat Khan. I watch small boys set out rows of prayer mats for the evening prayer, and rest for a long time near the cool ablution pool before returning to my cheerless room.

❁ ❁ ❁

I am crammed into the back of a small open jeep, with eight other people. The two small boys from the Karachi family on holiday stand first on my typewriter, then on my hand. My right leg is wedged between a tire jack and an old man with a bundle of rapidly rotting meat wrapped in a filthy cloth. My left leg is bent and bruised in an attempt to cushion my body against another bump and jump. My knuckles are white from gripping the crossbars which should support a canvas roof, as my nose and teeth bounce dangerously close to the bars with each yard of progress.

And for this I am paying more than it would have cost to fly. I curse my impatience. I had gone to the airport at 5 a.m., but the flight had been canceled due to bad weather. Even people with confirmed seats go to the bottom of the next day's waiting list, and so, unable to bear the dusty oven of Peshawar for another day, I had booked a bus ticket to Dir.

On the way, the bus collides with another bus. The children behind me throw up all the way. When I get to Dir I find out that the scoundrel jeep drivers charge whatever the market will bear, including extra for luggage. I get into an argument, but my choices are to pay or remain in Dir.

The two Karachi women get the front seat and take a little girl on their laps. Their husbands, the boys, and some locals, join me in the back. The journey is like some fiendish Disney nightmare. Out of nowhere huge construction machines loom, and cliffs suddenly give way. We pass over landslides, and as I look down at the left rear wheel I see the gravel giving way beneath us. My eyes draw a sickening line from the wheel to the muddy, rushing river a thousand feet below. I look up for relief, but see large rocks bounding off the mountain above. I close my eyes and pray.

The jeep breaks down on the high pass. The Karachi family passes out crunchy snacks with lots of chili in them. I miss the tasty, but not chili hot, Afghan foods, but gratefully accept the kind offering. The two men, businessmen on holiday, speak some English and make lots of jokes. By the fifth or sixth breakdown, even they are losing their sense of humor. The driver's mechanic, a teen-age boy who has been hanging off the back of the jeep most of the way, periodically leaps off and throws buckets of water from nearby streams on the engine to cool it. According to the Tourist Office brochure, this drive on the "jeepable road" is supposed to take five or six hours, but it is very dark by the time we break down for the sixteenth and final time.

A police van takes the Karachi family and me the last hour into Chitral. The night is slightly cool after the broiling day, and a near-full moon rises over forest-clad ridges, silhouetted against the sky. Though my whole body aches with bruises and muscle pains, I am inspired by this simple beauty.

By day, Chitral does not look so glamorous. It consists of a long strip of bazaar along a dusty road, intersected by another one, and some earthen houses climbing stair step fashion up the barren hills behind the town. Fida Hussain, Annick's friend who had treated her and her girlfriend so well the year before, is not at his Dreamland Hotel and won't be back for a few days. But his employees are kind and solicitous, though they don't speak much English.

The Aga Khan Real Estate Board is also on the premises of the Dreamland Hotel, and I realize that there is a small Ismaili community here in this out of the way corner of the world. I know something about this sub-sect of the Shiah sect of Islam because my close friend Bibi Versi, a Gujarati woman born in Zanzibar and schooled in England, is an Ismaili. Ismailis are followers of the Aga Khan, whom they revere as the forty-ninth Imam, a hereditary religious leader descended in a direct bloodline from Ali, the cousin of Prophet Mohammed who married Mohammed's daughter Fatima.

I admire many of the Ismailis I have met in England for their progressive views about women and modernization, mixed with respect for tradition, culture, and family, and with a deep spirituality based on the mystic practices of Sufism. Now I am even more anxious to meet Fida Hussain. I am eager to ask him about Chitrali Ismailis, and about Hunza, the mythical mountain kingdom of healthy, long-lived people, which I have just discovered is now part of Northern Pakistan, and is also mostly Ismaili.

The first morning in Chitral I book a flight back to Peshawar for next week. I rest a day, but Fida Hussain does not come, so I make arrangements to visit some villages in the area.

I soon find out all road travel in this region is as rough as my journey from Dir. But for a 50 cent surcharge, or sometimes merely for insisting on the peculiar "woman's privilege" in this male-dominated world, I can get a front seat. Front seats are far more comfortable, though one must still hold on for dear life, as there are often no doors on these jeeps.

I go first to Garam Chashma, a beautiful mountain village of hot springs. I am happy to be a few thousand feet higher than Chitral. In this summer heat I really want to be in the snows of Trich Mir, the conical mountain that looms at the head of the Chitral Valley like a beacon of hope of the season's change. But I am content by the river, basking in its cool spray by day and listening all night as it grinds its teeth on huge *grey* boulders.

I stay in the only lodge, a primitive earthen house built around three sides of a courtyard which is filled with string beds. Two Frenchmen sit and smoke hashish incessantly, raving about Chitral's apparently world-famous hash. I don't smoke, so we soon run out of conversation. Zafar, the owner of the lodge, speaks some English and seems very polite. He too is Ismaili, so I ask him questions about the area and about Ismailism.

The next day, Zafar offers to take me to the *hammam,* the baths. I expect turquoise ceramic tiles, but find instead a mud hut with a wooden door. I look at it nervously and say pointedly, "Will you go first, or shall I?"

Zafar lets me go first. He gets the bath started, directing the flow of water into the deep earthen shaft inside the hut, and then lets me go inside. I block the door with a heavy rock and take off my clothes, trying to find a place to put them where they won't get soaked. I relax as the hot, sulfury water rises up my body. When the hot water reaches my neck, I realize I don't know how to drain the water. I scramble out, quickly dress, and open the door to Zafar.

Zafar is solicitous the rest of the day. But I am annoyed to discover that the two Frenchmen have left in a jeep for Chitral while I slept in the stultifying afternoon but he "didn't want to wake me."

I don't much like the idea of being alone with Zafar, and am relieved when a large party of Afghans arrives at dusk. Some are from Nuristan, some from Badakhshan, and others from distant Panjsher. All are fighting Taraki's government. I am excited to meet these Afghan Resistance fighters, the Mujahedeen. These are the guerrillas Khalid had told me about.

I listen intently to their Persian-language conversation. I hear "war," "battles," "sixty people killed in a battle near the lapis mountain." One strapping redhead with a full head of hair speaks a few words of English and some French, so along with my simple Farsi, we are able to communicate.

"Taraki is a donkey," he says expressively. "We fight for Islam. The fight began in Kunar last year. We were the first to start fighting, and now all of Afghanistan is fighting."

He cheerfully asks me if I would like to come with them to Nuristan. It is a walk of only two or three nights over the mountain, he says. I look longingly at the steep mountains in the light of the full moon, and my heart wants to go with them, to cross the border illegally just for the sake of rebellion, and to see how the Mujahedeen live and fight. But better sense prevails. I am registered with the police in Chitral, and would soon be missed.

Zafar tells me I should sleep inside tonight, where he and his small son sleep. "It's not good for a lady to be alone with these Afghans outside," he says seriously.

I would prefer to sleep outside, where it is cooler, but I defer to him.

I trust him because he has been so polite. But in the middle of the night I hear a rasping voice: "Please, please, come here."

I wake up with a start, but don't dare move. I calculate my danger. There is a small boy in the room, and a dozen Afghans outside. If I screamed, the Afghans would come to my help, so I feel less threatened, but still do not move.

The voice becomes more pleading. "Please, I love you. Pleeease..."

I am ready to laugh, but pretend to turn in my sleep. Zafar sighs deeply, and gives up.

The next day he acts sheepish. He won't take money for the food and lodging, calling it hospitality. I accept, but leave him wondering whether I had heard his pleas. I am angry, but mostly just relieved to be going.

Fida Hussain is still not in Chitral, so I head for the Kalash Valleys, eager to experience this unique tribe, the only non-Muslim tribe left in the Hindu Kush mountains. I take a public jeep, which after a long delay takes a load of passengers to Bumburet, the largest valley. Entering the valley, I feel I have crossed the threshold to an ancient world of shamanic magic. In the balmy dusk, stark, blackclad figures stand in the middle of maize fields and stare at the intruding newcomers. Soft songs float on the tinted air, and small girls giggle and laugh at the new arrivals. Crystalline streams flow through green, rock-strewn meadows, and the corn stands tall and green in the fields.

I meet many Pakistani male tourists, most of whom say that the Kalash people are dirty pagans who worship idols. They are happy to come and stare at the pretty, unveiled faces of the Kalash women as they dance, but they moralize and disapprove of their way of life.

In the morning, I am awakened by the rising and falling of women's voices in a choral chant. A young girl has died, and the women of the valley have surrounded her body, placed on a string bed, to sing her praises. The gathering is right across from the Muslim-run hotel, so the Pakistani tourists flock to watch the funeral.

I watch from a respectful distance, and then head down the valley, since the other foreign tourists are heading up. I stop to rest under a mulberry tree, and listen to the whispers of the tree's thick leaves conversing with the darker green walnut tree nearby, and the cheerful gurgle of the stream. Although my stomach hurts, I am happy and peaceful in these surroundings. I feel inspired to play my little wooden flute from Kabul.

No sooner than I have played a few trills, three small children appear from around the bend. The two little girls in their miniature black robes and headdresses giggle and whisper to the little boy in his long shirt and trousers, and his miniature rolled wool cap. I stop playing and smile, and they come closer. I begin again, and they come still closer, like curious kittens. I offer them the flute, and the older of the two girls, who is about ten, takes it and after a few tentative notes begins playing a beautiful, simple tune.

She gives me back the flute and beckons me to follow her further down the valley. After a few minutes, we come upon two women and a man sitting under a mulberry tree. They smile warmly and greet me, gesturing for me to sit down. One of the women takes the flute and plays a sweet, fluid tune. The two girls start braiding my long hair in Kalash fashion, one braid from the center of the forehead, to be tucked behind the right ear, and two braids on each side. Their fingers are deft and quick from long practice.

The little boy takes my pen and draws a watch on his wrist, then takes the paper I give him and draws stick figures and designs. To my surprise, he draws a stick man with a large penis, but he doesn't seem to think it is funny or unusual. Later, I see his inspiration, a similar drawing on the outside of a Kalash temple to the goddess of home and family.

We try to talk, and I learn a few words of the Kalash language. *Baba* is sister, and all women and girls are called *baba.* Boys and men are called *baya,* brother. The whole tribe of 3,000 seems to be one big happy family of siblings. We tell each other our names, and I write the way I think theirs would be spelled in English, and give them the scraps of paper. The women send the small boy to climb a tree and shake juicy white mulberries into a cloth. These we eat with flat bread and bitter, hard goat cheese.

I am charmed by the innocence and unspoiled hospitality of these people. With virtually no words, we entertain each other all day. They spot my camera and gesture that they would like pictures. They pose, but don't ask for money like the Pakistani tourists said they would. Then one of the girls loans me her small, under-headdress, a wreath of cloth covered with cowrie shells, with a strip of cloth down the back. Everyone smiles with delight. I focus my camera on the children, sign for one of the women to stand where I had been, and join the children under the tree. The resulting picture will have fine composition and be much better than pictures taken by many Western tourists.

At dusk we part with regret and affection. I have nothing to give them but a few extra Bic pens. I am touched by their appreciation of these, and of my clumsy sketches of them.

After dinner, I walk up the valley in the dark starlight, listening to the continuing chant of sadness. I can already see that the sense of innocence in this valley is threatened. The whirlwind of change will soon reach these remote valleys and swallow up woodcarvings and cowrie shells, quaint clothes, and stone, wood, and earth houses adapted to the hillsides. An entire life of harmony with the mountain valleys will be choked as the Native American tribal ways have been smothered in my own country.

I approach the funeral scene slowly, keeping my distance in the dark beyond the great bonfire. A voice startles me.

"Be careful. There may be snakes."

I stop in my tracks. Two figures come slowly into focus.

"Are you interested in the Kalash?" continues the enthusiastic Pakistani voice. "Would you like to know more? You should meet my friend here, Saifullah Jan. He is fullblood Kalash and he speaks English."

I follow the two a little closer to the edge of the ring of firelight. "You like Kalash funerals?" asks Saifullah softly.

"Uh, I'm interested. I'm sorry there is a funeral. Who died?"

"A young girl in her twenties. She died in the hospital in Chitral and has left two young children behind."

"Ask him any question you want," persists the Pakistani voice. "He can tell you everything."

The three of us settle on a large boulder. I talk quietly to Saifullah, who has a deep, soothing voice. He speaks fine English, which he first learned in school, and then perfected working with foreign anthropologists. Saifullah answers my many questions about customs, beliefs, and the Kalash way of life.

Saifullah speaks calmly, quietly, telling me how his father had wanted his son to go to school, and how he had been mistreated in school by the Muslim majority. He had run away repeatedly, but each time his father had beaten him and sent him back. After he had finished high school, he had worked with the anthropologists for a few years. Now he wants to go to college in Peshawar, to become a lawyer to defend the rights of his people.

"I could tell you stories that would make you cry," he says passionately. "I cannot tell them without crying myself."

He tells me of many incidents of prejudice, and one sad tale of how the shrewd Muslim merchants had sold salt to the simple Kalash in exchange for the produce of their walnut trees. Walnuts would have been the only cash crop as the Kalash came out of their isolation and entered a cash economy. But now the trees were heavily mortgaged, for all practical purposes the property of the more worldly Muslims, either Chitralis from the surrounding area or Kalash who had converted.

I listen, thinking of all incidents of contact of traditional cultures with technologically more advanced cultures. "I am a writer," I tell Saifullah. "Maybe someday I can do a story on the Kalash and tell the world what is happening. Maybe someday I can write for *National Geographic* magazine."

Saifullah promises to help if I ever come again, to write or just to visit, and invites me to visit him in the Rumbur Valley, "which is quiet and has fewer Muslims," the next time I come.

I say good-bye, never having had a good look at the face which belongs to the melodious voice which tells such sad stories. I fall asleep to the drone of the women's mourning. When I wake up the next morning, they are gone, and some of the magic has dissipated. But I feel as if some spell has been cast on me, and I leave the valley feeling I am being torn away from yet another homeland.

6 Indian Pilgrimage

India
Autumn, 1979

As I crisscross northern India in the fall of 1979, I reflect that the spiritual pilgrimage that led me to India really began several years ago on the Mount of Olives in Jerusalem. There, in the Garden of Gethsemane at noon, the winter light was soft and golden on the torn and many times occupied holy city. There, at noon, the church bells rang as the call to prayer sounded from the mosques, and devout Jews lined up to mourn the destruction of the ancient temple at the sheer, stark Wailing Wall. There I first glimpsed the oneness of the spirit all too often encrusted with dogma, and there developed a hunger to explore the differing paths up the sacred mountain.

My pilgrimage is long, and at times wearying, as I cross the deserts, plains, and rivers of the Subcontinent, reading the history of millennia in the scattered shrines sacred to Hindus, Sikhs, Buddhists, and Muslims. As I enter India through the Punjab, I visit the Golden Temple of the Sikhs in Amritsar, unaware that in a few years the Pool of Nectar will run with blood. From there I journey to Kashmir, where I spend the summer in the cool solace of the Himalaya, where Muslim and Hindu holy places gaze at each other across the placid lake, and ancient Buddhist sites abound. As the nomads begin their autumn migration, I journey to the starkly beautiful high altitude plateau of Ladakh, perhaps part of the ancient Tibetan Bon-po kingdom of Zhangzhung, where Tibetan Buddhism is practiced today right beside Islam.

As autumn cools the Subcontinent, I descend to the Gangetic plain. During full moon in November, I roam the desert cities of fabled Rajasthan, dallying at a beautiful Muslim shrine in Ajmer. I stay at a guesthouse for Muslim pilgrims, recommended by Muslim friends in Bombay. The management is unused to foreigners, but accommodates me because I am a lone woman. At the shrine I join the steady flow of people around the saint's tomb. Like the pilgrims, I eat the dark pink rose petals given to me by an attendant, and sit cross-legged on the white marble floor, swaying to the music of the *qawalli,* the love songs to God.

The next day I take a bus to Pushkar, enjoying the spirited songs of the Rajasthani women wearing jingling bangles and brilliant colors that make them look like flocks of parrots. The pilgrims sing Hindu songs of praise to Brahma the Creator, whose temple was built here in the place where a lotus fell from his hand and formed a lake. The bazaars abound with *sadhus,* wandering mendicant holy men born in Bombay and Brooklyn. My senses are amazed, drenched in exotic and sensuous colors—the saffron, peacock blue, and marigold-colored blouses, veils, and skirts of the women, and dark, handsome men with drooping moustaches, their oversized cotton turbans spots of canary, persimmon, and crimson in the crowds of worshippers.

No matter how long I might spend in India, I realize, most of what happens around me I will never understand. India is an ocean, its Hinduism rising and falling in amorphous waves that absorb and swallow each religion that descends onto these plains, from Buddhism and Zoroastrianism to Islam, Christianity, and Sikhism. Each new religion floats bravely on the surface of the underlying ocean, allowed its moment of sunlight, and then waterlogged, sinks, its customs subtly altered from those of its place of origin.

Innocent of the Hindu mind-set after time spent in more egalitarian religious cultures, I wander the outskirts of Pushkar amongst nomads and camel traders, oblivious of caste. They are friendly, and beckon me to join them and share bread cooked over a late afternoon fire. Later, I wonder if these were untouchables, the outcastes Gandhi had called Harijans, the Children of God. Although castes are officially banned in India, caste-consciousness remains prevalent, particularly in food practices. This is a concept utterly foreign to me. I have not encountered it in my readings of mystical Hindu texts such as the Bhagavad Gita and the Upanishads. It shocks me to realize that I, as a foreigner not born a Hindu, am considered polluting to a Hindu's food because I have no caste and am thus the same as an untouchable. In years travelling around India, of all the Hindus I meet, only these nomads and the educated elite who have transcended caste will share their meals with me.

All the while, Afghanistan and the friends I left behind are never far from my mind. I seize English-language newspapers like an addict, and cut out snippets of news about Afghanistan, which is moving towards

Soviet invasion with the heavy-handed inevitablity of a Greek tragedy.

As I meander on my desultory pilgrimage, my heart is longing for Kabul, wondering and worrying about Khalid and Aiesha. I have decided to go to London via Kabul, but first must make the journey east. To understand India, I must see Benares, called Varanasi by the Indians, and Bodhgaya, where Siddhartha Gautama, known as the Buddha, the awakened one, attained enlightenment. Finally I must reach Calcutta and stand on the eastern pinnacle of this subcontinent. In my mind, Calcutta is like New York, a terminus which is both an end and a beginning. I am terrified to go there, but I feel compelled to visit the city. Then I plan to spend a few days in the hills of Darjeeling, with the Tibetans whose culture I have come to love.

I spend a few days in Delhi, recovering from my journeys south to Bombay and Goa, and west to the Rajasthan desert. Like many young travellers, I am hoarding dollars and pinching pennies, arguing over a rupee or two, so set in my penurious way of thinking that I forget that a rupee is only a dime. I am exhausted by poor food, heat, and too much walking. I buy a potion and cure my head lice, recover from my latest bout of dysentery by eating yogurt and rice for a few days, and lie under the fan in the dorm room, reading and resting my aching, bandaged feet.

Finally I feel ready for the next stage of the journey—until I try to find the railway coach for which I supposedly have a reservation. The huge, barn-like station is in its usual chaos. The passengers' names are posted on a glassed-in bulletin board around which a crowd of men push and shove. I stand on tiptoe and squint, but all the names are in Hindi. Finally, I find a man who speaks English and points out the coach number next to my name written in Devanagari script. Coach number 6361. I thank him, and find number 6358, 6359, 6360. But here the sequence is broken. I see only 2352, 2353, 2354 and so on. It is getting late, and the station's muted chaos turns to pandemonium as people and porters rush, and I dodge porters with huge tin trunks balanced on their red turbans, and families with children, and people asleep on the platform. I finally find coach 6361, at the opposite end of the train, where the Ladies Compartment has just been added on, as if it were an afterthought.

Ladies Compartments are supposed to be safer for women travelling alone. Indian friends had warned me to always get Ladies Compartments, or if that were not possible, to ask to share a compartment with a family. So far I have been lucky. The papers frequently report train robberies by dacoits, local gangsters armed with knives and country-made pistols. In Rajasthan I had awakened one midnight when the train stopped to see a hand reaching in through window bars. It disappeared when I screamed, and I slammed down the ventilator grill. I had also heard tales of travellers being offered cups of tea by hospitable coach-mates, only to wake up from a drugged sleep hours later with all their valuables gone.

Although I grumble about "another screaming baby car" when I see the number of infants and toddlers crowded into the compartment, I am grateful for the safety it provides.

To my surprise, the journey is pleasant. One of the women lives in Allentown, Pennsylvania, and is travelling with her family to visit relatives. She and her mother insist on sharing their food with me. They give me *puri,* a thin, airy, fried pancake eaten either with a sweet or with spicey food such as the potato and chili mixture they scoop onto the *puri.* At long stops, the husband comes in to check on the family, bringing sweet milky tea in a clay cup for me as well.

In Varanasi I find a cheap hotel recommended by a friend whose judgement I soon question. I am given a windowless room, whose front wall is not a wall at all. Only a thin plywood advertising billboard separates me from the din and traffic outside. Varanasi is one of the noisiest cities in the world. I do not see the Benares of the changeless Ganges, I do not hear the ceaseless hymns of praise, or find the peace and enlightenment promised by classical ragas and Vedic hymns. Outside, trucks and buses belch black smoke, and thousands of bicyles and bicycle rickshaws sound jangling bells as constantly as the buses and trucks sound the shrill whistles of their piercing horns, tuned to approximate the loudest screams one can imagine.

Exhausted, I sleep a little in between the evening bustle and the morning rush, which begins before dawn. I conclude that great meditation techniques had to develop here, as a sheer matter of survival. Maybe I can merge with God in mountains, or in the desert, or in a village, but in this madness? But it is here where contact with Spirit is most sorely needed.

The first day I rest until my feet are up to walking and the heat, still overwhelming in November, has abated a little. In the evening I wander the temple bazaars, disappointed that non-Hindus are not allowed inside the elaborate temples with their intricate carvings and symbolic forms. The bazaar shops sell every trash and treasure, from bright plastic buckets and cups to the finest Benares silk saris. I gladly sit and have tea while I buy many colored silk scarves as gifts for friends in England and America.

The dusk is magic, quietening, even though the din continues. I walk past the endless line of beggars, lepers, and men, women, and children deformed by polio, elephantiasis, and diseases I know nothing about, till I reach the ghats, the wide platforms that lead down to the Ganges. The river is low at this time of year. Mother Ganga is truly as placid and changeless as this modern India remains beneath its surface of glitter and color, squalor and ritual. In the plum-light, reflected on the water, I see a ring of marigolds circled with a swirl of ashes and human waste. On a ghat, two small boys do yoga exercises, not the way we do them on soft carpets in front of mirrors to see if we are doing them right, but naturally and intuitively. Beyond them, at the burning ghats where those who have come to escape the wheel of karma by dying in holy Benares are being cremated, dark smoke circles into the sky, looking like the trails of small trains bound for unknown destinations.

The next morning I force myself out of bed at dawn and make my way to the ghats, where I can hire a boat to go out on the river. I walk down the long flight of wide steps to the boats, and bargain in my limited Hindi with a bald older man who looks kind and placid. He gestures me to get in, and rows resignedly into the slow drifting current, reminding me of the Ferryman in Hermann Hesse's novel *Siddhartha.*

From the boat I can see the panorama of the river's life. Women bathe, fully clothed in saris, in the dirty sacred river; people drink the holy water oblivious of the burning ghats, dead carcasses, and floating pieces of bodies; and ordinary devout men as well as *sadhus* salute the sun with ancient and changeless Sanskrit words. I find a beauty in these timeless rituals, but also a denial of the change which is vitality. The rituals seem too often played out by rote, as Judaeo-Christian rituals seem to many in the West, all attempts to create a formula for salvation or enlightenment in three easy steps. Is there no middle way, I wonder, no way to both honor tradition and yet change and grow? Or is this just my Western addiction to change for change's sake?

The morning is as misty and grey as disappointment, but a golden light grows and turns rose-gold, and finally bright salmon in a mackerel sky. I am in awe of this grandeur, and suddenly see the paradoxical metaphor of sunrise—constant each day, yet changing moment to moment. I delight in holding this ungraspable paradox for a brief hint of time, and feel a spiritual centeredness which gives birth to a generosity and compassion toward all sentient beings.

When the boatman asks for *bakhshish,* a gift or gratuity beyond what we had agreed, I don't argue the way I often do. I smile tolerantly and make it a true gift. I watch a little girl with orange ribbons in her black pigtails selling marigolds and candles to put on leaf boats as offerings to the river. She prepares one for me without my asking, and mischievously asks a whole rupee, far more than the Indian price. I give her the rupee, and say my own prayers for peace. I light the candle and watch as the leaf soon sinks. The marigolds and the little yellow paper boat with the candle on it separate in the slow current, and the small flame of hope continues on its way to the endless sea.

It is good to get out of teeming cities and into rural India's heartland in Uttar Pradesh. Over two thousand years ago, when the Buddha lived, this land was lush and forested. Today it is overpopulated, exhausted, polluted, hungry and thirsty, but still carries the ancestral memories of a more peaceful time of Earth. I approach Bodhgaya by *tonga,* a two-wheeled horsecart, which collides with another *tonga* and sends it into a ditch, provoking a bitter argument between the drivers.

The little town is an oasis of peace. It is an anomaly in India, its architecture a hodgepodge of temples of different Buddhist sects, built by the Buddhist societies of their homelands. There is a spare and simple Japanese Zen temple, an elaborate Chinese temple with a sign advertising a Chinese restaurant in Kanpur right under the golden Buddha, and a Tibetan temple with a huge prayer wheel. The central temple is that built around the Bodhi Tree, where Buddha sat for 49 days, battling the demons of the world's temptations and at last achieving enlightenment. The present tree, a spreading peepul tree festooned with strings and scarves which represent the binding of the prayers and wishes of the devout, is from a sapling of the original Bodhi Tree sent by the newly-converted Emperor Ashoka to Sri Lanka over 2,000 years ago.

The Tibetan temple houses a huge prayer wheel which has multitudes of prayers inside. It is said that whoever turns it three times will be freed from the wheel of karma, and will never have to be reborn into this suffering world again. I turn it twice and find that though it takes effort, it is surprisingly easy, much easier than living in the world and maintaining constant compassion for all sentient beings. I stop after the second turn. It shouldn't be so easy to free oneself from the wheel of karma. Enlightenment requires far more responsibility and effort, and so I dismiss the legend as a comforting notion of popular religion.

I wish I could stay longer, but I have made a schedule in a scheduleless land, and must be back in Delhi at a certain time to catch my flight to Kabul. I talk with foreigners, monks, religious teachers, and Tibetan refugees. I sit and watch a Tibetan *puja,* and find the chanting and the clash of cymbals comforting, familiar, and exhilarating, perhaps echoing from some distant past of my own. My last evening in Bodhgaya, I watch Tibetan lamas clad in maroon robes light hundreds of butter lamps, pools of butter in softly gleaming brass lamps lined up nine-deep in the form of a square. The soft, natural light shines benevolently on the placid faces of these young monks who have never known their country, and I feel a keen sense of sorrow for a great culture and faith. I wonder what is in store for Tibet and Afghanistan, engulfed by powers beyond their material means to control.

I am in a nightmare. It is a very dark, steamy night, and I am trying to find my way onto a train in a crowded station. Everyone is shouting and pushing and elbowing, and my backpack and typewriter are heavy. My feet ache, and people are shouting at me, "Hurry up! Hurry up!" but no one is helping me hurry. The train starts up with the chug-chug of steam, and hands push me up from behind onto the steps of the train, as if I am an escaping refugee. I collapse to my knees and for a moment I am the victim of curious onlookers as the train lurches on its way, and I cannot regain my balance and hoist my load. I clutch at my necklace, a silver Allah, the name of God in Arabic, which I had bought in Kabul. It is gone, and I feel destitute and abandoned.

I am on my way to Calcutta at last. My feet throb even when I rest, and my head is stuffed with congestion. In the night, the train drifts to a halt in the middle of nowhere. The fan stops, and I watch as the filament of the electric lightbulb flickers and dims like a flame. It grows stuffier and stuffier, but no one dares open a window, and I'm sure the Indian ladies in the compartment are as glad for the bolt on the door as I am.

Calcutta has the paralyzing, frenetic intensity of New York. The train arrives some five hours late, and I am worried about finding accommodation so late in the morning. Howrah Station is a continuation of the nightmare. I don't understand anything around me, none of the shouting, or the blaring music of Hindi films, and none of the cries of the beggars with their appalling deformities, some of which are the result of intentional maiming of kidnapped children. Small dark children claw at me, looking winsome, pleading, and ragged. I give the remnants of two packets of glucose biscuits and two bananas to a boy and girl who look like they might be brother and sister, and flee the station, hardening my heart and closing my eyes and ears to the pleas of the hundreds I cannot help, even if I give a rupee, or ten rupees, to each of them.

In the late morning traffic jam, it takes half an hour for my taxi to get to the nearby bridge. What little patience I have developed in eight months of travelling in Asia is quickly exhausted, and I am near tears when I reach the Salvation Army Red Shield hostel. To my relief, I get a bed in a room with three other women. One is a Japanese woman who has worked as a volunteer with Mother Teresa for three months. The other two are Canadian nurses who also want to work with Mother Teresa. They welcome me and as we share oranges, they assure me that everyone is welcome to work at any of Mother Teresa's facilities. In fact, I can come with them tomorrow morning to catch the minibus across town to Kalighat, the neighborhood where the Home for the Dying lies next to the temple to Kali, Hindu goddess of destruction and regeneration.

7 A Dash of Inspiration, A Drop of Compassion

Calcutta
November, 1979

The only transportation in this misty dawn is a rickshaw pulled by a thin young man in a worn shirt and *lungi,* the wrapped skirt worn by men in some parts of India. The two Canadian nurses and I look at each other doubtfully, appalled at the thought of being pulled along by another human being. We start walking in the direction of the Mother House, where we are supposed to meet the minibus going to the Nirmal Hriday Home for Dying Destitutes, but the persistent rickshaw-wallah trots quickly alongside, badgering us. As we walk the fare he wants keeps going down and down; he does not understand that our reluctance is morally based, for his needs are immediate.

I explain to him in Hindi that we are three people, and this is too many for him. He shrugs and says this is no problem. The three of us finally climb in, perched uncomfortably on each others' laps. I wince as I watch the rickshaw puller's muscles strain as he balances and starts out. His dark face wears a concentrated expression, and he is happy for his first fare of the day. Not to hire him would only deny him his meager livelihood.

Several nuns and novices, and an efficient and dedicated French volunteer named Patrice ride with us in the minibus to Kalighat. When we arrive, Patrice directs us in her no-nonsense manner. We don faded, tattered blue aprons and set to work in the women's ward. It is spartan but cheerful, with beds clothed in alternating pink and turquoise sheets, and morning light shining in. No one is screaming and moaning with pain or insanity, but dozens of curious, quietly pleading dark eyes follow us on our rounds.

Some of the women are incontinent, and we must clean up after them as we change their sheets. As I concentrate on the faces of the fading women, compassion conquers my disgust. But involuntarily, my stomach heaves and I gag as I mop up the plastic sheets under the soiled bedclothes with a disinfectant-soaked rag. Ann, one of the nurses, tells me not to worry, that even nurses gag sometimes.

I help Ann carry some of the women, thin skeletons covered with withered flesh, into the adjoining room to be bathed. Some of them cry with pain or fear at our touch, and others are limp like dolls. We lay them on a concrete platform in the large room where the pots and dishes are washed, and those who have died during the night are laid on the floor. When I turn to fill a bucket with water from the concrete tank behind me, I stop cold at the sight of six pairs of vermillion-stained feet peeking out from under a canvas sheet. The feet have been colored according to Hindu custom, but I have no idea how the bodies of the poorest of the poor will be disposed of in a country where wood for cremation costs money.

When all the beds are changed and the women bathed, it is time to give out medicine. Many of these women have tuberculosis, which is curable with proper medication, care, and diet. Others have cancer, and some are simply dying from poverty and neglect. Most are old, but not all. One cheerful woman named Aida, who has tuberculosis and shuffles around on the thickened legs characteristic of elephantiasis, helps the volunteers and the sisters. Aida speaks fluent English, and I wonder what strange route brought her to homelessness and poverty.

There is a brief lull in our work. Women beckon to us, longing for simple human touch. I hold one's hand as she weeps and sobs out some words, over and over, in Bengali. It is similar enough to Hindi that I understand a few words. I wonder what happened to the children she is crying about—were they the victims of one of the kidnap and mutilate begging rings? Another woman curls up against me like an affectionate cat. She lays her head on my shoulder and stays there happily. I do not want to move, and just keep my arms around her until it is time to serve lunch.

The food, served out of big metal buckets, is good and nutritious—rice, *dal,* the curried lentils which are a staple dish in most of India, and a banana for each person. Some of the women are too weak to eat, and as the sisters ladle out food they ask the volunteers to help certain women. There are no knives and forks, so I feed one weak woman as one would a small child, supporting her with one arm and feeding her in small handfuls. I am careful to use only the right hand so as to avoid offending custom, since in the East the left hand is used for personal sanitation after visiting the toilet.

I am exhausted when the morning shift is over, but I feel satisfied as I hand in my apron. I look over the room, wondering who will die in the night. Most of them look all right; they seem to be dying slowly. Some may even recover. Aida at least is on her feet—she laughs and says she never wants to leave, that this is her home now.

As we are walking out, we fall into conversation with a tall, full-bearded young Englishman. "Are you a volunteer?" I ask.

"Not exactly," he answers. "We are here to make a film for Colombian television."

Peter introduces himself and his director, Hector, who speaks only Spanish. We chat a little more, and I offer my assistance when I find out that their crew is just the two of them. Peter confers briefly with Hector in Spanish, and then gratefully conveys their acceptance of my offer.

The next ten days are a whirlwind. I am finally putting my training in film-making to use on a meaningful project. We go everywhere in Calcutta, from the most miserable slums to the most elite hotels and theaters. Feverishly, I take continuity notes in detail, as I had learned at my father's sales promotion office in Los Angeles. Peter is glad for my careful note-taking, since he will be doing the editing when they get back to Colombia.

Hector treats us generously. We meet each morning for a Western-style breakfast in their posh, air-conditioned hotel, and then hit the streets. Sunil, a Spanish-speaking Bengali from Calcutta who is helping us, accompanies us each day. He not only translates for Hector, but acts as a liaison, introducing us to people and smoothing our way. He even introduces us to his personal friends. In this way we meet a lovely young couple, Jojo and Munia. Jojo is an aspiring film-maker who works in advertising. His wife Munia helps Jojo's parents run the Calcutta Social Project, a self-reliance project in the Rash Bihari slum.

I haven't met very many of this class of Indians, so well-educated, worldly, and travelled. They discuss world politics with us, and take us to their favorite local restaurants to eat beef kebab rolls. Munia says she likes to wear shirts and jeans most of the time, but wears a *shalwar kameez* or a sari when the occasion demands it.

One day, Sunil takes us to the burning ghats. These are not on the river bank like the ones in Varanasi, but in an out of the way enclosure. While Peter films, I take a few pictures. Most of the mourners are not miserable and weeping; many are singing, even laughing. They accept death as part of life, and have an unquestioning belief in reincarnation.

But I wonder if we are invading private moments, and cannot bring myself to take pictures of the actual cremation. This reluctance is not out of delicacy or queasiness, but out of respect. These bodies melting in the flames are not people any more, but only shells whose inhabitants have moved on. I remember the words of the *Bhagavad Gita:*

"Worn-out garments are shed by the body: Worn-out bodies are shed by the dweller within the body. New bodies are donned by the dweller, like garments."

I watch the flames lick at a face that was a woman, and feel an oddly detached sense of mortality. It is not fearsome, but somehow reassuring.

Jojo's parents, Mr. and Mrs. Karlekar, are dynamic and opinionated. They live in a spacious house bordering a very large slum made up mostly of immigrants from what is now Bangladesh, who came in two waves, one after Partition in 1947, and one after the India-Pakistan war in 1971. When Mrs. Karlekar retired from her position as head of a teacher training college, she wanted to keep busy, so started a Red Cross milk giveaway program. But as she saw how great the needs were, that initial start evolved into a multi-faceted program stressing self-reliance, literacy, and job training. Some of the current teachers of both children and adults were educated in the program in this very slum. Others have learned book-binding and other trades. Munia is now researching traditional embroidery and possible Western markets.

Peter, Hector, and I follow the Karlekars into the dingy lanes of the slum. The Karlekars are greeted with great love and enthusiasm, in the way I imagine Gandhi would have been greeted. We visit a school where children study for an upcoming exam by candlelight. The slum has electricity, but it is out, as is frequently the case in Calcutta, particularly during the monsoon.

Everyone seems to be bustling in order to survive. A few toddlers play, using stones as marbles, but older children all seem to be employed in some gainful activity. A girl and boy are busily making piles of cow and buffalo dung into patties for fuel. They pat them onto the walls to dry, their handprints making a decorative effect. They sell this handiwork for 10 paisa, about a penny, per hundred.

People work so hard for so little. The Karlekars tell us that rickshaw pullers work two six-hour shifts each day to earn about six rupees, around sixty cents. Then they have to pay rent to the rickshaw owner, usually a rich man who owns many rickshaws. They try their best to get as many customers as possible, and favor the rich neighborhoods and those frequented by foreigners.

Instead of the sense of misery and despair I expected in these slums, I find a resilient cheerfulness. But I sense an underlying anger, not only in the slums, but in all the frustrated classes of Indian society. It is an election year, and Indira Gandhi is hoping to be re-elected after being out of power for several years. The walls are covered with symbols and slogans. In a mostly illiterate country, symbols say a lot. Indira's party, Congress-I (the "I" stands for Indira) has the symbol of the palm of a hand, with a long lifeline and headline. The original Congress symbol was a cow and calf, a powerful symbol in nominally secular but overwhelmingly Hindu India, where the cow is held sacred.

Everyone thinks that Indira will get back into power. But here in West Bengal, a Communist bastion, the opposition has painted a garish wall painting, a horrifying image of Indira with her unmistakeable skunk streak, holding a bloody dagger in one hand and a bag of U.S. dollars in the other.

Hector falls ill with traveller's tummy, and Peter and I carry on working. Peter is like a kid out of school. He is thrilled to eat out of bazaar stalls instead of fancy hotels. After we film Mother Teresa's Home for the Children, we ride the train to Titagarh to visit the Gandhiji Prem Nivas (Gandhi's Abode of Love) Home for Lepers.

An American priest tells us more than we ever wanted to know about leprosy, while Peter films and I take notes. What stands out in my mind is that leprosy, known as Hansen's Disease in the U.S., is completely curable, and if caught early can be cured for literally pennies per day per person. Only one out of every 7,000 people has no natural immunity to the leprosy bacillus, which explains why some people live and work with lepers all their lives and never develop the disease.

In the center's two wards are people in all stages of the disease. The first signs are numbness and whitish patches on the skin. If the disease is caught then, the person wll never develop the deformities associated with leprosy. Fingers and toes do not "fall off," but are absorbed as nerve activity atrophies. One of the greatest dangers is that leprosy patients develop ulcers on their feet, as they do not feel anything and thus often are unaware that they have injured their feet.

Across the railroad tracks on an easement owned by Indian Railways, the recovered lepers have developed their own rehabilitation center. There they live, farm, raise pigs, dye thread, and spin and weave all the sheets, curtains, saris, and *lungis* needed by the leprosy center. They live

Gandhi's vision of the simple life around the spinning wheel. For these people who cannot ever go back to their villages because of the stigma of being a leper, even if they never developed severe symptoms of the disease, this is a godsend. Men and women work together, a woman holding a basket of cement on her head with stumps of fingers, a man limping slowly on the stump of a foot as he carries bricks.

Peter and I are profoundly moved, inspired, confused, and depressed. We return to Calcutta in silence, and eat at a small cafe, talking about being film-makers in the Third World, and wondering about the responsibilities inherent in filming poverty. Peter has lived in Colombia for several years, and enjoys some success as a cameraman. For a young man just starting out in his career, there are more opportunities to get actual experience in the Third World than in England or America, where students study for years, and then must spend more years assisting while others work. I tell him I would love to be doing what he is doing, and that I believe it does do some good to strive to record "the truth" and communicate it to others using the technologies available to us in the West. But we will always be unsure of ourselves, always wonder if we are stealing someone's image, invading their privacy, taking a job away from a local man or woman. And worse, wonder if we are doing any good at all, or if helping one woman die with dignity and grace at the Home for the Dying is worth all the films and articles I could ever write.

Calcutta is not yet awake as I stumble out the gate of the Salvation Army hostel into the dreary grey dawn. But as I make my way towards the Mother House of the Missionaries of Charity, I hear the first notes of the Muslim call to prayer, and here and there shrouded figures in the mist murmur words of ancient Hindu prayers. Pavement dwellers have lighted a few cooking fires, adding to Calcutta's daily pollution, and alongside the streets lie the carcasses of rats the size of American housecats, which the homeless have stoned to death during the night.

When I reach the Mother House, I feel shy and uncertain, even though I have been here before to catch the minibus that takes volunteers to the Home for the Dying. Today I am going to Mass, something I haven't done for at least ten years, and then I am going to interview Mother Teresa, who has just won the Nobel Peace Prize for her work among "the poorest of the poor."

Awkwardly, I add my ragged sandals to the rows of sandals and plastic shoes already in neat lines in front of the door to the sanctuary, as if in front of a Muslim, Hindu, Sikh, or Buddhist holy place. This is not quite the same Catholic Church that left me so disillusioned in the early 70's, and I'm not sure how to act. A smiling bronze-skinned South Indian novice dressed in a spotless white sari habit seats me on the floor at the back of a spartan white rectangular room. The congregation is seated cross-legged, in the manner of Hindus.

I grow absorbed by the atmosphere of joy and service in the room, a bastion against the horrors outside on the streets of Calcutta and hundreds of other cities in the world. As a quiet-voiced Indian priest begins the Mass, I slip into my own meditative prayers, in the personal and multi-religious form I have developed since I turned away from the guilt-laden, ritualistic, and socially unconscious Catholicism of my childhood. I hardly notice that someone has slipped into the space beside me, until it is time for the Sign of Peace, which apparently has been added to the liturgy since I left the church. I am surprised when everyone turns to their neighbors, hands pressed palm to palm in the graceful form of Hindu greeting. I turn quickly to keep up, and knock over the alarm clock and stack of books belonging to the woman next to me. She is a small woman with an androgynous face and merry blue-green eyes, whom I recognize as Mother Teresa herself. I am slightly awed and embarrassed, but as I gather books and apologize, she laughs and puts me at ease.

I'm in for a further shock when Mother Teresa helps dispense Holy Communion. The Roman Catholic Church still doesn't allow women priests, though there were women priests amongst the early Christians, and I wonder if some special dispensation has been given to this humble woman regarded by many as a living saint.

Carried along by the moment, I am tempted to receive Communion myself. The symbolic aspect of the transmutation of wine and bread to spiritual food of blood and body attracts me, and I wish to share in the miracle, though I am no longer a literal believer. Some respectful, perhaps fearful part of me holds me back—I have not been to Confession. Not that I believe it would be a sin, but somehow it would be false. Peter, however, surprises me by lining up and reverently receiving the Communion with closed eyes. Later he confesses ingenuously that he thought it was expected of him.

I am moved by this simple Mass, though I know I could never return to the confines of even a liberalized Church. This return to a Catholic ritual imbued with the essence of the cultures and faiths native to this land to which it has been transplanted, is a completion, a higher point on a spiral journey which has taken many years. At last I can look at Catholic nuns without fear, and can appreciate ceremony and ritual for their beauty and symbolism, rather than a pre-interpreted meaning. It is a joy indeed to see the teachings of Jesus translated into service and sacrifice.

After the Mass, Peter and Hector interview Mother Teresa on film, while I grow increasingly nervous at the prospect of interviewing her. I admire her greatly, how could one not? But I am also aware of her positions on birth control and abortion, those that can be expected of a Catholic nun loyal to the Pope. She believes in "fighting abortion through adoption," and points to the success of the Children's Home, where children are taken in off the streets and trash heaps, and often adopted, even by people in other countries. But I have seen the horrors caused by overpopulation and dwindling resources, and feel strongly in favor of birth control, and a woman's right to control her own body and take responsibility for her own soul's choice.

A journalist's role is not to argue, I remind myself. In any case, she immediately puts me at ease. "This must be the thousandth time you're being interviewed this month," I say, referring to the recent announcement of her award of the Nobel Peace Prize.

"All for Jesus," she says, grinning.

I ask her many philosophical questions, and I depart from my prepared script to discuss my own feelings about the days I spent working and filming in the Home for the Dying. "They are not a burden," she says, "but a joy."

I ask the eternal question–"Why suffering?"

"We can all participate in Redemption," is her practical answer.

For a moment, I envy her certainty. It would make life easier and more simple. But for me this simplicty does not ring true.

"Don't you get depressed when you read the newspapers about all the wars and..."

She interrupts my sentence. "Never! Little drops make the ocean. Our work is only a small drop in a very great ocean."

Certainly I cannot argue this, as I have personally experienced the greatness of the work. I have little more to say, as I don't want to take her time, since I don't know if my free lance article will ever be published. But I can't resist asking her about a statement she recently made in Delhi that "women should leave the greater things in life to men." I quote it to her, and she remains smiling.

"Have you not done great work?" I ask.

"The greatest part of a woman is to be a mother and a wife," she answers promptly.

"But have you not done great work?" I insist.

"According to the mind of God, I have given love and compassion, which is the gift of women."

I thank her for the interview, and say a silent prayer that Mother Teresa, regarded by many as a saint, and by some as just another flawed human being struggling to do good, may continue to inspire both men and women to give the compassion that is the gift of being human.

8 Reunion— Into the Whirlwind's Eye

Kabul, Afghanistan
December, 1979

The Afghan Customs Inspector politely asks to see what is in the bulky package wrapped in brown paper and string. I try not to show my annoyance. He tries to help, and apologetically scrambles to pick up the small wooden chess pieces that scatter on the ground as he drops one of the chess sets I'd bought in Delhi.

He carefully rewraps the package. I am disarmed by his polite manner, so different from that of the officious security woman at the airport in Delhi, who had disdainfully made me unzip my boots, suspecting who knows what nefarious contraband. He waves me on into the airport arrivals area, where a knot of eager Afghans is waiting. Men are greeting other men with effusive hugs, and women greeting other women with kisses and tears. I know no one will be here to meet me, as Khalid wouldn't dare to be seen meeting a foreigner. I don't even know if he has received any of my cryptic letters, but he must know am coming, since Annick will have arrived by now to see Parwez, and will have left a message at Khalid's friend's hotel

To my disappointment, Khalid is not at the hotel to meet me. But Hakim, the manager, has prepared a warm room for me. He brings tea, and I settle in for the night. Kabul in winter is very different from Kabul in spring or summer. I huddle by the wood-burning stove to warm my hands, then curl up under heavy quilts supplemented by my down sleeping bag, reading *The Far Pavillions.* I am enjoying this romantic tale about the Second Anglo-Afghan War, caught in its word-spell of insight. I am struck by how M.M. Kaye's words "the Afghans had never been dominated by any foreign power," echo eerily in the present, a harbinger of a greater struggle soon to come.

I don't know if the situation here is better or worse than it was when I left in July. The Indian papers had pictured President Taraki embracing

Brezhnev in Havana at a world Communist conference. Then suddenly Taraki had resigned "due to ill health." He had subsequently been reported dead, and had been succeeded by Hafizullah Amin, who as Minister of the Interior had been responsible for the detention, torture, and death of thousands of prisoners who had opposed the great new dawn of socialism.

The same searchlights still leap off the mountaintop, but they appear harsher in this cold, black winter night, heavy with silence. I look out my window and then walk out into the shivering night. The full moon shines serenely above the spotlights, disdainful and oblivious. I feel a strange urge, and after looking around to make sure no one is watching, I stoop down and quickly kiss the frozen ground. With this ritual, I feel I have truly returned to the home of my heart.

Khalid comes to see me early the next day. My first impulse is to hug him and tell him how much I have missed him, but he is reserved. We kiss each other's cheeks formally, in the Afghan way, right-left-right. We are awkward, avoiding unspoken memories, but he is kind and solicitous, and brings in an armload of wood before he settles down in a woven-rope chair near the stove.

I nervously offer him my gift of a wooden chess set. He accepts, but looks embarrassed. He is less reluctant to accept the bottle of Chivas Regal. I am at first happy to have pleased him, but then have second thoughts about having given him alcohol. I try to give him the gifts I have brought for Aiesha and his sisters, but he brushes them aside.

"You will see them. We will invite you one night."

Aiesha is six months pregnant, but Khalid seems more worried than happy. Many, many people are in prison now, he says, and things are much worse than when I left. He lapses frequently into silent gloom, and puffs on the pipe he has taken up in order to stop smoking cigarettes.

"My uncle, who was a teacher at the university, is in Pul-e-Charkhi prison now," he says quietly.

"Do you know if he is alive?"

"We think so. No one is allowed visitors. Family members can bring things, but they have to leave them with the guards, and no one knows if the prisoners get them. But we think that if the guards accept the gifts, then the prisoner must be alive. We don't know how he is being treated, or how long they will hold him, or even why. But it is very cold in the cells in winter, and he's always had a good life, so he is not used to this." He pauses and looks thoughtfully at my sleeping bag, wrinkling his high forehead. "If we had a sleeping bag, I think we could bring it to him. I've looked all over the bazaar and can't find anything. There were hardly any tourists this year." He hesitates. "Maybe you could sell us yours before you go."

My sleeping bag has been a good companion for some years, and has warmed me through winters in England and Asia. It's a good down bag and will be more expensive to replace than Khalid realizes. But Mother Teresa's words come to me: "Give not from the abundance, but give until it hurts."

"Here, take it now," I say, moving to roll it up.

"No, no, not now. You will be cold in the night."

I gaze at his eyes, the blue-green of spring waters, and think, "I wish I had you to keep me warm," but say nothing.

"We will be very grateful to accept it when you leave. I am Afghan, and I am proud. Normally, I would never ask for anything, but now..." He sighs deeply.

"Khalid, are the Russians going to invade?"

"It's only a matter of time." He drops his voice and out of habit looks about, in what some foreigners have come to refer to as the "Kabul twitch." "My information is that a very high official of the Soviet Foreign Ministry is in Kabul now. It may even be Gromyko himself, or someone directly under him. What do you think that means?"

"Maybe they are just assessing the situation."

"Fool. They are preparing the invasion, because they have been losing to the Mujahedeen in the mountains, even though the Communists have planes and bombs. The Mujahedeen are waiting for the snows. The planes can't fly in bad weather, and they'll have the advantage then. But I think the Russians will come before that."

My heart is sinking with the weight of the truth of his words. What will America do, I wonder? But America is preoccupied with the fate of the 49 embassy employees recently taken hostage in Iran, and is paralyzed with ineffective anger. My mind clings to shreds of vague hopes, rationalizations for why the Russians shouldn't invade, why they wouldn't want to alienate the Third World and the Muslim world, or abrogate the SALT II treaty, even though it hasn't been confirmed by the U.S. Senate.

Khalid gets up abruptly. "I will talk to you soon."

"When?"

"Soon. We will invite you. And I will come to see you every day. Only I will not come to see you in the night," he says mischievously. He moves to give me a brotherly kiss on the cheek, then for a moment his barriers drop and he kisses me lightly, slowly, on the lips, tossing me a look of longing.

I smile, but do not return his look. He is married now, and a child is on the way. He is my friend and brother.

He stands near me, and runs one finger along my lips. "I shouldn't be doing this," he whispers, smiling. "We're friends now."

He knows what he is doing, and I am a little angry. I pull away, and repeat firmly, "Yes, we are the best of friends."

I am glad to be in Kabul again. On this clear winter morning, the trees are etched against a blue sky the shining color of the fine blue pottery glaze of Istalif. I know this city like the lines in the palm of my hand, and it speaks to me as eloquently. I breathe deeply and look all around me as I make my way to Parwez' restaurant. Annick and Parwez are waiting for me with kisses and hugs. Parwez has ordered a great feast of kebab and rice prepared, and seems more excited to see me than Khalid was.

"We came to the airport to meet you," says Annick, "but the plane was delayed for hours. We'd gotten a bottle of champagne to celebrate your arrival, but we drank it ourselves."

I laugh, glad to be back among friends. I am touched by Parwez' ingenuous hospitality. During winter, he is free from his teaching duties, as schools have a three-month break. His friend Wali soon shows up, and greets me effusively, and then Aziz comes in with his beautiful girlfriend, who speaks no English but laughs with the giddy abandon of youth in love.

Annick and I go to visit the families of the two brothers who own the hotel attached to the restaurant. Annick had become close to them during the summer, even though the two wives could not speak a word of English, and not much Farsi, as their native language was Pashtu. These traditional women live in *purdah,* literally behind a curtain, in two small rooms. Whenever they go out, which isn't often, they must wear a *chadori.*

I had always wondered who the women behind the *chadori* were. Now I see two of them, young, bright, and beautiful, with black hair and exquisite alabaster skin. They wear ornate heavy silver jewelrv, and embroidered caps under their veils. Their flowered dresses, bright pink and bright green, are in the style of Ghazni, and their baggy trousers fall to their ankles in pleats of many yards of material. Their veils are thick, stiffly edged with silver and gold embroidery, but these women are graceful in their accustomed clothes. They move like birds to bring us pillows, serve us tea and sugared almonds, and play with their children.

Annick's favorite, three-year-old Siah Mui, is shy at first, but finally remembers her. She is a China doll of a girl, porcelain-faced and somber, her black hair cut in a blunt bowl cut. Her name means "black hair," and her shiny hair matches her dark eyes.

We never learn these two women's names. When we ask, they giggle and hide their faces under their veils. They will only tell us the children's names. Their husbands allow us to take pictures, after we promise never to show them to a man, and to send copies when we get home.

Annick is troubled as we head for the bazaar afterwards. "What kind of life is that?" she asks. "What kind of life will Siah Mui ever have? She is free to run around now, and maybe she'll go to school for a few years, but when she is twelve, or fourteen, her father will put a veil on her and marry her to someone, and that will be the end."

I am more hopeful. "Things are changing. Look at all the girls going to school, and the women on the street without veils, and working in all kinds of jobs. At least Siah Mui is here in Kabul."

Kabul's bazaar is colder in winter, and there are none of the oranges and pomegranates of early spring, or the mangoes and bananas of summer. Now is the time of staples: mounds of wheat and pinon nuts, *nan* fresh out of underground clay ovens, beans, spices, and vegetables. The low angle of the winter sun softens everyone's faces, but there is a hard edge of anxiety beneath the banter and bartering. I take pictures, and look at many faces and scenes, trying to memorize things that may never again be the same. Some of the images I want to remember forever: the moment the flat piece of *nan* is lifted out of the clay oven, a turbanned man with a woman in a *chadori* filling a goat skin with water from a public tap, and men with deep red Bukhara carpets slung over their shoulders, walking around in hopes of finding a buyer .

There are many more soldiers on the street than before. I pass two men, Uzbeks with Mongolian features, and hear them talking about Tashkent in excellent Russian. Khalid has told me that many of the 10,000 Soviet advisers in Kabul are dressed in Afghan uniforms. I feel sure that these are two of them.

In a horrifying moment, a man is hit by a bus. Chaos erupts as a crowd runs toward the scene. The man is screaming, and blood is all over. People are shouting, but we can only watch, feeling powerless to help. I wish I knew First Aid, as no one else does. We stay until the poor man is put into a taxi, presumably to be taken to a hospital.

We are still shaken when we arrive at Chicken Street to visit some of our friends. Feda is glad to see us, but is gloomy about the future. He hasn't been paid by most of his foreign clients, and many of his regular clients cancelled their trips this year, preferring to deal with more stable countries like India. He gives us tea and baklava, and we sit quietly, just looking at people float past the open door of the shop. Some have the overlong ornamental sleeves of their striped silk *chapan* coats wrapped around them against the cold, and others wear rolled woolen caps, with camel-colored blankets flung around them like cloaks of courage.

This part of the bazaar, the shops that sell antiques and tourist trinkets, is nearly deserted. Some shops offer bargain prices, and others desperately try to overcharge.

"Everything half price today," one young man shouts at us as we walk down the street. "They have just taken my uncle to the jail, and I must buy some things for him." We buy a few gifts for friends in Europe and America, as it is nearly Christmas, and accept the young man's prices without the usual bargaining.

A Russian family in heavy coats comes into another shop while Annick and I are having tea. They are looking for furs and *posteens,* embroidered sheepskin coats. Annick's smiling friend Hafiz, who speaks a few words of Russian and now has a new Russian sign outside his shop, offers them exhorbitant prices, which they accept. "For you, we give a good price," he explains afterwards, "but from the *shuravi* we try to get whatever we can."

The shops, restaurants, and hotels are all deserted. We go to lunch in a restaurant whose owner we know. We are the only customers.

"Who comes to your restaurant?" I ask him.

He shrugs. "The locals–those who are still alive."

It is no joke. "If every family in Afghanistan has ten persons, one person is in prison," another friend tells me.

I want to warn the American Embassy, to ask them to send cables to Washington. But surely they must know. Will America stand by and watch an invasion of an innocent people? Or has America written Afghanistan off as "not within our sphere of influence," meaning "not an oil-producing country that affects our vital economic interests?"

I must write an article once I get out of the country. I can begin in Istanbul, where I will be for a few days. When I get to London, I'll try to publish it. I'll send it to America, I'll let the world know that Afghanistan is in danger of invasion, and the world will care.

I dream of walking barefoot among snakes, into the rat temple in

Rajasthan. The rats are feeding everywhere, but they are ignoring me, just running over my feet to get from place to place, like the snakes are slithering. I feel sick with fear, but know I will survive.

I spend mornings working on my novel. Being in Kabul again has made me feel creative and inspired. Darya and her tribe witness the terrible destruction of Bamyan, and know they must flee from everything they have known. They set off into the unknown, into Kafiristan, but while crossing the river on inflated skin rafts they are attacked by local tribes. Darya loses her beloved father, and the child growing within her.

Darya's loss reflects my own sense of regret. I feel an era slipping by, and there is nothing to prevent it. I write feverishly, and wait for Khalid to visit. For a few days he does not come, and I grow angry, remembering his glib promise to visit every day. I have only ten days here, and I long to talk to him, to have my familiar key to Afghanistan for a moment back in my hand.

I wonder if I will ever see Khalid again. If there is an invasion, who will die, who will fight, who will be conscripted? How can I ever reach him or anyone else here again? What will happen to Feda , to Siah Mui and her family? Parwez has spoken to Annick of coming to France and marrying her, but Khalid has said nothing about leaving. I had asked him once if he would fight against the Soviets, but he had answered only, "I am Afghan."

When Khalid finally comes to visit, I forgive him instantly and treasure our moments of conversation. I am in a strange emotional state, full of fear for him, trying to hold on to an icy wind that rips through my fingers and bites at my cheeks.

The ten days pass with the immediacy of a dream, and I must again say good-bye. On my last night, Khalid ivites me to his home. His parents greet me warmly. In the corner of the modern living room a wood-burning stove crackles and hisses, keeping the room warm. Aiesha, who is happy to see me, looks the way pregnant women are supposed to look, round-faced and content.

For a moment I wish it was I who would be sharing Khalid s life, fears and hopes–but I see him pouring another drink, as his mother speaks to him in a sharp tone. He gives the defensive reply of a spoiled child, and my fleeting longing dissolves and turns to compassion for Aiesha.

When I say good-night, I want to hug him, but I know it would not be proper, so I dutifully shake his hand and give him the formal kisses on the cheek. Even this, I realize, is a mark of respect, as Afghan men and women who are not related never greet or say good-bye with kisses.

The next morning, I feel heart-broken as I watch the taxi's exhaust steam into the chilly air. The garden is desolate, but there is beauty in its loneliness, in the way that the sharp-edged trees are etched against the pale silver sky. And I know that the grapevine will again have lush green leaves, and will bear small green grapes in another autumn, regardless of the doings of humans.

Khalid comes running across the courtyard just as my taxi is pulling away. I stop the taxi and jump out. Oblivious to all social customs, I hug him, biting back my tears. He cheerfully wishes me a good trip, and promises to write, though we both know he won't. I get back in the taxi and wave, until he turns away, and I too turn away.

I feel pulled when the plane takes off, as if I am attached to a long invisible, unbreakable, substanceless cord being reeled off further and further into space. The moment I leave, I long to be there again, even to share the fear and uncertainty. I have spent 99 nights in Afghanistan, and it has been a symbolic tale of transformation. But I know that my destiny is different; I am a wordsmith, and must forge swords and plowshares, guns, needles, and lanterns out of experiences and words. The whirlwind's eye has stayed too long over Central Asia, and now I sense that the whirlwind itself is beginning to move, with its fantastic power of destruction, and potential for rebirth.

9 Borders and Barriers

Istanbul, Turkey
December, 1979

"May I help you with your luggage?" asks the slight, fair-skinned, brown-haired young man politely.

I look at him suspiciously, but my luggage is heavy, and he does seem sincere. "Yes, please."

He helps me on to the airport bus, and we pull off through the dismal rain toward Istanbul.

"Where are you from?" I ask.

"Afghanistan."

"Oh, that's why you're so nice and polite! Thank you so much for helping me."

"No problem. Where are you from?"

"America. But I love Afghanistan and wish I could stay there."

"Afghanistan is finished," he says sadly. "I am on my way to Germany. I just got out of the army. In Afghanistan, to get out of the army is like being reborn again into life. So my family in Herat told me to leave, to go to Germany where I know people because of our carpet business. They gave me a few very valuable carpets," he continues, gesturing at the bulky bundle at his side, "and told me to sell them and just stay there. I don't know when I'll see my family again."

I look at him with sympathy. "I have very good friends in Kabul, like family. I don't know when I'll ever see them again either." A heavy lump blocks my throat, and the pouring rain makes me want to cry.

Before Daoud catches his bus for Germany, he helps me find a hotel, carries my luggage, and eases my transition into Istanbul, a schizophrenic city astride East and West, unsure of its identity. After eight months in Asia, I perceive it as very Western, very European, grey, wet, and cold, its streets filled with people in Western clothes, its traffic clotted, most of its buildings the characterless international style of blocky modern architecture.

But as usual, I find kindness. The two brothers and their elderly mother who run the tiny hotel offer me small glasses of strong Turkish tea with lots of sugar, and teach me a few Turkish words.

My days in Turkey pass in a blur of shivers and fear. Soldiers are everywhere in the streets, guarding against urban terrorism. The rain never really stops, and when it thins to a drizzle, an icy wind springs up off the Bosporus. Turkey is in a severe economic crisis, and there is no heating oil anywhere in the city. I go into a five-star hotel hoping to have tea and get warm, but leave because it's just as cold there as it is in my hotel.

I miss the down sleeping bag which I gave to Khalid for his imprisoned uncle. I spend the days half-heartedly sightseeing—half of my broken heart remains in Afghanistan. I realize I'm not seeing Istanbul at its best. I can't get my hands warm enough to enjoy anything, and give up even on the Topkapi Museum. I resolve to return in a better season, when the people of the city might be happier as well. Faces are angry and closed, in the manner of city-dwellers in the West, and too many men accost me, one even in a mosque. I finally kick one man's houndstooth trousers with my muddy boots, and wickedly enjoy his shocked expression.

All I really want to do is write. The only reason I have stopped in Istanbul is because my plane ticket allowed it, and I am always eager to see a new place. But as I sit in my narrow hotel room, typing with numbed fingers on a typewriter balanced on my knees, I wish I would have gone straight to London.

❂ ❂ ❂

I am relieved to be leaving Turkey, glad to run the gauntlet of luggage check-in, customs, and airport security. Finally I go to change my Turkish lira to dollars or British pounds. I am astounded when I am told that I can't change my money because I haven't spent $20 a day.

"No one ever told me," I sputter. "I stayed in a cheap hotel. What could I spend money on?"

The man behind the counter is as adamant as he is indifferent. This makes me angrier. "What am I supposed to do with it?"

His face remains blank and impassive.

"Here, give it to beggars!" I say, flinging the money on the counter.

Some of the coins and notes fly onto the floor as I start to walk away. A dark, moustachioed man grabs my arm. "Now you've done it."

"Done what?"

"What would happen if you threw dollars on the ground?"

"Someone would pick them up and keep them."

I continue to walk away, wondering what I've done, when a security man muscles his way through the line and starts shouting at me in Turkish.

"What have I done?"

"You threw money on the ground," says the first man. "That shows disrespect to our country, and to the father of our country, Ataturk."

"I'm sorry, I didn't mean any disrespect," I explain, chastened. "I didn't even mean to throw it on the ground. They wouldn't change my money, so I told them to give it to beggars."

The security man demands my passport. He takes it and beckons me to follow him.

Now I'm getting scared. Visions of the movie *Midnight Express* are dancing through my head. I haven't done anything wrong, certainly not intentionally. All I want to do is to catch my flight to London, which is being announced right now.

"That's my flight," I say cheerfully, putting my hand on my passport.

The man snatches it away and leads me into an office.

I begin to panic and turn pleadingly to the line of people waiting for the flight to London. "They've taken my passport just because I threw some money," I say loudly. "Can someone please help me?"

The line of sober British businessmen and Maggie Thatcher look-alikes turns away, seeking to avoid a scene at any cost.

Another uniformed man takes my passport and looks at it. I hold out my hand and smile, pointing to the clock and the line. "It's my flight. No problem, I am leaving the country." He slams my passport into a desk drawer and smiles gloatingly.

I am terrified. All I want to do is to get on that plane. I consider making a run for it, trying to get on without a passport. Another man enters the room, his shoulders full of epaulets, his demeanor puffed up. I don't know if he understands English, but I plead with him.

"Please don't arrest me. I didn't mean to do whatever I did. I just want to go to London. Just let me leave."

He looks at me and takes the money off the desk. Suddenly he kisses it, then thrusts it at me. I follow suit, fervently kissing Ataturk's picture.

The officer is at last content. He motions to the other man to give me my passport, and I run to get on the plane, shaking all over.

Even before I land in London, I am in high gear culture shock. The in-flight magazine has an article on how silicon chips could eventually be implanted in human brains to create a future generation of super-intellects. I am so fascinated and horrified by this prospect that I write it down in my journal.

I can't wait to land at Heathrow, as I haven't seen my friends for eight months. Toni and Bibi have promised to meet me at the airport. I am one of the first people off the plane and up to the immigration booth, behind the yellow line.

"Good afternoon," I say brightly, presenting my passport.

The balding, steely-eyed immigration officer nods curtly and looks at my paper. "Where have you come from?" he asks crisply.

"Istanbul."

"May I see your ticket?" He peruses my ticket and says, "I see, Delhi, Kabul, Istanbul. What were you doing there?"

"Just travelling. And writing. I'm working on a novel."

He gives me a withering look. "How long do you intend to stay?"

"I'm not sure. My parents want me to come back to America to work for them, but I'm not sure if I'll do that. I may stay here for a few months and visit friends. I used to go to Sussex University and have lots of friends here."

I know I am rambling nervously, telling far too much, giving all the wrong answers. I should say breezily, "Oh, I'm here a week, and I'll be putting my ticket to America on my American Express card." But I am not yet a savvy traveller.

He squints at the card I've filled out. "Who is Miss Hertenstein?"

"She's one of my dearest friends. I've known her for years, since we met in the Caucasus. I always stay with her." I realize that my accent and choice of words are getting more British, due to my unconscious habit of mimicry that makes it easy for me to learn languages, but sometimes disconcerts or even offends people.

"Come with me please," he says.

"Why? Is there a problem?"

"Just come with me."

My visions of warm reunion freeze up at his icy tone. I begin to wonder if I will be admitted to the country at all. I follow him to the baggage claim area, while he resists all my attempts at polite cheerful conversation, even about the weather.

My throat is dry, my heart is pounding, and I know my cheeks are flushed. I am furious at this man for treating me with such disdain, and not even telling me what he suspects.

I hate the uniform that seems to cause the attitude, and wonder if he's like this with his family, if this sort of job simply attracts a naturally authoritarian personality.

He leads me to the customs area. "Do you have anything to declare?"

"No."

"What a pity. All the green channels are crowded. We'll have to go through the red channel."

He speaks quietly to the customs man, who manhandles my bags and roughly opens them. The customs man takes out each piece of clothing and shakes it out, even the dirty underwear. Then he starts on my hand luggage. He hands my packet of letters from friends, my journal, and the manuscript of my novel over to the immigration officer.

I am livid at this indignity, my blood pressure ready to explode. I swallow hard and literally bite my tongue to hold back a string of curses and vituperative language. "Can you please tell me what you are looking for?" I finally manage to ask with relative calm.

The immigration officer glances at me coldly. "I'm not required to tell you anything."

The customs officer, a little more human, says, "You know what I'm looking for. Do you have any?"

"No, I don't use the stuff."

The customs man helps me put my disarrayed belongings back in my pack. My hands are trembling uncontrollably with anger. The immigration agent, I notice, has worked his way through my personal journal, and is now glancing through my novel.

"That's a novel," I tell him. "You're the first person to read it. I hope you enjoy it."

He doesn't look up, but goes on to my personal letters, picks out a few from Bibi which mention an Iranian friend's experiences during the revolution, and takes them away, perhaps to photocopy them.

I can't believe this indignity, even though I have heard similar horror stories. A Mexican poet had told me how British immigration officials had made him wait until they found a Spanish translator to read his personal journals, and an Indian friend had also had his journals read. I wonder if a traveller has any rights at all, or if all are surrendered when one crosses a border.

The worst is yet to come. I am forced to undergo a strip search. Finally I start to cry. The young blond woman goes about her job, then tells me to get dressed. "I don't use drugs," I sputter angrily, "I don't even like drugs. How can you possibly do a job like this?"

She shrugs. "Just a job like anything else, I guess."

My tormentor returns. "You'll have to have a health check. The doctor isn't here. We haven't reached him yet."

I look at the clock and see that well over an hour has gone by. "May I page my friends? They will be waiting for me."

"In a while."

He takes me to another booth, where we both sit. He is taking all this time, and taxpayer's money, just to deal with me, an innocent person. "Why are you doing this?" I ask.

"To protect the country," he answers, surprised that I should question him.

"To protect it from what?"

"Everything."

I realize I won't get an intelligent, thoughtful, or compassionate response from him. I sink into gloom at the state of the world, and watch the minute hand go round the clock on the institutional wall.

He looks again at one of my letters from Bibi. "According to this, you have head lice, an intestinal infection, and a skin infection. We can't have all that entering the country."

My stomach is boiling. "At the time she wrote that letter, she had just received a letter from me in Delhi, when I had the same stomach trouble everyone else has, a heat rash, and yes, I did have head lice from staying in a middle class family's house, but I took care of it immediately. I had written to her when I was depressed about these things, and she was concerned."

Finally the doctor shows up. I rip off my scarf and say, "See, no head lice. There's nothing wrong with me."

The doctor seems to think the whole affair is ridiculous, and quickly gives me the all clear. I am led back to the immigration booth in the now deserted hall, and given a six-month visa. "Have a pleasant visit," echoes ironically in my ears as I run, sobbing, to see if Bibi and Toni are still waiting, after nearly two hours.

They are relieved to see me. I find out that immigration had paged them, and Toni had answered. Unlike Bibi, a woman of Indian descent born in Zanzibar, Toni is white, a teacher who owns her own house, and solidly middle class. She has the "right" accent despite her foreign sounding Swiss surname, and she has vouched for me that she has recently visited my respectable family in California. At last I am in Britain, but hardly welcome.

I am deeply culture shocked, though my friends take turns hosting me and making me feel at home. All I can talk about is Afghanistan, and like Cassandra, all I see is doom. When I finish my article, I dress up in my proper woolen suit and go with Bibi to meet an acquaintance of hers who is an editor at the *Guardian* newspaper.

"I've written an article on Afghanistan," I tell the receptionist.

"Would that be domestic or foreign?" My heart sinks. I can see that education is going to be a challenge.

The editor is eager to read my article, and before I leave London, tells me they are going to publish it. I am excited about having my first article in a major publication, but I insist on using a false name to protect Khalid and other friends in Afghanistan. I choose Jennifer Baker, after a character in a novel I have written about Africa.

It is nearly Christmas, and my parents want me to come back to America for awhile. They really miss me, but their words say only that they need me to help them finish editing a big film project in their sales promotion business, and so I resist. Half of me wants to go back and see them and my friends in L.A., and half is rebellious and wants to stay in England.

Suddenly they call again. My father had sent the article I had written in Peshawar last summer to *National Geographic.* The magazine has just written a nice letter asking to see more of my writing. It's too great an opportunity to miss, and it swings the balance. I buy a ticket to L.A.

L.A. is hot and smoggy, in the middle of a December heat wave. I am full of Afghanistan, but my father is talking about motorcycle sales training films, and solicitously telling me to write to *National Geographic* as soon as possible. Two days after I arrive I am back in the pressure cooker of the business world—high stress, competition, urgent deadlines. I discipline myself to the job at hand, and drown worries in frame counts and splices.

At noon I go out and see the banner headline, "Afghanistan Coup!" The Soviets have invaded, removing Hafizullah Amin and replacing him with Babrak Karmal. I buy the paper and in a haze of tears read it as I walk into the photo store to buy film. Tears are streaming down my face, and the clerk just stares at me.

"I have friends there! I ve just come from there, and now the Russians have invaded."

"Oh."

My parents understand my concern, but no one seems to realize the implications of this invasion, least of all the U.S. Government, which appears to have been taken by surprise. America is obsessed by the Iran hostage drama, and every night tunes in to network news programs with catchy titles like "America Held Hostage," and special computer-designed logos and hostage theme music. There are Khomeini dartboards and "Nuke the Ayatollah" bumperstickers, and Iranians, Indians, Mexicans, and other brown-skinned people are being attacked and villified on the streets.

I write frantic letters to the President, Congress, the Governor, singers and stars who have helped other refugee causes. There are already 400,000 refugees in Pakistan, and the number will grow quickly now that the country has been invaded. I know the Afghans, know that it will be a long war, but don't foresee the magnitude.

I conquer my fears of rejection and call the *Los Angeles Times* op-ed section. Jennifer Baker publishes another piece, called "Afghanistan's Lonely Rebellion."

I scour Hollywood bookshops for books on Afghanistan. One bookshop owner suggests I look under Africa.

"But it's not in Africa."

"Oh, I thought it was near Morocco."

I work long hours to finish our film project, but my mind and heart are in Afghanistan. I realize I have no way to find out if Khalid and his family are all right, as I don't dare to phone them. I wait and pray.

President Carter speaks strong words to the Soviet Union, and declares a wheat embargo. The farmers are up in arms. He threatens to boycott the Moscow Olympics, and the athletes get up in arms. He gives the Soviets a deadline and they ignore it. Americans don't care about Afghanistan; they are angrily focused on Iran. I call up bookstores, asking for Persian dictionaries, and get cold responses. One man snarls, "If we had any, we'd burn them."

Borders and barriers, cultures and walls. I dream constantly of war, but all I know is that I want to go to Pakistan to find a way to help with the refugees. I want to write and publish more, learn more Persian, maybe write for *National Geographic.* An editor writes me a kind letter, but rejects my proposals to write about the Kalash or the refugees. Though I am disappointed, I make my plans to return to Pakistan as soon as I can save up some money.

10 Ups and Downs: to a Magic Valley

Islamabad, Pakistan
Spring, 1980

My suitcase full of clothes donated for the Afghan refugees arrives at the office of the U.N. High Commissioner for Refugees at the same time I do. It has come a circuitous route—from Dubai, where I have just spent two months helping my friend Bibi's family with their business, to the Tourist Office in nearby Rawalpindi, where I had gone to ask what to do with the heavy case, to this office—by who knows what means.

I view the simultaneous arrival as a good omen for my plans to find work in the refugee camps. Even the Pakistan International Airlines check-in man had been understanding about my 16 kilos overweight. When I had explained that the beat-up old vinyl suitcase tied with green plastic twine was destined for the refugees, he had put his hand on his heart and said simply, "I believe you. Go."

I am ushered into the office of a Danish woman who shares my enthusiasm for Afghan culture.

"Hello, I would like to work with the Afghan refugees," I begin. "I speak some Farsi, have been studying the culture, and I want to do all I can to help. I know there is a need for women medical workers in the camps, as women won't see male doctors. I thought maybe I could be a liaison."

She listens politely, then informs me gently that the Pakistanis allow very few foreign workers. Even though there are over two million refugees just five months after the invasion, and the numbers are swelling daily, the Pakistanis prefer to handle the situation themselves.

But she gives me an application anyway. "Don't get your hopes up," she warns. "By the way, what is your degree in?"

"I don't have a degree. But I know some of the language and I'm learning more every day. And I'm a good photographer and writer, and could get into the tents and take pictures and write articles to tell people about the situation. Doesn't that count?"

My Danish friend sighs. "It should, but it probably doesn't. Go ahead and try anyway. And don't talk too much about what you want to do. The Pakistanis are very suspicious of people wanting to help the refugees."

I return to my tiny hotel room in Rawalpindi in low spirits, pressed down further by the overwhelming pre-monsoon heat. I sweat and wilt as I ride the "wagons," the mini-vans which take passengers the 21 kilometers between the old city of Rawalpindi and its manufactured twin, Islamabad, the capital of Pakistan. The wagons are a poor solution to a major public transportation problem. They wander desultorily, stopping and starting, often packed full, especially the two front seats reserved for women. Often I am squeezed between a modern young woman in a well-tailored *shalwar kameez,* and a mysterious figure in a black *burqa,* a heavy veil with a long piece of thick black chiffon covering the whole face.

My room depresses me further. Its single window lets in no light or air, as it gives onto a brick shaft. When the electricity is out, which is often, I am in total darkness until I can find a stubby candle, which gutters as I light it. Stoically, I type out my application to the U.N., hoping that some bureaucrat in Geneva will see the value of experience over a mere degree.

As there is virtually no chance of working with the refugees until I hear from the U.N., I decide to go to the mountains of Hunza, an isolated valley high in the crumbling, starkly beautiful snowpeaks of the Karakoram range in the far north of Pakistan. I had been enchanted when I had visited last year. As I worked to make money to return to Asia, and sweltered in the deserts of sand, oil, and money in the United Arab Emirates, I had often longed for Hunza's remote splendor and peace. There I hope I will work on my novel and on short stories, as I had done little writing while working full-time in the U.S.

With a lot of help from kind fellow-passengers in the wagons, I find my way to the Ministry of Tourism, and ask for a permit to stay in Hunza for six weeks. The Karakoram Highway, which runs from Islamabad to the Chinese border, is at this point open to foreigners only by special permit, as it is considered a sensitive area.

The man who grants permits looks at me sternly. "The longest time I can give you is two weeks."

My face falls. "Oh, please, isn't there anything you can do? I promise I won't cause any trouble, and will respect the customs. All I want is to find a peaceful place to work on my novel and to study Persian and Urdu."

He looks at me with new interest. "Are you a Muslim?"

"No, but I am studying Islam, as well as the languages. I have studied Sufism for about five years now."

He orders tea for me, leaves the room, and comes back about ten minutes later. "I will recommend that they look kindly on your request. Come back on Wednesday. *Inshallah* you will have your permit then."

As promised, I get my precious permit. I even miraculously get a ticket to Gilgit, the airstrip nearest Hunza, for the next day. All I want is to get out of the hazy sauna of the plains, relieved only by the blue-violet lace of jacaranda trees in bloom. I hardly sleep, and get up well before dawn to catch a taxi to the airport for the 5 a.m. check-in. I pass through security and sit in the passenger's lounge, waiting...and waiting, and waiting. Just past 6 a.m., the flight is cancelled due to bad weather.

I should be rational, should realize that the flight is cancelled for our own safety, as the Fokker-27's, which fly at about 18,000 feet, must fly on visual up valleys between mountains up to 25,000 feet and more. But I am not rational. I just want to get to Hunza. Angrily, I take a seat in the bus going to the PIA office, ready to bully the ticket man into a seat for the next day. But the mild soft-spoken man says he is from Hunza himself, and his smiles immediately deflate my anger.

"But where shall I go?" I ask. "I don't want to go back to the terrible hotel I was in."

"There is a hotel where PIA puts passengers," he says hesitantly, "but foreigners usually don't stay there."

"Does the PIA bus pick up passengers in the morning?"

"Yes."

"Good, I'll take it."

The Deluxe Hotel does not live up to its name. I still don't have a window, but the grillwork below the ceiling lets in some natural light as well as smells. I read, and sleep, and pray the plane will go tomorrow.

I am again up before dawn. Two men from Hunza are also trying to get on the plane. They buy me tea from a nearby tea stall, and together we wait for the PIA bus. When it doesn't come, we share a taxi to the airport, which they insist on paying for. From this point on, the universe shifts slightly and events flow in a comfortable synchronicity.

A handsome young man whom I have never seen before comes up to me and takes my luggage. He takes my ticket and presses into the melee of pushing people to get my boarding card. I am confused, wondering who this fair-skinned man with brown hair and blue eyes could be, when another man greets me by name. He is a friend from Dubai, an Ismaili Muslim born in East Africa who hopes to go to Hunza to meet the community there, said to be pure and uncorrupted. The other man, Samsam, is the brother of a friend of his who lives in the Emirate of Sharjah.

My friend from Dubai doesn't get a seat, but I am lucky. The flight steals away my breath as I look out the window to the awesome mountains. I see Nanga Parbat, the Naked Mountain, and a hundred cat's tooth peaks whose names are known only in local legends, and a hundred more nameless peaks. We fly up the Indus Valley and then make a sharp left where the Indus is joined by the Gilgit River. An hour after we have taken off, we land at the airstrip, gracefully clearing a stand of almond trees. I say a quick prayer, thankful that I have avoided the 17-hour bus ride.

The spring morning is bright, the air refreshing, the sky a brilliant blue. Karim, the owner of the Tourist Cottage, where I had stayed last year, recognizes me and greets me warmly.

"Will you stay?" he asks.

I tell him that I've come to stay in Hunza, and will undoubtedly stay at his Tourist Cottage on my way back.

"Well, let's book your bus ticket. My place is on the road to Hunza, so you can have breakfast there and wait for the bus. I will tell them to pick you up."

Within minutes, I am eating Karim's famous pancakes and honey, which he won't let me pay for. When the mini-bus comes to pick me up, I see Samsam is also a passenger. He looks after me, and insists on paying for my tea at the rest stop.

The road is as treacherous and terrifyingly beautiful as I'd remembered. The landscape changes with each sharp turn over a precipitous drop, the bus toots its horn loudly around each curve, and I still worry about landslides. There are plenty of small rockslides, but we don't meet any just as they are tumbling down. Finally we round the last few bends and the Hunza Valley opens up in front of us, in tones of emerald green and gold, beneath sapphire skies and opalescent mountains gleaming with caught sunlight.

I feel instinctively home, much as I had in Kabul. Years ago, I had read about Hunza, in a health class at Hollywood High. Halfway through the semester, I and another girl who had gotten "A's" on all the tests were banished to the eccentric instructor's library and told to spend our time reading. I was charmed by the story of the high Himalayan valley of

Hunza, where people were unusually healthy and many lived to well over a hundred. I read of their diet of apricots and green vegetables, whole grains, meat only on feastdays, and virtually no salt or sugar. I envied their stress-free life, and dreamed I would someday visit.

I had been surprised to learn that Hunza, an autonomous state until 1974, was now part of Pakistan and could actually be visited, albeit for a limited time. I was even more surprised to learn that it was a bastion of Ismailism.

Hunza was full of surprises. People were warm, spontaneous, open, and calm. Their health, however, had deteriorated alarmingly. There were still many elderly people who were vigorous and full of life, still an active, useful, and respected part of the community and family. A couple were even centenarians. But salt, white sugar, synthetic cooking oil, white flour, black tea, and even cigarettes had arrived with various invaders. Smokers hacked, shopkeepers drank heavily sugared black tea all day, some people had goiters the size of grapefruits protruding from their necks, and others suffered the common Third World curses of dysentery, decayed teeth, and even cancer.

Hunza has long since been a society in flux. Once the British invaded in 1895, there was no going back. But the Hunzakuts have maintained many of their traditions, and I am elated to be coming home again.

A jeep waits for the mini-bus at the village below the capital of Karimabad, high on the hill. Most passengers, sturdy mountain folk, wind their way up on foot. A few people with luggage sit in the jeep, which makes three-point turns on each switchback. When we finally get to the top, Samsam helps me get a room at the small hotel where I had stayed last year. Bargaining starts high, but I end up with a room with an attached bathroom with a flush toilet, a basin, and a shower that gushes forth silty glacial water, ice cold and pearlescent, all for about a dollar a night.

Calm and happy, I sit on the steps drinking spiced green tea and watching the sunset rose-gold on the snow-cloaked shoulders of the great mountain Rakaposhi. In this healing place, my worries dissipate in the lucid sky.

I fall into a pleasant routine. I rise early, drink tea and eat delicious *pfitti,* a thick, whole wheat round bread, with apricot jam. I study the Quran in English, then study a little Persian and Urdu. Then I walk, and sometimes in the afternoon I write.

My young friend Amjed Ali, the 12-year-old nephew of the owner, often comes to visit. He speaks excellent English, and is precocious and mature, despite his child's voice and body. He asks me questions about America, Islamabad, and other parts of Pakistan, since he wants to travel someday. I give him a penknife, because he doesn't ask. Delighted, he digs into his pockets and offers me a handful of opaque, dark maroon garnets which he has found near the river far below, and in the crumbling rock at the foot of the sheer cliffs far above, on the way to the high pastures below the glacier.

A few foreigners come and go, most only for a day or two. I check the post office, and find no letters, but often people who live alongside the soft, dusty irrigation channel road that leads to the post office invite me in. Farida, a pretty young girl, shows me how to rhythmically beat wool with sticks to clean it. I try to help her and her friends, but my fingers are soon blistered, and half the time my sticks lift the wool in the air and it flies away. But no one is angry. They all laugh good-naturedly. Further on, a woman named Bibi Amina invites me into her home. It is a fairly prosperous mudbrick house, three rooms and a covered veranda, neatly plastered and well kept up. She gives me tea and *pfitti,* and we exchange a few words in Urdu. I try to teach her a few English words, and she tries to teach me Burushashki, the tongue-twisting language of Hunza that has no known relation to any other language. English is equally daunting for Bibi Amina, as she can't pronounce "v" or "th," and confuses "p" with "f."

There is never any mail at the post office, but I learn more and more, and enjoy my new friends. I sit peacefully watching, and sometimes take pictures as Bibi Amina and her mother bake bread, sew on a sewing machine on the floor, or do fine needlepoint designs of stylized flowers, birds, and bands of dark green, yellow, orange, and dark pink. They urge me to try, but my unaccustomed fingers are clumsy, and I cannot master the tiny "x" stitches in one day. We have more tea, and chat a little. These friendly women wickedly make fun of the Shiah women of Nagar, the land across the river, and Ganish, the village at the bottom of the valley. They mock the way the Shiah women turn away and hide their faces, for Ismaili women are bold and relatively free, "equal but separate," as one anthropologist described them.

One day I go to the post office with Michael, an independent young Australian with little formal education but insatiable curiosity. The women don't invite us in, but they do greet us, shouting from down the road. I am disappointed at the post office yet again, but when Michael hears my name he tells me what I had feared: he has seen letters for me in Rawalpindi.

I talk a lot to Michael, and find out that he knows my Kalash friend Saifullah. Michael met Saifullah at a cheap hotel in 'Pindi and they became good friends. Saifullah had told Michael all about the sufferings of the Kalash people, and had invited him to come and visit.

Michael is the perfect brother. We talk late, but always in the kitchen/dining room. He is considerate and sensitive, and knows that going to each other's rooms, even just to talk, would be an occasion for gossip.

Lots of local men stop in at the teahouse in the morning and sit smoking, talking, and drinking tea. One of them comes over to the steps where I am studying Urdu, and stares over my shoulder. I look up with a friendly smile to see a tanned, lined face watching me. The man has blue eyes, like many Hunzakuts, and wears the usual soft rolled wool cap, with a bright yellow flower tucked jauntily into the cuff.

He introduces himself as Imam Yar Beg Sany, and invites me to come meet his family. I follow him slowly up the steep path toward the old Baltit fort, a massive stone and wood building now fallen into disuse. The present Mir, the son of the former ruler, has a more modern, rectangular-cut stone edifice further down the mountain.

Hunza lies at about 8,000 feet, and I huff and puff, stopping a lot. Sany greets passers-by and waits for me until I catch up. At the village square, a low stone wall under a shady tree, I stop to rest so I can enter his family's home presentably. Several old men sit around the square. Sany says one, Juno, is the oldest man in Baltit, 106 years old. He looks old, but his eyes are bright and his white hair is dyed partly black, and partly hennaed orange. A few of these elders speak Persian, the language of the former court, and are delighted that I can speak a few words.

To my surprise, it is Samsam's house to which Sany takes me. Samsam's sister is married to Sany, who is also his mother's cousin, quite close ties in the East. Samsam's father, Haji Qudratullah Beg is a spry old man, thin, wirey, and strong, with a prominent nose and a gleam in his eye. He speaks excellent Persian and a little English. He is a scholarly man, from the family of the Wazir, the adviser to the Mir in former times. He has worked with foreign anthropologists, and has written a history of Hunza in Persian.

"But, my head is not so good anymore," he says. "I was kicked in the head by a horse during a polo match, and it has not worked well since."

Aside from Haji's weak eyes, I see little evidence of age. He is a piece of living history, a wise and strong elder who solves disputes over water rights and village matters. At 73, he still works in the fields, while his wife, a slight, thin woman of 67, chops wood every morning.

My life is filled from morning to night with studies and conversation with my many new friends. I hear nothing of the outside world, and don't miss it. I know there isn't much good happening out there, and I want to run away. But when the hotel owner plays the radio and I hear the news in Urdu, I strain to pick up words, and I am frustrated when I recognize a few words like Afghanistan, war, refugees, F-16s.

One day a foreigner brings up a recent copy of *Time* and leaves it in the restaurant. I open up the pandora's box and read of horrors—Mt. Saint Helens has erupted in the Northwest, destroying forest and blanketing the region with ashes; but worse, Miami has erupted in bloody race riots.

As I read the stories, my tears fall and dampen the glossy color pictures of death. I know I can't stay forever in this valley whose magic is its isolation. The world marches inexorably up the valley, and I must bravely go to meet it.

11 Remembrance of God

The dark man with long, unruly hair is not like the other Hunzakuts I have met. He seems nervous, and he does not quite connect with the other people around him. I sense that he is distrustful, and reluctant to answer the German woman's anthropological questions, which a translator asks in his native language, Burushashki.

His distrust is understandable. The young man is Hunza's last *bitan,* a shaman in the old, pre-Islamic tradition. He replies somewhat noncommitally to questions about his life and the traditions surrounding his profession. He watches our reactions, and occasionally changes his story, which frustrates Irmtraud Muller, a scientific anthropologist intent on gathering and analyzing consistent data to support and further her considerable research on Hunza.

I am fascinated that belief in shamans, witches, fairies, and various other spirits such as *boyo* and *raachi* can exist side by side with such devotion to the Ismaili sect of Islam. But the Hunzakuts appear to have happily interwoven their indigenous beliefs and spirits with the new faith, which only came to this valley a little over a hundred and fifty years ago. Perhaps it is a reflection of what went on in Europe when the new Christian religion began to supersede the older, animistic beliefs and Goddess religons, or in the New World, where Catholic Pueblo Indians light solstice bonfires on Christmas Eve.

The young shaman's dark eyes are intense as he weaves stories of the fairies who have adopted him. He describes his twenty-one helpers in detail. He can see them all the time, he says, and he hears their voices in the drums when he dances under a walnut tree. The fairies are beautiful to him, but they have very long fingers, vertical mouths, and feet turned backwards. They live mostly in palaces made of crystal high on the mountain, where some of them herd the Ibex. He has sucked their milk, and has been adopted by them. Some men marry them, he explains, but he preferred to be adopted so he could marry a human woman.

In childhood, the *bitan* had often fallen unconscious unexpectedly. Eventually, his talent for foretelling the future, healing, and consulting the fairies for advice was recognized. He is subject to falling into trance any time, even without dancing to drums and juniper smoke under a walnut tree. To prevent this, his wrist is bound with a twisted iron bracelet made by a blacksmith who rubbed cowdung on it to repel the fairies.

Irmtraud is methodical, intent on objectively examining this alien culture. But I am free from the need to be scientific, and look on the *bitan* with understanding and respect. I can see that his reality is simply different from our ordinary consciousness. His belief system allows him to see and experience what most of us can only know in the world of dreams. He lives in his world, and interfaces with the ordinary world of his people in order to serve them. A Sufi would see the fairies as perhaps another of the multi-faceted manifestations of the Oneness that is Allah—perhaps this is why the Ismaili Hunzakuts have been able to integrate the two traditions so gracefully.

Irmtraud who is one of the foremost authorities on the customs of Hunza, has recently received permission and a grant to make her first visit to the region, to conduct six months of field studies on pre-Islamic traditions. One afternoon, while Sany and I are having tea on the steps, she arrives in a jeep with Sany's cousin, Ghulam Mohammed Beg. Sany, ever full of curiosity, rushes to meet the foreign woman, using me as the excuse.

Ghulam Mohammed is stately and reserved, his dignity increased by his peaked karakul Jinnah cap. Behind his tinted glasses, his eyes are sharp and observant, but he is watchful, slow to judgement, and slow to humor. Over tea, Irmtraud explains her plans, and I in turn tell of my interests. Ghulam Mohammed is especially keen to hear of my interest in Sufism, Ismailism, and the Hunza language and culture. He invites me to visit his bookshop in Gilgit, and promises to lend me some books on Ismailism that he feels are important for my further education.

I invite Irmtraud to meet me later in the afternoon for tea on the verandah. She seems nervous and reserved, but soon warms up and jokes with me and my Australian friend Michael about the rustic kitchen and the staple food, an oily meat curry with chapatis. I assure her that Hunza food is delicious, when one can get it, especially the *pfitti* with apricot jam or stewed apricots that is available every morning.

Irmtraud confesses that it is good to have a Western woman to talk to. I feel the same, since my Hunza women friends and I can't converse freely. I ask if I might accompany her on her investigations occasionally, and she readily agrees.

Ghulam Mohammed arranges for a young man named Murtaza to translate for Irmtraud. He comes from a village down the valley, and is Shia, but not Ismaili. His English is quite fluent, and he is somewhat Westernized. Unlike most Hunzakuts, who look with disdain on the plains culture, he loves Lahore and 'Pindi, and longs to live there. He admires the Iranian revolution and wants to marry an Iranian girl and become a judge in the *shariat* court of Islamic law. But he wears jeans and a Leo belt buckle, and hungers for the West as much as for Islam.

I learn a lot about the anthropological method of inquiry, as well as about Hunza culture. People tell Irmtraud about seeing witches, and one man claims to be a "witch-chaser." A number of people recount dealings with fairies, and one or two older people remember seeing the *boyo,* small spirits native to the valley, who live under certain trees. One evening Irmtraud comes home with handfuls of sweet golden apricots, annoucing, "The first ripe apricots in the valley are always from the *boyo* tree."

The fairies, the *boyo,* and the *raachis* that sit on our heads and shoulders are usually benign spirits. But the idea that witches and witch-chasers inhabit the valley scares me. I had never imagined evil in this valley, but now begin to feel its possibility.

One night Michael and I are talking late. He too is bothered by what is revealed by scratching the surface of this society. By day, everyone is cheerful, working in the fields, beating wool, weaving, cooking. The sunsets are glorious, shell-pink and pomegranate, the mountains are proud and near, sometimes blowing angry breaths off the glaciers above. The land seems in harmony. But witches? What primal forces and fears do they touch?

I leave the warm light of the kitchen to get something in my room. Outside is the blackest night I have ever seen. The stars are obscured by clouds, and there is no light of a large city to reflect back on them. I literally cannot see my hands, my feet, the nearby drop into the valley, or the mountain peaks. This is truly the darkness which swallows mountains, the possibility of annhilation which precedes rebirth.

I dream of Afghanistan. I am on a bus, being warned by one faction of Mujahedeen not to trust another, that they may ambush us. I am travelling by night through a dark land full of fear.

I dream of Khalid, but in these dreams I never get the chance to talk to him. It has now been many months since I have heard from him or anyone else in Afghanistan, and I don't know whether he and his family are dead or alive.

One day, Irmtraud very awkwardly asks me to stay home. Later she tells me that someone, "I promised not to tell who," says that I am a danger to her because I am American. I am angry, but contain myself in front of her. I ask, coax, beg her to tell me who said these things. She is apologetic, but explains that she can't jeopardize her work.

I understand, I tell her, but feel unfairly judged. Resignedly, I stay home and continue my language studies and read the esoteric books Ghulam Mohammed has loaned me. I resolve to get up early each morning and meditate, just as the Ismailis do. I am undisciplined and usually fall back to sleep while meditating, but have vivid dreams.

One morning I come out of my room to find five men sitting on chairs in a circle, waiting for me. My shopkeeper friend, who speaks good English, courteously says, "These are some people from the Special Branch. They want to talk to you."

I am paranoid, and underneath fiercely angry. Every one of these men has been in the teahouse at some time in the past two weeks, posing as an ordinary citizen. I keep my temper and show them my passport and permit, saying mildly, "Is there any kind of problem?"

"Problem? No, no. We are from police, we have just come to investigate. It is our duty."

"I am writing a novel and some short stories. Would you like to see them?"

"No, no, no," says the head officer, embarrassed.

"So, is there much crime in Hunza?" I ask.

"No, no crime at all."

"Then what do you do all day?"

They are all nonplussed.

"I know. You sit around and drink tea all day, just like Ainul Hayat the shopkeeper, just like the hotel owners, just like everybody else."

Finally they all laugh and invite me to have tea with them.

I think I won't be watched anymore, but over the next days I develop an intuitive sense of who is Special Branch. My Hunza friends confirm my suspicions, whispering a few words in Burushashki, or muttering "donkey ears" in Persian.

"What do you do here?" asks one of these agressive plainsmen sharply.

"I write. I study the Holy Quran, Urdu, Persian, and the Hunza culture. Would you like to see my lessons?"

I pull out my notebook with the scribbled Urdu lessons, and he is impressed. "Why do you want to learn Urdu?" he asks suspiciously.

"Why not?" I reply, in a wide-eyed paraphrase of a common Pakistani expression. "So, what do you do?" I ask, going on the attack.

"I am a teacher," he answers promptly.

"Oh, what do you teach?" I see he is thinking quickly.

"Uh, literature."

"Where?"

"In 'Pindi."

"Oh, where in 'Pindi? I know it quite well," I lie.

He names a neighborhood I've never heard of, and I nod. "How much money do you make?" I continue. I am delighted to finally get revenge for all the people who have asked me this question on trains and buses, in teahouses and hotels. He is getting flustered, and mutters something about having to go. I smile sweetly, and wish him luck with his teaching.

I am a little lonely, now that Michael has gone and I am not allowed to accompany Irmtraud on her excursions. But one day Ghulam Mohammed makes a special point of inviting me as well as Irmtraud to visit his home in the village of Hyderabad. He sends a boy who leads us along paths covered with thick, soft, glacial dust that kicks up as we walk. Then we pick our way through dry irrigation channels, and jump over wet ones. Finally we arrive, to find tables, chairs, and carpets set out under the thick leaves of a white mulberry tree. Ghulam Mohammed and his elderly mother, a woman with a crinkled face and bright eyes, are there to greet us. He proudly introduces us to some of his younger children, affectionately cuddling them as they come forward.

Through Ghulam Mohammed, Irmtraud questions his mother. Because she is a *siligus,* a pure woman, a feast of merit was given in her honor many years ago. Now she is a widow, but still active in volunteer service to the Ismaili community, despite her advanced age, somewhere in the eighties. She smiles at me a lot, and when she finds out my stomach is bothering me, sends for the leaves of a plant from which I can make a healing tea.

Ghulam Mohammed respectfully greets a bald, portly man striding slowly up the stone steps to the garden. Though his physical figure is unimposing, I have an intuitive sense that this man is a spiritual teacher. He is introduced to us as the great scholar Haji Nasir Hunzai. Although he has only finished the fifth grade, he reads and writes nine languages, writes and translates Sufi poetry, and has just returned from a stint as a visiting professor at McGill University in Canada.

Irmtraud asks general questions about Ismailism, and then I get the chance to ask questions based on my readings. In a few hours, I learn more than I have in years of reading. Haji Nasir's energy is concentrated, quietly intense. He explains the stages of spiritual growth, from *shariat,* the law which every Muslim understands and obeys, through choosing the Sufi path, the *tariqat,* through the overall truth, *haqiqat,* which the Ismailis believe they are following, to *marifat,* recognition of God. For the first time, I see the Aga Khan the way the Ismailis view him, not as a rich, sophisticated jet-setter, but as the hereditary "Imam of the time" who must always be on Earth as the symbol of the perfected human, as a conduit between God and creation.

We are honored with *diram pfitti,* the greatest delicacy in Hunza. It is a slightly sweet pancake made of wheat sprouted for seven days. But the real delicacy is the very old butter which is poured over it. Hunzakuts bury a portion of their butter each year, in a special hiding place known only to each family's patriarch, who must confide it to his heir before he dies. Some butter has been buried for up to 30 years. Ghulam Mohammed apologizes that this has only been buried for about a year.

Haji Nasir and Ghulam Mohammed attack the dish with great relish. Irmtraud smiles and waves away the butter with what she hopes is a polite gesture. I know I must try it, so as not to offend. To my palette, it is almost unbearably sour, but I hold my breath and chew, and thereby cease to taste. Because of the company and the honor, it becomes sweet to me.

Haji Nasir and Ghulam Mohammed make a program for us for the next few days. I am specifically included. Tomorrow we will go to Mohminabad, a village of musicians and blacksmiths who are from a separate race and speak a different language, and have historically been outcasts. Two days from now they will arrange a special *zikr,* the group meditation practice of "remembrance of God."

After Nasir has left, Ghulam Mohammed tells us more about him. Haji Nasir used to be an Ismaili missionary to Chinese Turkistan, now known as Sinkiang, where there are many Muslims and Ismailis. He was imprisoned there, but meditated every day until he saw *noor,* the light. A voice told him that he would be tied to an electric torture device the next day, but not to be afraid, for he would not be tortured, but released and deported. He returned to Hunza, but was not allowed to bring his Chinese wife, who later died of cancer, or his son. He remarried a Hunza woman, and one of his sons died in a jeep crash not long ago.

I am stunned by this tragic story. How can someone who has suffered so much remain so full of compassion and quietude? Haji Nasir is both more and less present than anyone else. What is his secret? I leave the garden, longing to see the light he has seen.

The religious leaders of Mohminabad ceremonially place shining tinsel garlands over Ghulam Mohammed's and Haji Nasir's heads. To my surprise, Irmtraud and I are likewise honored.

Abdullah Jan, the most famous drum-player in Hunza, proudly leads us to the construction site of the first Jamaat Khana, the Ismaili house of worship, in Mohminabad. The village looks the same as any other in Hunza, the Jamaat Khana and villagers look the same. I can hardly believe that these musicians and blacksmiths have been outcasts, that this is the first time ever that Hunza religious leaders have visited this village.

We are guests in Abdullah Jan's house. The villagers are of the Dom, or Berisho, people, and speak a different language from the majority Burusho people. Formerly, no Burusho would have eaten with a Berisho. There was even a special place on the doorstep for a Berisho to sit, and special bowls from which they had to eat.

Pungent scents waft into the room, where we are seated on the floor around a clean cloth spread for our meal. While we have tea, Irmtraud asks questions through Murtaza.

Abdullah Jan matter of factly recounts stories of the prejudices to which he and his people have been subjected. Ghulam Mohammed and Haji Nasir add their own stories. I listen, and reflect on these strange circumstances. Why musicians and blacksmiths? Why cast out such useful members of society? Yet throughout the Himalayan regions, including Tibetan cultural areas, one finds these outcast classes, usually musicians, blacksmiths, carpenters, and miners who pan for gold in mountain rivers. Did these people inspire fear in working with their magic of fire and rhythm? Did their command of technology, and their contact with spirit through music imply a threat to established rule?

This is a historic meal, as Ghulam Mohammed and Haji Nasir, two of the highest status religious leaders in Hunza, break bread and eat meat with the musicians and blacksmiths. I am moved by the excited, slightly nervous graciousness of the hospitality, and the kind eagerness of

Abdullah Jan and his wife and daughters. Before and after we eat, his small son brings a metal pitcher of warm water, with a basin, a cake of soap, and a towel, for us to clean our hands and faces. Nasir prays before and after the meal, and we all share the delicious spiced mutton stew, rice, and chapatis with great gusto.

Abdullah Jan also has serious business with the religious leaders. Mohminabad is a new name, meaning "place of the believers," and removing the stigma of the old name Berishal, which meant "place of the Berisho." Now the people of Mohminabad want a seat on the regional Ismaili council. Ghulam Mohammed, President of the Council, listens carefully and promises to do what he can.

It seems like the whole village is gathered to watch us as we file out Abdullah Jan's gate and head down the tiny path back to Karimabad, hardly half an hour's walk away. When we get back to the hotel, I am happy, feeling that we have taken a big step toward breaking down ancient prejudices. But when I tell Amjed Ali and his uncle that we have been to Mohminabad, Amjed Ali laughs, and his uncle smirks and says, "Berishal." I give Amjed Ali a short lecture on the equality of all people, and hope I've made an impression on his young mind.

As we enter Haji Nasir's courtyard, Irmtraud and I are garlanded with sweet-smelling, dark pink roses. In an inner room, bare but for an exquisite Persian carpet, we join the crowd assembled for the special *zikr* meditation. About forty people are packed into the room, a knot of brightly dressed women in traditional needlepoint pillbox hats on one side, and somberly dressed men on the other. Irmtraud and I are seated on the men's side near our host and Ghulam Mohammed. Haji's son bustles about, making sure we have pillows to sit on and rest our backs against.

An air of expectation fills the room, a tension between the present moment and what is about to happen, or perhaps a border between worlds. Two *mukkis,* or prayer leaders, cradle guitar-like rebabs, and another man holds a flat skin drum. Slowly, the drum begins to thump a rhythm, and then the rebab players join in with their rhythmic strums. The players begin to sing in Burushashki, songs in praise of the Aga Khan, the Imam of the Time, the channel between God and Earth. Then Nasir takes a rebab and begins to sing, his eyes squeezed shut, his face beginning to sweat with emotion. A subtle change infuses the tiny room as the energy grows and begins to swirl about, and the men and women begin to breath in rhythm to the drum and rebab, chanting, "Ya Ali, Ya

Ali..." over and over.

My own breath and heartbeat are caught in the pounding rhythm. I look at Irmtraud, but she remains an observer, rather surprised by what she is observing. I sink into the waves of sound, and watch the woman we know as the Lady Teacher weeping profusely, then comforting others who have begun to weep and sob. A young man, wracked with sobs, clings to Haji Nasir. Tears stream down Nasir's face as he hugs the young man, like a father hugging his small son. Even the normally stoic Ghulam Mohammed has tears streaming down his face.

My face, too, is wet with tears. The room is expanding, and I feel us all becoming one in this sound, in the scent of my rose garland, in the single breath of a crowd of one purpose. I close my eyes and see a ladder of light, with four steps. It is so bright I cannot see where it begins and where it leads, but I slowly begin to climb it, and reach the second step before the cleansing wave of emotion begins to subside. The music stops, and everyone smiles at each other, dabs their eyes with handkerchiefs, and breathes more slowly, harnessing the power of breath that had run wild.

I am in love, but not with a person. I don't know where these feelings are directed, but I want to hang on to them, to take them down from these sacred mountains where peace is so easy to find, into the teeming plains and choked cities of the world. I wonder if I have the strength to hold on to this feeling, or if I must keep this newfound treasure locked in my heart until someone again finds the key. But having tasted this boundless compassion and love, I now know that it is not a phantom, but truly exists.

As is fitting after ceremony, we share a scrumptious feast. We dine on mutton and rice, salad, chapatis, a special dish of thin bread and fresh cheese, and a wonderful sweet dish which Ghulam Mohammed's mother cals "Hunza Halvah," made of ground walnuts, apricots, and apricot oil.

One by one, the women bid us good-bye, hugging us, kissing our cheeks and hands. Haji's wife presents us both with brightly colored Hunza hats. Everyone smiles when I put mine on, and Ghulam Mohammed says, "Now you look just like a Hunza girl."

Outside, we say our farewells to Ghulam Mohammed and Haji Nasir. Impulsively, I kiss Haji's hand and hold it to my forehead, as I have seen others do to honor him. To my great surprise, he kisses my hand and does the same. As we take our leave, the scent of roses follows us.

I dream that I die into a new body, in appearance exactly the same as the one I've got, but subtly transformed. The old body I roll up and put in a white cloth sack. When my parents come home, I call out to them so they won't find the body and think I'm dead. There is an undertakers strike, but finally someone comes and takes the old body away, and I go on living in the new body.

Each day in Hunza is sweet, as little time is left on my permit. The days are growing longer and hotter, and the nights warming up, bringing tourists from the seething plains. Pakistanis come from 'Pindi and Lahore and Karachi, with large radio-cassette players and a supply of Hindi film tapes and Western disco music, which they play full blast until late at night. At dawn, I think they are getting up for their morning prayer, and listen as they clear their throats and spit—and then click on the cassette player.

I escape into the meadows beyond the hotel, and watch sunrises, sunsets, and starlight. I derive comfort from these scenes, which I seek to imprint in my mind, but when I return to my room it is to the shrill of popular film songs, or the hard beat of disco. I beg the hotel owner to do something. He yells at them, but most of them turn their players up as soon as he leaves. "Bloody Pakistanis!" he snarls, using the only English he knows. But it makes me laugh and cheers me up.

I visit all my friends to say good-bye. Haji Qudratullah Beg seems tired and sad the day I visit. We take family pictures, and I set the camera's timer so I can be in one. Then Haji asks Samsam to bring out an old, heavy book. In the back is a yellowed letter, which he asks me to read aloud. It is from Lt. Col. D.L.R. Lorimer, a former Political Agent of Gilgit who became an expert on Hunza. Lorimer too sounds old and sad, aware that a graceful way of life is fading and giving way to something new and hard, as brittle as the old ways were soft and flowing. I read from Lorimer's last letter to Haji: "The time is coming when your sons must seek their fortunes in Pakistan or in the wider world, where they will perhaps cease to be Hunzakuts."

But still, I am hopeful for this valley, for Hunzakuts have the power of the Remembrance of God. Young and old, they may drink from the fountainhead of existence, and find sweet annihilation of the pain of the material world in the boundless world of Spirit.

12 Many Returns

Peshawar
Summer, 1980

I walk slowly through the steamy, dusty streets of Peshawar toward the Afghan Consulate. The city is more crowded and chaotic than it was last year. The sleepy town, now on the fringes of war, has become a booming frontier town reliving its history as a center of smuggling and storytelling.

But I find nothing romantic about Peshawar on this unbearably hot July day. All I want is to go to Kabul and see if Khalid and his family are all right. I dodge the ever-buzzing, tooting, three-wheeled motor rickshaws with the colorful paintings on their back panels. I avoid the crowds of turbanned men, and try to look as Pakistani as possible in the new maroon cotton *shalwar kameez* and matching flowing chiffon *dupata* scarf which I bought in the Rawalpindi bazaar a few days ago.

At the gate to the rather seedy consulate building, a Pakistani soldier rises from the sweltering interior of an army-issue tent by the side of the road and "takes my particulars." I wonder if merely wanting to go to Afghanistan, now a country under Soviet occupation, is enough to bring a person under suspicion.

I sit for a long time in an empty waiting room. Finally I am ushered into an office where a young man with a heavy moustache sits drinking tea. He looks surprised to see me, and his surprise increases when I tell him I would like a visa to go to Kabul.

"No visas," he says brusquely.

"What? Why? Is it just because I am American? I have heard of other people getting visas."

"Let's see your passport."

He peruses my passport to gain time, then says, "No visas until after Ramazan, the fasting month which begins next week."

"Why?"

His broad shoulders shrug. "Orders from Kabul."

"Then give me a visa before Ramazan."

"Why do you want to go to Kabul?"

My inclination is to answer honestly, "To visit friends," but I stop myself. "I was there last year. It is a beautiful country. I wanted to study at Kabul University." I switch to Persian and tell him, "I speak a little Farsi."

His dark eyes warm slightly, and his lips curve into a slight smile as he asks where I learned Farsi, and flatters me that I speak it with a good accent.

I get embarrassed and stumble on my next phrase, then say in English, "I would like to learn more."

We are finally in a human to human communication. He hands me back my passport, saying, "You come tomorrow morning 10 o'clock. Maybe God will help you."

"Inshallah. Khoda hafez."

Outside it is noisy and hot, a vision of the urban districts of hell. But because I am hopeful, I take less notice. I phone the head of the U.N. High Commission for Refugees in Peshawar and leave a message. I spend long hours in the air-conditioned American Library and have many fresh lime drinks in air-conditioned hotels, using an English-Persian copy of the *Rubaiyyat of Omar Khayyam,* as a shield against unwelcome men.

The next morning I return to the consulate promptly at 10. My would-be benefactor is quiet and reserved, a little intimidated when he ushers me into his superior's office. His superior is an imperious man who speaks no English. He does not even deign to look at my passport. He merely says something in Pashtu to my friend, which I get the gist of.

My friend looks at me apologetically as we walk out of the building. "Not possible till after Ramazan. There is nothing further I can do."

Tears brim in my eyes. He offers me a cup of tea, which I refuse. I almost feel I can trust him, that I can ask if he knows Khalid, if Khalid is all right...but better sense takes over. I thank him for trying and start to leave, then in a moment of pure frustration turn and say, "What are they afraid of? Are they afraid foreigners might see something they don't want us to see?"

He avoids a confrontation. "Better you go now," he warns.

At the hotel, I try to phone the U.N. again, but the phone in the downstairs office/store is padlocked, and no one knows when the owner will be back. I go upstairs to take a shower, but the pipes only hiss and whistle, and no water comes out. Grimly, I get dressed and go downstairs.

Haji Qudratullah Beg, a venerable elder of Hunza, ponders the past and the future. Baltit, Hunza, 1980.

Mir Azam Khan, one of the author's Mujahedeen escorts on her trip into Kunar, Afghanistan, 1983.

Afghan soldiers and friends take refuge from a thunderstorm in an ancient cave at the foot of a monolithic Buddha. Bamyan, Afghanistan, 1979.

In a quiet moment between battles, a Mujaheed smokes tobacco in a chillum. Kunar, Afghanistan, 1983.

Mujahedeen, Afghan resistance fighters of the jehad, pray for victory.

Many of the Mujahedeen are young, "not yet with a beard."

The varied faces of children weaving an Afghan carpet show the richness of the ethnic heritage of Afghanistan. Barakai Camp, Pakistan, 1984.

Chilling harbinger of the future. Kunar, Afghanistan, 1983.

Afghan refugee man with orphans from his destroyed village. Orphaned children are adopted by members of the extended family, clan, or village. Munda Camp, Pakistan, 1984.

As in all war-torn regions, this girl already bears the psychic scars of war, as reflected in her art. Nasir Bagh Camp, Pakistan, 1984

Afghan mujahedeen. Kunar, Afghanistan, 1983

Wounded warriors waiting to be fitted with prosthetic legs so they can return to battle. Peshawar, Pakistan, 1983.

Afghan refugee girl near Peshawar, Pakistan, 1984.

The owner is back. "There is no water," I say with frigid politeness.

"No water?"

"I am hot and would like to take a shower."

"I will send the manager."

The manager follows me up the stairs, and looks into the shower stall. "No water," he says.

Now I am really getting angry. "Yes, that's right, no water. When is water coming?"

He shrugs. "Water turned off. Many Afghan refugees here, and they take showers and use water. Very expensive, so *sahib,* he turns the water off."

"But I am paying for a shower."

He shrugs and turns to leave the narrow room, followed by my shout, "What am I supposed to do?"

There is no answer. I throw a book at the closed door, cursing and sobbing.

There is a knock at the door. "Go away! Don't come back till the water is on!" I shout.

Another knock. I fling the door open, ready to confront the manager, and instead find a thin young man in wire-frame glasses. "Please don't be angry," he says. "Are you hurt? Can I help you?"

I feel foolish. "No, not hurt, just angry. I want to take a shower, and there is no water."

"I understand. My friends and I have been here for weeks, and they turn off the water during the day, when it is hottest."

I sit down on the bed and begin to cry. "I'm sorry. It's so hot, and I want to take a shower, and I want to go to Kabul because I am worried about my friends, and I can't get a visa..."

"Don't go to Kabul!"

"Why not? What will happen to me?"

The young man rolls up the sleeves of his shirt. "I've just come from Kabul, from Pul-i-Charkhi Prison. They cut me and tortured me there. Look at these scars. Kabul is not a nice place anymore. You don't want to go to Kabul."

I stare at the mottled scar tissue on his forearms. "I'm sorry," I say quietly, looking him full in the face. "I had no idea."

He sticks out his hand to shake mine. "I am Zabi. I was a student in the Engineering Faculty of Kabul University. Now I am a refugee."

I introduce myself, and he calls down the hall to his six friends, with whom he shares a small room. The polite, well-dressed young students crowd into my room and introduce themselves in halting English.

My heart nearly stops—one of them looks so much like Khalid that for a moment I think it is him, or his brother. But I bite back my questions, and invite them to share tea with me.

"No, no," says Zabi. "You will be our guest. We are Afghan." One of the boys goes to their room and returns with a boiling kettle and some small glasses, which he fills with light, fragrant Afghan tea.

We drink many cups of tea as one by one, they tell me their stories. I forget about the shower, the cockroaches, the noisy street below, the heat and palpable pollution. I am engrossed by their tragic stories and the pictures of the beloved sweethearts they have left behind, the mothers still in Kabul the sisters in Germany or America. "The cream of the nation has been skimmed off," says Zabi sadly.

Finally I ask them about my friends in Kabul. One man had been Parwez's student in high school, and he thinks Parwez has gone to France. Aziz, they say, has been arrested. Another man knows Khalid's brother and thinks that Khalid and his wife have left Kabul. But someone else disagrees, and thinks he saw Khalid on the street just before he left Kabul himself.

My mind is spinning in confusion. Is Khalid in Kabul or not? If not, where is he? Could he and Aiesha be in Peshawar? Did they have a baby? Will I ever hear from them again?

The seven young men become my brothers. They keep me full of tea, and insist that I am their guest. I don't have to eat alone in restaurants anymore, as they bring in kebab and *nan*. They accompany me when I must go out into the streets, which makes it possible for me to take walks in the cooler night air without fear of harrassment.

My "brothers" go to secret political meetings of Afghan resistance groups, and return to have keen discussions on world politics, the American hostages in Iran, Carter, Brezhnev, Khomeini. They practice martial arts in the park, sweat gleaming on their bare chests as lightning flickers in the grey-green pre-monsoon sky.

After a few days, I finally reach the head of the UNHCR. He is understanding about my desire to work with the refugees, but tells me it is nearly impossible. The Pakistanis don't want foreigners meddling in this sensitive border area, and so he has only tiny staff to cope with nearly two million refugees, whose number is growing daily. But he suggests that I talk to the Pakistani Commissioner for Afghan Refugees, and makes an appointment for me.

The Commissioner is a kindly, elderly man, soft-spoken but regretful. "Unfortunately, madam, I can do nothing for you. I understand your desire to help. If you were to work with some voluntary agencies, I don't think anyone would take any notice. But to do so officially would take months, and your visa will run out in three months. So, go with my blessing. I'm sure no one will trouble you."

I am wilting in the heat, and suffering from fever and intestinal cramps. I long for the mountain valley of Chitral, where it is cooler. Remembering the discomforts of the journey by road, I make my way to PIA, only to be told there are no air tickets for weeks.

I sit in the ticket manager's office, tears of frustration and self-pity welling in my eyes. The ticket manager, a good-looking youngish man, ignores me as he deals with a succession of locals. Finally, after everyone has left the room, he turns to me curtly. "What do you want?"

"Is there any way to get a ticket to Chitral?" I plead. "I just can't bear this heat anymore, and I went by road last year. It was a horrible experience."

His interest perks up "You have been in Chitral before?"

"Yes, last year."

"You went to see the Kalash?"

"Yes."

"They are a special interest of mine."

I brighten up. "And mine. I want to go visit them again, and learn more from Saifullah Jan, the only full-blood Kalash who speaks English."

"I will see what I can do for you."

Sadar Gul orders tea. He busies himself with papers while I sip at the spiced green tea, then looks up again. "Let me do you a favor. Let me be honest with you. You look like a hippie. That's why I didn't talk to you. But as soon as you began to speak I could see that you are educated and intelligent. Why don't you wear proper *shalwar kameez?*"

Today, unfortunately, I am wearing my oldest set of clothes, which have slightly freyed sleeves. I had intended to go to the arms-making village of Darra, and had dressed to sit on a bus for three hours, then had come to PIA on an impulse. When I explain this, he laughs and loosens up.

"I really do have decent clothes," I say. "I do try to wear *shalwar kameez,* as they are very comfortable."

"I'm sure you look very nice in them. Let me give you advice. Take those clothes and put them away. Maybe in the villages, okay, but you should always look like a lady. Our people are funny, and they won't respect you otherwise. And don't wear those big silver earrings. Only the nomads and villagers wear them. I know you people in the West think they are exotic. But here you must wear gold."

I walk out of the office a few minutes later with some good advice and a coveted ticket to Chitral.

My Afghan brothers are sorry to hear that I am going to Chitral. I buy them a chocolate cake at Jan's Bakery, the best bakery in Peshawar, and that night we all feast on it. They ask me a big favor—will I write a letter of recommendation for them to the American Consulate? I am glad to comply, though I know in my heart that it will do no good.

The Chitral flight is delayed, but finally leaves only an hour late. In another hour I am at Chitral Airport. The jeep from the Dreamland Hotel is there, and Deedar, the manager, recognizes me and greets me warmly.

This year Annick's friend Fida Hussain is in town. He is a handsome, robust man with dark hair, a salt-and-pepper mustache, and twinkling black eyes. He is a leader of Chitral's Ismaili community, and I have heard many good things about him in Hunza, where he has relatives. Fida's father was a Hunza missionary in Badakhshan, Afghanistan. There he married a Badakhshi woman, and when Fida was a small child, the family made the long trek back across the mountains to settle in Pakistan.

Fida is one of the warmest people I have ever met, and I immediately feel welcome. It is clear that he is an honorable man whom I can trust.

"Yes, I had heard about you from Ghulam Mohammed," he begins. "He wrote and said an American woman may come."

"I am also a friend of Annick's. You remember the French girl from two years ago?"

"Yes! She was with her friend, and I took them to Garam Chashma, and to some of the villages."

We have tea, then lunch, and I tell him about my stay in Hunza while Deedar prepares a room for me.

In the middle of the meal, a middle-aged Afghan man walks in and greets Fida with hugs and kisses. "This is Abdul Ahad, an Afghan friend of mine," says Fida.

I surprise them both by greeting Abdul Ahad in Farsi. Abdul Ahad answers rapidly, but I manage to understand that he is a lapis merchant from Mazare Sharif. He joins us for tea and opens up his briefcase, which is full of fine lapis. Nonchalantly, he pulls out a pyramidal chunk of the deep blue stone and hands it to me.

"Because you speak Farsi," he says in Persian. "You are our countrywoman."

I am amazed at this rich gift. Fida nods as a sign that I should accept it. I do so with all the grace I can muster in my limited Persian.

After lunch, Deedar shows me to my room. It is a spartan room with a floor fan which marches across the floor when I turn it on to high. I am unpacking when Fida knocks at the open door.

"There are some letters for you. Also a telegram."

"A telegram?" I take the stack of mail worriedly, and puzzle out the handwritten telegram on top.

"Khalid wife and daughter refuge in Germany. Write soon. Love Mother."

Slowly the meaning dawns on me. Khalid is alive, and he, Aiesha, and their daughter are refugees in Germany! "He's alive!" I shriek, holding the telegram to my heart and jumping up and down, crying and laughing. "He's alive!"

Fida is confused. "Are you all right?" he asks worriedly.

I brush the tears away. "Yes, everything is wonderful. I have a dear friend, an Afghan friend, and all this time since the invasion I didn't know if he was dead or alive. Now I hear that he and his wife and daughter are in Germany. And I was trying so hard to get to Kabul to see them!"

Fida orders some tea to be brought to my room, and discreetly leaves me alone to read my stack of mail. Most of it is addressed to Hunza, and seems to have been forwarded from Gilgit by Ghulam Mohammed. There are letters from friends, from my parents, one with a copy of a letter from Khalid in Germany, and one sad letter from my grandmother, almost incomprehensible as she descends into the halfway state between life and death.

In the next days, I spend much time resting and writing. I immediately write to my parents and to Khalid. I run into Michael, my Australian friend from Hunza, who is on his way to the Kalash Valleys. I give him a note for Saifullah, hoping he will remember me from our brief meeting last year.

Fida looks after me well, but he is often busy with work for the Ismaili community, or with his family, who live in a village about 10 kilometers out of town. In the evenings, though, I am never lonely, as Abdul Ahad and his entourage of Afghans sit in a circle on the rooftop, sharing delicious food cooked by his servant, Mohmin. Nearly every night we eat sweet melon from Kunduz in Afghanistan while listening to radio broadcasts in Persian–from the BBC, Voice of America, Radio Kabul, and even Moscow. These men are keenly involved in their country's struggle for freedom. Fida tells me that Abdul Ahad, the happy-go-lucky businessman, contributes large amounts of his profits to one of the Mujahedeen parties.

Not one of these men speaks a word of English, so I go out to the rooftop each night armed with a dictionary and a notebook, and get lessons in Farsi. I also pick up words and phrases I don't quite understand, but start to use anyway. Abdul Ahad has a habit of shouting at his servant and even his friends, "*Mordah gau*" This means "dead cow," so I start to tease him, saying "dead donkey," "dead horse," "dead fly," all of which provokes general laughter. Only much later, in embarrassing circumstances, will I find out that *Mordah gau* is Kabuli slang for a pimp, a terrible insult indeed.

One night, Fida invites me to his home. I am delighted to meet his two wives, one a traditional woman from Chitral, the other an educated woman from Karachi, and his many charming children. Shamsa, who is 13, is exceptionally affectionate and curious. She stays around all evening, and it is she who puts me to bed in a comfortable *charpoy* rope bed under a tree.

In the evening, we listen to Afghan music, and Fida loans me many books on Rumi from his personal library. Fida's Badakhshi mother is happy to meet a foreign woman who speaks her mother tongue, even though I am slow and find her dialect difficult.

I fall asleep to the roar of the river, a sound which accompanies all my travels in these mountains, sometimes louder, sometimes softer, but always present as the boulders grind their teeth on the riverbed. A full moon rises and shines silver on the bare rock mountain opposite Fida's hillside house.

Fida, ever generous, invites me and Abdul Ahad to accompany him on a business trip to Garam Chashma. Though the road is rough, his jeep is far more comfortable than the public jeep. And he and Abdul Ahad are great company–the irrepressible Abdul Ahad dances in his seat to blaring Afghan music all the way to Garam Chashma.

Fida arranges for me to stay with some friends of his. He leaves me with the small family, none of whom speak any English. Somehow we get by. I have copied a few Chitrali words from a word list in a book on the area, and when I am at a loss try Persian or Urdu words. There are enough words in common that it often works.

The temporary head of the family, the son-in-law of Fida's friend who is away, does his best to offer hospitality, but I can see that there is little food in this remote area. He goes out to catch fish in the river, but is not lucky. We dine on rice and green onions, and they insist that I eat the single egg they have cooked.

I sleep well, and arise at dawn. With the constant lullaby of the river, this is a peaceful place. I take pleasant naps during the long, warm afternoons, and look up at the rock-sealed cave, decorated with white flags on sticks, where the Sufi ascetic Nasir Khusrow had meditated for 40 days.

In the village, I meet a troupe of Mujahedeen, as friendly and warm as any Afghans I have met. Even though Ramazan has begun, they insist on giving me tea, stew, and rice. I am reluctant to offend custom, but they explain that the fast is not incumbent on travelers.

After lunch, two ragged men greet me shyly and respectfully. I don't understand most of what they are saying, but hear something about a wounded girl. I follow them across the river, through the stones of a dry streambed, and up onto a bluff where a bright yellow refugee tent is pitched. The womenfolk cover their faces and disappear into the tent, as some Mujahedeen are behind me.

Inside is a young, very beautiful girl with the face of a madonna. She is obviously in great pain and very tired. One of the thin bearded men draws aside her red-printed veil to reveal a horribly infected wound in her neck. It is swollen, red and white and yellow, and her black hair is matted into it.

I lose all my Persian words, then focus and get them back. "I must get medicine in my house," I tell them, and ask one of the men to come with me so I can find my way back.

I run wildly, tripping on the stones, slipping into the water. I have never seen a war wound before, and I'm not sure what to do. When I return with medicine, I ask them to boil water, then clean the superating wound first with soap and hot water, then with Q-tips dipped in antiseptic. The mortified skin moves around the lip of the wound, and my hand shakes. I don't know if antibiotic cream and tetracycline will cure this—no, it won t. This girl must go to the hospital in Chitral and have the piece of shrapnel lodged in her neck removed. I tell them this, and leave them a course of antibiotics along with some antibiotic cream and bandaids.

That night I dream I am on a raft on a river. Helicopters are above me, and I am about to be arrested because my bright orange rucksack and my journal are visible, and have marked me as a foreigner. I am relieved to awaken to uneasy reality.

Back at the Dreamland Hotel in Chitral, I am reading about Rumi's life when there is a knock at my door. I answer it and find myself face to face with a handsome, European-looking man with green eyes, but wearing a *shalwar kameez.* I look at him questioningly, and he looks equally uncertain.

Then the features resolve, fade into darkness, firelight, and the sound of mournful song. "Saifullah?"

"You are Debra, aren't you?"

"Yes, please, come in."

He sits down on the bed. "I got your note, from Michael."

"Oh, I didn't expect you to come here!"

"I didn't think you should travel alone. I have come to accompany you to Rumbur."

He closes the door and lights a cigarette, explaining that Muslims do not like to see anyone smoking or eating during daylight during Ramazan. After we talk for awhile, our warm friendship is restored to its easiness.

"Can you leave today?" he asks.

"I don't have a permit."

"We will go to get one."

We wind our way up the hill to the Deputy Commissioner's office. Saifullah hangs back at the gate, and I wish I could hang back too once I see the imperious man behind the huge desk.

He frowns when he looks at my request. "Seven days?" He looks incredulous. "Impossible!"

"I know that you have given other people seven days."

"Do you know what can happen in these border areas?" He picks up an artillery shell from his desk and bangs it back down for emphasis. "An Afghan shell. On Pakistani territory. This is what can happen to you, and you are our responsibility."

"If it can happen in seven days, then it can happen in five, or in three."

He is flustered for a moment. He picks up the phone and shouts in Urdu into it, finishing with an English, "And that is an order!"

I refuse to move. Finally I slam my passport down and say, "It's because I am American, right? You're just being prejudiced. You'd give it to someone with a British passport, wouldn't you? You're not being fair."

He is nonplussed. I don't mean to be dramatic, but I am tired of being blamed for policies which in many cases I don't even support, made by people I didn't vote for.

My speech from the heart works, and I walk out with a seven-day permit.

It is about noon when Saifullah and I get places in a jeep, sharing the front seat. It is a beatup old vehicle, with suspicious-looking wires and twine holding on door handles, and probably important internal parts as well. At Ayun, an unimposing village which is a transfer point for jeeps to the Kalash valleys, we get into an even worse-looking rattletrap, which groans its way up the switchbacks, bouncing and jostling. Every turn is a thrill as we climb higher and higher in the barren landscape, which reminds me of the dry, eastern side of the Sierra Nevada Mountains in California.

Suddenly the steering gives out, and the driver takes his hands off the wheel and begins to pray loudly. We crash into the side of the mountain. Luckily, no one is hurt, as we weren't going very fast. Saifullah is unruffled, but I am shaking, looking down a thousand feet toward the river below, thanking God we hadn't been pointed in that direction.

We wait for hours as the driver tinkers with the jeep. One of the passengers has walked ahead and gotten another jeep from Bumburet, so we pile onto that one, abandoning the broken jeep and hapless driver in the deep twilight, and continue on to the lodge in Bumburet.

The next morning, Saifullah and I decide to walk to Rumbur, where he lives. I don't want to waste the precious time of my seven-day permit waiting for a jeep. So we start out along the dusty path, Saifullah carrying one of my bags and me struggling with the other.

I had not expected to walk much, so have only brought the thin, worn Indian buffalo hide sandals on my feet, which are clearly not up to the long walk. But the beauty of the unfolding land captivates me. It is summer, a dreamtime of wind in tall maize fields, soft and loud roars of rivers and streams, and thick, cool deodars on the hillsides. Women in cowrie shell headdresses and long black robes greet us enthusiastically. We also pass Kalash men who wear feathers and flowers in their rolled wool caps, to distinguish themselves from Muslims.

At last we reach a tiny settlement near the bridge across the roaring river, where there is a hotel of sorts. The dirt-floored lodge is owned by Saifullah's father-in-law and run by his brothers-in-law. It has many *charpoys* in a large room, which I will have to myself.

I soon fall into a routine. I arise each morning at dawn and go to the chilly irrigation channel to wash. Saifullah joins me for breakfast, then returns to the village if he has business. I write down Kalash words and phrases, which I practice with villagers when he isn't around.

I am content to simply watch what is going on around me. I sit on the ground by a large boulder with a group of women and girls and help them crack apricot kernels, which are strung into long necklaces. The women chat and sing as they work, and sometimes make simple jokes that I can understand. Mikinili Bibi, a green-eyed beauty with especially shiny long black braids, gives me an apricot kernel necklace, which I put over my head. Some of the girls braid my hair in Kalash fashion, unable to bear the sight of only two braids when there should be five.

I soon find out that there are lots of subtle prejudices on the part of both the Kalash and the Muslims. The small mosque in this village has a provocatively loud loudspeaker. Many Muslims, I discover, are not Chitralis, but ethnic Kalash who converted, or whose ancestors were forced to convert. The practicing Kalash have good relations with their Muslim neighbors, but are openly hostile toward Muslims from outside their valleys, whom they view as interlopers. Among themselves, my girlfriends joke and call each other "Muslim" as an insult.

I am the only foreigner in this little-visited valley. Word spreads quickly, and various friends and relatives of Saifullah's come to have tea and take a look at me. Saifullah makes a lot of time for me. His English is excellent, quite idiomatic. Occasionally he even lets out a string of four-letter words, learned from tourists and anthropologists. He is easy to be with, but smokes constantly, and I can tell that inside he is nervous and frustrated, longing to finish his education as a lawyer, and for the money to make that possible.

On our long walks, he opens up to me. He tells me how his father had sent him to school as a child, after his elder brother had died. He had walked down the river, three hours each way to Ayun and back, and there had endured insults even from the teachers, some of whom called him "dirty Kalash." He had come home crying and refused to return to school, but his father had beaten him and sent him back. In the end he had emerged literate in several languages, including Urdu and English, and ready to take up his destiny as *de facto* tribal leader.

Saifullah's destiny lies heavy on his thin shoulders, and there is often sadness and pain in his clear eyes, the green of this mountain river. He is a living contradiction, an educated man living in a village, a man who looks like a sophisticated Frenchman on a devil-may-care holiday, but who is utterly entwined with this land and people.

On my last day, Saifullah and I visit the hillside graveyard of the Kalash. We sit on the crisp brown leaves of many sad years as I ask him endless questions about gods and creation, and funerals, marriages and feasts of merit. Patiently, he answers all of them. He even tells me the story of how he had fallen in love with his wife when she was married to someone else, and according to custom had had to pay twice the original bride price to the ex-husband. Marrying his wife had cost him a lot of bulls and goats, and a couple of radios and alarm clocks, he explains ruefully.

"Where is she now?"

"Up at the summer place."

"Can I meet her?"

"Next time you come, I promise."

Finally I run out of anthropological questions, and we just sit and look down at the river, listening to flies buzzing in the summer heat. The leaves crackle as I move, and I become aware that sparks are flying on another plane. I feel a strange love for Saifullah, and a strange attraction. I sneak a glance at his profile, and notice how handsome he is, with his high cheekbones, wide green eyes, sensual lips, and touseled brown hair. But when he turns to me, I dare not look into his eyes.

The moment passes, and Saifullah lightly takes my hand to help me off the steep hillside and lead me back to the village.

That evening, we sit in the garden of the poorly stocked dispensary, watching the moon rise and talking about America–Disneyland and movies, freedom and spirit and men on the moon. I want to comfort him, but I don't know how. I want to tell him that the Kalash will get back their walnut trees and their land, but I don't know if they will. So I sing him a song, Todd Rundgren's "Love is the Answer," and he listens enchanted.

That night, on an impulse, I insist that he take all the cash I have except what I will need to get back to Chitral. He is at first reluctant, then gratefully accepts it, knowing that it will help his cause.

The next day he accompanies me to the end of Rumbur Valley, and sends his cousin with me the rest of the way to Bumburet. It is a long hot walk, and I feel a sense of regret and sadness I cannot define. At Bumburet, the only jeep driver wants 60 rupees instead of the usual 20. Since I don't have that much, I argue vehemently, using two Afghan refugees as translators. The driver remains adamant, knowing he will get passengers eventually. I have no choice but to head for Ayun on foot, leaving Saifullah's cousin looking very worried.

I fill my water bottle at a spring seeping out of the hillside on the first steep ascent to the pass. The bottle is heavy, but I don't dare pour any water out. The adrenaline of my anger keeps me going even in this heat. I curse my inconvenient shoulder bags, and my flimsy sandals. The sandals soon get revenge by breaking. I try going barefoot for awhile, but the sharp stones cut my feet, so I stumble along with a broken shoe that flies off every few steps.

I begin to count the number of steps I can take without losing my shoe or hurting my foot. I get to the point where I can take over 600 steps at a time. I concentrate on this, not on the heat, my thirst and hunger, or my fears. When I stop to rest, which is quite frequent, every rustle I hear sounds like a snake, and I turn suddenly to realize that it was my own clothing that rustled.

I find short cuts by following the prints of someone's rubber sandals, rows of little circles in the dusty sections of the path. Sometimes I lose them, but I keep on, and pray silently. I have only dried apricots to eat, which make me thirsty, so finally I start on the apricot kernel necklace which Mikinili Bibi had given me.

I try to keep courage by thinking that I am, after all, where I want to be. I remember my junior high school English teacher, Sandra King, who had given us a reading unit called "Venturing into the Unknown." Yes, that's what I'm doing, venturing into the unknown. And I wouldn't have it any other way. I wouldn't be tied to a desk or a classroom or a schedule, or a numbing freeway commute. I am living my life in an unorthodox manner, but I am doing what I want to do, even if I must pay different prices.

I walk until it is nearly dusk. I see the village of Ayun far, far below, still miles away, and I know I cannot make it before dark. Then I see a path leading down to a mud house, and rejoice, sure that some villagers will give me shelter. I practically run down the steep ridge, only to find the hut deserted.

I shout to the sky, to God, "What am I doing here?" "Here, here, here..." my words reverberate from the ruddy stone walls of the barren mountains. "Help!" I shriek. "Help, help, help..." the mountains mock me.

I begin to cry hysterically. My water is nearly finished and I have little food, but I do have a sleeping bag, though I don't know what kind of wild animals might be in these mountains.

I force myself to keep going, sobbing and breathing hard, stumbling and hurrying. I pause at the place where the shortcut rises to rejoin the road, and above my harsh breathing hear a motor. I turn and see a cloud of dust, and begin shouting at the top of my exhausted lungs. To my joy, the jeep stops, and someone runs down to haul me up the last few agonizing steps into the back of the jeep. A miracle has happened. As my shoe falls off for the last time, someone stoops in the dust and puts it back on my foot.

13 Hellish Trains

India
Summer, 1980

The train jolts me awake, and I squint at my watch. Four-thirty a.m. The train will probably arrive late in Jammu, but I should put my contact lenses in now, so I'll be ready to rush to find a bus to Srinagar. I stretch my aching limbs and grope around my sleeping bag feeling for my small shoulderbag with the contact lenses and mirror in it.

I curse and grumble sleepily, looking under the wooden seat with my flashlight. Shoulderbag and camera are nowhere to be found. Like a cold slap it hits me that they have been stolen—I start shrieking for help.

The German women in my compartment wake up terrified, but no one else comes to my aid. They comfort me as the enormity of my loss sinks in—passport, all my money and travellers cheques, all identification, my camera, and a box of jewelry collected from years of travel. I am sobbing furiously when a strong man's shoulder forces open the door to our compartment, which had been stuck shut.

"What is wrong? Are you all right?" demands the handsome Sikh.

I cannot answer, but the German women tell him I ve been robbed.

"This is an outrage!" he shouts angrily. "You must search everyone on the train. I will help you."

He starts questioning everyone in the compartments near us, while I put in my extra pair of contact lenses with spit and shaking hands. When I can see this disastrous scene more clearly, I ask him to stop questioning people.

"It's none of them, I'm sure of it." I tell him about the leering faces that had looked in at me through the open window from the platform when the train had stopped at about 3 a.m., and how I had moved my camera and bag closer to me, but had not closed the window because of the heat, and had fallen asleep again. My big mistake must have been to have gone to the toilet—even though the train had been moving, and our door had been stuck at a narrow opening which I had barely been able to squeeze through.

The Sikh shakes his head. "Every night it happens on this train, in the second class compartment. It happened to my wife two weeks ago. I am an army officer and normally I would travel first class, but I travelled second class tonight just to see what would happen.

"The conductor is in on it, and the driver is in on it. I know. They are organized gangs. They give the conductor and driver *bakhsheesh.* The conductor points out who is not paying attention, which ladies are alone and unprotected, which travellers seem to have money, and then the driver stops or goes slow at a pre-arranged time, so the thieves can abscond with the goods."

My heart is sinking to the bottoms of my feet. All of my things are really gone. The camera I had travelled with for years, the jewelry with sentimental attachments, and every cent I have in any currency. I am enraged at myself for being so stupid. I berate myself for having slept with the window open, for having slept on top of my sleeping bag with my valuables outside, for having left anything for even a moment, for not being as alert as one has to be when travelling alone, especially on an Indian train. After four months in India last year, I should have known better.

I am still sobbing when the train pulls into Jammu station. The German women take up a collection and give me a few rupees each. One gives me a hundred, and I ask for her address.

"Never mind, never mind," she says hurriedly, "It could have happened to us."

But I insist, and she scrawls out her address at home so I can return the money.

The Sikh officer, in civilian dress, leads me to the Railway Police office, a dank cell on a lower level, with peeling, ice-blue paint and a lazy fan.

The scene takes on an increasingly nightmarish quality. I am in shock, feeling angry and violated. The thought of some thief's hands on my camera, and smearing gold charms and silver earrings given to me by my parents and friends, or collected in faraway bazaars, churns my stomach into a hard lump of anger.

The officer goes to find someone in charge, and I am left alone. Everyone from police officers in uniform to sad-eyed sweepers peeks in to look at me. Many of them seem to find my tears amusing, and I get angrier and angrier. Someone finally brings me a cup of tea and slaps a piece of stale, dry white bread on top of the cup. Gingerly, I eat it, staring at the chain-style handcuffs hung on a nail on the wall next to two ceremonial turbans, and feeling like a victim taken to prison.

Much, much later, the Sikh army officer returns in full dress. He takes me to the office of the Chief Inspector, who salutes smartly. In English, the Sikh demands redress for my grievance. "This is a disgrace to our nation," he says fervently. "You people are obviously not doing your job. You should make sure that this young lady gets safely on the train to Delhi to replace her passport and papers. You should buy her a first class ticket and put her on the train yourself."

The Sikh leads me back to the first office. "He says for you to wait here," he says kindly. "He assured me that he would take care of you, but he needs a statement first. I will come back later, if I can." He shakes his head sadly. "This is truly a disgrace to our country. You should write to the Prime Minister about this. She is a woman and she should understand."

We shake hands good-bye. "Luckily, I was in India for four months last year," I tell him, "so this is not my first impression of India. Thank you for your kindness–I would rather remember that as more typical of India."

I spend eight hours in the police station. They tell me to write out a statement and a list of the valuables stolen. I am to write it on the back of reservation charts. When no one comes for a very long time, I drag out my typewriter and my own stationery supplies, and type out a more official-looking list, in quadruplicate. The date is very important, as my insurance is due to expire in three days. I begin stoically, but let out repeated gasps and groans of anger as I remember some piece of jewelry I will never see again–the Arab silver ring from the island of Lamu off the coast of East Africa; oh no, not the Islamic seal ring from Jerusalem! And the bastards got the amethyst earrings that Mother had bought me in Bukhara...on and on, until I remember that even the lapis bracelet Khalid and Aiesha had given me was in that box.

I have plenty of time to think of the long jouney which has led me here. I remember as if recollecting a dream, Fida Hussain's kind face at the bus station in Peshawar when he put me on the night bus to Lahore, just two days ago. Then the pouring grey-brown rain in monsoon-flooded Lahore, the closed Salvation Army hostel, and my decision to get out of Lahore and leave for India. The heat was driving me mad, and I decided to make a run for the cool hills of Kashmir.

I begin to realize what sleep deprivation does to a person. I hadn't slept on the bus, hadn't rested in Lahore while trying to turn in my Foreign Registration form, which no one knew anything about; hadn't rested on the border train to India, which had smacked up against the border like a moth against glass.

At the border, I had mislaid some necessary piece of paper, and in my flustered state, had broken the zipper to my shoulderbag. With a sinking feeling of ironic shame, I remember cursing the purse, then noticing that my silver Allah had broken off its loop and was lost. Just like the moment when I had discovered the robbery, when my hand had automatically clutched at my necklace, and the double-heart protection against the evil eye had also broken in two.

I asked for it all, I berate myself. I cursed my purse and lost my temper, and taunted the universe. I deserve my bad fortune.

The letters I had collected in Lahore had been depressing. Khalid's heartbeaking letter describing how he and Aiesha had escaped on foot and on donkeys with their two-month-old daughter, who had been severely ill at the time. Mother's letter telling me how my grandmother was losing her mind, and another incoherent letter from Grandmother confirming it. A heart-wrenching poem called "Ash Wednesday," written for me by my dear friend, poet Susan D. Baker, full of images of Afghanistan. Yet I had rushed on headlong to Amritsar, and then miraculously onto the train to Jammu, the railhead for the buses to the vale of Kashmir. I had been so happy to get a berth in the Ladies Compartment, where I felt safe.

But, I had not been alert. My throat had begun to rasp and hurt, my joints had ached, and I had a fever, from the heat or from flu I couldn't tell. But in my mind and heart remained the vision of the beautiful lodge where I had stayed last year, in a clearing in the pines above the village of Pahalgam.

In this dark room lit by dim fluorescent light, I try to recreate Kashmir. But I can't go now. I must go deeper into the furnance of August in India, to Delhi, which I had hoped to avoid till autumn, and replace my passport and travellers cheques.

Finally, a police inspector comes in and slowly reads my statement aloud in English to a table full of stenos, each of whom laboriously copies out the statement by hand. Then the same process begins in Urdu. Someone takes me to buy a ticket on the train to Delhi but no one buys me a first class ticket as my Sikh friend had suggested, and I must pay out of the money the German women had given me.

I try to sleep on the hard wooden pallets of the retiring room. I tie a long scarf around the handles of my typewriter and the straps of my rucksack, and knot it around my body. I drift off into spurts of anxiety dreams, but wake up periodically to find that there really is a black dog snuffling just under my ear, or a man standing over me staring at me blankly. Police officers keep bringing me statements in Urdu, which I sign even though I can't read them. I have a typed copy of my statement and a list of my losses signed and sealed by the police, which I will need for the insurance company.

Things could be worse, I muse. This could have happened next week, when the insurance had expired. But nothing can replace my sentimental items, and my blood boils again in this heat.

I don't sleep well on the train, which is late and arrives in Delhi at mid-morning. The rickshaw driver overcharges me, and there is no room at my usual rooming house. I am allowed to store my luggage and take a shower, then hurry to the U.S. Embassy.

The Embassy is miles from the city center, and thus expensive to get to. I have to wait to place a collect call to my parents, who are not happy to be roused at 1 a.m. by bad news. The Consular officials are polite but businesslike. I am relieved that I can get my passport in a day, even with no identification other than a few letters addressed to me.

At American Express, a kind, cheerful man named Mr. Om Prakash offers me tea and makes good on all those advertisements that they replace your cheques immediately. They cancel my old card, and tell me to come back tomorrow for new cheques, and in a few days for a new card.

But life remains Kafkaesque. The owner of the rooming house decides to overcharge me for sleeping on the floor, then tells me I wouldn't like my dorm mates anyway, as they are noisy. I remember the heroin addicts who had stayed there last year, and decide she's right. But all the cheap hotels are full, and I am getting desperate until some kind strangers lead me to a place where I can sleep on the balcony. Two Italian hippies decide to smoke endless rounds of hash on the same balcony, and get terribly offended when I tell them I need to sleep. Finally, after three nights of virtually no sleep, I fall asleep out of sheer biochemical depletion.

The next day, refreshed, I spend my last few rupees on passport photos, which don't come out, and have to be redone. American Express has my cheques, but needs identification. I can't pick up my passport because I have no money, and can't cash my cheques without a passport.

American Express solves the problem by calling the Embassy, which gives them my passport number.

I think my ordeal is over, but the Embassy tells me I must go to the Foreigner's Registration Office to get my visa replaced. This sounds simple enough, but at that office I am informed that it will take three weeks to replace my visa, as they have to send a telex. But telexes are instant, I protest. The *Babu,* as Indian bureaucrats are called, looks annoyed at my impertinence and tells me to come back in three weeks.

All I want is to get out of this heat, and then as soon as possible to get out of India. Back at American Express, I find out that all the cheap flights are booked for weeks. I make a reservation for three weeks from now on a more expensive flight and charge it on my replaced American Express card, grateful for my middle class privilege.

I decide to go to Kashmir and wait for my visa in a cooler, more healing climate. To my horror, I have to deal with railway booking offices again. The short-tempered and rude *babus* inform me that there are no Ladies Compartments on this train. I give up and take what I am given.

I finally find a halfway decent hotel and spend many hours beneath a fan, feeling chilled and fluish in the nearly 100% humidity. The oppressiveness is relieved when a few cool drops of rain fall on the parched city. I lie musing on fantasies of the lost city of Kabul, and Khalid. I've reconciled myself to the loss of my things—what can the bracelet matter if Khalid and his family are alive? Having surrendered, I find my silver Allah at the bottom of my denim bag, and feel God has returned to me.

Back in Jammu, my luck turns. I find a bus going directly to Pahalgam, carrying pilgrims joining the August *yatra* to the Amarnath caves. I jump at the chance to avoid the humid, teeming city of Srinagar, and bless my changed luck.

The bus is filled with *sadhus,* wandering holy men on their way to the cave of Amarnath, high in the Himalaya. Inside the cave is an ice lingam, the phallic representation of Shiva, the Hindu god of destruction and regeneration, which is said to wax and wane with the moon. But despite the sacredness of the journey, many of these *sadhus* are most unholy in their behavior, arguing and shouting boisterously. The other pilgrims range from poor Rajasthani women in brightly colored saris with no blouses underneath to solid middle class folk. Most of them seem unusually ill-tempered and sullen for people about to embark on one of the holiest pilgrimages of Hinduism.

The bus arrives well after dark, at about 9 p.m. Feeling invigorated by the cool air, I walk through the village, cross the bridges over the two rivers, and start up the steep path toward the Aksa Lodge. But in the pitch darkness, I put my bags down for a moment to rest and take out a flashlight. Foolishly I wander a few steps off the path. I become totally disoriented, and can find neither the path nor my luggage. I am starting to panic when I trip over the wooden strip that marks the steps cut into the hillside leading up to the lodge. I abandon my luggage, reasoning that if I can't find it no one else could either, and climb the hill, finally stumbling onto the verandah.

Mohammed Yasin, the proprietor, remembers me from last year. He sends two servants with a flashlight to look for my bags, and sits me down in his office with a cup of *kahwa* the Kashmiri spiced green tea. The only vacant room is the big room on the ground floor, but he tells me to take it for tonight, and not worry about the price.

The Aksa is like paradise after the purgatory of the plains and the hell of the trains. The night sky is brilliantly clear, and soft breezes confer in the tops of pines. I smell the scent of mountains, which I had missed so much in just these few days, and the sweet and heady scent of the colorful flowers in the garden. It is a great pleasure just to be cold again, and unimaginable luxury to think that I will have a hot shower in the morning. I drink another cup of *kahwa* and snuggle into the warm quilts, with thankful prayers.

Kashmir is balm for my wounded soul. I am overjoyed to be in mountains again, to see the varied hues of green, from the misty, deep green of the forest to the more intense, sunnier greens of blades of grass and leaves of plants. Mohammed Yasin has planned a brilliant garden, somewhere between the order of a Persian garden and the chaos of natural growth. I eat breakfast in the garden and then explore, looking at the tall, waving cosmos blossoms of white, purple, and bright lilac, and the zinnias of every color an artist would struggle to blend, from straightforward red and orange, deep yellow and rose pink, to subtle salmon and lavender, peach delicately edged with light purple, and lavender with apricot centers.

Yasin and I have tea, and agree on a price for the room. It is more than I had intended to spend, but a bargain for that wonderful room. I decide I need to be kind to myself after all I have been through. I enjoy talking to Yasin, a handsome young man who dresses like an Englishman with fine tastes, favoring sleeveless wool pullover vests over elegant shirts. Yasin is constantly making improvements on the lodge, which he excitedly points out to me. I am again impressed by the rustic lodge with the textured panels of pine bark, the smoothly varnished pine, the bedspreads and batiks in subtle, tasteful colors, and the delicious food and cool spring water. It is one of the nicest places I have ever stayed anywhere. Best of all is the soothing music, Western classics and Indian classical, that floats quietly across the verandah and into the garden.

In a moment of spontaneous generosity, Yasin offers to loan me his camera. I accept, and set off for the village. There I have my silver Allah and my evil eye charm repaired, and feel whole once again.

As the days pass, I relax into my surroundings. I wake up at dawn to the sound of conch shells and chanting, fall asleep again, wake up again. I shop for shawls and papier mache and embroidered table linens, as I will be going back to England and America soon. For once the thought is a relief. This year India has beaten me, and I seek comfort in the familiar, though Kashmir tempts me with its allurements.

I write letters home, and on a whim I write two important letters—one to Indira Gandhi about my train robbery, enclosing a photocopy of my police report and a list of my losses, and one to *National Geographic.* I write to the editor I had spoken to before, Jim Cerruti, telling him that the magazine is missing a big chance if they don't do a story on the Kalash. I explain that I have visited there again, and will become a bloodsister on my next trip, which I would like to make during the winter festival in December. I figure I have nothing to lose, and send these two letters.

Although all around me is peaceful, I am disturbed inside. I have dreams of war and violence. A pregnant woman is walking along by the sea, her husband far ahead. She falls and drowns, and he says, "At least she died a natural death," and then he is shot. In other dreams, my visa is expiring, and everyone else's visa is okay, and I am trying to get to Kabul.

I read *Time* and *Newsweek* and realize that the world does not welcome refugees. Khalid and his family arrived in Germany just before they started requiring visas of Afghans. Congress has just liberalized U.S. refugee laws, but budgets have been cut, and quotas are tiny.

I begin writing a play called "Visa—An Absurdist Play Based on Real Life." A woman, arrested for writing poetry in a meadow, is being held prisoner in a jail by a man in a uniform with a paper bag over his head.

"What did I do?" she asks.

"Your visa expired."

"But it expired after you arrested me"

"Yes, exactly."

"Then just deport me."

"We can't deport you. Your visa has expired. You need an exit visa, and you can't get an exit visa without an entry visa."

One day, I am photographing flowers in the garden. I balance and bend to get just the right angle on the peach zinnias edged with lilac, and bump the camera against my left eye. Out pops my contact lens, into the long, lush grass. I freeze. I have never lost a contact lens in twelve years, but I've always had an extra pair. Then I realize that the extra pair was in the bag that was stolen. I take deep breaths and feel the folds of my clothing. I stoop into the grass and feel. I can hardly see out of my left eye, and my balance is thrown off. Yasin sees me from the verandah, just as I start to cry, and he and a Canadian woman come running out to help me.

We spend half an hour looking, then hire a shepherd boy with sharp eyes. I take out my right lens, very carefully, to show him what it looks like. He is amazed, and looks diligently, but finds nothing. At night I go out again with a flashlight, but dewdrops all over the grass shine like a thousand diamonds, or a hundred contact lenses.

I stay in Kashmir as long as I can. I am off-balance, emotionally and physically, as I am so near-sighted without my lens. Finally I can put off my departure no longer.

In Delhi I find an unusual guest house that belonged to a wealthy family. I sleep in the library, which has been turned into a dorm, complete with high green velvet drapes and floor to high ceiling glass bookcases. An American woman practices her sitar on the verandah each day, and when the monsoon finally hits, her music echoes along with the irregular rhythms of the life-giving rain of the Subcontinent.

I find myself falling in love with India again, half-unwilling, just as I am ready to leave. I send a telegram to my mother, asking her to please replace my contact lens. I go to get my replacement visa, but the *babu* tells me it isn't ready. I show him my ticket to London, my voice lowering and growling as tears of anger and frustration spring to my eyes. I tell him that I can't see well and Delhi is dangerous for me. Finally he relents and gives me the visa confirmation–it was there all along, somewhere in a file no one had bothered to look in.

At dawn on my last day in India, I am sad. I go out on the marble terrace and feel the heat beginning. I sniff in the fresh scent of night rain, dew, and tropical plants, and watch the red-orange flame trees take shape against the opalescent sky. The sky fades from black to lapis to pale opal, and the morning star fades as I remember it fading in Kabul. Morning birds which I cannot name call, and I know I will return to India. India will make me angry, will wound me and caress me; I will love her and hate her by turns, but I will never be indifferent.

14 Culture Shock

Germany
September, 1980

"Hello. I'm sponsoring an Afghan refugee family, and I've just come all the way from Pakistan to Germany. I'd like to know what I can do to expedite their U. S. visas.

On my way to visit Khalid and Aiesha, in a small city near Cologne, I have naively decided to see what I can do to help hurry the political asylum process.

Obviously bored, the receptionist in the refugee section of the American Consulate in Frankfurt directs me to another office. I go through my speech again, acting confident and official, and ask to see Khalid's files. The young secretary goes to the tall filing cabinet and finds the file. It is in my hands when a heavy-set American man sweeps into the office and snatches it away.

"What do you think you're doing with that?"

"Oh, this is my friend's file," I say in innocent surprise. "I am his family's sponsor, and I've just come from Pakistan so that I can get them to America as soon as possible."

The official sighs. "Young lady, you have a lot to learn. Come into my office."

I hate people who call me "young lady, " but I follow him. "All I want to know is when they might be able to come to America."

"Do you have any idea how many people we have on our waiting list?"

"No, but I thought I could find out if I came myself..."

"They ll be given a number like everyone else, and they'll wait their turn," he snaps. He stares at me for a moment, chagrined. "Are you an only child?"

"Yes. Why?"

"I thought so. You look like you're used to having your own way."

"Well, I do try to get my own way when I see it as a question of justice," I reply, dusting off my dignity.

My official antagonist softens. He explains that he and his staff are overworked, and are way behind in processing a flood of refugees. He looks at Khalid's file and tells me which refugee agency his family is registered with, and whom to speak to there. Then he gives me a lecture on the intricacies of the Refugee Act of 1980, which has brought U.S. refugee laws into accordance with the U.N. definition of a refugee as someone with a "well-founded fear of persecution" due to race, religion, nationality, ethnic group, or beliefs. Previously, refugees wishing to enter the U.S. had had to prove "specific personal danger."

The magnitude of the world refugee problem in 1980 is awesome. There are well over ten million refugees in the world, and over two million are Afghan. Afghans in Pakistan are the world's largest concentration of refugees. In addition, tens of thousands of educated Afghans, mostly the cream of the nation, have fled to exile in America and Western Europe. Several thousand landed in Germany before it began requiring visas for Afghan nationals in mid-1980.

Khalid and his family made it just in time. Frankfurt was already closed to refugees, who had a choice of finding a small city which would accept them, or living in the refugee dormitories outside the city. A few Afghans opted to settle permanently in Germany, but most applied for resettlement in America. The quota for refugees from what the State Department calls the Middle East is small, only about 1800 places this year–including Afghans, Iranians, Turks, Palestinians, Lebanese, Syrians, and Iraqis, most of whom are from troubled, politically repressed nations.

This man with such great power over people's lives hands me a copy of the guidelines for accepting or rejecting refugees. There are thirty-three reasons why refugees can be rejected, ranging from illiteracy in their native tongues to insanity, homosexuality, and polygamy.

The refugee laws are more complicated than I had realized, and will become more so over the next few years as regulations change and tighten. Sometimes, unmarried refugees won't be allowed in; in other cases, they will be preferred over married refugees. Family reunification will have major gaps, and parts of Afghan families will end up stuck in Pakistan or Germany. The officers who interview Afghans, Vietnamese, Cambodians, Africans, and Salvadorans will be mostly men and women who scrupulously go by the book, and must have some mental mechanism that allows them to ignore the human pain of the people whose lives are in their hands.

I leave the office with lots of food for thought, but no real information, and a vague assurance that *if* my friends are approved, they will be sent to America "in a few months." I visit Rafaelswerk, the Catholic refugee agency, where I am warmly welcomed by dedicated people who are happy to meet the sponsor of one of their refugees. They speak in idealistic, compassionate terms, and offer me tea. They find Khalid's file and let me look at it–luckily, for I find that Khalid has not given them his new address.

I stay for a long time talking to these kind German women and asking many questions about the conditions of refugees in Germany and throughout the world. They are optimistic about Khalid's chances, and one remembers interviewing him. He is due to be interviewed by the U.S. Consulate any day, and they see no reason why the family won't be accepted.

For a moment, I don't recognize Aiesha as she opens the door to the tiny hotel room, then in a rush all recognition and emotion come back. We embrace and kiss, and laugh with joy. Khalid is standing behind her, and he too embraces me and kisses my cheeks. On the bed is a small, beautiful baby girl, just six months old, with deep, liquid black eyes. Aiesha picks her up proudly and shows her to me. I touch her cheeks gently, thankfully, secretly wistfully.

Aiesha's cousins crowd into the room, all eager to meet me. There is a flurry of happy greetings in Farsi, and tea is soon served, followed by delicious *pilau* with carrots, raisins, and chicken, which Aiesha and her cousin have cooked on hot plates in their tiny rooms.

We all talk about Germany, and make lots of jokes. I am in severe culture shock after months in Asia, and this Afghan enclave is a comfort to me. Germany seems more modern, more American than America. In Frankfurt, I ate at a Burger King because it was relatively cheap, listening to American pop music and musing on the Teutonic incarnation of the "Burger King," like an Elf King spiriting away the innocent into a kingdom of endless fast food. Everything is glitz and glitter or shiny sleaze, and technology runs on time, without a trace of obvious human interference.

I cannot believe that Frankfurt is the romantic city which had been my first sight of Europe at age twelve, only fourteen years before. I can't believe the dizzyingly high prices, and the homogenized food and decor which seems so alien after the tawdry, intimate bazaars of Asia.

I try to practice the Sufi saying, "Be in the world, but not of the world." It is easy to feel close to God in Hunza, in the Kalash valleys, or in Kashmir, and hard in Delhi, London, and Frankfurt. New York and Los Angeles will be nearly impossible, and the thought of going to L.A. fills me with trepidation.

But for now, all I can think of is my Afghan friends, and the irony of their wishing to go to America even more than I dread returning. Like most immigrants, they think of America as a wealthy land where they will find a good, dignified job and work hard to live in freedom and buy lots of consumer goods. I don't disabuse them of these notions, but gently hint at unemployment, problems learning English, and culture shock.

Khalid and Aiesha have adapted remarkably well to Germany. She has lost the weight of her pregnancy, and is slim and fashionable in the elegant European fashions she has managed to buy at discount stores. Khalid looks handsome in a leather jacket and jeans, and is trim because he plays soccer with a local team.

While Aiesha is talking with her cousins, Khalid speaks to me in English in a corner of the room. He tells me that all along he had been an army deserter and had finally been informed on. I am shocked, and wounded that he had never before trusted me enough to tell me. He sees my hurt, and tries to reassure me that it was for my own good. He tells me how he was inducted into the army, and refused to join the ruling Communist party. He was punished by being put in solitary for nine or ten days, then sent to Kunar Province, where he was one of the first of many conscripts to desert from the Afghan Army. Amazingly, he had lived openly in Kabul, had even married, but had had virtually nothing to do with the government until he was warned that some neighbors had informed on him, hoping to gain a business advantage.

He and Aiesha had had little time to prepare for their flight. With her married cousins, they had quickly dressed as villagers, and had set out in the night. Aiesha, who has just joined us in our corner, listens to the story and adds, laughing, "I had never worn a *chadori* before and I kept falling. One time I fell off the donkey and tore the bottom of the *chadori*. If anyone had seen me walking they would have known that I wasn't used to wearing a *chadori.* "

I am amazed at how brave Aiesha is, and how cheerful. Khalid tells me he has stopped drinking and smoking, and is playing lots of soccer and keeping in good health, just waiting for the day they are accepted to go to America.

The days of my visit pass swiftly. I want to stay, though my room is expensive and Khalid repeatedly apologizes that they cannot pay for my room or let me sleep in theirs. But I know I must leave soon. I must visit Paris, where I will see Annick and Parwez, and return to London to prepare for my further work on articles about the refugees, and see if my contact lens has finally arrived.

I take walks with Aiesha and get to know her better. To my relief, my attraction to Khalid has faded, and only a tender pang remains. I enjoy Aiesha's sense of humor, and together we suffer German racism. An old man on the bus pushes past us and mumbles, "*Auslander*—foreigner." And in the markets, more than once, checkout women scowl at us for our poor command of the German language.

Khalid is under great stress. Aiesha doesn't understand enough German or English to realize how difficult their lives really are, and he holds his feelings from her, finally confiding in me. Up till now, they have received a housing allowance, but they are notified that the government will no longer pay for a hotel, and they must find a flat, or move to the refugee camp. Their stipend doesn't leave much for clothes or other necessities, and one day Khalid is nearly in tears because the baby needs a crib. His throat is tight with unshed tears as he tells me how hard it is to sleep in the narrow bed with the baby between them, afraid they may roll over and crush her.

I offer to loan them money. At first Khalid is reluctant and proud, but he finally agrees to accept my loan of $350, which will be enough to buy a good crib and some other things they need for the baby.

"You did a lot for me in Kabul," I explain, when I come out of the bank with a handful of Deutschemarks.

He looks at me ruefully. "I did nothing for you in Kabul."

Together we go to a big department store, to the baby department. Everyone thinks we are married, I think ironically. A part of me surges into a wish that things had been different and I had married Khalid and together we were picking out things for our baby. But I know that it is not my fate. Part of me realizes that even if someday I become a wife and mother, my work and love will expand beyond the house and into the community and the world.

Word comes that Khalid's interview at the American Consulate will be on the next Monday. He and Aiesha are excited, but rushed. They must get photos, and phone relatives in Frankfurt, as Social Security won't pay for a hotel, only their train ticket.

On Sunday we all go together to the station. I will stay in Frankfurt until their interview is over, and then catch a train to Paris. Aiesha's brother meets us in Frankfurt, and takes us back to his family's flat. There we have a delicious meal, while I worry about where I am going to stay. In true Afghan fashion, no one else worries until about 11 p.m. Then Khalid and Aiesha's brother take my luggage and begin wandering the streets of Frankfurt with me. It is a nightmare. Every decent hotel, and many indecent ones as well, is full. There is a convention of some sort going on. We start out with Khalid asking for me, then we decide to let me go in alone to ask, thinking that maybe the managers think we want the room for immoral purposes.

I am exhausted by the time one manager snarls, "It's not my problem that you have no place to go. You should have made a reservation."

As I break down into tears, Aiesha's brother insists that I stay with them. Though the flat is very crowded, I gratefully accept. Amidst all the rejection and alienation of this impersonal city, I feel loved.

The next day, I watch the baby while Khalid and Aiesha go in for their interview. We wait for four hours for their names to be called, and their interview takes a long time. The baby sleeps peacefully until they go in, then wakes up and begins to cry. I am at a loss as to what to do with a crying baby, and rock her in her stroller, humming softly and clucking to her. Finally I begin making quiet animal noises, mewing and barking, and keep her attention for a long time.

Khalid is cautiously optimistic when they return. "The man says my English is good," he says proudly. "We didn't need to use the translator."

There is no certainty, but their refugee agency had told me that they would probably be flown to the U.S. soon after being accepted, as had been the practice with previous refugees. So when they accompany me to the railway station, we are all hopeful. It is hard to say good-bye, but I am sure that I will see them again soon, in America, just as I had once dreamed.

"They'd better let you in soon," I tell Khalid, "or they'll have me to fight with. I'll do anything to get you and Aiesha in to America!"

Khalid tells me not to fight with people so much. I smile inside, thinking of the many fights I've seen him have with everyone from authority figures to family members. "Sometimes you have to fight for justice," I remind him self-righteously. "I know I lose my temper too easily, and fight over small things, but sometimes you have to try to teach people about justice and mercy and compassion."

"The world needs a million teachers like you. Not just one."

My reunion with Annick and Parwez is another joyous one. But I soon find out that Parwez has not adjusted to life in France. Every time we eat, he says, "The melons are tasteless here. They are much bigger, and tastier, in Afghanistan."

Annick and I try to tease him. "There are melons this big in Afghanistan," I say, holding out my arms full length.

"Yes, really," says Parwez. "From Kunduz. The biggest and best melons you can find."

We go to La Mercerie, one of my favorite restaurants in Paris. "The meat is much better in Afghanistan," says Parwez. "These French don't know how to cook anything."

Annick is sometimes sad, sometimes angry at him. She does everything she can to please him, and when nothing works she gets frustrated and goes out with her friends, leaving him home alone to think of Afghanistan. I understand his sorrow, his longing for his family, his country, anything familiar. But I'm glad I don't have to live with it.

"I don't know what to do," he tells me many times, echoing Khalid's words. "I have lost the way."

I realize that these personal stories of lost souls can be multiplied by millions. These stories need to be told, and I want to tell them so that people throughout the world will know that a nation is dying. The educated are confused, many unable to find a niche in the Resistance based in Pakistan, or unwilling to make the sacrifices of living permanently in Pakistan. Some unmarried young men have stayed. Parwez tells me that our old friend Aziz has been released from prison and has joined the Mujahedeen. But most of the married men worry about their families, and want their children to have educations in America or Europe.

The Afghans in France and Germany eagerly await news of the war, news of Soviet-American relations, of anything that relates to their country, however remotely. They are hopeful and blustery, and believe that the same peasants many of them once scorned, and few of them really knew or understood, will win Afghan freedom. Most of these educated refugees expect to go back and resume their former positions. A few believe that Afghanistan is lost, and fall into despair, mourning for a way of life that will never come again, while obstinately refusing to adjust to any other way of life.

My second day in Paris, I get good news. My friend in London has left a message telling me to call *National Geographic.* My hands are shaking when I call, and I can hardly believe the news—the magazine is giving me an assignment, sending me back to the Hindu Kush to write about the Kalash winter festival and becoming a bloodsister to the tribe. I can hardly hold the phone as I listen to the editor's voice. When he says, "We'll pay you a dollar a word, and give you expenses," I am sure I am dreaming. I hang up feeling elated, confused, scared, apprehensive. My mind is racing, and I am writing letters in my head, to Saifullah, to Fida Hussain. I hope that there is a new Deputy Commissioner. I worry about what will happen if Khalid and Aiesha arrive in the U.S. while I am gone, how my parents will cope with them and communicate with them. In the middle of a lot of problems—the train robbery, amoebic dysentery, and the contact lens that still hasn't arrived—suddenly my prayers have been answered. I've been stubborn and have done everything my way, the "wrong" way. I've dropped out of college, never studied journalism or writing, never worked for a newspaper or a magazine, and suddenly I am being offered the plum assignment for a magazine writer. All I had to do was find a "lost" tribe, and have the patience and faith to finally arrive at the right place at the right time.

15 Adoption in the Hindu Kush—The Baptism of Fire

Northern Pakistan
December, 1980

Small groups of black-clad women in cowrie-shell headdresses converge at the Jestak Khan, temple of the Kalash goddess of home and family, carrying flat baskets full of dried fruit and nuts as offerings to honor their ancestors. It is a joyous, informal, yet reverent procession. The late afternoon sun shines its rich tones on the overflowing baskets, evidence of a fruitful harvest of grapes, apples, apricots, mulberries, and walnuts.

I do not linger outside in the chill of the late autumn day, as a welcoming bonfire sparks and crackles inside the dark wooden temple. Women are separating out handfuls of fruit and nuts from their households' baskets, and putting the offerings outside in communal baskets for the spirits of the ancestors of the clans that built this temple. The sacred space grows more crowded and chaotic as the light outside dims, and the firelight grows brighter.

Small sticks of pine are passed around until everyone holds a makeshift torch of three sticks. Then the *kotik,* a light for the ancestors to see by, is lit outside the single door, and the last worshippers retreat inside the temple. Two men hold a thick cloth over the entrance, while we raise our torches aloft so no one will be frightened by the rumblings of the ancestors' annual visit. I am in a hushed sea of cowrie shell headdresses and feathers, black dresses and men's woolen caps. The fire of anticipation throws the rough geometric carvings on the four pillars into sharp relief, as the temple is brought alive by belief in an ancient, living religion.

When the *kotik* has burned out, the heavy cloth is dropped, and our joyous cries, unsealed, ring into the night. We throw our torches into the fire, and laughter begins anew. In the chaos, families, clans, and neighbors celebrate the initiations of children who are around seven years old.

Small girls are given their first *kupass,* a miniature headdress, and in turn give their mothers' brothers colorful sashes woven on finger looms by their older sisters and mothers. Little boys are initiated in the *goshnik* ceremony, marking the first time they are allowed to wear trousers.

Everyone feasts on the food which remains in the household baskets, but the food placed ouside, whose taste has been sucked by the ancestors, is now considered impure for men, so the women good-naturedly quarrel over its division.

Everyone drifts home to prepare for the official start of Chaomos, the winter solstice festival. Tonight they will bake bread and make dough effigies of the markhor, an antelope-like animal that lives in the high Hindu Kush mountains. The last of the flour has been ground, and the elders have declared the festival's imprecise beginning for the next day. The valley will be sealed against outsiders, and all the Kalash women will be purified. For seven days, no flour will be ground, and no Kalash will make love. They will dance, sing, pray, sacrifice goats, and taunt each other into a joyous frenzy to light up the dark winter days.

In the long, desultory days of my visit here last summer, Saifullah had said, "If you want to understand the Kalash religion, you must see Chaomos." I had hoped to celebrate with them someday, but had never dreamed I would return so soon, especially on a *National Geographic* assignment.

I am travelling with Steve McCurry, a young photographer from Pennsylvania who is also on his first assignment for the magazine. As both of us have experienced the delays of travel in these regions, we had allowed for plenty of time, especially since Saifullah had been unable to pinpoint a date for the beginning of Chaomos.

Steve and his girlfriend Lauren Stockbower, also a photographer and writer, meet me in Peshawar in early December. Day after day, we are stuck there under the dismal grey skies, as no flights went to Chitral.

Steve, who was one of the first American photographers to enter the war zone in Afghanistan, spends his time looking up old friends from Nuristan. I take the time to find Aiesha's parents, brothers, and sisters, who had fled Kabul and now share a small room on the outskirts of Peshawar.

On the second day, outside the PIA office, Lauren and I run into Fida Hussain, who has made a special trip to meet us in Peshawar. He and our old friend Abdul Ahad prove to be godsends in our ongoing negotiations with PIA officials to get tickets on the first plane going to

Chitral. After four days of cancellations, we obtain a letter stating that we are "very important passengers".

On the fifth miserable morning, Steve and I get onto the plane. At the last minute, Lauren comes running on, breathless and thankful. Fida's friend in PIA had saved him a seat, and Fida had gallantly insisted that she take it.

In Chitral, we hear from foreign tourists that the festival has already begun. We anxiously rush to the Deputy Commissioner's office to get our permits, only to be told to come back the next day. Steve is ill-tempered and withdrawn, and I am frantic, still worried about whether the Deputy Commissioner will agree to our request for the three-week permit we need to cover the festival.

The next afternoon we meet the handsome, sophisticated young man who is the new Deputy Commissioner. Shakil Durrani is unlike any high official I have yet met in Pakistan. He apologizes for having been "out of station," but explains that he is trying to see all of the area he administrates before the snows set in. He offers us tea, gives us our requested permit for all three Kalash valleys with no questions asked, and wishes us a good journey. He speaks enthusiastically of Chitral's beauty and of the fascinating Kalash culture, and even tries to call someone to find out when the festival is due to begin. He reassures us that he is quite sure it hasn't started yet.

Steve and I leave for Rumbur feeling optimistic, with Lauren promising to join us in a few days, after she has investigated the Afghan refugee situation in Chitral. Durrani's helpful attitude is a good omen, both for our assignment and for the Kalash. I feel sure that he will be a fair administrator, one who will zealously carry out the official policy of the Islamic government of Pakistan to protect the rights of religious minorities.

The walk to the valley is long and familiar. Although I am unaccustomed to the high altitude and the sharp winter air, my heart and pace quicken as I approach Saifullah's home. I have not heard from him since I left, and I don't even know if he knows we are coming. It is pitch dark when I hear an instantly recognizable deep voice a few yards ahead. I run forward toward the voice, shouting, *"Saifullah! Ishpatah, mai baya, prusht taza?"*

Impetuously, I hug him, knowing no one else can see in the dark which always seems to hide intimate moments.

Saifullah takes us to the lodge where I had stayed during the summer. Someone has scrawled a sign that says "Palace Hilton Hotel," and a wood-burning stove with a hot water tank has been installed. Kata Sing, Saifullah's handsome father-in-law, and his two sons are there to greet me. I introduce Steve as my cousin, so no one will mistakenly think he is my husband.

During the next few days, I greet old friends and observe preparations for Chaomos. Young girls are busy finger-weaving, making sashes in complicated and artful patterns for their little sisters to give to their uncles. Some women are washing dresses and headdresses on the flat grey rocks by the rushing, winter-clear river. Others are thoroughly cleaning their earthen-floored houses. A few women sit in the water mill, in clouds of flour dust and smoke, warming their hands over tiny fires and gossipping and telling stories to pass the time as their grain is ground.

On the day of the *Manda'ik,* the ceremony of the ancestors, Saifullah leads me across the narrow bridge to his village, Balanguru, and into his house. His neighbor and clan sister Batan Gul, has finished sewing my very own *cheo,* the voluminous black dress that Kalash women wear. I put it on over my woolen sweaters, trousers, and long underwear, and Batan Gul ties a woven magenta sash very tight around my waist, forming the pouch where Kalash women keep everything from sewing implements to food to knives.

I sit on the wooden terrace in the wintry sun as Batan Gul combs my hair and braids it into the five *chui,* the braids worn by all Kalash women. She begins with the braid at the center of the forehead, and then completes the other four. Saifullah observes from the door of his house, then brings a *kupass* and ceremonially places the cowrie shell headdress on my head.

"Now you are really Kalash," he says, green eyes crinkling into a teasing smile. And now I am your uncle."

Saifullah introduces me to his wife, Washlim Gul, who welcomes me with apricots and walnuts. Her face is warm and brown, her features regular. What I realize only dimly then, and later, much more clearly when my own mother mistakes a picture of her for me, is how much we resemble each other.

Saifullah goes off with Steve to translate while he takes pictures, leaving me to practice my Kalasha with Washlim Gul, his mother, and the rest of the family. Washlim Gul is shy at first. She casts quick glances at me and giggles softly as she suckles Wazir Ali, her nine month old baby. But each time she looks back at me, it is with greater warmth. She speaks slowly, clearly, so I will understand.

"How old are you?" she asks.

"Twenty-six."

"He is your husband?"

"No, my *baya,* my brother."

"No husband?" she asks in disbelief.

"No. Maybe after two or three years."

"You will be old then! I am 23 and already have two children."

For a moment I am nonplussed, but she starts laughing and says wickedly, "Husbands are no good. Husbands are a lot of trouble!"

Washlim Gul, Saifullah's grey-braided mother, and a whole host of neighbors and clan sisters, mostly teen-age girls, come to sit in the one-room house around the fire and look at me. They inspect my braids, my *kupass,* my beads and bangles, and pass judgement. "Your hair is long, but your *kupass* is too small," says one. Chus Namah, a vivacious girl who won't live with her husband because she considers him too short, appraises my silver bangles from India and offers me red plastic as a trade. I refuse, and we both laugh. To my surprise, my gold earrings don't interest them, as they think they are brass, but the cheap silver Kashmiri earrings I wore the day before are coveted and praised.

By the time we head for the Jestak Khan, I feel a part of the clan. The dress and heavy headdress, which weighs several pounds, give me dignity and make me walk like a Kalash. When I see Saifullah standing outside the Jestak Khan, laughing with abandon as he jokes with other young men, I have a powerful sense of *deja vu,* and this whole village, this whole culture seems all at once familiar.

In the icy mornings, when I put on my Kalash dress as soon as I get up, I feel as if I am putting on another persona. Steve and I have agreed that it is my job to run down to the river and get a bucket of water, while he starts the fire in the stove. Dutifully, my face smarting from the wind, I dip the bucket into the achingly cold water, which numbs my hands instantly. I drag the heavy bucket back to the warmth of the lodge, momentarily wishing I were anywhere else.

But by the time the fire is roaring and we have warm washing water, I am glad to be here, and ready for the day's adventure.

Today I will be purified with the other women. Saifullah comes early to take me to Kata Sing's house in another village.

Because I am living in a house owned by Kata Sing, I must be purifed by his clan. We climb the steep path to Kalashagrum, on the other side of the valley, where the houses jut out over the steep hillside on cantilevered terraces.

Kata Sing's pretty daughter-in-law leads me down to the river. There, in a sheltered spot, women are bathing and washing their hair. I am thankful that my period has just ended, or I might have been sent to the Bashali, the menstruation house, and missed the entire festival. I view with trepidation the icicles clinging to the dark rocks, but I take a deep breath and peel off my many layers, and plunge in. It is so cold I want to yell, but I shiver and laugh as the women pour warm water over my head.

"Cold water is better for the hair," says one older woman, but I disagree vehemently.

I sit on a boulder by the river's edge, soaking in faint warmth as the girls braid my wet hair. I watch a young woman washing her hair, which falls down to her knees. When I tell her how beautiful it is, she laughs and tells me it is a problem.

All along the hillside, in the early morning sun, groups of men are baking *shishaou,* the bread of purification. This must be baked outside the village, or in the cattle house, where women are not allowed. Blue-grey smoke curls gracefully up past the dark hillsides, to merge with the lake-blue, cloudless sky.

The ceremony takes place in the late afternoon. Groups of women gather in small circles and sing slowly, reverently, in rising and falling choruses. Their sacred songs sound like Gregorian chants in a magnificent outdoor cathedral of rocky pillars and mountain spires. I hum with them, and join in the chorus, "*Utchun dao*–He came down," These chants are songs in praise of Balamaiyin, the legendary prophet who once lived among the Kalash and did great miracles. Every year at Chaomos, the Kalash celebrate his return. It is said that his spirit walks through the valley and counts the people and their prayers.

I follow the women of my clan out of the village and up the trailless hillside. The men stand apart, watching, as we go forward in small groups to be blessed and purified. At last it is my turn. Water is poured on my hands, and I am given five round flat loaves of bread, which I hold between my hands while a clan brother waves a sprig of pungent, burning juniper over my head, and murmurs, "*Such, such*–Be pure."

I am hushed and reverent, feeling like a small girl at her First Communion. This ritual has truly made me feel purified, and ever more a part of the Kalash sisterhood.

Back at Kata Sing's house, we begin to celebrate. Three French anthropologists, who have up till now kept their distance, join us for homemade cloudy wine in bottles corked with corncobs.

I am glad for a supplement to our diet of rice, bread, and potatoes. Kalash consider chickens impure, and only Muslims raise them. As Muslims have not been ritually purified, the Kalash will not have any contact with them during this holiest of times, and we won't have any eggs for the duration of the festival.

The pinkish, bubbly wine is surprisingly strong. When Saifullah knocks over a glass and breaks it, I find myself saying, "I remember when I was a child, if a glass broke I always felt sorry for it."

"Ah, this is a wise woman," Saifullah replies. "She knows that everything, even a glass or a stone, has a spirit."

Steve looks skeptical, but thus encouraged, I launch into a simplified explanation of the connection between subatomic physics and mysticism. I am halted only when one of the French anthropologists says, "Pour another glass! When others begin to talk about God, we French begin to talk about wine..."

The festival continues in a rich mix of reverence and ribaldry. I never know which is coming next, or in what proportion. The next morning, all the men of Balanguru herd thirty goats through the village, past the huge spreading walnut tree, and up the valley to the altar of Sajigur, god of flocks and shepherds. The women gather solemnly, decked out in their finest ornaments, headdresses crowned with feathers dyed lavender and purple, shoulders and waists circled with newly woven blankets striped blue, green, and white. A sloe-eyed baby girl balances a headdress on her tiny head, looking serious and not too happy.

The women sing more Balamaiyin songs, and I join them. It is a moment of great reverence, and I am suitably solemn. Then all of the sudden, two figures dash down from the village, their faces covered with bright cloths, and begin a wild dance. They are immediately encircled by teen-age girls who taunt the boy dancers dressed in girls' clothes, and try to guess their identities. As the boys in drag run back up to the village, the girls break into another laughing dance, gathering the ends of their blankets into phallic parodies, and thrusting at each other as they shout.

When the men come back, carrying the bloodied carcasses of the slaughtered goats, there is again reverence. The men form a large circle around the women and rotate slowly, adding their deep bass voices to the alto and soprano of the women. They are led by Baraman, one of the elders, who is dressed in a long coat of green and gold brocade. His woolen cap is crowned with hollyoak and juniper, and he reminds me of the Ghost of Christmas Present.

Then the men start to shout, "Oh, ho, ho, oh, ho, ho," and jump laciviously upon each other's backs, while the women continue their sacred songs unperturbed. The whole group files up to the Jestak Khan in Grum, the village on the cliff above, where more boys' and girls' initiations are performed. This time the dances turn into a contest between boys and girls vying to sing the most explicit lyrics.

Saifullah is laughing uproariously. At first he won't tell me what they are saying, but he finally translates: "The girls are singing, 'Your penis is red with shame because we are closed for seven days.'" Embarrassed, I try to maintain anthropological objectivity.

The men begin to drift away. Saifullah says they are going to the cattle house for another goat sacrifice, and purification with the blood of the sacrifice. I accompany Washlim Gul back to her house, where we bake special bread filled with goat cheese and crushed walnuts. I help the women shell walnuts, and then help bake bread, but my unaccustomed fingers make clumsy shapes.

"Don't you bake bread in America?" asks Washlim Gul.

I explain that most people buy bread from big, big shops. This my friends find unbelievable and funny.

When we are finished stuffing the unbaked loaves, she takes the first two and puts them in the embers to bake. "One of mine, one of yours," she says. Mine is easily recognizable by its odd shape, but when she tastes it she pronounces it good, and I am proud.

The next night is the culmination of the festival in Rumbur, the *tranjah rat,* or "torch night." Saifullah takes Steve and me up to Kata Sing's house for a meal of chewy goat tripe. I discover another use for the wide sleeves of my Kalash dress when I find I cannot chew one particularly tough piece and discreetly hide it.

The usually effervescent Chus Namah is here too, but tonight she is drunk and in a bad mood. The women are nagging her for having drunk too much, and this is making her angrier. Noor Jan, Kata Sing's wife, tells me that Chus Namah is crazy. As an afterthought, she mentions that Steve, whom everyone sees rushing around taking "thousands of pictures," is also a little crazy.

I try to cheer Chus Namah up by joking, "Why don't you marry my brother?" but this puts her in an even blacker mood.

Then suddenly it is time to leave. I am given a long torch made of split pine cut and bound with willow. On a hilltop above the village is a large bonfire. There we light our torches, and then begin our slow procession down the steep path to the valley floor. Fire is everywhere around me, embers falling from my torch and everyone else's torches, burning sticks falling into dry grass at the edge of the path. The night is filled with smoke and flame, and I am terrified and exhilarated as I hurry through the breathless air.

Across the valley, a small constellation of torches appears in the village of Grum, and snakes down the side of the mountain. Our two processions meet at the narrow bridge to Balanguru, and the jostling crowd of fire and bodies somehow crosses the river and reaches the village, where a glowing bonfire ten feet high reaches higher into the black-glazed dome of winter sky. I throw my torch into the fire with the others, glad to be rid of it, and dance in abandon with Saifullah and my teen-age friends. Taigun Bibi, a pretty young girl with a beautiful voice, shouts the words of the songs loud into my ear so I can learn them. I sing, whether I know the words or not, and laugh and dance. Frantic groups of boys and girls chase each other, shouting insults, and running in mock fear.

The night is full of moonlight, and the stars are icy crystals strewn across a shiny black sky. The snow peaks that wall the valley are vast and awesome under the full moon, wild and primal.

My voice is nearly gone when an old woman with a wrinkled, nut-brown face and an Eiffel tower earring kindly takes me into her house for some tea. There I meet Bashara Khan, who may be one of the richest men among the Kalash, but is rather a buffoon.

"When Chaomos is finished, you take a Kalash husband," he says, grinning wickedly.

"Oh no, husbands are much trouble," I say with a smile.

"No husband then. Just one night?"

I laugh, and dance out of the situation, grabbing the old woman's hand and pulling her with me back into the melee of fire and song.

Saifullah tells us that the dancing is over in Rumbur, but we can see more in Bumburet, which began its festival a few days after Rumbur did. Steve is eager to go, to make sure we don't miss any photo opportunies. I am somewhat reluctant, as I would prefer to spend time with my friends in Rumbur, but agree to accompany him for the sake of our story.

Saifullah warns us not to eat anything offered by the Muslim jeep-drivers, or to touch them, even to shake hands. Inevitably, the friendly drivers offer us some dried fruit. Steve and I politely refuse, but I feel guilty at the men's hurt looks, as I know it is an insult to refuse their hospitality.

But when we get to Bumburet, we are not allowed inside the houses merely because we have sat in the same jeep with Muslims. Even Saifullah is astounded, and tries to reason with Bumbur Khan, a village notable and the owner of the house where Lauren has been staying while Steve and I were in Rumbur. Bumbur Khan is adamant—Steve and Saifullah must sacrifice a goat, and I must bathe in the river. "He said, '*Buy* a goat' first," says Saifullah sourly. "Then he said 'sacrifice.' He is just making this up to make himself richer."

I look down towards the river at the bottom of the snow-covered valley. My throat is raspy and painful, and my voice is barely a whisper. The thought of another bath in an icy river is too much to bear. I stomp off angrily, and watch from a distance as a goat is sacrificed on the roof of the cattle house, and Steve and Saifullah are sprinkled liberally with its blood.

I stare at the valley before me and the high, dark mountain walls behind, powdered with snow, What makes one place or person pure and another impure? I wonder. Why is this rock holy and not that one? Is an "out" group just waiting to become an "in" group so it can oppress others? I am deeply disappointed in the Kalash. I don't want to admit it, but though I understand their anger at the Muslims who have oppressed them, I can't laugh with sincerity when they throw sticks on a fire, whispering the names of Muslims who have offended them, like college fraternities burning their rivals in effigy.

I am shivering and crying quietly when Saifullah comes up to me, still spattered with blood. "Bumbur Khan says we can wash your hands in wine," he says gently. "I told him you are sick, and he said you don't have to bathe in the river."

I am relieved, but think how easily religious principles are sold, once the required goat is sacrificed.

I join Saifullah next to the fireplace of the room where the four of us will sleep. But he won't respond to my jokes, or even my questions, and I start to get angry. A small boy stands in the doorway, staring at both of us and making me even angrier.

Saifullah stares moodily into the fire, and finally says, "I will leave tomorrow."

"Why?!"

But he does not answer me. "Did I do something wrong? Or did Steve?" I feel a flash of anger, sure that Steve has overworked Saifullah.

"No, not you. Not Steve either."

"Then why?"

After I beg him many times to be honest with me, he confesses that his son Yasir is sick, and he had a fight with Washlim Gul in the morning. The last he had heard she had run home to her father, leaving the sick boy and the nursing baby crying for her.

"I want to die from this life," he says miserably.

I urge him to return to Rumbur, assuring him that we will do fine without him. I know Steve will be angry to lose our translator, but I only want Saifullah to feel happy. "Why was Washlim Gul angry?"

"She does not understand what I do for the people. She says I am educated and I should get a good job, work in an office. She says I could get a good government job."

"But you're working for us now, and you ll be working for the French anthropologists after we're gone."

"Yes, but she does not understand."

"How can she understand? Maybe you could teach her some English so that she could talk to people and deal with foreigners when you are out of the valley. Maybe then she would feel she had her own work for the Kalash people."

"Maybe..." He stares into the fire, tears of despair in his eyes.

"But tomorrow, you must go back to Rumbur. We will be fine. I speak some Kalasha, and I will work with Steve. You can meet us later in Birir. You must take care of your own life first."

A shout interrupts us. Saifullah shouts back, then says, "We must go up. They are going to sacrifice a sheep to Jestak, on the hearth."

The sacrifice is simple and straightforward, but profoundly upsetting to those of us who grew up far from the edge of nature. There is a sacred awe to this act, a fascination that does not permit one's eyes to wander. Lauren and I stare as Bumbur Khan matter-of-factly slits the throat ot the large, four-horned sheep she has bouqht, then twists the head to finish it off. There are a few terrified gurgles and cries, and it is over as the blood gushes and spurts all over the hearthstone sacred to Jestak, and the sheep's life energy ebbs. Steve dutifully takes flash pictures with his motor drive, but I have no such barrier to the intensity of this moment and find myself in an altered state.

The four of us retire to the room below, where we drink several bottles of wine and begin to relax into laughter. Lauren and I try to explain "Star Wars" and the concept of "the Force" to Saifullah, whose eyes are wide with amazement as we act out scenes.

The dancing begins again at night, and we join in for awhile under the wild stars thrown by some god in random anger. We go to sleep late and a little drunk, not paying much attention to the fire as long as it keeps us warm. I wake up in the middle of the night in a smoke-filled room, staring sleepily at a firey, dragon-shaped log which is spitting sparks. I realize that we are being choked by the smoke and come fully awake, flinging the door open and dragging out the large smoking log as it spews embers into the night and burns my clothes.

Saifullah sleeps late and does not leave for Rumbur. He avoids my questions by standing on the roof of the Jestak Khan, which is forbidden to women, while Steve takes pictures. Then the two of them disappear for the day, taking our key with them. Lauren and I are left to practice our Kalasha and shiver in the chill wind as girls paint our faces in dotted patterns of black paste made from burnt millet seed.

The two men return in fine spirits at the end of the day, we suspect many rupees poorer from consuming copious quantities of homemade wine. Steve, who is in a cheerful, joking mood, wickedly makes fun of our painted faces. Saifullah is boisterous and laughing, though I can tell it is a thin veneer over his underlying pain.

We are looking forward to a hearty meal of fresh mutton, but Saifullah discovers that Bumbur Khan's family has already eaten the choice pieces, and has left us only a thin broth. "I've been fleeced," jokes Lauren wryly. "First on the price of the sheep, according to Saifullah, and then we don't even get to eat any of it,"

Again we join in festival revelry, but we are called away to help bandage a man's head wound, and to take a look at a woman who is very ill.

Lauren assists as, with hot water, I clean the wound which is covered with a pomegranate paste. We have no proper bandages, but Lauren goes to our room and comes back with an old pair of Steve's underwear, which we cut into strips.

The sick woman is not very old. She has pains which are variously described as in her chest, breast, heart, and lungs. Saifullah finally tells us he thinks she has pneumonia, so I take a chance and give her some antibiotics with careful instructions as to when to take them. I leave for the moonlight dancing wondering once again if I have misprescribed, if she really has angina, or cancer. I know that many people don't believe travellers, qualified or unqualified, should be dispensing medicine, but in cases where I know medical help is unavailable or inaccessible, I cannot in good conscience watch someone suffer without tring to intervene. I walk the line, trying to do no harm, and if possible, to do good.

It is a few days before Christmas when Steve and I decide to visit Birir, the one remaining Kalash valley. We arrange to go with Saifullah, and meet Lauren back in Rumbur on Christmas Eve, in three days time. But in the jeep we hear a news broadcast saying that today is December 23rd. I look at my journal, usually written in morning sunlight as my fingers slowly unnumb, and discover that I dated two entries December 17th.

I am disappointed, as I want to be in Rumbur to share our "foreigner's Chaomos" with friends and family there. Everything seems to go wrong on this journey. The overloaded jeep breaks down, and the driver carelessly throws Steve's blanket into the dirt. Steve flies off the handle and threatens him, but suddenly we hear a few stones falling high above, then a few more and in a breathless moment see a long log shooting down the mountainside towards the jeep.

I scream, "Landslide!" and run, thinking only to grab the bag containing my notes and Steve's exposed film. The log comes to rest in a cloud of dust under the jeep, which teeters gracefully a few times, then stops.

We walk the rest of the way to Birir, where we take lodgings in a newly built room overlooking the valley floor. Chaomos, we find, is a little different here, just a few miles from the other valleys. The boys and girls do slow, swaying, circular dances, and sing slow chants in perfect harmonies, unknown in the other valleys. Saifullah wildly plays a drum, unique to Birir, while a Pakistani policeman sidles up to Steve and asks him for wine.

The three of us sleep on straw mats on the earthen floor. A warm fire roars as I fall asleep, but hours later I wake up in complete darkness and in a different position, far from the fireplace and parallel to it. I start as someone touches the braid at the center of my forehead and then flips it to one side. I hear stifled laughter, then hold my breath. I peer into the blackness, but this time I do not see the figures which had floated above my bed in Rumbur, sometimes children and sometimes old men. I see only darkness, and finally fall asleep. I awaken at dawn to find myself exactly where I had bedded down last night.

It is a dismal Christmas Eve, dull and chilly. There is only tasteless gruel for breakfast, and we leave the house hungry and unfilled. In the nearby village where we take pictures, no one invites Saifullah for a meal, and he grows angrier and angrier. Saifullah tells Steve about a big drum at the last village, far up the valley, and Steve is immediately obsessed with that drum. I start up the narrow, slippery, muddy path with them but Saifullah notices my exhaustion and insists that I return to the village and rest. He sends someone to show me the path, and by the time I make it back I am grateful that he is taking better care of me than I am, for my throat is sore, and my body is feverish and weak.

I fall asleep, oblivious to the hordes of small boys peering in my window. When I wake up it is nearly dusk and Saifullah and Steve are still not back. There is no sign of food, but the owner of the house comes in and lights a fire. It is so cold that I crouch by the fireplace, my breath coming out in clouds of steam, and warm my numb fingers by the fire so I can write by its dim light.

Christmas Eve, and I am cold and hungry. I look out at the powdered mountains in the gathering dusk, and think of powdered sugar on chocolate. Clouds in the golden sky remind me of *oeufs à la neige*, a French dessert I have had at Christmastime. I make myself very hungry, and finally pour the contents of a packet of powdered orange drink into my hand and greedily lick it up.

Hundreds of jumbled images, some from childhood and some from the past few years, pass through my mind like a video collage. The papier mache elves and glitter snowflakes of early childhood turn up next to images of Soviet tanks in Afghanistan last year, and a Santa in red velvet my mother recently bought is juxtaposed with the planet Earth seen for the first time from space one Christmas Eve only a few years ago. I think of the cold and hungry barefoot guerrillas in Afghanistan, and the naked brown babies of Calcutta. I seek images of comfort, and find them, but their flip side is always one of crying need.

I think of Saifullah, of the Kalash, of the injured man and the severely ill woman in Bumburet, of a simple way of life and the price a fragile culture must pay for basic comforts. I have the sense of participating in ancient rituals which may soon be forgotten, and must be valued even more for that reason. And I suddenly see Saifullah as completely vulnerable, and fear greatly for him.

I stare into the ever-changing fire and begin unconsciously to hum a tune. Words come to me and I sing them, verse after verse. I see Saifullah and myself on a path by a green summer river and I see the seasons change, and how he leads me across an icy bridge, clasps my hand, and then returns to his side of the river. "I must walk on the other side of the river," I sing, "Please understand, let go my hand..." On and on, words flow like water to the sea, and my tears flow with them as I sing a song I can never recreate, a poignant song of destiny and necessary separation.

I know I can never stay here, though at times I long for the simplicity of this life. But I know that we are not on a safe island here. If there is a global environmental catastrophe, even this and other Shangri-las are not exempt. Global warming and a tattered ozone shield will flood, blind, and starve urban clusters, remote villages, and the shyest wildlife without prejudice. This planet, after all, is one whole, one world, fragile and strong, but belonging to all of us. Only our faith and love, and our sense of being one, can turn threatening fires into the fusion fire of creation.

Christmas morning we arise before dawn, as the fat moon, just past full, is setting in a pale blue half-light. To catch a jeep to Rumbur today, we must rush to Ayun by mid-morning. I am freezing and miserable, but the beauty of the vast mountain winter lifts my spirits, and as the sun rises I sing traditional Christmas carols, and with a full voice echoing, snatches of Handel's "Messiah." The energy of song courses through my body and wakes me up to life and joy. Dawn, a daily occurence, today seems incalculably old.

When we reach Rumbur, Lauren is overjoyed to see us. Steve rushes off to take pictures, while Saifullah goes home to reconcile with Washlim Gul. His brothers-in-law tell him that she is back in the house, and he is relieved, but anxious. Lauren and I decide to make Christmas for our friends, and go to the tiny store where we buy socks and cigarettes for Saifullah, and odds and ends for Steve. We take the silver paper from the cigarette boxes and cut snowflakes, which we paste on the windows, decorated with boughs of hollyoak, and a "Merry Chaomos" sign. We use my long Afghan socks as stockings and put our gifts in them, along with two certificates we have made—for Saifullah, "The Best Advocate of the Kalash People," and for Steve, "The Best Photographer in the Valley." As an afterthought, I give them both certificates for Tarot card readings.

When Saifullah and Steve come back, we all go to the *Tum Kuchawao*, the Bow-shaker oracle. Steve wants pictures, and offers to pay for Saifullah to ask a question. Saifullah is suddenly frightened, but I tell him that I believe that the future is largely made by our mind, and that we can change it for the better. He asks his question: "When will I achieve my goal of working for the Kalash people?"

I stare at the intense eyes of the Bow-shaker, and watch his hands, still in the winter cold, until the bow begins to move as he prays to the gods for an answer. He says a few serious words to Saifullah as the cameras whir and click. Saifullah turns to us in relief: "He says I will attain my goal, not next year but the year after."

Steve suggests that we invite Kata Sing, the village elders, and some other people to join us for Christmas dinner. Chaomos is over now, so we can get chickens from the Muslims down the valley. The Kalash don't mind eating chickens even though they won't keep them. Fazli Azam, the carpenter who had once worked as a cook for some anthropologists, carefully slices potatoes very, very thin, to make excellent chips. Steve starts to act gruff again, but Lauren and I smile at each other, knowing how soft he is under that hard crust, and how much he too cares for the Kalash.

I tell the Christmas story to our guests, knowing that missionaries would be horrified. Jesus is a little like the prophet Balamaiyin, but is the son of Dezao, the Creator. The parallels work quite well. My listeners are rapt though a little confused. Lauren and I sing Christmas carols over wine and walnuts, and then I sing a Kalash song that Washlim Gul has taught me. Saifullah gets a little drunk and sings lustily in a full voice. The others join in, and the Christmas night is filled with song that some might call pagan, but which is born of that love which is Spirit, be it called God, or Dezao.

I dream that the *Tum Kuchawao* offers to teach me his art and knowledge. Then the dream shifts and I am in a gallery helplessly looking at photos of various nations at war.

It is nearly time to leave the valley, and time for me to become a bloodsister, as Saifullah had promised on a summer day. I am reluctant to remind Saifullah, not wanting to be too forward, but Steve brings up the subject. Saifullah is noncommital, but in private he confesses, "It is a very serious thing. An anthropologist who was my friend had asked me to be his bloodbrother, but when I thought it over I thought it was too much responsibility and I refused."

I think of the responsibility, something like being a godmother in Christian cultures, and I agree. I let Saifullah make the decision, and he goes to arrange things–I will become bloodsister to his wife Washlim Gul, and he and I will be sister-in-law and brother-in-law.

Washlim Gul's brothers procure a sheep, slaughter it, and roast it. I visit her and Saifullah while we wait for it to cook. I am nervous, wondering if she really wants me as a sister, but as soon as I see her warm face I know it is the right decision.

"She says it is good to have an American sister," says Saifullah, "but she is sad that you are going soon and you will be so far away."

I am sad too. I tell him that I am an only child, and that I have found family here, where I did not expect it, in this remote village high in the Hindu Kush.

Akbar Hayat, Washlim Gul's brother, officiates when the sheep is cooked. The ceremony takes place outside, on the front porch of Saifullah's house, which is the roof of his neighbor's house. We sit in snow flurries, shivering, giggling, and hiding our cold hands in our sleeves while Akbar Hayat takes my Swiss Army knife and cuts the sheep's kidneys in half. He feeds half to me, and half to Washlim Gul, and the ceremony is completed. I am elated, and feel changed. Whatever else I may become, I will always be Kalash, and wherever I may go, there is a home for me in this simple house of earth, stone, and wood.

I send portions of meat and rice to my new extended family, and Washlim Gul and I exchange gifts. I give her a silver bracelet from India, and she gives me a brass bangle engraved with ancient patterns. Then we return to the lodge for a feast with my newfound family and friends. I look from face to face in the soft golden glow of the lanternlight, and feel sad. I have found a family, only to lose them to distance, borders, and visas.

Kata Sing, one of the best Kalash orators, gives a speech which Saifullah translates. "You are our guest in the Kalash tribe, and yet you have made us your guests twice. Now you have become my daughter. We have had foreigners here before but never have they shared their Christmas with us. In the past we have been made many times to feel low. But because you have made us your guests, we feel we are something high."

"But Saifullah, why should such good people ever feel low?" I ask, tears blocking my throat.

"We have been told so many times that we are low that it is carved on our brains, like the carpenter carves on the wood."

I want to forever erase these carvings and patterns, and replace them with pride and dignity. Out of love, I will do all I can to tell their story, in the hopes that it will help create a world where people will never be made to feel low simply because they are "other."

16 The Baptism of Ice

We are given a respite by the thick snow swirling in the icy morning. My aching heart is soothed by the knowledge that we don't have to leave Rumbur today. Lauren and I burrow deeper under thick quilts, but Steve throws the door open to the frigid winds, shines the flashlight in Lauren's face, and pulls the covers off her bed.

Still, I don't mind the hardship, as I will have another day to see Saifullah, Washlim Gul, and others I don't know when, or if, I will see again. Steve is elated at the chance to photograph the valley under snow, especially when the weather breaks in the late morning, leaving a bright layer of pristine snow under a translucent blue sky.

Lauren, Saifullah, and I accompany him, enjoying these moments of transient beauty. Icicles cling to dark, lacy branches in fantastic patterns, sparkling like jewels in the strong sun. Kalash children are playing barefoot in the snow, oblivious to discomfort. Two little girls in long black dresses and miniature headdresses delightedly help a small boy roll a huge cylinder of snow in the flat space beneath the walnut tree where dancers revelled by firelight a week ago.

We soon forget our frozen feet and play like children. I show Saifullah how to make snow angels. Even Steve, ever the serious professional, loosens up enough to sneak up behind Saifullah and me and make devil horns over our heads as Lauren takes a picture.

The extra day gives us time to take pictures that are an unexpected bonus. Taigun Bibi and some of the other girls paint their faces with masks and designs in millet paste while Steve avidly shoots. But the girls soon get bored and ask, "How many pictures is your brother going to take?"

"Thousands and thousands," I answer. I stand behind Steve and joke with the girls in Kalasha. "My brother is a little crazy," I tell them wickedly. Steve occasionally turns around and glares, suspecting something, but he is captivated by the girls' pretty and disarming expressions.

We also photograph another Bow Shaker, to give the editors a greater choice. Saifullah and Steve decide that I should be the one to ask a question. I am reluctant. "I want to ask when I will come back to the valley. But what if he says five years, or ten, or never?"

Saifullah reminds me of my belief that our minds can make and change the future, and I relent. I nervously watch the dangling bow, willing it to move. I listen intently as the Bow Shaker tells Saifullah his verdict. I understand the words "six months" and "one and a half years." Saifullah explains that I will return before a year and a half has passed, but not before six months. I am relieved, and much less anxious about leaving.

As a parting gift, Washlim Gul sews some feathers on my *kupass*. Some are peacock, but she also gifts me with tiny irridescent feathers of the monal, a rare Himalayan pheasant. Saifullah and I spend some time translating songs I have recorded, and have some precious time alone to talk about our hopes for the future.

That night, I suddenly cannot bear the merrymaking which will end so soon, and quietly walk out of the firelight into the darkness. In the wild and starry mountain night, a shooting star streaks by, as ephemeral and yet as everlasting as love, and I make a wish, not for myself, but for Saifullah and the Kalash.

It is New Year's Eve, and we can delay our departure no longer. A thin layer of snow and ice coat the ground, but the sky above is cloudless, so we say our sad good-byes. Saifullah will accompany us to Chitral, as we do not have enough cash left to pay his salary. I had wanted to say good-bye to him in the valley, where he belongs, not in the mean bazaar of Chitral, but I am glad for his company.

We slip and slide on the icy path. Saifullah takes my hand and leads me across one particularly nasty bridge, constructed of two narrow planks leaning together at the center and covered with a thick layer of ice. I cross gingerly, feet splayed, and then we throw dirt onto the surface to make the crossing easier for Steve, Lauren, and the porters. Steve crosses without incident, but Lauren freezes in the center and starts to topple, then reaches for her swinging camera and loses balance.

Before I know it, Saifullah is thigh deep in the icy current, reaching up to steady her. I decide right then that whoever I marry must have such gallantry.

Lauren is shakey, but has the presence of mind to find an extra pair of tennis shoes and dry socks for Saifullah, who is shivering in his light cotton clothing. Fortunately, the day is warm, and he warms up by the time we come around a bend and are dwarfed by the spectacular snow-clad massif of the Hindu Kush rising above the Chitral Valley.

We spend New Year's Eve at the Mountain Inn, Chitral's finest hotel, trying to stay warm. I am looking forward to the privacy of my own room with attached bath. But the room is far from cozy, and the bathroom is icy. The bucket of hot water for bathing and washing my hair takes hours to come, and is delivered lukewarm. Cursing and shivering, I soap down and shampoo my hair, using this single bucket of water.

The management won't give us extra wood, even for money. The fire burns so low that it reminds me of the blue-green flames of fake logs, and throws out far less heat. For dinner, we order a "feast" of chicken and chips. The broth is cold and too peppery, the chicken scrawny and skinless, and the chips congealed with grease.

Just before midnight, we have burnt all the decorative pine cones on the mantlepiece, and Saifullah and Steve have gone out to look for wood. They come in with a thick broom made out of twigs, which Lauren and I put on the fire, puffing and blowing on it while they go out into the cold again.

The door flies open, and in walks the portly Prince of Ayun, whom we have met before. "Happy New Year!" he says. "I have just come from my brother's party and thought I would wish you a Happy New Year."

I am unsuccessfully trying to hide the burning broom with my shawl. The prince peers at us bleerily and says, "What is that you are burning?"

"I'm afraid you've caught us at a bad time," Lauren says seriously. "We are burning a broom."

"That's not a broom, it's a lawnmower."

We offer him tepid green tea as Saifullah and Steve enter in a puff of cold air, and the turning of the year passes unnoticed. Saifullah shrinks into a corner, and the Prince likewise ignores him, as the Prince and the Kalash are engaged in a land dispute and neither will speak to the other.

After some moments of silence and spiritless, kissless "Happy New Years," the Prince leaves. We drink another few rounds of green tea, and Saifullah leaves for the small hotel in the bazaar where he prefers to stay.

I go to my room and spend a long time writing, thinking, praying. I want to be hopeful for this New Year, but this gloomy December has not been hopeful for the world at large. A hundred thousand Soviet troops are wreaking havoc in Afghanistan, detente is in disarray, and it looks as if Poland may be invaded soon. American hostages remain in Iran, and cross-cultural understanding and tolerance have reached new lows as America prepares to enter a decade of greed and selfishness.

Our real celebration comes the next day, when Fida Hussain invites us for dinner. We can't find Saifullah in the bazaar, so go to Fida's hillside house by ourselves.

The atmosphere is warm and joyous, everything that last night was not. We feast on kebab, *pilau* with mutton, Chitrali bread, and delicious apricot kernels roasted with clarified butter and salt or sugar. We listen to Afghan music, and speak of the Kalash. Fida says the Kalash are peaceful people, and wishes all the Muslims of the area were peaceful and tolerant. The new Deputy Commissioner, Shakil Durrani, is a strong man and a good man, he says. Maybe he will make a difference.

It is hard to say good-bye to Saifullah the next day, there in the middle of the dusty bazaar by the jeep stand. I want to embrace him, but many people are standing around watching and Saifullah looks uncomfortable. Lauren and Steve have already said their good-byes and have tactfully walked on ahead. I am left for one last moment, clutching Saifullah's hand through his heavy leather gloves, memorizing his face and staring into the green eyes that remind me of long summer days and dancing leaves.

Once Saifullah has gone, I am anxious to get back to Peshawar to get news of home and find out whether Khalid and Aiesha have arrived. Steve too is eager to leave, as he has an appointment in Baluchistan to cover another story.

But the weather is again cloudy, and no planes go. For three days we wait, while the food at the Mountain Inn gets colder and greasier.

We are diverted by a charming young Frenchman named Guillaume, who invites us to dinner and shows us magic tricks. He says he is a journalist, and certainly knows a lot about the Afghan war. He seems to be trying to impress us, and Steve, never gregarious, remains taciturn and silent.

Lauren, however, is captivated. She eagerly practices her French with the dashing young man with the bright, seductive eyes and the dramatic Chitrali wool cloak floating after his tall thin body as he walks down the bazaar. His magic tricks are very good, but I decide he is an adventurer, not to be taken seriously as a journalist. He is learning

Russian, and carries around a "Teach Yourself Russian" book, which greatly offends the staunchly anti-Communist Prince of Ayun, who also happens to be Commissioner of Afghan Refugees.

Guillaume is like a poorly drawn character in a movie. He has only a vague background, and no visible motivation. He says he was on his way to Nuristan with a porter/guide provided by the Nuristan Islamic Front, a young man who speaks no English. But the Nuristanis here say the passes are closed for the winter, so he is on his way back to Peshawar.

Guillaume suggests that if Steve and I are in a hurry, we should walk over the Lowari Pass to Peshawar. "I came that way just two days ago," he says in his disarming accent. "There was just a few inches of snow, maybe six inches at the top. You can take a jeep to below the pass, then walk, catch another jeep, and you will be in Peshawar by the nightfall."

He goes on to suggest that Steve and I take only our essential equipment. He and Lauren will wait another day for the plane. If it doesn't go, or they don't get on, they will find porters and follow with the rest of the luggage.

Steve cares only about his cameras, which he won't let anyone else touch, so there is just my luggage, and most important, our exposed film and my notes, to worry about. Guillaume generously offers his Nuristani porter, Dilaram Shah, to guide us and carry my luggage.

The next day dawns grey and gloomy. It is obvious that the plane won't go, and neither Steve nor I can bear the thought of another day waiting in Chitral.

Fida Hussain looks worried, his eyebrows furrowing into a deep frown. "I don't think you should go. It will be snowing on the pass."

"No, no, no," says Guillaume disdainfully. "You don't know. I was there."

Fida looks doubtful, but by now knows how stubborn and impatient both Steve and I can be. He finds us a jeep driver who is willing to go as far as he can toward the pass, and says, "If you must go, go with God."

Fida, Lauren, and Guillaume fade off behind us in the thick mist. Before long, we start to climb into the mountains, and it begins to sleet. The driver is unhappy, as the wheels slip out from under us, and the road disappears beneath a cover of white. Finally he stops and refuses to go any further.

I am angry at the unrelenting weather, which seems determined to keep us in Chitral. I refuse to turn back. So does Steve. Stoically, he dons the plastic cape and trousers Guillaume had loaned him, and shoulders his camera bags. I pick up the bag with the film and notes, and put it under the heavy wool blanket Guillaume has loaned me.

On and on we walk, slower and slower as the blizzard thickens like whipped cream. My burden becomes heavy, and my breath comes more slowly. Dilaram Shah keeps up with Steve, but stops often for me to catch up. Steve forges on ahead, his angry mood giving him a good supply of adrenaline.

After a couple of hours, which seem like days, we come to the last teahouse below the pass. It is late afternoon, and it is clear we must spend the night here.

"I don't know if you'll make it tomorrow," says Steve as I trudge in, dripping snow.

"Of course I'll make it," I snarl, wishing I felt so certain. We've already come too far to go back. I don't want to go back down that mountain in the snow any more than I want to go forward.

Before dusk, a party of nine Chitralis arrives. At first I don't want to share our room, and am about to bad-temperedly invoke the woman's privilege of privacy, but Steve reminds me that if I refuse to share our warm room, the men will have to sleep outside with scant protection from the storm.

Then it's Steve's turn to be bad-tempered as the boisterous group enters, clearing their throats, spitting, and talking loudly. His eyes jealously guard his valuable camera equipment, and he whispers that we must set off well before dawn, before these guys do, because there are only three of us in this isolated place.

We get up at 4 a.m. Steve and I each eat two boiled eggs for strength, and offer some to Dilaram Shah. He doesn't understand that we want to save most of them for later, and promptly wolfs down the eight remaining eggs.

Outside, the snow is a ghostly spirit in the forest. By the tiny light of our flashlights, we can't see much. The snow has all but obliterated the trail, but Dilaram claims to know the way. We plod through knee-deep snow, which becomes thigh-deep. Steve goes on ahead, forging a trail, but even he is soon exhausted. When we come to a deserted hut, Dilaram makes a small fire and we rest, sharing two precious oranges. I notice then that Dilaram has only sandals and thin socks on. Though he is not complaining, I am horrified, and find thick wool socks and plastic bags for him, as I have no extra shoes.

While we are resting, the nine Chitralis pass us. We soon catch up with them, as no one can go very fast in this thick snow. The day warms slightly as the sun rises, but all around us is only white snow, the black silhouettes of trees, and the blinding blue of the sky reflected here and there on a patch of snow.

I've read many books about climbing in the Himalaya, but I am far from snow-wise, having grown up in Southern California. I vaguely remember something about not eating snow, but I can't remember why, so I now dismiss it as an old wives tale and scoop up handfuls whenever I am thirsty. When the Chitralis tell me not to eat it, I pretend not to understand their Urdu. It momentarily quenches my thirst, and I do not realize that I am getting colder and colder.

My hands and feet are numb, and I keep moving my toes to see if they will still move. I feel guilty about Dilaram, who has so much less protection than I do. I grow tired under Guillaume's heavy blanket, and Dilaram carries this, too, for me. Whenever we rest, I lie down in the snow. I notice small details, like the perfect ice crystals on the bright yellow woven cloth bundle of a man in front of me, and the way the individual crystals of snow lie on top of the snowdrifts and blow in the breeze.

The layer of snow gets thicker, and the drifts deeper as we climb. First one man leads, then another breaks trail, each taking turns at the exhausting job. I fall far behind, my feet feeling heavier and heavier. Even Steve is having a hard time, and Dilaram, with his heavy burden, is the only person behind me. Sometimes when I rest, I just want to lie there in the pleasant sunlight and go to sleep. I do not recognize this as a symptom of hypothermia, but Steve does, and he keeps yelling at me to make me angry enough to go on.

I keep thinking we must be almost at the top, and then round a bend and see the rest of the party far away, like tiny insects appearing to climb straight up the sheer mountain face. The snow stings my face like a thousand tiny needles, but I am too tired, and my hands too numb, to pull my woolen shawl closer about me. The bottom of my tunic is frozen solid, and my two pairs of gloves have likewise frozen.

"You're going to end up like that body in the snow if you don't hurry up!" yells Steve.

I am furious at him, and speed up on a rush of adrenaline, wanting to catch him and smear snow all over his face. "I'll kill the bastard," I mutter. "Making up horrible stories like that..." I don't see the dead body in the snow alongside the trail, a lone victim of a fall or an avalanche, and don't believe there was one until Dilaram tells me later.

But again I slow down, despairing at yet another steep ascent. "Why don't you ask that guy behind you to pull you up?" shouts Steve.

I think he is being sarcastic again, and look back towards Dilaram, but out of the thickening mist walks a healthy young mountain man, his woolen cap at a jaunty angle. He seems to be walking over the surface of the snow with catlike grace. He smiles, says *Salaam,* and immediately sees I am in trouble. He loans me his walking stick, and uses it to pull me up the steepest places, where the slick soles of my boots, never meant for snowy mountainsides, slide back to the bottom. He even loans me one of his big leather gloves to cover my frozen, bare hand.

This cheerful, kind man is a life-saver. For some time I have felt as if I am walking beside myself, but with him helping me I return to my own center, and feel alive again.

Just below the top of the pass, Dilaram stops and starts looking in the snow for something. The frame of the old backpack which I have carried from the coast of Kenya to the Hindu Kush has just broken. Bolts have worked loose and fallen in the snow. I am ready to leave everything except the bag of film, but the mountain man dashes back to help Dilaram wrap the canvas part of my backpack in a blanket so he can carry it. He returns carrying the broken frame—nothing is ever allowed to go to waste if it can possibly be repaired and used. Dilaram shoulders the film bag, which I can hardly lift, then tightens my shawl around my face and over my head, like a mother tying a parka around her child.

At the top we say, *"Al-hamdulillah!*–Thanks be to God." I feel I will survive now, for as hard as it is, the rest of the way is downhill.

Five ghostly figures pass us going the other way followed a little way on by another group of four. They are local men, taciturn, and obviously tired. I whisper *"Salaam"* and look into their dark eyes. They each meet my eyes and nod silently.

A few yards ahead smoke puffs from a wooden shack. I think it is a snow mirage, but hope that it is a hotel. Two Chitrali men, who speak a little English, have waited for us in the wayside shelter.

"Sit down, sit down, we knew you would be tired. Warm yourself by the fire and eat."

I can hardly believe my eyes, can hardly believe the warmth of the tiny fire. The men, a soldier and a teacher who turn out to be Ismailis who know Fida Hussain, are chatty and good-humored as they hand us chunks of cold meat and dried apricots. I ask if they have water, and they regretfully say no, but offer me a pear. It is the sweetest ambrosia on earth to me as I suck its delicious moisture into my dehydrated body.

"The weather is getting bad," says our mountain man urgently. "Let's go, quickly."

I don't ever want to leave this place. I would be quite happy spending the night here, so I move slowly, but he urges me on again.

A few minutes later we discover how right he is. A thick fog envelopes the mountain, and we experience the whiteness that swallows mountains. I am disoriented, unable to see more than a few feet in front of me, and I am almost too paralyzed with fear to move. But I take deep breaths in the thin air and stop my sobs of fear, concentrating on the hollows of the footsteps ahead of me, following one by one each deep depression in the snow.

Finally we come out of the cloud, and see the village of Gujar far below. We all begin to hurry, as the day is late. The mountain man walks swiftly down the trail; he is carrying the film that makes or breaks our entire assignment, so Steve summons his strength and hurries after him, doggedly keeping him in sight. I fall repeatedly in the icy snow, and weep out of frustration and fear that I am going to break a limb or fall off the mountain. The teacher and the soldier stay near me, and they also fall a lot, but laugh each time. At first I am angry, and finally it becomes a welcome release as I too grasp the absurdity of the moment.

The villagers are amazed to see any of us, especially a foreign woman. I mumble "*Salaam*" to a few people who stare back, and we make our way to the teahouse, where we spend the coldest night I have ever spent in my life, warmed only by a fire in a tiny tin box. I sleep lightly, turning from side to side, warming first one side, then the other, like a rotating spacecraft with one side turned toward the distant sun, the other toward eternal night and cold.

The plane flies overhead as we set out the next morning in melting slush and ice. Some of our Chitrali companions spit in disgust, and I shake my fist. But we are all glad to be alive. A few hours along, a jeep splashes up out of the village of Dir, and takes us all the rest of the way. We hear that five people have died on the pass, victims of an avalanche. Vividly, I see the group we had passed, and realize with a chill that had we been a little slower it could have been us. The teacher helps us send a wireless message to Fida Hussain to assure him that we are safe, but we have little hope of it arriving, as the wireless operator cannot read or write.

The owner of the hotel in Dir knows he has a monopoly on jeeps, especially at this time of year. Everyone else decides to wait for the bus, but Steve and I are willing to pay almost any price to get to Peshawar, so we agree to the owner's outrageous demand and take our two friends, the teacher and the soldier. The journey is unremarkable until we reach a town in the foothills where the driver is fined for being out of Dir State. Our friends tell us that the driver isn't supposed to take us to Peshawar, and would like us to take another car.

"Oh no," says Steve, "we paid him to go to Peshawar and he agreed. He's taking us all the way to Peshawar."

The driver gets his revenge by driving agonizingly slow and taking all the back ways to avoid police. Then we run out of gas, and he leaves us stranded while he catches a bus somewhere to get a can of gas.

By the time we arrive in Peshawar, it is nearly nine o clock at night, and we are exhausted. Steve wants to find Lauren, and we are both ready to kill the Frenchman, who we suspect of wanting to do us in. But when we finally find them, Lauren can't stop hugging us, and Guillaume is mortified at our misfortunes.

"The American Consulate thinks you are dead," she says urgently. "They heard there were Americans lost in the Hindu Kush, and..."

We check into the Intercontinental, so we can place long distance calls. The first thing I want to do is to have a hot bath—I slip on the marble floor and nearly fall, then can't stop laughing at the irony of having survived the last three days only to fall on a marble floor.

My parents are glad to hear from me. Khalid and Aiesha haven't arrived, and don't know when their number will come up. The good news is that I have a mysterious check from Indian Railways for $900 as compensation for my robbery. There is no note, no explanation, but I assume this is the answer to my letter to Indira Gandhi. I tell my parents to put the check in the bank before it bounces.

On the sixth day of the year, Lauren, Steve, Guillaume and I celebrate New Year's. We eat fine fish, and drink champagne in the almost empty Permit Room where foreigners are allowed to drink alcohol in Islamic Pakistan. Together, we all drink to life, to the Kalash people, and to freedom for Afghanistan. As the bubbly, fiery liquid tumbles down my throat, I know that my work has only begun.

17 Like a Moth to a Flame—I

Northern Pakistan
Summer, 1982

A year and a half passes before I return to the Hindu Kush, just as the Kalash Bow Shaker prophesied.

On the plane to Islamabad, I feel that peculiar detachment that comes with air travel, as one is suspended between worlds, and all the petty disturbances of the world left behind fade into insignificance. Like a child, I am mesmerized for hours by the pale crests of mountains and the brown baking plains far below. I muse on how river systems in the eroded desert are macrocosmic images of the veins in a leaf, the circulatory systems of animals, and the complex, intertwined nerve synapses of the human brain.

The past year and a half has been marked by both triumph and discouragement. I am proud and excited that my article on the Kalash, along with Steve's pictures, was published in the October, 1981 *National Geographic.* I sent a copy to Shakil Durrani, the young Deputy Commissioner of Chitral, who replied with an appreciative letter and enclosed a copy of a report he had submitted to the Government of Pakistan, entitled "The Kafir Kalash–The Urgent Need to Save a Vanishing People."

In these days of Islamic rhetoric, Durrani has stood up for the rights of a tiny non-Muslim minority, probably at some risk to his career. I am glad to know that at last the Kalash have a real friend in an influential position. I hope, too, that my article has made some small contribution by bringing the Kalash culture and its plight to world attention.

When I think of my long wait for Khalid and Aiesha to be admitted into the U.S., I grimace. I have felt lost in the tortuous bureaucratic corridors of a Kafka novel. I had written over fifty letters to government and refugee agencies in a vain attempt to get a probable date of arrival so I could continue with my own life. But not a single person or agency was able to give me an answer, and so I could not pursue my career as an international journalist, for fear that Khalid's family might arrive while I was away and have no one to sponsor them and help them adjust to life in America.

After twenty-one months, just as I have written a letter to Khalid suggesting they consider settling permanently in Germany, the news comes that they will arrive in two weeks. In some ways, their arrival is an anti-climax. Our family had closed the business which would have given Khalid a job, and we were worried about how we could help them. We need not have worried—when they arrive, they thank us appreciatively, but head the next day for Aiesha's brother's house in San Diego. There, with the help of extended family members who have arrived in the U.S. before them, they quickly settle in to life in the U.S., with all its disappointments and joyous discoveries.

But my long vigil in the U.S. has not been for nothing. I have worked, along with both Afghans living in America and Americans who lived in Afghanistan as Peace Corps volunteers, to bring the plight of the refugees to a world increasingly obsessed with its own comforts. I have published a few articles here and there, and have raised small amounts of money for the International Rescue Committee, a low-overhead group doing fine work running medical clinics in the refugee camps. I have even spoken at a few demonstrations, honing my various skills and knowledge for an unknown future when I will be able to use them to reach a greater number of people.

The time spent with Afghans in America improves my Farsi and my knowledge of the culture. Although I am disappointed by some of the Afghans I meet, who are interested in little other than the material well-being of their extended families, many others are dedicated men and women who do their best to help their countrymen who have remained to fight the Soviets. I watch sadly as some new refugees become angry and disillusioned, pining for a lost world of comfort and status and spending their days watching TV, smoking, and drinking. I actively seek out those whose hearts still have strong ties to their country.

I have learned a lot, and planted many seeds. I have reminded myself that seeds first grow downwards into darkness before reaching up towards the light, and I know that like the people of Afghanistan, I must have patience. Over and over, the Persian saying echoes, "Patience is bitter, but bears a sweet fruit."

Now at last I am returning to lands and people I have missed greatly.

Soon I will see Saifullah, Washlim Gul, Fida Hussain, Ghulam Mohammed Beg, Shakil Durrani, and Hamid, a handsome, bright young Afghan man Steve and Lauren had introduced to me in that dismal winter in Peshawar. Hamid had taken me to a refugee camp and had translated the refugees' tragic stories. The image of a boy and girl, their eyes hard with fear, has haunted me. In a dream, these two children had dipped their hands in pools of blood and rubbed them on my palms in a ritual of shared responsibility. And I have often wondered, am I doing enough to help?

Hamid has kept me up to date with news of the war and the camps. I enjoyed his frequent correspondence until the letter in which he said he loved me. But after looking into my own heart, I answered with a gentle and serious, "But I always thought of you as my brother..." Hamid never acknowledged either his letter or my response, but continued a lively correspondence, passionate about freedom, but never again mentioning personal feelings.

Now he has found a good job at one of the big international hospitals in Peshawar. He has promised to do all he can to help me, to take me to camps and hospitals so I can talk to people and take pictures. I'm looking forward to seeing him again, and my luggage is filled with jeans and books for him, as well as gifts for my other friends.

As I approach the center of Asia once more, memories, so long held frozen, suspended like a precarious glacier, cascade back into my consciousness. I remember the price I have paid to see these mountains and know their people, the weakness, hunger, and illness suffered to view the delectably forbidden vistas. When I am away in the urban deserts of the West, I remember only the majestic scenes of mountains and clouds, the sweetness of fresh apricots, the bright and welcoming eyes of those who are kind to me. I forget the cold and heat, the insects, the amoebic dysentery, the stomach pains and blisters.

Yet even when I remember all this, I am drawn back, like a comet in an eccentric orbit.

In my journal, I write a reminder: "In Asia, everything is impossible, but nothing is completely impossible." Nearly everything is difficult, and half the time "Impossible!" is the first answer. But I have learned that with persistence, sometimes patient and sometimes stubborn, difficulties usually dissolve into friendship over tea, which has been called "the social lubricant of Eastern society," whether in the city or in a tiny village police post.

As the plane nears Islamabad, I look at my calendar. I have less than two months in Pakistan, and have planned an ambitious journey. I have promised to take pictures in Baltistan for an exhibition on the Silk Road curated by friends I had met through my Afghan work; my promises to myself include revisiting the Kalash, visiting Afghan refugee camps, assessing the greatest needs and which organizations best meet them, and finally, returning in time for a friend's wedding in Canada.

I realize the folly of trying to plan in the East, and simply hope for the best. And so, a little riper, I again approach my beloved mountains, the dwelling place of God.

Pakistani popular music is blaring out of loudspeakers as the minibus pulls up to what only two years ago was the peaceful village of Karimabad, capital of Hunza. Paper pennants of pink, yellow, green, and blue festoon the mud-plastered shop where Dad Ali Shah, one of Hunza's premier entrepreneurs, exhuberantly greets each foreign tourist fresh off the bus, offering to sell them Coke and Fanta chilled in the irrigation channel.

In the mind-numbing heat, the Cokes are tempting, but mindful of cultural norms, I ask Dad Ali for tea instead. Like the older generation, I cling to comforting tradition in the face of bewildering change. The hotel where I spent such happy weeks in the spring of 1980 is full. The owners, Ibadat Shah and his brother Sadat Ali are happy to see me, and arrange a room somewhere else, assuring me it will only be for one night. Ibadat Shah leads me down a path to where there was no building two years ago, and shows me a simple room with a *charpoy* and an earthen floor. In the clear light of day it looks clean enough, so I cheerfully accept. I unpack and look out the wooden framed windows to the U-shaped valley below, its terraced sides patched with irregular emerald and gold patches of ripening grain, and feel a sense of peace to be back in this place which holds so many happy memories.

On my way back to the hotel, I am accosted by children trying to sell me apples, Hunza hats embroidered in bright, non-traditional colors, and "rubies," actually large garnets like Amjed Ali had given me two years ago. One or two kids even beg for a rupee or a pen. In the space of two years, they have become aggressive little businessmen. I shoo them away with a few words of remembered Burushashki, and they laugh and look friendlier.

Dad Ali is still sitting outside his shop, doing a thriving business in chilled soft drinks and Hunza handicrafts. At the hotel, which has been expanded since I was here, young foreigners wearing shorts, inappropriate in Muslim Pakistan, lounge on the steps, camp in the courtyard, and play rock music on boom boxes. The scent of hashish smoke wafts sweetly in the otherwise unpolluted air. I cannot believe that the opening of the Karakoram Highway to travel without a permit could have had such an effect so quickly.

Most of the guests don't seem particularly interested in Hunza culture, and a few of them cast me strange glances. I finally figure out my *shalwar kameez* and cotton veil must be putting them off. But on this trip I have made a conscious decision to follow the advice of an Afghan woman friend in America and respect the culture. I have no wish to wear a veil all the time, but find it convenient as well as culturally appropriate—the veil keeps sun and dust off my head. And in my brief visit to Peshawar before coming here, I realized how easy it was to blend in, and how much more seriously I was taken. Ironically, I feel I am more likely to influence the freedom of Afghan women if I take on this habit which to Westerners, and to some Muslim women, is a symbol of oppression.

I am here to see old friends, and am glad to share tea with Ibadat Shah, Sadat Ali, and their nephew Amjed Ali. Amjed is now a mature thirteen, and his English is excellent for a young boy who has never been out of Hunza. His eyes are as bright and quick with intelligence as ever, and I am relieved that he hasn't picked up any bad habits from foreigners. I shudder to think of Hunza becoming like some places in Nepal, where small children smoke cigarettes and joints and sell hashish and magic mushrooms.

I take a walk up the familiar steep, dusty path to Haji Qudratullah Beg's house. The valley is still beautiful, though it is baking under this relentless sun, and seems to be fading away, like Brigadoon, into another existence. The dark green poplars still rise to the brilliant cobalt sky, the imperious jagged white peaks still overlook the golden barley fields and apricot trees laden with more fruit than they can bear. But the children don't offer foreigners handfuls of apricots anymore; they sell them by the bagful.

Haji's house, at least, has not changed. Haji's hawknosed face still wears a warm smile, and his pale eyes still twinkle, but his sight is fading, and when he gets up to show me something, he is stooped over and walks with a cane. He has arthritis now, and no longer spends so many hours working in the fields.

In the evening, the hotel is so noisy I go to sit by myself on a hillside above the village, from where I can watch twilight suffuse the valley. The apricot light of dusk soothes my soul as I look out at the white cone of Rakaposhi, serene and slow to change. I am moved to tears at the beauty, and feel a hard ache inside and a sense of loss of something intangible but irreplaceable. So far this road has brought sugar, tobacco, white flour, black tea, and cooking oil. It has brought a few people a little money, but I'm not sure if it has really brought anyone any happiness.

The sky deepens to plum, and the crescent moon begins to rise. My old friend Ainul Hayat, the gem dealer, walks by and invites me for tea in his shop. I am comforted, again feeling a sense of belonging in this valley which was once only a childhood dream.

Dinner at the hotel is no longer in the cozy, intimate kitchen, but in a crowded dining room. The electricity is more consistent, but the light is bright and garish. I miss joking with Ibadat Shah and Sadat Ali as they cook. Only the table is the same, and I stare at its pattern, remembering quieter days.

Over tea, I reread a satirical story I wrote when I was in Hunza before. It is about the village of Salaamabad, where a dare-devil American motorcycle rider wants to jump the junction of two rivers. Thousands of American tourists converge in the area, encouraged by a Third World government eager for foreign exchange, bringing with them their beer cans and boom boxes. The locals are bewildered when the star, Bad Joe Becker, arrives in a helicopter painted to look like a well-known brand of American beer, and climbs down a hanging ladder followed by a scantily clad woman. The American Cultural Attache, horrified by the whole circus, quietly gives children gifts of Swiss Army knives, secretly hoping they will damage some of the telelvision equipment. When Bad Joe insists on meat, the villages sell his entourage a diseased goat. When he gets sick to his stomach, he overdoses on diarrhea medication and collapses just as he and his fancy machine soar off into the canyon.

I am afraid to write satire ever again. What if I am helping create reality? Should I write only about an ideal world?

At night I go for a walk, rejoicing in the coolness of night after a broiling day. I look at the stars through the arms of the stately poplars, and watch the Big Dipper slide behind the high wall of the mountains. I walk along the wide, dusty road, now a jeep and bus road, and enjoy the soft, cool moondust under my feet. But behind me I hear footsteps, and taunting male voices ask, "Are you Pakistani?"

"No," I say shortly, not wanting conversation. But they continue to follow me, so I quicken my pace and around a bend I dash through a gap in the thornbushes and hide until they have passed.

When I return to my tiny room, I discover that daylight was deceptive. By night, the room is alive with insect life. At first, I ignore the big black beetles, the large leaping bugs, and even the centipede on the wall. I throw off the mattress full of bedbugs, and lay out my trusty sleeping bag. I read and write for awhile by the light of the bare electric bulb, then try to fall asleep.

I doze off, but a terrible prickling feeling on my cheek wakes me up. I switch on my flashlight to surprise a horde of tiny, blood-gorged transparent insects. I turn on the light and again try to sleep, but the light attracts even more vermin, and worse, I can see them. I try to sleep sitting up, I meditate, I go out for walks, but every time I think I am tired enough to sleep, the prickling of biting insects wakes me up.

In my exhausted daze, I begin to think that these insects are an incarnation of evil, a metaphor for the outside influences on this valley, for disease, pollution, and change for the worse. I feel overwhelmed by the magnitude of this change, and the presence of so many insects, and all this gets confused until just before dawn I doze off sitting up, like a Tibetan hermit.

As soon as it is light, I hurry to the hotel restaurant, knowing Ibadat Shah will be up. I don't know the word for insect in either Burushashki or Urdu, but an insect has conveniently died in my orange plastic bowl, so I take it to show him. "Thousands and thousands and thousands," I tell him expressively in my limited Urdu.

He shakes his head and laughs sympathetically. "Tonight, good room," he assures me, shaking his head apologetically.

I spend most of the day catching up on sleep in the good room. In the afternoon, I go for a walk. Suddenly a violent duststorm kicks up, the familiar huge, powerful wind which picks up the fine glacial dust on the valley's paths and blows a thick cloud across the valley towards Hispar glacier.

I seek shelter in Ainul Hayat's shop. We have tea, shielding the small glasses to keep the dust out. "They say that Ultar, the glacier above Baltit and Karimabad, is male, and Hispar is female," he tells me. "When this happens we say that Ultar has broken. These winds are so strong that, they say, chickens have been picked up in Baltit and landed in Nagar."

We also talk of the influx of tourism. It is good for business, he says, good for gems and handicrafts and hotel-owners, but not good for the people. Hunza people don't like the long-haired hippies who bring hashish. He has seen foreigners throw cigarette butts in the irrigation channels, which are the source of drinking water for most villagers, and some people have even seen French tourists bathing nude, men and women together, in the channels. So far, it is only in the summer that the tourists come in such numbers, but it is not like the old days, he says regretfully. Then the tourists who came had gone through some difficulty to get here, and really appreciated the place and its beauty.

That night, there is a tremendous single peal of thunder, followed by heavy rains and even hail, as if the valley is cleansing itself. The next day is a most sacred day to the Hunzakuts, the celebration of the Aga Khan's Silver Jubilee, marking 25 years since he became the spiritual leader of the Ismaili sect.

In the morning, I head across the terraced fields and through the stony irrigation channels towards Hyderabad to meet Ghulam Mohammed and his family for the celebration. The path is familiar, but this year the heat is unbearable, and I am dehydrated and nearly collapsing when I reach the village. A young man recognizes me and leads me to a tent where I can have tea. When I have recovered a little, he escorts me to the dais where the dignitaries are sitting, and I see all the familiar faces: somber Ghulam Mohammed in his safari suit and peaked karakul cap, the serene poet Nasir Hunzai, and exhuberant Dad Ali Shah. I am welcomed to sit among them.

I listen to many speeches in Burushashki. A *ferman,* a command from the Aga Khan, is read in Burushashki, Urdu, and English. It tells the Ismailis that they must find a balance between spiritualism and materialism, and must guard against becoming too materialistic.

Alama Nasir, whose title means "the scholar," speaks with great fervor, and I understand a few words of Persian origin. The Aga Khan is the fountainhead, the source of the spring, the light of God. Ghulam Mohammed then gives a serious speech about the importance of education, and ends with a phrase I understand even in Burushashki—"one world under the sun."

After the speeches, the dignitaries proceed to the Jamaat Khana, the Ismaili mosque. I hang back, knowing that outsiders, even other Muslims, are never allowed in, but Nasir turns to invite me, and Ghulam Mohammed says, "You are our honored guest today. And someday, *inshallah,* you will be Ismaili."

After the meal, Ghulam Mohammed invites me to his home, where I see his dear mother again. She has made me a small purse out of camel-colored wool, which she has embroidered herself. His sister presents me with a pillbox Hunza hat embroidered with colorful needlepoint designs. "She says you look Hunza and should always wear this hat when you are here," says Ghulam Mohammed. "In fact, many of the people thought you were an educated Hunza girl who had come back for the Jubilee."

Ghulam Mohammed is eager for me to take pictures of the Volunteer's Band. The volunteers are a community service group which he had organized years ago, and they are proud of their band. I am astounded to see about twenty craggy-faced Hunza mountain men in spotless white British-style uniforms with tartan sashes and caps, playing bagpipes and drums. I follow them on their procession to all the Jamaat Khanas in Hyderabad, moved by the devotion that these simple people have for their spiritual leader, who lives a life most of them cannot conceive.

When I return to Karimabad, I notice cans full of sawdust and oil all along the path. At dusk, the entire village lights up in a fiery tribute to the Aga Khan. Even the sides of the steep mountains are lit up with orange flame spelling out "Silver Mubarak," or "blessings," in English, and the name of Ali in Arabic letters. The valley is ablaze in the darkness, and on the rooftops people stand in silence, watching the awesome display, quieter and more reverent than fireworks. It is a moment of magic regained, and I know that this Brigadoon will never entirely fade away. It may remain invisible to most, but beckons to those willing to step off the beaten path.

Late at night, I again go for a walk to look at the stars in peace. I have always felt absolutely safe here, but now I feel fear and mistrust creeping into the valley. I am sorrowful, but my faith has been renewed by the fire on the mountain, which is stronger than any evil. I stand in the thick, soft dust, gazing in enchantment at the stars, like silver grains in an utterly black sky, the Milky Way like a gossamer veil. I think of how these stars have come down to earth tonight, simply to honor a people's love for the light of God. I close my eyes in peaceful meditation and suddenly feel someone grab my elbow. A rough male voice says something in a gutteral tone, but I twist away, screaming in English, "Who are you? What do you want?"

I run back towards the hotel in a panic, then stop and turn to look back. In the darkness I can't see anything. I shout, "*Sheitan*—Satan" and reach the hotel out of breath. I want to tell someone, but no one is awake, and I must keep this in my heart until the morning.

The next day, I return to Hyderabad for more festivities. I quietly tell Ghulam Mohammed about last night's incident. He listens and frowns. "Do not go walking at night," he tells me sternly, his eyes hard behind his tinted glasses.

"But I always used to. This is Hunza. I have never had anything to fear here."

"It is not the same now." Things have changed, he tells me. Outsiders are no longer welcome in the houses, since a visiting Pakistani policeman abducted a Hunza girl some months ago. People are more and more suspicious of outside influences they cannot control.

His answers do not satisfy me, but I promise to give up walking alone at night. I settle down to watch the speeches and skits, one encouraging little girls to become nurses. Children play tug of war and run three-legged races, and boys jump through flaming hoops and play musical chairs, sitting on big cooking oil tins.

The best part of the spectacle is the Hunza dancing. Handsome dandies of all ages leap and cavort to the frenzied music of a country that once excelled at polo. The musicians, who play drums and the wailing, clarinet-like *surnai,* are all friends from my last visit. Ghulam Mohammed says it is fine to take pictures, but when I come down from the dais one of the marshals grabs my arm and starts shouting. The dancers stop, the music fades, and people start shouting at each other. Ghulam Mohammed takes command and tries to smooth things over. In the middle of all the anger, a man signals the musicians to play and begins a magnificent sword dance. The crowd stops shouting and watches him swing the sword under his legs, leap over it, swirl it, and cut through the air in huge, dramatic sweeps. He is given a prize for his display of virtuosity of this almost-lost art, and perhaps for his diversion as well.

A village headman later comes to Ghulam Mohammed to apologize for the confusion, explaining that some people were angry that not all the dancers from all the villages were in the photos. Ghulam Mohammed, always the diplomat, invites the village headman along with me and several others to his home for tea. There I give a donation to the Jamaat Khana, and Ghulam Mohammed proudly announces it.

That night, I float in and out of consciousness, listening to the German tourists outside spraying against insects and singing to the accompaniment of a harmonica, and the Pakistani tourists angrily banging on a jeep that won't start. But I keep slipping into dreams of the golden stars come down to earth on the sheer cliffs of this valley of refuge, by turns heaven, hell, and paradise lost.

18 Like a Moth to a Flame—II

I sit in the Mohammed Book Stall, Ghulam Mohammed's tiny shop in Gilgit's dusty bazaar, seeking meager solace from the baking heat outside. I am content to sit fossilized under the lazy fan, when the electricity is on, drinking hot cups of sweet milky tea which are surprisingly refreshing, just watching Ghulam Mohammed's varied clientele come and go.

I am actually in a hurry to find a jeep going over the 12,100 foot Shandur Pass to the Chitral Valley, but no one would guess it from watching my sluggish pace. In my mind I am already on a jeep high in the mountains, licked by cool breezes; but my body is motionless, my mind dulled, hardly able to make a decision. Luckily, Ghulam Mohammed has the uncanny knack shared by merchants in all Asian bazaars—he always knows what is going on, who has just arrived, and who is soon to go.

"You just wait here," he tells me, and sends one of his teen-age sons to speak to a jeep driver.

Content and well cared for, I browse through his extensive collection of books on the area, and on Islamic philosophy and Sufism, and watch the procession of foreigners, Pakistani tourists, Hunzakuts, and Shins from Gilgit. As I sit in the shadows at the back of the shop, wearing a maroon embroidered Afghan shawl as a veil over my head and shoulders, most of the foreigners assume I am a local. When Ghulam Mohammed introduces me in Persian to a scholarly personage from Hunza, the gentleman at first assumes that I am Iranian. Until I speak, even some Pakistanis assume I too am Pakistani, despite my fair skin.

"This is the University of Gilgit!" I joke to Ghulam Mohammed. "Everybody comes here, and you introduce everyone to each other. I name you the Dean of the University of Gilgit."

He looks every bit the part in his trademark peaked karakul cap, called a Jinnah cap in Pakistan because Mohammed Ali Jinnah, the founder of Pakistan, always used to wear one.

In the stultifying heat, we continue to gaze out on the dusty bazaar, waiting for customers or visitors. A wizened Afghan Kirghiz man in a white embroidered black skullcap approaches tentatively, offering Ghulam Mohammed a silver-trimmed bridle with both hands. Ghulam Mohammed takes it politely and appraises it, then tells the man in Farsi that he regrets that he cannot buy it, because he does not think he can sell it. The man looks at me questioningly, but as I too regretfully refuse, he moves on slowly down the bazaar, clutching a lost piece of his culture.

"The Kirghiz refugees are leaving in a few days," says Ghulam Mohammed. "Now they are selling everything. I have bought as much as I can, to help them, but I can't buy everything."

This particular band of Kirghiz, from the remote Wakhan corridor of Afghanistan, has an unusual history. Once these nomadic herders roamed freely between Afghanistan and what is now the Soviet Union. In the 1930's, Stalin sealed the border, cutting off a million Kirghiz from their ethnic cousins in Afghanistan and China. Haji Rahman Qul, the Khan, or chief, of this band, led his people to China on their migrations. Then in 1949, during the Communist revolution, they had to fight their way through Chinese border guards to return to Afghanistan. Because the borders were closed, they were forced to change their migration patterns and remain within the Afghan portion of the Pamir, high altitude plateaux where they could graze their yaks and sheep. To help his tribe survive, the innovative Khan also developed new methods of livestock management and encouraged some agriculture.

Rahman Qul proved an apt leader, and the tribe thrived, despite the harsh conditions of life at 12,000 feet. But when he heard that Soviet-supported Marxists had taken over the Afghan government in April, 1978, he had led most of his tribe into yet another exile, this one likely to be permanent. About 1500 Afghan Kirghiz crossed the mountains into Pakistan, leaving their round felt yurts set up as a decoy to gain time. In Gilgit, the Pakistani government allowed them to settle in a refugee camp, but the high altitude nomads were not used to the extreme heat of the valley, which lies at only about 5,000 feet. Three hundred people, mostly children and the elderly, died the first year. The rest of the tribe suffered terribly. The Kirghiz women were for the first time cooped up inside tents or houses and forced to wear veils if they walked in the conservative town, where women are rarely seen. Everyone suffered from heat-induced illnesses, much as Tibetan refugees have suffered in the steamy plains of India.

But Rahman Qul had once seen pictures of Alaska. Ever ready to take a risk, he decided that the terrain and climate were similar to that of the Pamir, and one day walked into the U.S. Embassy in Islamabad and applied for 1300 visas. U.S. officials were nonplussed. Official reaction was that visas would be decided on a case by case basis, thus consigning the Kirghiz, who wanted to remain together, to a bureaucratic limbo.

"They are going to Turkey," says Ghulam Mohammed. "After five years, at last they are leaving this camp."

The government of Turkey, in a display of pan-Turkish solidarity, has just accepted several thousand Afghan refugees of Turkic descent, the Kirghiz among them. They will be resettled in Turkey's mountainous Van Province, and allowed to stay together and continue some form of their nomadic life. I look around Ghulam Mohammed's shop, and see the flotsam of their exile–embroidered hats, lacquered spoons, wood-carvings done by one of Rahman Qul's sons, and watercolor paintings done by another. A way of life is forever passing, and I have the urge to see its last days.

I rouse myself from my stupor to visit the Deputy Commissioner, since access to refugee camps is strictly controlled. I've been in Pakistan long enough to drop whatever names I know, and luckily this official turns out to be a friend of Shakil Durrani's. He readily gives me permission to visit the camp and interview the Kirghiz Khan, asking only that one of his men be present. We arrange for the man to meet me later at Rahman Qul's cloth shop in the bazaar, and I go there to wait.

The shop is in sad condition, most of its stock already sold off or given away. Two of Rahman Qul's sons are there. They are delighted that I speak Farsi, which is a second language for many Kirghiz, especially the men, who used to trade with Kabul. At first they think I am Iranian, and are surprised when I tell them I am American.

"Is one of you Abdul Malik?" I ask.

One nods his head.

"You are the artist. I have seen your beautiful work in Ghulam Mohammed's shop, and also in a film about the Kirghiz."

Abdul's Malik's work was featured in a documentary by British anthropologist/filmmaker Andre Singer. The film showed how the young man's paintings had changed from peaceful mountain scenes to depictions of war and Islamic victory over godless Communist aggression.

"Where did you learn to paint so beautifully?" I ask Abdul Malik. The bronze cheeks blush dark. "The rivers and mountains of Pamir were my teachers," he answers ingenuously.

Haji Rahman Qul has sent a message that he will meet me later in the afternoon, so while I wait for him and for the man, I pass the time drinking tea and conversing with a growing crowd of curious Kirghiz. Ghulam Mohammed has loaned me a copy of a book on the Kirghiz by Afghan-born anthropologist Nazif Shahrani. Many of them remember Shahrani, and they eagerly look at the pictures of their Khan, of people they know, and of the meadows and mountains of their Pamir homeland. Many of the men are sentimental, and obviously homesick. As they pass the book carefully from hand to hand, their narrow black eyes glisten with tears, even as their brown, Mongol-featured faces glisten with sweat.

I am trying to explain a picture, at a loss for the proper words in Farsi, when Abdul Malik says, "Ask Hamid. He is Afghan and speaks very good English."

I am shocked to see the small figure of my friend Hamid at the edge of the crowd of Kirghiz. When I had last seen Hamid in Peshawar, he had been angry at me because I had told him I could not travel with him in this strict Muslim country. When he had told me he was going to take his holiday from work while I was in Pakistan, I had told him, truthfully, that I was unsure of my itinerary.

But here he is. My emotions are mixed, but he is smiling, and seems genuinely glad to see me.

Hamid helps me translate to the Kirghiz, and then we speak in English. I am slightly embarrassed by his presence, and don't want to seem too closely connected, but agree to meet him for dinner at the Tourist Cottage, where I am staying. What will Ghulam Mohammed think? I wonder. What will Karim, the proprietor of the hotel, think? I am surprised at my own reactions, but here in Pakistan traditions and customs are different. Life is so much easier, and homes and families so much more open, if one simply observes rather than fighting to change. For now, I am relieved that Hamid is wearing a *shalwar kameez* rather than the peg-legged jeans he had worn in Peshawar.

The crowd parts when Haji Rahman Qul arrives. He is not a tall man, but is charismatic and commanding. He is at the same time dignified and friendly, and I feel that he is assessing me with a shrewd eye as I explain that I would like to visit the camp and write something about the Kirghiz.

"Most people forget us," he says.

"I will not. I promise to send you the photos I take, and a copy of anything that I may write and publish."

He nods slowly, considering, stroking his thin white beard. "Where did you learn Farsi?"

"A little in Kabul, three years ago. And more in Pakistan, staying around Afghan people."

"Your Farsi is good," he says approvingly.

We talk about the war in Afghanistan, the Jehad against the atheist invaders, and he asks if I have been there with the Mujahedeen.

"Not yet," I answer, "but *inshallah* one day I will go."

We wait around awhile longer for the government man, but when he doesn t show up, we decide to go to the camp anyway. Rahman Qul orders a jeep, as the camp is a long way on the other side of the river. He invites Hamid, but the young man declines politely, then tells me in English that he has often been questioned by the Pakistanis because he is Afghan, although in theory all refugees are free to move around Pakistan.

The camp is a depressing row of yellow UN tents on stony ground that radiates heat up to the mountain walls. I understand why the Kirghiz are so glad to be leaving in a few days. The women, who like most nomads traditionally mingled with the men in the course of their work and did not veil their faces, come out and look at me with open curiosity. They are sweating in their heavy velvet vests, bright red and pink-flowered dresses, and bulky trousers. Most of them wear white veils over high-peaked red caps, and their silver jewelry jingles softly as they shyly pour me cups of salt tea and offer me an enamel plate of fried bread. A beautiful little girl in crimson satin stands nearby, carrying her brother on her back. Beads of sweat stand out on her high Mongolian cheekbones and forehead, and she symbolizes to me the sad state of the Kirghiz in Gilgit.

Rahman Qul asks me to take a picture of all the men in the camp in a big group. I walk far, far back to get them all in, knowing that this life will be over in a matter of days, and that their old way of life is over forever. Yet another traditional way of life has fallen victim to the mysterious forces of world politics and the struggle between industrialized capitalism and industrialized communism, both inexorably wiping out the old ways of harmony with the environment.

On the way back to the road, we pass a family waiting for a bus to Gilgit. A beautiful young Kirghiz woman wears a black *burqa*, which covers her from head to toe. For now, her face is left uncovered, the thick chiffon veil thrown back, but she is already dripping in the heat.

Rahman Qul invites me to his rented adobe house in the back lands behind the bazaar. He has just sold a small herd of sheep that his family had kept in the high pastures far from Gilgit, and the Kirghiz are celebrating their impending departure with a feast of mutton kebab.

"You will forget us," says one of the Kirghiz headmen. "Everyone has forgotten us. The Americans have forgotten us, the Pakistanis have forgotten us."

"We are not angry with Pakistan," Rahman Qul hastens to add. "Only with the heat. We are grateful for all that our Pakistani Muslim brothers did to help us."

I promise never to forget them, promise to send the photos to them in Turkey. Rahman Qul's wife, a pretty, well-aged woman, presents me with two lacquered spoons as a memento, and I sadly take my leave, wishing them a journey of good fortune.

On my way back to the hotel, I run smack into a Pakistani who asks me where I am from. One too many strangers have asked this question, so I answer flippantly, "*Dunya*–Earth." Unfortunately, this Pakistani is not just a nosey tourist from Karachi, but a local policeman.

"You were visiting the Kirghiz without permission," he says.

Chastened, I explain to him that I do have permission, but that the Deputy Commissioner's man never showed up. The policman is suspicious, and demands to know where I am staying. Later, he phones an apology, saying, "The D.C. says you are very genius woman and I should not bother you."

Hamid is in a black mood by the time I arrive at the Tourist Cottage. "Where were you?" he asks dramatically.

"With the Kirghiz. You knew that."

"It is nearly dark. I was very worried."

"I was with Haji Rahman Qul."

He looks as if he doesn't quite believe me, and I too begin to grow angry. I am not accustomed to someone questioning when I come and go. Our dinner conversation is strained, but he talks animatedly to the table full of foreigners. I am relieved when he tells me he is leaving for Islamabad tomorrow, and we finally part on amicable terms, agreeing to meet in Peshawar. I feel less exposed in a larger city, especially where my work provides a reason for us to be seen together in public. Hamid's good-bye is intense, but I know that I cannot return this intensity. "Good-bye, my dear brother," I tell him, with an honest fondness for this passionate, bright, and eager man.

The next day, I am back in Ghulam Mohammed's shop. "An Afghan boy came looking for you," he says.

"Yes, I know. That is Hamid. I know him from 1980, and he has been very helpful to me in Peshawar."

"Be careful of him."

"Why?"

"He came here and was saying bad things."

"What?!"

"He said that you were like his sister, but I didn't like the way he said it. It was not good."

I smile inwardly, aware that I have another protector.

"You know who is here?" asks Ghulam Mohammed. "Mr. Hugh Swift, the author. He has just completed a long journey, and has given me a copy of his book."

Proudly, Ghulam Mohammed shows me the copy of Hugh's trekking book, and the acknowlegements page. "All I did was talk to him for a few hours," he says, "and yet he is so kind to thank me. Not everyone is like this. There are others I have helped much more, but they forget. Anway, you can see him and his friend Mr. John Mock, who speaks excellent Urdu, in the Hunza Inn."

Over a delicious meal, I have a reunion with Hugh, whom I had met in Hunza in 1980. He has just finished an eight-month journey, the Great Himalayan Traverse, trekking along the length of the Himalayan range with mountain-climber Arlene Blum. They started in Bhutan, walked the length of Nepal, and into India in Ladakh. Hugh, the thorough perfectionist, has come to Pakistan to complete the journey to his own satisfaction. He and John have just been trekking in Baltistan, as close to the Indian border as they could legally get, and have ended up in Gilgit.

"I guess we're just going to keep running into each other in different parts of the Himalaya," I conclude. "We're all a bunch of assorted Himalayan nuts."

When I return to the shop after lunch, Ghulam Mohammed has good news. He has found a jeep for me that leaves in the morning. I go to his house to say good-bye to his wife and children, and they present me with a pair of gold-embroidered wedding shoes from Peshawar. Then his wife impulsively takes a bracelet off her arm and gives it to me.

"She says it will protect you," says Ghulam Mohammed. "She wants you to have it. It has the names of God, Mohammed, Ali, Hassan, Hussain, and Fatima on it, as well as 'In the name of God, the compassionate, the merciful.'"

I feel happy to know that here too I have a family, and that wherever I go, they are praying for my well-being and protection.

When I see the jeep driver the next morning, I realize why I will need protection. The jeep is a shiny new bright blue, but the driver chain-smokes hashish-laden cigarettes. It doesn't seem to affect his driving much, but he laughs and jokes without language with a French Canadian man who also chain-smokes joints and keeps insisting that I try one.

I pretend neither of them are there, and watch the scenery. On the Gilgit side of the Shandur Pass, the valleys are wide and lovely, with small circles of golden, ripening grain appearing suddenly between serrated mountain walls beneath cat's teeth peaks. Clear rivers run over snow and become blue-green streams, and later converge with brown floods, rushing beneath swaying suspension bridges.

We stop in a tiny village below the gently sloping meadows that lead to the top of the pass. The night is cool, and breezes carry sweet scents. We are given different varieties of apricots, some soft and golden, others white and firm. A bright gibbous moon shines on our string-beds beneath the open sky, transforming the mountains and giving the scene a dreamlike quality.

We begin talking about the moon, in mixed languages, and I take out a picture I carry everywhere, a view of Earth from the moon's surface. The villagers crowd around in the flickering, ancient lanternlight, looks of amazement on their faces as I tell them that this ground is the moon and this blue and white half circle in the black sky is Earth. My words are translated from English to Urdu to Chitrali and Shina. This is what Earth really looks like, I tell them. Can you see countries? Can you see any borders?

Thoughtfully, our gathering disperses, and I soon fall asleep, watching clouds spread wings of light across the moon-fed sky.

Shandur Pass is another landscape from a dream. The land spreads out to a flat plateau with an indigo lake in the distance at the foot of a massif of pale blue mountains which suddenly rise from the earth-toned plain. This view holds me for a long time, but when we begin to descend toward the Chitral side, we are slapped with a vicious wave of heat reflected off the bare mountainsides.

The Canadian gets off in a village not far from the top of the pass. I drink and drink, till all the water I have in my bottle is gone. My throat goes dry, and I doze, waking up to realize in a panic that I have stopped sweating and my skin is dry, a dangerous sign of impending heatstroke.

"Pani, Pani," I whisper, calling for water in Urdu. But the driver doesn't hear me over the grinding of the rocks beneath the jeep's wheels.

I have ceased to worry about his drug habit, as I am too ill to be terrified as he backs up the jeep on each hairpin turn, seeming about to catapult us into a chasm of hell.

When he finally stops on the outskirts of a village I throw myself into an irrigation channel. I know that I must cool my overheated, dehydrated body quickly. The driver is angry, not understanding, and all I can do is repeatedly rasp, “I am too hot, too hot. Give me water.”

Now looking concerned, the driver helps me out of the channel and into a nearby shop. I keep asking for clean water, but they bring me cloudy water directly out of the irrigation channel. Another jeep stops, and two Punjabi doctors jump out to see what is wrong. They speak English, and I again ask weakly for clean water. They tell me there is none, and suggest that I drink some packaged rehydration solution. I hold my breath and drink the foul water, vaguely hoping it is not full of parasites and viruses. Under the circumstances, it is my only alternative to heatstroke.

I rest for awhile until the solution begins to take effect. Then I am able to drink some tea, which is safer because the water is boiled. But I am weak, and will never quite feel well until months later, when I have recovered from infectious hepatitis.

When I reach Chitral, I find out that Fida Hussain is out of town, and Shakil Durrani has just been transferred to a new post.

Disappointed, I go to the Mountain Inn, where I am given the same room I had frozen in during the winter. I lie in bed, trying to remember being cold, thinking that cold couldn’t possibly exist. I have a feeling of dread, and I don’t know it if is just the delirium of illness. The air feels electrically charged, and I sense an impending doom. I watch the sky and listen to the wind beating my door, slamming it again and again. It is the sound of fate, and the roses in the garden are the pale scent of fate on this harsh wind. I feel caught between the lightning and the moon, my soul at last ground to powder by these mountains, and thrown to this wind.

The next day, I discover that I am lucky after all. Shakil Durrani is still in town, having decided to stay for the big Chitral-Gilgit polo match on top of Shandur Pass. He readily gives me permission to visit the Kalash valleys, and invites me to meet his wife and take tea at their house. The Deputy Commissioner’s house has a cool, pleasant garden, and it is an improbable luxury to sit and eat spiced chickpeas and chocolate brownies in the cool evening breeze.

Shakil's wife Sabrina is an elegant and perfect hostess, even in this rural outpost. The three of us chat about Chitral, and Shakil's next job as Political Agent of Khyber. Shakil is a modest, unassuming man, and is worried that he might be seen as patronizing toward the Kalash. I assure him that he has done a lot of good already, and tell him how glad I am that someone has stood up for the rights of the Kalash.

"The Kalash have few real friends," he answers. "Just you, and a few others who have stuck with them. The rest just come for a few days, take photos, and go."

We discuss future plans for a museum and a Kalash Foundation, which would spread the material benefits of tourism among the Kalash people rather than outsiders. Shakil has commissioned several Kalash wood-carvers to carve the statues that used to adorn the tombs of the dead when a feast of merit was given by descendants. He was looking forward to administering the Kalash Foundation, he says, and is concerned for its future. Though he is pleased about his promotion to a plum job, he regrets that these two years have passed so swiftly.

The next day, I am on my way to Rumbur with Robert, a young Australian whom I had met at Shakil's office, and who had turned out to be my old friend Michael's brother. We are in Chitral bazaar sitting in a jeep and waiting for it to go when suddenly I see Saifullah. Laughing with excited joy, I jump out to greet him. He can't stop smiling either, and can hardly believe that Robert is really Michael's brother.

"I saw you, and I thought, 'That boy could be Michael. But I was too shy to say anything.'"

We eat in the Shabnam, the small hotel by the jeep stand, with a group of Kalash men including my adopted father-in-law, Kata Sing, who also greets me enthusiastically. Already, as I ask questions about my *dari,* my bloodsister Washlim Gul, I feel I have come home. Saifullah, Robert, and I talk all the way to Ayun, and I forget my strange weakness until we are walking up the river from Ayun. I am suddenly overcome with vertigo just as I am climbing down a rough-hewn ladder made of a log set at a crazy angle on a sheer cliff. Saifullah has to support my legs while someone else holds onto my hands to lift me down. For a long time I lie on the flat rocks by the river, the world spinning, until I recover enough to go on.

Every bend of the Rumbur Valley is familiar, and my pulse quickens as we walk past the fields of tall green maize, drawing nearer to the villages. But my eyes see what my heart wishes to deny–like Hunza,

Rumbur has changed. The hotel is now two stories high, and Balanguru is deserted, as most of the people are at the summer farmland higher up the valley. Worst of all, the huge walnut tree where we danced the Chaomos dances has been cut down, as its dying branches had become a danger to the village houses.

The first night, Saifullah enjoys the bottle of whisky which Robert has brought him, and later the coffee which I brought. The three of us sit and joke late into the night, but I feel so weak that I lie down and half listen while they talk.

Saifullah is full of admiration for Shakil, and regrets that he is being transferred. He tells many stories of what Shakil has done for the Kalash, and I begin to think that Durrani has become a legendary figure for them.

"I had come from Islamabad, and I had no money and no idea how I would get back to Rumbur," begins Saifullah. "Then Shakil sees me in the street and stops his car. He asked if I needed anything, but I was shy to tell him, so I just said no. But he put his hand in my pocket and came up with a few paisa coins, and just laughed and told me to tell him what I need."

The next day, I feel a bit better, and very eager to see my bloodsister. Robert and I follow Saifullah to the summer p]ace, where Washlim Gul and I have a warm, affectionate reunion. She can't seem to stop laughing, and her dark eyes shine with delight as she proudly shows me her new son, and calls him my nephew. All of Saifullah's family is here–his gentle, elderly mother, his cheerful father, his other two sons, and various relatives. I am surprised at how much Kalasha is coming back to me. I remind them that the Bow Shaker was right–here I am home again in a year and a half.

I feel serene and peaceful, but again weakness suddenly overtakes me. Washlim Gul leads me to a string-bed beneath a walnut tree, and I fall asleep in the afternoon sunlight while Saifullah and Robert visit the altar to Sajigur. I have strange, restless dreams, falling in and out of sleep, and for brief moments I think I catch glimpses of the fairies who live in the dappled green leaves above my head.

The next day I am dehydrated from vomiting and diarrhea. I do not want to leave the valley so soon, but Saifullah is concerned, and insists that I go back to Chitral. Robert isn't too well either, so Saifullah accompanies both of us in the jeep which delivers provisions for Afghan refugees from Nuristan. The driver hurries, hoping to reach a gas station before he runs out, but to no avail. We refuel from a passing jeep, and make it as far as Ayun. There we lie in the heat in a dismal teahouse where chunks of fly-encrusted meat perched on top of a wooden door lend a surrealistic atmosphere.

Saifullah is gloomy. "This is not a good place to be sick," he says. "I am worried for you, as the toilet places are very far away in the fields. And there are mosquitoes here, more than you have ever seen anywhere. This is the worst place in the world."

By now, Robert and I are ready to pay any price to get to Chitral. Luckily, Saifullah finds a jeep and bargains a fee that is not too outrageous. At the Mountain Inn in Chitral, there doesn't seem to be any food for people who aren't in tour groups, so we eat corn flakes and feel hungry and dejected, each of us trying to cheer the others up.

The next day, Robert feels well enough to return to Rumbur with Saifullah. Saifullah had hoped to say good-bye to Shakil Durrani, but he is still up at the polo match, so Saifullah leaves disappointed. He is reluctant to leave me in Chitral, and I can hardly bear to say good-bye after such a short visit. In private, I give him some cash to help in his legal battles. This time, at least, I can say good-bye with an embrace.

It seems I will never get out of Chitral. I am too ill to go by road, and the PIA office won't promise me an air ticket. Fida Hussain's relatives and friends try to help, and finally I am given a seat. At the airport the next morning, I am sent to the women's *purdah* room, a tiny room with no fan, where I begin to feel hysterical. There is a close, evil feeling in the air, and all I want is to be out of Chitral.

The plane does not go that day, but I am befriended by two Jordanian students who look after me and make sure I get to the airport the next morning. Miraculously, I am given a seat—and find myself sitting next to two empty seats.

Much later, I find out that Chitral went mad the next day. A *mullah* of the majority Sunni Muslim community incited people against the minority Ismaili Muslim community, taking advantage of the change of Deputy Commissioners. The previous year, Durrani had met their challenge by deploying an armored vehicle with a machine gun at the bridge leading to the Ismaili part of town. He told the rioters that if they set one foot on the bridge, he would be forced to open fire. The mob had dispersed without incident.

But this year, no action was taken. The rioters crossed the bridge unchecked and attacked Ismailis and Ismaili property, burning and looting. Three people were killed in this small town in the peaceful mountains; one old man was thrown into the river after being beaten.

Fida Hussain's life was saved by the fact that he was far away, visiting relatives in the high pastures near the Afghan border. The rioters came looking for him, but Sunni neighbors saved his family and some of his possessions by hiding them and claiming they didn't know where anyone was.

Fida's Dreamland Hotel was burnt, along with a student hostel and a health center, and his house was looted of whatever remained. Far more than the financial loss, the hurt was that fellow Chitralis, fellow Muslims, could do this to their neighbors.

Violence and change, cruelty and kindness, hospitality and bureaucracy. All are mixed in this summer journey, after such a long absence from these mountains which are the dwelling place of God. And yet I write a short song:

"I am drawn to these mountains
Like a moth is to a flame
I am drawn to these valleys
Like a flower to the rain
and I can't explain,
No I can't explain."

19 Into the Crucible

Peshawar, Pakistan
Summer, 1982

"This house is your house. Come to stay any time," the hospitable Afghan family had told me before I went up to the mountains. But did they really mean it? Or did I misunderstand? I sit anxiously in a motorized rickshaw at Peshawar Airport, wondering if I am about to make a fool of myself.

Peshawar is much hotter than Chitral, but I am relieved to be out of the strange, thick atmosphere in that dusty valley. I direct the rickshaw driver to Syed Ishaq Gailani's house, which is well-known because of Ishaq's prominence as a Mujahedeen commander and his uncle's role as leader of one of the Afghan political parties. I will play it by ear and see if the generous invitation was merely obligatory polite phrases, or if I am truly welcome.

Ishaq's beautiful wife Fatana, a woman only a few years younger than I, dispels all my fears at once. She greets me warmly in her flowing, precise Farsi, her rich, soothing voice speaking a little more slowly and clearly than usual so that I can easily understand. This sensitivity endears her to me, and soon we are laughing with the sisterly familiarity we had established during my brief visit last month.

Wana, Fatana's four-year-old daughter, runs in excitedly from outside. She politely tells me she is glad I am back. The little girl, who already has the charismatic beauty and irresistible charm of her mother, asks me to play with her while I am waiting for Lala, the cook, to fry me an egg. I sit on the floor on a thick red Afghan carpet and color with her while Fatana asks many curious questions about my journey, and about Afghan refugees in Chitral and Gilgit.

I am given the room I had when I first met the Gailanis a month ago. It is a cozy room, formerly inhabited by one of the Mujahedeen Resistance fighters. I am again struck by the young man's choice of decor:

the black flag of the Resistance party headed by Ishaq's paternal uncle adorns one wall; on the other are three posters—Charles Bronson, a Sioux warrior on horseback, and a huge pink rose.

I am glad to get out of my already sticky clothes. As I rest beneath the fan which only slightly cools the humid air, I remember the day I first met the Gailanis. I had been eager to meet Ishaq, as I had heard high praise of the young Resistance leader from journalists and Afghans in the U.S. Unlike most of the leaders who never left their comfortable, even luxurious homes in Peshawar or Islamabad, Ishaq actually went inside Afghanistan and commanded the Mujahedeen on operations. He was gracious and helpful, and Westernized enough to understand the importance of publicity. And, a woman journalist friend of mine had mentioned, "He's really good-looking—and I've heard he's not married."

But when an Afghan friend who had been a classmate of Ishaq's had taken me to the house, we had been greeted by an exceptionally beautiful woman whom I had correctly assumed to be Ishaq's wife. A peek at a framed photo on the bookshelf, however, confirmed what my journalist friend had said—Ishaq is an unusually good-looking man by any measure with fine, strong features, charismatic black eyes, and black hair and a well-trimmed beard contrasting with his fair skin.

Ishaq had been welcoming, but formal at first. His unnerving eyes were usually hidden behind tinted glasses. Possessed of a commanding quality, he was at the same time an intensely private, even shy man. From the beginning, he had spoken to me only in Farsi, though I knew he spoke some English. I was at first taken aback, but he had insisted, "You must practice your Farsi."

Ishaq had immediately offered to arrange a trip "inside" for me. I was tempted to forget about my trip to the mountains and follow my heart to Afghanistan, but I had a commitment to keep to take photos for the Silk Road exhibition. Besides, I knew I would find travelling in the heat difficult. I had reluctantly told him that this was not the right time for me to go into Afghanistan. Without judgement, he had accepted and arranged visits to an Afghan hospital and a refugee camp during my short stay in Peshawar.

Fatana, for her part, had been the perfect hostess. All our conversations were in Farsi, as she spoke no English at the time. This was a constant challenge for me, especially first thing in the morning. She had immediately noticed that the few *shalwar kameez* I had were not suitable for city wear, and one morning had brought me one of her own outfits, saying tactfully, "All your clothes are too warm for the summer. Here is one that is light and cool. Please, it is yours, a gift from me."

The day I left their house for the mountains, she had come to my room and said slowly, clearly, "This house is your house. Ishaq has told me to tell you that anytime you are in Peshawar, you must come to us, you are always welcome. You are a girl alone, and it is not safe for you to be in a hotel. It is better that you should be with us. Besides, I like to talk to you. You can learn Farsi, and you can teach me English!"

The Israelis are invading Lebanon, and each night the TV screen is filled with images of death and destruction. With Fatana and Ishaq, I watch helplessly as shells explode, buildings crumble, young men run through streets and alleys shooting guns, and children cower and bleed. We know the same thing is happening in Afghanistan. Kabul would be an eight-hour drive from Peshawar, if there were no war and no borders. Jalalabad, where Ishaq's family owned land, is only six hours. There his orchards are heavy with oranges, and there the Soviets bomb and destroy.

Each night, if he is home, Ishaq watches the news keenly. His pale face looks horror-stricken at the evolving destruction of Beirut. These are not his people, but he has seen enough of war to respect it. Fatana watches with him, shaking her head and clicking her tongue.

Ishaq goes out of his way to arrange trips for me, as if I were a correspondent from a big news magazine instead of an uncertain freelancer. He wants me to understand the plight of the refugees, and simply hopes that God will give me the means to tell the world about it. He sends his own jeep and driver with me whenever he can, and I am treated with respect everywhere I go, because Syed Ishaq sent me. I appreciate his help and esteem, which gives me the resolve to publicize the struggle of the Afghans in any way that I can when I return to the West.

I find out that Ishaq is loved and admired both for his own character and because he comes from a family of hereditary religious leaders. After six years of studying Sufism, the mystic, esoteric side of Islam, I have fallen into the family of the great thirteenth century Sufi saint, Abdul Qadir Gailani. But no one comes out and tells me this. I know that Ishaq has a philosophical bent, and like most educated Afghans, he and Fatana read the poetry of Rumi and Hafez for inspiration and enjoyment. But it is only after I ask Fatana about the big photo on the wall, which turns out to be Abdul Qadir's mausoleum in Baghdad, that I realize I am amongst the leaders of the Qadiriya sect.

The Mujahedeen and the refugees I meet speak of Ishaq with devotion. His father's brother is the titular head of the Qadiriya, as well as political head of the National Islamic front of Afghanistan. I see many refugees and fighters greet Ishaq by kneeling to kiss his hand. These devoted followers, many of them hereditary *murids,* or disciples, send him gifts—honey from Kunar Province, fresh cheese and fruit from Jalalabad, and colorful, elaborately embroidered traditional silk dresses for his wife from Katawaz. Yet he treats everyone as an equal, deferring to the experience of an old guerrilla fighter, or feasting a ragged party of Mujahedeen just back from the front. At these times he requests the women of the house, including me, to observe *purdah,* separation of women, in deference to the strict customs of rural Afghans. Although I chafe under the restriction, and I am dying of curiosity about the men's discussions, I accept this as the price of the protection, respect, and insight that being accepted into an extended family gives me. And I have privileges other women don't—when it is important for my work, Ishaq always invites me to speak with the men.

Fatana receives many female visitors, refugees and wives of Mujahedeen fighters. She listens to their problems, and tries to help them if she can. She is egalitarian like her husband, and has no qualms about embracing a ragged refugee woman in dirty clothes. She takes off her fashionable high heels and sits on the floor with these women, pouring them glasses of tea and offering them sugared almonds sent from Kabul by a friend or by a disciple of her husband's.

I wonder what Fatana's life might have been, had there been no war. She and Ishaq come from well-educated, Westernized families; he would probably have been a lawyer, judge, or diplomat, and she might possibly have worked if she had wished, perhaps as a teacher like her mother's sister. Certainly they would have had a comfortable life with few worries. I watch them laugh, and wonder how most wealthy Americans would adjust to such a radical change in circumstances.

One night, when Ishaq is late coming home, Fatana tells me the story of her trek to Pakistan in spring, 1978, just after the first Marxist coup in Afghanistan. Ishaq, then a student in Tehran, could not return to Kabul to rescue his wife and baby daughter, as the Gailanis, along with many other prominent families, were on the government's list of opponents to be arrested and/or executed.

Fatana's deep brown eyes are dry as she tells me of her fears on the journey with Ishaq's brother and his family. She and her sister-in-law, dressed as villagers, had prayed they would not be questioned, as they spoke no Pashtu, the language of the border provinces. Wana was a small baby, and Syed Hossein's children were too young to understand, but old enough to say the wrong thing. But luck held, and they arrived in Peshawar to meet a relieved Ishaq.

"We had no home, nothing anymore," she says. "We had one glass between us. Now, by the grace of God, we have more. I know people say Ishaq is rich and has a good life but it is not all what it seems. Look..." She walks to a table and lifts the yellow-gold cloth. "These tables are all made out of rifle crates. Every one of them. This material I bought for a few rupees a meter in the bazaar and stitched myself. All the other things are gifts. Many people love Ishaq, his followers, and Afghans who live in America or Europe and now have lots of money, and Pakistanis he knew before the war. We are so fortunate, because they all love him and are generous."

Even the carpets, which look so impressive, are either gifts from friends or loans from Afghan friends and relatives who have gone to America as refugees.

"So many Afghans say, Why don't you go to America? Ishaq knows lots of people and could get you a visa. But I say I don't want to go to America. I want to be here, near Ishaq and near Afghanistan. Ishaq goes to the front with the Mujahedeen many times, sometimes for a month, two months, four months. When I am here I get messages every few days, and when he comes home I am here to greet him. If I were in America, I would never know where he is, or if he is safe.

"This is not such an easy life here, not what we were used to in Kabul. Here I can't go out, and I have to wear *shalwar kameez* and a *chador* all the time. But I would rather have that than go to America and paint my nails and have my hair done and put on make-up. All those things are nice, but not while Afghans are fighting and dying."

Conversations like this make my efforts to learn Farsi worth it. My language subtly improves, as I learn from Fatana on an intuitive level. Even if I don't understand her words, I know what she is saying, and learn quickly from this total immersion in the gestalt of another culture. She affectionately calls me her sister, and introduces me that way. When I can't understand someone else's rapid or unclear speech, she always quietly "translates" into simple, clear language. As we grow closer, sharing fear and laughter, I appreciate my newfound sister more each day.

❁ ❁ ❁

Several doctors are bustling about, getting everything in order for the opening ceremony of the Ibn-i-Sina Balkhi Hospital. The facility is run by Afghan doctors and surgeons, and supported by one of the two current "Islamic unities" of Afghan Mujahedeen. This one is the "moderate" or "traditionalist" three-party alliance, in contrast to the more fundamentalist seven-party alliance.

The hospital is in a new two-story building around a courtyard, much brighter and airier than the cramped rooms of the previous facility, and more likely to live up to the literal meaning of the Afghan word for hospital, "healing house." Dr. Assefi, a thin, young, bespectacled, energetic doctor I had met in Peshawar two years ago, proudly shows me around. There is even a surgery room with a proper light. And there are many more beds than before, and more room for the beds. Patients don't have to be out in the halls like they were in the other place.

I recognize some of the patients, all male fighters recovering from their wounds. They call out warm *"Salaams,"* remembering the American woman who speaks some Farsi. A few bold souls shout out some variation on the theme of, "Tell your President we need arms. We can't fight airplanes with rifles."

It is a cry I will hear a thousand times in the coming years. Most of the men are improving, but one old man's eyes are glazed with pain as the dressing over his abdominal wound is changed. Dr. Assefi, passionate and compassionate, shakes his head and says indignatly to "look at what the Soviets have done to so many innocent people."

The beds are clean, and the men all have new striped pajamas. Some come out in wheelchairs to watch the ceremony, and others watch from their rooms. In a corner room sit three men who are shell-shocked. They don't understand anything going on around them, and barely speak to anyone. "Afghans are strong," whispers Dr. Assefi, "but some men experience psychological trauma after they have seen something terrible. We try to treat them here."

Leaders of the Mujahedeen parties speak about the future, and quote the Quran on the importance of cleanliness, health care, and healing. There are a few other journalists, one woman dressed as a man so as to be less conspicuous, and a whole group of somber Afghan men.

We are served a buffet of Pakistani snacks and sweet cakes, but as I look through the windows at the patients, I do not feel much like eating.

When the crowd begins to filter out, Dr. Assefi introduces me to Dr. Abdullah Osman, the chief of surgery. Dr. Abdullah is a tall, distinguished man with deep-set eyes and silver-grey hair. His manner is serious, low-key, and somewhat harassed. Everybody seems to want to talk to him at once. When he has a free moment, he offers me tea in his office, and I offer him my personal donation to the hospital, $100 in Pakistani rupees.

"It isn't much," I say, "but I wanted to give something, because I am so impressed by what you are doing." I know that the money will go far in this economy.

Dr. Abdullah graciously accepts. "We will use it well, I promise," he says with a tired smile.

When I walk out of the office, Dr. Assefi shakes my hand and says, "I knew you cared from your heart when I saw the tears in your eyes for the wounded people. None of the other journalists cry from their heart."

A few days later, I visit the office of the Afghan Doctors Society, a non-political group of Afghan doctors and other medical personnel who have chosen to remain in Pakistan, rather than going into exile in a Western country. I had met some of the doctors two years ago, and had observed one of their morning clinics, when the doctors see about 150 patients a day. They are seeking to fill the gap between the care offered in the refugee camps and the needs of refugees who aren't living in the camps. Many patients come from the camps as well. They claim the mostly Pakistani doctors who staff camp clinics don't understand their problems, but maybe they just trust their countryfellows more.

The stream of patients has not decreased in the past two years. There are more refugees than ever, and the Society is outgrowing its facility. I watch as an Afghan dentist extracts a woman's tooth without novocaine. The middle-aged village woman stoically grabs at her cheek and grimaces, then turns to spit without ever making a sound.

I watch as children are given injections, and abcesses are cleaned. They too remain silent, large black eyes staring in sad, brave dismay.

I also visit a couple of refugee camp clinics to assess the health care needs of refugees for possible donors in the U.S. I am particularly concerned about women and children, as the orthodox interpretation of Islam forbids male doctors to treat women. The Austrian Relief Committee agrees to take me on a day-trip to Baghicha, a camp some miles from Peshawar, where I can watch an Afghan woman doctor treat refugee women.

Dr. Sima works for hours in the stifling heat under the yellow canvas tent, which gives shelter from the direct sun, but nonetheless collects heat. She is sweating, as are the women she is treating, and as I am while I photograph them. Over her head, she wears a thin white cotton veil.

Obviously not accustomed to it, she tugs at it impatiently, and constantly readjusts it. It finally falls off while she is examining a child with her stethoscope, but no one seems to mind.

The health problems of the refugees are appalling. Small miseries like gastro-intestinal infections, upper respiratory infections, and skin problems are rampant. So is tuberculosis, which flourishes in crowded conditions. Most of the refugees have some basic staples to eat, as their rations include wheat, dried skim milk, cooking oil, and occasional tea and sugar. But here and there I see a child with the stiff, reddish hair of malnutrition

Dr. Sima looks overwhelmed. She listens patiently to one overbearing woman, and later tells me resignedly that the same woman comes every week, probably because she wants attention. Loneliness and idleness are great problems in the camps, she explains, especially for women. Afghan women who lived in small villages suddenly find themselves in huge aggregations of people. Their neighbors are not members of the same extended family, and may be from an entirely different part of the country with different customs. Hence the men of the family don't allow the women to go out much, except for essential business. A visit to the women's clinic provides an excuse for an outing and some much-needed attention.

After the long morning, which has stretched into afternoon, I return with Dr. Sima and her team to the Austrian Relief Committee's quarters in Mardan, where we all share a delicious lunch. Dr. Sima and her colleague Dr. Anisa speak with great animation. They don't want to go to America or Europe, they say, but some Muslim fundamentalists don't approve of women working as doctors, even though without them these same men's wives and daughters would go without medical care. Dr. Sima has even received death threats. Up till now she hasn't taken them seriously, but she is wary of offending the religious elements.

We talk about politics and war, and I tell them about the big anti-nuclear demonstration I had gone to in New York in June. "I would have a world passport if I could," I tell them. "I believe in one family of humanity. I have no brothers or sisters, but I have adopted and been adopted all over the world. The whole world becomes our extended family."

Dr. Anisa, tears glistening in her black eyes, agrees. "Yes, I would have an international passport too," says the fervent dreamer.

❁ ❁ ❁

My friend Hamid has returned from his holiday in Gilgit and is eager to see me. He is also angry at me.

"I took my holiday because of you," he says petulantly as we sit in a rickshaw going to the Afghan silver market in the old bazaar.

"I told you it is not proper for me to travel with you. What would people think in this society?"

His dark face goes darker. "Something else you said really hurt me."

"I'm sorry. What was that?"

"When you first came to Peshawar, and you called me on the phone, you said, 'Don't cry.'"

"So?" I can't even remember the conversation.

"I missed you so much, and you were telling me not to cry."

"What?" I am still not quite sure what he is angry about. "I didn't mean any insult. I just wanted to comfort you."

Hamid has been kind to me, but I am uneasy with him. Two years ago, he had helped me a great deal, taking me to refugee camps and the Afghan Doctors Society. He had given me a cassette of Afghan music before I left, and then had written letters every week. He had escorted Lauren into Kunar Province, and they had arrived to find his village still in flames from a bombing attack. She had written me in horrified detail about the war, and had described the look on his face when he had opened a cupboard which had belonged to his grandfather. He had written to me about the dead bodies of Afghan soldiers they had found, and the terrible stench.

When Hamid wrote confessing his love for me, I had agonized. Could I ever love him? I thought of his handsome face, quick wit, and caring intense manner. But no, I did not feel that indefineable spark of attraction. I had been relieved when he had continued to write to me after I had written telling him I look upon him as a brother.

But his possessive, moody behavior when I had run into him in Gilgit had not endeared him to me. Still, I am ready to forgive, and we are here in this rickshaw, on our way to the silver market.

Hamid introduces me to some of the Afghans who sell crafts in the silver market. Some of the silver is new, modern minimalist designs set with lapis. But much of it is old, chunky pieces worn by Kuchi nomads and Turkomans from the north. I buy some gifts for friends, and Hamid insists on buying both me and Lauren a gift. I finally pick out two simple silver bracelets.

Afterwards, we go to the international hospital where Hamid works. He clearly enjoys introducing me to his colleagues, who seem to be quite fond of him. He is in his element, and I can see that he feels great compassion for the wounded war victims. I greet the patients, and those who can speak Farsi answer me enthusiastically. I tell them that I am a journalist, trying to tell the world the truth about Afghanistan. Some of them ask if I have been "inside" yet, and tell me that I have to go there to get the real story. Others ask the inevitable questions about why America doesn't send them more arms. They don't seem to mind me visiting, and some even insist that I take pictures of their terrible wounds, or the stumps of their legs or arms. Their faces, young, old, bearded, lined, fresh, beardless, are all stoic, their eyes piercing into some collective vision of victory and freedom that only they have the faith to see.

But the hardest is the children's ward. Here Hamid too has tears in his eyes. I see a boy with a stump where his arm used to be. "He picked up one of the green butterfly bombs," says Hamid. "And this one, he stepped on one," he continues, motioning toward a thin boy of about six or seven.

A four-year-old lies on his back, both of his legs bandanged and in traction, staring but not focusing, even on his old father who is sitting in vigil beside him. Hamid says a few words to the man in Pashtu, and the man smiles at me. My tears brim over as I try to focus the lens. I turn quickly away, not wanting the children to feel worse.

I know that I must say good-bye to Hamid today. I sense that, in his eyes, I have somehow failed him. We have lunch in a kebab shop, and then in the bazaar he stops a rickshaw for me. I shake his hand formally, since we are in the middle of a Pakistani bazaar, and thank him sincerely for all he has done for me.

His grasp is cold, and he is shaking. "Learn how to be with the friends," he says, angrily pulling his hand away from mine.

"What?" I am in the rickshaw, and a piece of Peshawar's dirty air has flown into my eye, causing it to tear.

Hamid sees my tear and softens, thinking it is for him. He shakes his head and says more gently, but with great emotion, "*Khoda hafez.*"

I wish him the best of luck on his upcoming exams to qualify for a scholarship to study in England. I assure him that he is smart and will score high, and ask him to let me know what happens. Finally I tell the rickshaw to go, but I don't look back anymore. Hamid too is among the victims of this terrible war—his is a brain waiting to be drained away from his needy nation, a soul burnt out by trying for so long to be of service, now longing only for comfort and the illusions which we in the West are so good at creating.

In Ishaq's house I meet many people, all of whom give me some personal insight into the Afghan heart. The vast majority of the educated refugees I meet are using the house, and Peshawar, as a way-station to the West, just as Khalid had two years ago, when he and his family had stayed in the same room I am sleeping in.

A few stubborn souls, in love with their country and the cause of freedom, choose to stay. They too pass through the house, rootless and filled with longing. They work hard on Mujahedeen newspapers and magazines, translate for journalists, take people on tours. Many are doctors, a few of whom plan to set up clinics in liberated areas of Afghanistan under the auspices of the Afghan Doctors Society.

On my last day, Fatana makes me a tasty soup called *aash* full of noodles, vegetables, and *qurut,* a rich, salty dairy product made from boiling yogurt. I am moved by all the trouble she has gone through, and suddenly realize how much I am going to miss her.

Later, as I am packing to leave, Fatana knocks at my door. In her hand is a beautiful silver charm on a silver chain. The workmanship of the egg-shaped locket is fine, a technique little used nowadays in which a black powder is rubbed into engraved traceries. The charm was originally used for *surmah,* the black powder called *kohl* by the Arabs and traditionally worn as eye make-up. But Fatana smiles mischievously and says, "*Inshallah,* when you next come back maybe you will be in love, and you will have the picture of a man to put with yours."

At Islamabad Airport, I am exhausted, unaware that I am incubating hepatitis virus. The lines are endless, and the PIA officials are as bad-tempered as one can expect people to be if they have to work the 3 a.m. shift in a huge building without air conditioning.

In the passenger lounge, there is air conditioning and relief from the late August heat. I have been in Pakistan less than two months, but I have seen heroism, kindness, sacrifice, bravery, purities mixed with the impure elements of earthly life. I have seen love of peace, and love of freedom even unto death. I have seen the innocent wounded and left homeless, and the triumph of ignorance and hatred, and sometimes just petty bureaucracy. The world is in flux. It is not the same world I found in 1979, nor the same world I will see in a year.

And yet, I have an image of subtle silken cords which bind and support our world, which hold together even the enemies. I have a sense of what the philosopher Teilhard de Chardin meant by the noosphere, the envelope of thought which surrounds the earth. All thoughts go into it; positive, loving, compassionate thoughts build it up, and angry, hateful thoughts tear it down. We are all together, in a race for our own existence. I catch a glimpse of destiny, and know I will return to this crucible, to face my terrible fear of war, and to test my faith that I am doing the work the God-spirit intends me to do.

Ironically, war and exile have given these young girls a chance at an education they probably would not have had in rural Afghanistan.

Afghan refugee girls are eager to learn. Camp near Peshawar, Pakistan, 1984.

Noor Jehan, widow who sang the eloquent song of the "burning pain of widows and martyrs" in "A Nation Uprooted," the video documentary co-produced by the author. Nasir Bagh Camp, Pakistan, 1984.

The author applying millet-paste "makeup" during the winter solstice festival. Rumbur Valley, Pakistan, 1980.

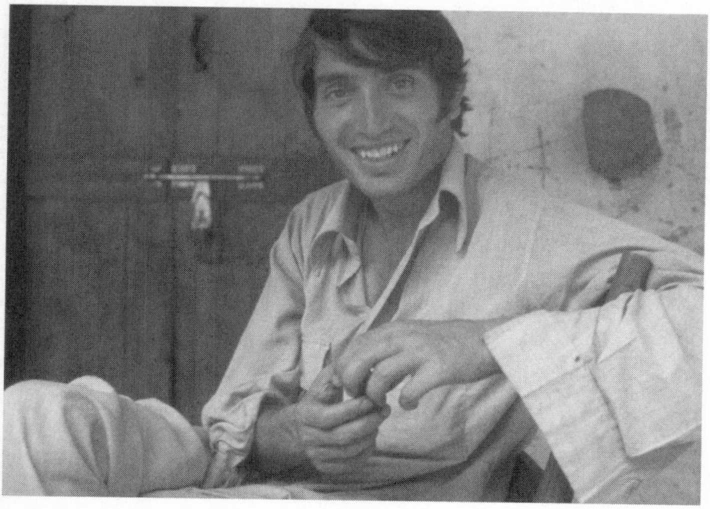

Saifulla Jan, a fighter for the rights of the minority Kalash tribe. Rumbur Valley, Pakistan, 1980.

Pashtun mother and child. Kunar, Afghanistan, 1983.

Friendly women of Hunaz, wearing their trademark needlepoint pillbox hats, 1982.

Political wall painting of Indira Gandhi in a Calcutta slum, 1979.

Boatman ferries pilgrims out upon the Mother Ganges at dawn.
Varanasi (Benares), India, 1979.

Buddhist monks make a mandala, a cosmic diagram, out of colored powder in a process reminiscent of Navajo sandpainting. Spituk Gompa, Ladakh, India, 1979.

A crowd of celebrants gathers on the temple steps as they enter into the sacred Cham dance, Thicksey Gompa, Ladakh, India, 1983.

20 Cultivating Courage

Peshawar, Pakistan
Spring, 1983

Fatana playfully lifts up Ishaq's pistol, closes one eye, and aims the gun at me.

"Don't do that!" I cry. "It's dangerous." I don't know a thing about guns, but I know I don't like that small black hole staring at me from across the circle of family and friends.

She puts the gun down in her lap. "Don't be afraid, it'snot loaded. You're afraid of everything, and yet you want to go inside Afghanistan. Ishaq, don't send her, she's too scared."

"Of course I'm scared," I say, laughing nervously. "I never said I wasn't afraid. I've never been near a gun before. But I *do* want to go to Afghanistan."

"She's afraid, but she's going to Afghanistan anyway," says Ishaq. "Courage doesn't mean not being afraid, but doing something even if you are afraid." He takes the gun, a Soviet officer's service pistol which he captured in battle, back from his wife, and shows me the clip in his other hand. "It's not loaded. We Afghans have been around guns since we were children, and we know how to be careful. Don't worry, I will send you with Mujahedeen who will take good care of you. It will be as if I myself were with you."

The conversation moves on to other subjects, more tea is served by Ishaq's maternal uncle's wife, and a plate of pinion nuts is passed around. My eyes are stinging and brimming with tears as my nails tear at the thin brown shell of the sweet white nut. Does Fatana really consider me a coward? Or is this more of the rough teasing that Afghans seem to like so much?

When we leave to walk home through the alleys between earthen walls, Fatana comes close to me and whispers. "Ishaq says I shouldn't have joked with you that way. He is angry with me now."

"It's all right," I reassure her, relieved. "I'll tell him it's okay. I guess I will have to get used to being around guns if I'm going to Afghanistan!" But I don't want to tell her that my heart jumps and shudders every time I see the Kalashnikovs in her bedroom, and whenever Wana and her small cousins insist on posing for pictures with guns bigger than themselves.

This time, returning to Peshawar has been like returning home. In early spring, after a rigorous trek in Nepal, I brought my mother to meet my dear Afghan and Pakistani friends. To my relief, I have recovered completely from the debilitating hepatitis I had suffered last autumn. The trip to Nepal had been a test run for my planned trip into Afghanistan. The journey was an eleven-day walk up the Kali Gandaki gorge, finally ascending to 12,500 feet at Muktinath, where a shrine marks the place where fire, in the form of natural gas jets, comes out of the rock over pure springs. In the vast blue silence, I understood why both Hindus and Buddhists had consecrated this place where the Four Elements meet. The high peaks whisper of holiness, and in a consciousness altered by thin air and high winds, I have seen a grand metaphor for the cyclical nature of life in the hard grey-black fossil of a spiral sea creature that I found along the path, perhaps lying there from the time when the Himalayas were a seabed.

My return to Pakistan is part of this grand cycle. When Mother and I arrive, Ishaq is not in Peshawar, but his brother Ismail offers to set up a trip into Afghanistan for my mother. She laughs nervously and refuses.

"How do you feel about your daughter going in?" he asks her ingenuously, oblivious to my whispered entreaties in Farsi.

"She's going to do what she's going to do," says the woman who knows me best.

We don't talk about my planned journey anymore. We stay in Dean's Hotel, visit museums and bazaars, and dine with friends. Shakil Durrani is now Political Agent of Khyber Agency, sort of an ambassador from the Pakistan Government to the independent Pashtun tribes of the Tribal Areas. Khyber is now closed to foreigners, because the government is cracking down on opium growers and heroin producers.

Shakil and his charming wife live with their two small sons in Khyber House, an imposing, cannon-flanked compound dating from the British Raj. It is obvious that he enjoys the challenge of this free-wheeling job, where personal charm and diplomacy count for more than mere law. Beyond the easement of 50 feet on either side of the road, the land is governed by tribal law and the ability of the Political Agent to persuade.

Right now, Shakil is doing his best to persuade the elders that opium and heroin production is un-Islamic as well as socially harmful to the youth of Pakistan. He is making considerable headway in Khyber, where several heroin factories have been closed down with great fanfare, and poppy fields have been destroyed. For this he's become somewhat of a celebrity, and has even been interviewed by *Time* magazine and filmed for "60 Minutes."

Mother and I try for several days to get a plane to Chitral so we can visit Saifullah and Washlim Gul. But rain continues to pour unseasonally, and all the help from Shakil's and my friends at PIA can't get us a seat on a plane that won't fly. "Do you want to go to Khyber?" Shakil asks us. "Why not?" we answer.

The journey is arranged like so many things in Pakistan, mysteriously and without communication. We are listening to the rain pattering on the tin roof of the hotel when there is a knock on the door. At the door stands an officer of the Khassadars, the tribal frontier force, who ushers us into Shakil's private car. Neither he, the driver, nor our other bodyguards speak English, but I manage to establish that they are taking us to the Khyber Pass.

For me, it is a journey back in time as the road unwinds like a reel of film of the past few years. I am returning to Khyber, at another season, a more beautiful but sadder time. Beyond the miles of squalid refugee camps lining the road, spring spreads a textured carpet of purple flowers on the grey-green land, and the hills rise craggy beyond the flatland. Khyber always holds an excitement, a romance beyond what it actually is, for here is history. Here are many ghosts of men and dreams of conquest, which have died in these rocky defiles. And there, beyond the rolls of barbed wire at Michni Point, where we are served a delicious curry lunch, is the beloved land of Afghanistan, barely greening in the spring. Down there in the clump of mud buildings are Afghan border guards, and maybe Soviet officers. To my surprise, trucks are coming and going with fruit from Afghanistan and foreign-manufactured goods and cigarettes from Pakistan.

The Khassadars are fascinated by my mother, whose blond hair peaks out from under the printed silk scarf she wears over her head in deference to custom. They all want their picture taken with her. I take a few photos, then linger. Black crows caw overhead, respecting no border. Then, in a small miracle, a white dove lands and balances delicately on the barbed wire fence. But she does not stay long, perhaps sensing that this is not yet her time or place.

When Mother has gone back to America, I move into Ishaq's and Fatana's house. Their extended family is always large and lively. Ishaq's brother Ismail, who was wounded in a battle at Kandahar a couple of years ago, is leaving for London to get married. He still limps a little as he walks under the Quran held above him in the farewell ritual. Wana and her young cousins throw rose petals at him as he and Ishaq laugh and weep at their parting.

Another brother, Hossein, and his wife Leila and their two daughters and one small son, move into the house. But room is made for me as well, and I again have the small corner room.

Hossein's family has voluntarily returned from several years in America, going against the westward flow of most Afghans. But adjusting to life in Pakistan is hard, especially for the kids. Samira, at twelve, does not like the idea of wearing a *chador* outside, and Leila, too, considers it an inconvenience. She was used to working in America, and even in Kabul the educated women never wore veils. She worries that the children will forget their English, and asks me to help them. She also practices English with me every day so she won't forget. For Hossein, the adjustment is not so hard, as he is out in the world dealing with the Mujahedeen every day.

I never forget that my real reason for being here is to write about Afghanistan, but in the evening, after I've been to refugee camps, secret guerrilla training camps, hospitals, clinics, and bureaucratic offices, I enjoy talking with Fatana and Leila, playing with the kids, and listening to music. The kids all call me *khala,* which means "mother's sister." They love to talk to me, but always leave me alone if I am working in my room.

When the men are out late, Fatana, Leila, and I laugh, gossip, and joke. The two of them ask if I have ever been in love, if I've met any Afghan in America or here whom I would like to marry. They want any and all details of love stories, mine or my friends', for they are romantics at heart. Fatana prefers Afghan music, or Iranian, Urdu, or Hindi love songs, while Leila and the kids like American pop music. Leila listens to "Endless Love," and Fatana starts to like some of these songs too. We drink tea late into the night, and get as silly as teenage girls at a slumber party.

"Laughter is the salt of life," says Fatana, quoting an Afghan proverb. We jokingly call midnight the "hour of madness." But all too often, Fatana's laughter is suddenly caught in her throat, and her face turns dark and pensive. Something in her feels guilty for laughing when she is separated from her mother and brothers, when people are dying every day, when others are shivering in refugee camps. Sometimes bad news is suddenly brought in by a messenger, and sometimes she just stops laughing, then abruptly gets up and tells us it's time to go to bed. Often she wakes up with terrible migraines. She rarely complains, but I grow to know her face and feel when she is in pain.

Ishaq too is similarly moody. He is quiet, always lost in thought, his high brow furrowed. His shiny black hair is now shot with silver, which has appeared in the last six months. He eats small portions, even when Fatana serves a dish he especially likes. She implores him, me, and Wana, "Eat, eat more. You'll get sick, you'll get weak. You need your strength."

"Ishaq is like a saint," she says one day at the table. "He eats little, sleeps little, and talks little."

That gets a laugh from him. "And what are you?"

"I eat a lot, talk a lot, and sleep a lot. I'm not a saint!"

All the time I speak Farsi, never dreaming that Ishaq speaks quite fluent English, until one day I come home to find photographers Steve McCurry and Lauren Stockbower there. Ishaq is speaking quite beautifully, joking, telling stories, making plans.

"You never told me you speak English!" I tell him accusingly.

"You never would have learned Farsi if I'd spoken English to you," he replies in Farsi. "You must keep practicing."

One night, Ishaq comes home very tired and drawn. He unstraps the pistol that he always hides under his long shirt, and lets it fall heavily on the floor, like a sheriff turning in his gun. "I'll be glad when Afghanistan is free and all this is over," he says. He tells us the latest bad news—twenty-four Mujahedeen killed in Kunar Province, where I am planning to go. And many wounded who have arrived at the hospital.

Fatana too grows quiet. None of us speak, the television plays unwatched. Ishaq leaves the gun on the floor, and goes to a bookshelf where he pulls out a thick volume. It is the *Diwan-i-Hafez,* the works of Hafez, one of the greatest and most profound Sufi mystic poets in the Persian language. Following an old tradition, he prays, says, "*Bismillah*—in the name of God"—and opens the book at random. He reads the poetry aloud, in an expressive, ringing voice, and all are comforted by the sweet words and spiritual perspective of one who recognized the Oneness of all.

As days pass, Ishaq becomes less formal. He jokes a little, and begins to use the familiar pronoun, as he would to a sister. I remain a little in awe of his knowledge, presence, and experience, and stumble when I answer. But his patience is endless, and he is never angry. One afternoon when Fatana is out, we talk about my upcoming trip into Afghanistan. I have decided to go to Kunar to see a clinic set up by one of Dr. Abdullah Osman's colleagues, and Ishaq has promised to arrange the trip. "I will find you someone who speaks English," he promises, "though your Farsi is very good."

Embarrassed, I murmur, "Thank you. But I still need to learn so much more."

We listen quietly to music, and he asks, "What religion are you?"

It is a difficult to answer in this culture so defined by religion. "I was born Christian, Roman Catholic. But now I study all religions. I read the Bible, the Quran, the Hindu and Buddhist books. I have studied Sufism for seven years. I believe that all religions are the same, that they are different paths to God, to Oneness."

I have said this in simple Farsi, and I don't know if he will understand or approve, as he is a devout Muslim. But he is also from a Sufi tradition, and he merely smiles thoughtfully. "That is good. In some way this is also true. There are good and bad people everywhere, in every country, in every religion, good and bad Muslims, good and bad Christians. The important thing is not to lie, steal, cheat, murder."

"You are a true Muslim in my view," I tell him. "For Islam is truly merciful and tolerant of others. Doesn't the word *Islam* mean 'surrender,' and the word *Muslim* 'one who has surrendered to the will of God?'"

"You know a lot. Maybe you will become a Muslim someday. Maybe you already are."

"Debbie *Khala,*" says Wana's cousin Samira, "There is a commander in the garden to meet you."

I fling on a chiffon *dupata,* which is an acceptable veil within the family compound, and go to meet the commander. He is indeed a commanding man, tall and sinewy, giving the impression of an officer in uniform, though he, like the rest of the Mujahedeen, wears a *shalwar kameez.* After our greetings, during which I feel he is sizing up my handshake, my physical fitness, my courage, and my Farsi, he begins speaking very rapidly in Farsi. "So, you want to go to Kunar?"

"Yes, to Deh Wagal, to Dr. Farid's clinic. Will that be possible?"

"Yes, why not? When do you want to go?"

I am trying my best to keep up with his clipped Farsi. "As soon as possible."

"Good, I will find some men for you." He sticks out his hand to say good-bye.

"Uh, is there much fighting there now?"

"It changes from day to day. No one except God knows. You want to see fighting?"

"Well, no. Uh, yes, but not to be in the middle of it. I mostly want to see the doctor's clinic, and see how people are living in the liberated areas."

"We will do our best to help you and keep you safe, *inshallah.* Thank you."

The interview is over almost as soon as it has begun. Ishaq reassures me that Commander Jan will find good men for me. "He has found two men who speak good Farsi," he says a couple of days later. "I told him to find some English speakers, but when you spoke to him in Farsi, he said your Farsi is so good you don't need English speakers, and it would take longer to find them."

"Maybe I should have spoken English. I didn't know he spoke English. When are we leaving?"

"Tomorrow, *inshallah.*"

But tommorow, and the day after, it is raining. On the third day, in the afternoon, a tall, clean-shaven man in a karakul hat shows up and says, "Let's go."

"Where?"

"To Kunar."

I am packed, but not ready. "Come back tomorrow, first thing in the morning," I tell him.

I am glad that he and his companion arrive an hour late. I had not wanted to wake Ishaq and Fatana, though I had wanted their blessings on my journey. "Go with God," says Ishaq, "and don't worry, it is as if I am with you."

But I'm scared. I'm scared of being caught while still in Pakistan, scared of having an accident in the Datsun taxi that drives so crazily and careens through brown rivers in spate. At last we reach a haven, a small village in Bajaur Agency, a tribal area where Haji, my guide, has a house. But his younger brother fails to reassure me. "You are going to Kunar?" the teen-ager asks, eyes wide.

"Yes, *inshallah.*"

He shakes his head. "We came from Kunar. Our home was there. Every day, the planes and helicopters come and bomb the valley."

"Every day?"

"Every day," he says solemnly, and shakes his head.

That night I do not sleep well, even though I know it will be my last night with the luxury of knowing I will not be wakened by bombs.

21 Facing Fear

"'I will not fear. Fear is the mind-killer. Fear is the little-death which brings total obliteration. I will face my fear. I will allow it to pass over me and through me, and when it has gone past, I will turn the inner eye to see its path. Where it has gone, there will be nothing. Only *I* will remain,'" I murmur, repeating over and over again the Bene Gesserit Litany Against Fear from the science fiction novel *Dune.* It is a calming mantra, and helps me to go on putting one step in front of the other in this dusk of human bird calls and a near-full moon.

My work in Kunar is done, and I am anxious to leave. My right knee, injured days ago, is aching badly, and my stomach is subject to sudden and severe cramps. I am tired, and have lived through lifetimes in a matter of days. My Circadian rhythms are more askew than if I had flown around the world, and my body is nearing its limit.

But I must cross the Kunar River again, on the inflated cowskin raft. My companions and I have joined the men at Babur Tangay once again, and I am glad to see them safe. Some Mujahedeen from Hisbi Islami, one of the fundamentalist parties, are also there, and I am glad the parties are cooperating in the field. One of them has brought two anti-tank rocket launchers and three rockets. Not much for an ambush, but more than I've seen so far. I'm getting used to having guns around all the time—pistols and bandoliers hung on hooks above beds, Kalashnikovs laid out on blankets as offerings while Mujahedeen pray, rifles stacked in corners, and small black holes staring at me as the Mujahedeen slip and slide their way down steep mountain paths.

In the mauve dusk, the watchmen call out to each other with sweet birdsongs. We proceed slowly, carefully, from rock to rock, for we are nearing the main road, a dusty white ribbon running along the skirts of the mountains. We have to walk along this road, glowing in the light of the rising moon, and that frightens me most. I murmur my mantra, and walk automatically, matching my footsteps to those of the men in front of me.

"If you hear a shot, lie down," whispers Kamal. I am glad that he is beside me, as he has been all along.

We reach the river without incident. The Mujahedeen point out signs of their victories, the sad remains of a school that was "against Islam" because it had fallen under the control of the Communist government, the burnt-out skeleton of an armored personnel carrier, the big holes in a bridge which the Mujahedeen had mined against tanks. What the government and Soviets were not destroying, the Mujahedeen were being forced to destroy, and the countryside was being laid waste.

The men stop to pray, and I sit on a rock. Haji throws a tin at me, which startles me. "Food of the devil," he says afterwards, and spits in the dust. On the rusted can is the Russian word for meat, and I try to imagine the Soviet solider eating C-rations as he fought. Was he some true believer, some maddened patriot ready to massacre and torture villagers, or just some poor conscript who wants to be back in Moscow or Tashkent with his girlfriend?

The river is in spate, rushing heavy and bright in the moonlight. Much snow has melted in the week since we came this way. Kamal has to carry me to the raft, and I almost fall in the water as my injured knee gives way. I shiver, though it's not that cold, and the memory of a dream comes to me. I am a teen-ager, and shadowy totalitarians have taken over America. After an earthquake, Los Angeles is all lakes and rivers. I am floating down a river at night, beneath guardtowers, listening to the guards shout, "Spike anyone who sets foot in the river." The guards have bows and arrows, but somehow they don't see me.

It takes ages to get across the Kunar River, and all the time I feel a target in this bright moonlight. I wish I had never written the scene in my historical novel about the attack on the rafts. What if fiction is a form of prophecy?

I can hardly walk when we reach the shore, but grit my teeth and keep chanting my quiet mantra. We reach a villlage where we had stopped before, but this time the lady of the house doesn't let us in until there is a big argument and her husband wakes up. "They don't have any food," Kamal tells me, "and they were afraid we were asking for some." I pull out my secret supplies of salted peanuts and toffees, and share them. The peanuts are gone before I realize what has happened, but the poor lady of the house doesn't get any. I ask Haji about the toffees, but he gestures that he has hidden them.

It is a nightmare walk across the plains and ridges. The moon is bright, and silhouettes are sharp. My knee is excruciating, and every time we stop, I feel I can barely go on, but I have no choice. I want to scream, but dare not. The men seem cheerful. They joke and romp, picking golden wildflowers silvered by the moon. This annoys me because they aren't paying attention, and I don't know if we are in any danger or not. They speak Pashtu amongst themselves, and it begins to sound harsh and grating to my ears.

Kamal settles next to me, and I am comforted. Then he whispers, "When we get to Haji's village, you and I can sleep together, in one place."

I can't believe what he has just said, and play dumb. "Oh, I'm very happy with the women in Haji's house. I am very comfortable there."

He does not respond, then says casually, "We are going to attack the Parchami village over there."

"Oh, what am *I* going to do?"

"Haji's brother Jamil can take you to Dunahi. Or do you want someone else?"

He wants me to ask *him.* I still can't believe he is propositioning me, knowing it is perfectly ridiculous, impossible, not to mention un-Islamic. "To hell with all of you!" I say in English, then add in Farsi, "I'll go on my own if I have to."

Haji calls us to continue, and I raise myself painfully. Kamal reaches out to steady me, but I am furious with him and with adrenaline energy I stumble back to the path. I walk alone, dark and angry, covering my face and biting back tears. When we halt again, one of the men who knows massage reaches for my knee out of compassion, but I pull away. Haji, not the most sensitive of men, reaches toward me with his well-meaning but rough hand, and I turn on him like a cat.

"Why are you angry?" he asks in surprise.

I don't want to tell him, and start to cry. "All of you are making a joke of me," is all I can say, all I want to say.

"Who is making a joke of you?" he asks angrily. "Tell me, and I will shoot them!"

"Just leave me alone!" I shout in English, and stumble to my feet and out across the rocky plain.

Haji grabs me with his vise-like grip.

"I'll go alone," I say in Farsi.

He keeps holding me, until I calm down, realizing that it's not a good idea to set out by myself across an area that might be mined.

"Who upset you? I'll kill him, whoever it is." He turns toward Kamal and begins to shout at him, holding his rifle threateningly.

I am about to scream when a loud birdcall sends all the men scrambling for their guns. It breaks the tension, and I start to giggle, then laugh aloud. It is only a nightbird.

Haji and Kamal walk on, again companions in arms and the best of friends. They hold hands, and both pick yellow flowers which they give to me. I cannot remain angry at them.

At last we reach Dunahi, where Haji's parents and brothers live. Bibi Halima is aroused by Haji's quiet scratching on the door, and welcomes him with fervent embraces. She holds me close and says, "I am so glad you are safe. I saw in a dream, just after you left, that you were in trouble. I am glad you have returned."

Kamal and the others have gone to other villages, Haji tells me the next day. They want to rest for a couple of days, and have things to do here. Tonight is the anniversary of the first Communist coup, and there will be an attack on the Soviet post four kilometers away.

I am weak, tired, and sick to my stomach. I want to go back to Pakistan, and I don't particularly want to see the attack on the post. I stay in bed for hours. Bibi Halima comes in and practices Pashtu with me, and teaches me the Kalima, the Muslim profession of faith, in Arabic and Pashtu. "There is no God but God, and Mohammed is the Messenger of God." To them, because I know the Kalima, and because I have gone to Jehad, I am already a Muslim.

Life goes on, even in a war zone. Jamil's pretty wife and her sister-in-law bake bread in a traditional clay oven. Bibi Halima rolls the bread into round balls, and then the women flatten them against the inside wall of the oven. The old grandmother, who must be eighty or ninety, insists on posing for a picture with Haji's Kalashnikov. Helicopters fly over, high overhead, and artillery fire rattles the windows all day, until the sky clouds over in the afternoon.

"When are we going?" I ask Haji.

"Tonight, *inshallah.* Maybe tomorrow. The Mujahedeen need to rest, and so do you."

Something does not feel right. I want to leave this village, I feel a sense of stifling panic. It is not logical, but a deep pit of the stomach, gut-tightening feeling of fear. I try to tell Haji, but he is not interested.

Haji's father, a gentle old man with a silky white beard and a light blue turban to match his eyes, is more understanding. Though we have few words in common, he comforts me. He sends one of his sons to fish in the river, and asks his wife to cook the two tiny fish that his son caught. He brings me a strange, sour, stubbly yellow-orange fruit, and three pink roses. He takes me into the small mudwalled orchard, fragrant after the rain, where we sit quietly and have tea.

At dusk, it begins to pour. Haji shrugs and says, "It's too muddy to go tonight. We will go after tomorrow."

When the rain breaks, a battle begins. Haji is excited, and takes me up on the walled roof so I can watch. It is an astonishing fireworks show as golden arcs of tracer bullets fade to red and a second later the sound of the shots reaches us. Flares fired into the air light up the sky, white, red, green, like dying stars. There are pops and explosions, and a deadly beauty to the whole scene, counterpointed by jagged purple lightning to the north, and the throaty growl of thunder.

Finally I begin to shake. I am overstimulated, ready to explode. I want to be alone and cry, for these people, for all of Afghanistan, even for the Soviets embroiled in this crazy war by some bureaucratic ideologues far from the fighting.

Inside the house, Haji's father is sitting with his younger son, patiently counting out a thousand grains of corn by the flickering light of a lantern. The scene shimmers like a medieval illumination. Each golden grain represents a prayer, as the old man and his son, Haji's young brother, murmur the many names of God to keep the house safe.

For a long time I watch, consumed by dread. The rain begins again, and Haji says, "It always rains after a battle." I try to sleep, but wake up in the middle of the night and hunker at the edge of the muddy courtyard, trembling and full of fear. A scene keeps returning to me–I see the Soviets coming to this village, to this house; I see bombing, and something to do with the tower. With all the force of my prayer I put a blessing on this house, and all in it, and then begin to sob.

Bibi Halima awakens and comes out to hold me. But I cannot stop crying. Haji finally wakes up, and is angry. "Do you want to leave in the rain?" he shouts. His father wakes up, and when he sees my face he tells Haji to prepare to leave, as soon as the rain slackens.

I feel better as soon as we are out of the village and into the foothills, well before dawn. My stomach and knee are cramping, and I stop to rest. Haji isn't angry anymore, so I explain to him, "It was the voice of my heart telling me to leave. I don't know why."

He accepts this, and tells his father, who nods thoughtfully and says good-bye. In this culture a dream, a vision, a feeling, has reality.

The day brightens as most of the Mujahedeen rejoin us. Kamal is not among them, and I find that I miss him, despite his rough and disrespectful joke. I doubt he has ever spoken to a foreign woman before, and in my heart I forgive him.

As I pick wildflowers and press them in my notebook, the nightmare of the previous night fades. We are in daylight now, in no more danger, at the ridge which marks the Durand Line, the border between Afghanistan and Pakistan. I must be crazy, I think. I didn't have to inconvenience everyone by insisting on leaving.

When we get back to Peshawar, I don't see Haji and Kamal for a week or so. One day they come and invite me to Kamal's family's house for the next day, but no one shows up to get me. After another week, they come again. "We were in Kunar," says Haji. "We had to go fight, because we received word that the Soviets had come to Dunahi, into our house."

"Is your family all right?"

"My father was arrested, but they set him free after some days, because he said he was too old to fight." Haji laughs. "Even though he was wounded before, and he is a commander, but they don't know. My brother escaped by way of the tower, but they took my brother-in-law for the army. He will escape soon, no doubt, and will bring weapons with him. My mother and sisters and everyone else, by the grace of God, are fine. There were no weapons in the house, so no one was arrested."

No one can know the timing of visions, or the power of blessings. Haji's family lived to fight another day, and their house was not destroyed–then. Two years later I will see the name Dunahi on a list of destroyed villages in a human rights report. But still this village exists inside me, giving me momentary shelter from fear.

22 Being and Becoming

"When I was in Afghanistan, I was really afraid, and I prayed a lot. I got the feeling that if I made it back to Peshawar safely, I should become a Muslim."

Fatana listens intently to my account of the journey to Kunar. At these last words a surprised smile plays about her lips, and her dark eyes sparkle.

"Mubarak," she says approvingly. "Blessings."

I tell her of my years studying Sufism, and of how the quiet, non-fanatical, simple faith of the people of Kunar has moved me deeply. I want to express solidarity with their faith, to be a part of it. It simply feels like the right thing to do. I don't care about sects of Islam, about Sunni or Shia or Ismaili, or about schools of Sufism. I approach this faith with a mystical perception of the Oneness of God, by whatever name God is called, in whatever form He/She may appear. Islam, I reflect, means "submission to the will of God," and after the experience of facing my worst fears, surrender seems the most reasonable, natural thing in the world.

"So, how do I become a Muslim?" I ask Fatana.

"Say the Kalima in front of witnesses."

"I want to say it in front of you and Ishaq, because you are like my family."

She smiles, and her eyes grow animated. "You can say it in front of Pir Sahib, Ishaq's uncle. He is the head of the family, and that will be a great honor. I will ask when he will come from Islamabad, and you can do it then. You must give sweets to everyone, and we will have a nice feast. I am so happy for you! Really, you are like my own sister. I forget that you were born in America and I was born in Kabul. It is as if we grew up together in the same house."

"Come closer, my daughter, and say the Kalima after me," says the old man, speaking in English. I am confused, for this is not Pir Sahib, but Hazrat Sahib Mojadidi, another Afghan religious and political leader. How does he know that I want to become a Muslim? I am here for the interview which my friend Safiullah has set up with him. Safi has even brought a tape recorder, which he now turns on and sets up near me.

"I have heard that you wish to become a Muslim."

So has everyone else in a two hundred mile radius, I think. "Yes," I answer quietly.

"So, you will say the Kalima in front of me, and I will teach you some other words in Arabic. Just repeat after me."

I realize that Safi had never intended for me to interview Hazrat Sahib, and the tape recorder is to record my conversion. I feel caught in a political undercurrent of one-upmanship—it seems that the one who is seen to "bring me to Islam" gets spiritual Brownie points.

I feel vaguely guilty as I struggle to repeat the Arabic words and phrases with correct intonation. Some of what I am saying, I already know, but I am not comfortable in front of this group of strangers. I respect Hazrat Sahib, who is an important figure in the Naqshbandiya sect of Sufism, but I don't know him. And I am disappointed that Fatana and Ishaq are not here to share this moment with me.

The brief ceremony is soon over. "It is because of my teaching that she has become a Muslim," I hear Safi say, and I want to shout out, "No, it is because of Sufism, because of the Mujahedeen, and because of Fatana's and Ishaq's gentle example." But I don't want to cause a scene.

A Pakistani journalist congratulates me, and asks a few questions about why I wanted to become a Muslim. I talk about Sufism, and Kunar, and the faith of the Afghan people, while he takes notes avidly. But I am disconcerted by the attention to something I regard as a personal matter, and I don't want him to use my name. I am, after all, American, and raised to believe that religion is between the individual and God. I cannot get used to individuals and whole cultures being defined on the basis of declared faith.

I am ushered behind a curtain, where I join the women of the family, several of whom I have met before. Most of them are very conservative, despite their advanced academic degrees, and wear their veils even in the house. I don't know how to tell them this is not my vision of Islam, and I wonder just how misunderstood I will be when my own vision becomes clear.

The endless feast has been prepared especially for celebration of this blessed occasion. The chicken is succulent, the *pilau* with raisins, carrots, and almonds delicious. But I taste a sourness of betrayal by Safi who knew that I had planned to profess my faith in front of Ishaq's family.

When I reach Peshawar that evening, I am not sure what to tell Fatana. She rushes in to greet me, and immediately sees that I am troubled.

"Safi took me to Hazrat Sahib today," I begin.

"Did you interview him?"

"Well, no. He asked me to say the Kalima."

Her dark eyes go darker as she begins to understand.

"So, I guess I have become a Muslim."

"Mubarak," she says, and kisses me lightly. "I thought you would wait for Pir Sahib." There is disappointment, even a hint of accusation in her voice.

"I did want to wait. I didn't know what to do when he asked me to say the Kalima. I was shocked, since Safi told me I had an interview."

Her beautiful face creases into a frown. "But I have told the whole family you will say it in front of Pir Sahib."

"Maybe I could do it again for Pir Sahib."

I keep asking if she is hurt or angry, but she denies it. "No, no, I am glad for you. Never mind, it's not important."

She leaves abruptly, and I feel miserable. I feel I have offended my beloved adopted family, that I got caught off guard and gave away my power.

I sit in the dark and cry quietly, but when Fatana finds out from Wana's cousin that I am upset, she comes to find me. "No, no, I promise I am not angry. It would have been good to say the Kalima in front of Pir Sahib, but it doesn't matter. What does matter is that you are Muslim now, you have the light of God. What name did you choose?"

"I didn't choose a name. I didn't have time, it was such a surprise."

A smile grows on her lips again. "Then we can have Pir Sahib name you, and all will be happy."

But Pir Sahib does not come for a very long time. Fatana and I discuss names, and I have to discard some beautiful ones because they are "not really Islamic." Finally I come to her and Ishaq and tell them, "I like the name Rabia, after the Sufi Rabia Basri, and the Afghan poet Rabia Balkhi. What does the name mean?"

Ishaq looks it up in the dictionary. "Rab'a is the correct pronunciation in Arabic. It is the fourth month, and it means spring. It is a good name for you."

Nothing is turning out as I had expected or hoped. My naming is an anticlimax, just as my conversion had been. What is the lesson in this? Perhaps names are not so important. Perhaps fixed being is not as important as constant becoming.

This is a culture that respects the opening of the heart, and Fatana and Ishaq accept me as a sincere seeker. But others seem to think that I should become one of those converts who is more zealous than those born to a religion. "Are you going to give up journalism and get married?" asks Safi's wife.

"I'd love to get married to the right person, someone I'm in love with and who is a poet, a Sufi, and wants to serve God and humanity. But no, I won't give up my career."

Some women, I know, are angry, bitter, and jealous of my freedom. But I am steadfast in my beliefs and cite examples of Afghan, Pakistani, and other Muslim women I know who are very devout, but also have successful careers and are free to choose whether, when, and whom to marry, and how to live. I quote Muslim sayings I have read in English like, "Women are the twin halves of men," and like many Muslim women, argue for contemporary interpretations of Islamic laws. If the spirit of the law was to give greater protection and more rights to the Arab woman of the seventh century, then the spirit of the law in today's world should surely be updated to one of true equality.

Simple, religious people come to me and embrace me when someone tells them I am Muslim, or when I tell them my new name. "You have the light of God, the light of Islam," one woman murmurs. "You will go straight to Paradise. But you must convert your parents, or they will go to hell."

I am anxious to learn the *namaz*, the Muslim prayers, so I can join my friends in their prayers. I admire the discipline of remembering and honoring God five times a day, but I don't know if I can live up to it. Wana's mullah agrees to help me after her afternoon lessons. But being an impatient and busy American, I record a tape of the call to prayer and the entire *namaz*, and practice it on my own.

The mullah is a kind man, well-versed in Islam, but literal in his interpretations. When I can't escape his attention, he drills me in the *namaz*, then tells me endless stories about Paradise and Jehad.

I find these fascinating at first. Paradise has four rivers, and trees of gems. The walls are of garnet, ruby, and pearls. Everyone is beautiful, and wears white silk. Twenty thousand years of earth don't equal half an hour of Paradise. Hell, on the other hand, is fiery and interminable...

Like the mullah's speech, I think. I blank out until he moves on to Jehad. "In the days of Abraham, Jehad was not like it is now. There were no bombs, no planes, no guns. There were only arrows, and stones, and swords..." The mullah drones on, not even looking at me, and I meditate on the parallelism of his sentence structure until I am rescued by Fatana.

As I write many versions of stories about different aspects of my trip to Kunar, I reflect that this journey has forever marked my soul. In those mountains and valleys, I lived many lifetimes in a span of days. The first night back in Peshawar, I had suddenly burst into tears, because I was comfortable and safe, and those left behind, who gave me so much hospitality, were not.

I want to give back something, and finally decide to offer a hundred dollars to Ishaq for the Mujahedeen of Kunar. He thanks me gravely, as I suggest that maybe they can buy some of the guns they need.

But he laughs. "A Kalashnikov costs hundreds of dollars. But the Mujahedeen will be happy to have this to buy food. And they will be very happy to know you have become a Muslim."

I go to visit Dr. Abdullah Osman at the Mujahedeen hospital. He is glad to hear good news of Dr. Farid, but he is gaunt and pale, just back from a long trip to Farah Province in the south of Afghanistan. He is distracted as he speaks to me in between the demands of patients. There is never enough medicine, money, or staff, he explains. And every Mujaheed who comes has to be given some medicine, even if only a vitamin or an aspirin, or they feel cheated.

"It is we who have done this to them," he says resignedly. "We don't know how to stop it now. Some unscrupulous doctors used to give an injection whether people needed it or not, so they could charge more money. So now the favorite of the people is an injection. Next is a suspension, especially if it fizzes. Then finally a tablet. Sometimes they throw the tablets at you, because they think you are just making them go away. If you don't give them something, they will just find another doctor, maybe a worse one. We are trapped."

Dr. Abdullah invites me to his home, where he is having some of the Mujahedeen from Farah as luncheon guests. We listen to a tape one of them has made of the frequent, continuous bombing, and the overpowering sounds of helicopters, and I fall into fear, sucking in a collective feeling of dread One tall turbanned man is recording a commentary in Pashtu, and when he finishes, the men are nearly in tears.

Dr. Abdullah turns to me. "That is a wonderful story. He tells of a small bird who was afraid of all the bullets that were like rain. The bird landed on the shoulder of a young Mujaheed, and hid beneath his arm. Somehow he knew that the Mujahedeen wouldn't hurt him. He stayed there during the whole battle, and then when it was over, he flew away, but he was hit by a stray bullet. He gave his life for the Mujahedeen."

I work hard to finish the stories I am writing about Kunar, and start sending them off to magazines and newspapers in America.

In the middle of May, I decide to take a break and fly to Chitral to see Fida Hussain and my Kalash friends. Chitral is very green, and this is the most beautiful time of year I have visited. But the Dreamland Hotel is a black shell, burnt by the rioters last summer, and Fida is noticeably subdued.

The Kalash will be celebrating Zhoshi, the spring festival of dancing and flowers, and in Chitral, the Ismailis are excitedly waiting for the Aga Khan's visit. I feel very lucky as it appears that I will catch both celebrations. But will either group of friends understand my conversion to Islam?

Fida takes it with a grain of salt. Although I have previously considered becoming Ismaili, he doesn't see any problem, for he is a Sufi at heart. One of his Ismaili colleagues is more disturbed, for he thinks I should become Ismaili, and he is stern with me. I must go to Karachi, he says, for instruction in Ismailism. And I must change my lifestyle, and stop doing things like "sticking my head under a helicopter." I should get married and settle down.

I can never figure out who it is all these people want me to marry, and so reply with my cheerful litany of what I want in a man: a pure, intelligent, poetic Sufi who wants to serve God and humanity and work with me as a partner. They shake their heads and say, "This will be hard to find." "I know," I reply, "but if it is in my fate I will find him. We cannot hurry God or Fate."

I am a spiritual chameleon, I find. My substance and beliefs are the same, but my method of worship changes to match the culture I am in. I see beauty and blessedness in all religions, and want to worship in whatever way feels right at the time, whatever way the land and people call out for. Organized religion appeals to me less and less. In fact, one of the appeals of Islam is its lack of hierarchy. In true Islam, faith is a matter between the individual and God. But I had not reckoned on seventy-two different sects. Like many Sufis of the past, I too find myself in trouble.

I don't know if Saifullah will understand, and decide not to tell him now. I will write him a letter later, once he has seen that I have not changed. I will tell him that now that I have become Kalash, I will always be Kalash, no matter what else I may become in addition.

I am overjoyed to see Saifullah again, and my bloodsister Washlim Gul. They have a new son, and I am glad that she and Saifullah seem to be close again. Saifullah and I talk for long hours, and I urge him to teach Washlim Gul English, so that she can share in his world, and help foreign visitors when he is not there. "She wants me to get a government job," he complains. "She says I am educated and could get a good job and have money every month. She doesn't understand what I am doing."

I understand his dilemma, and wish I could talk to her and explain. But it is up to Saifullah to take action to change their lives.

I have brought photos from previous visits, along with some small gifts for Saifullah's family and other friends. The most popular gifts are several plastic goats that I had taken off someone's birthday cake in California. I had thought they might be nice toys for Saifullah's sons, as goats are so important to the Kalash, but the adults appropriate them for themselves. The men engage in long discussions about whether they are male or female goats, and what type of goat they are. Saifullah explains that in Kalasha, there are different words for black goat, white goat, spotted goat, one-horned goat, almost any imaginable sub-category of goat.

Fida has asked me to return to Chitral for the Aga Khan's visit, so I leave Rumbur, promising Saifullah to be back for Zhoshi in three days. Fida invites me to stay at his lovely home outside of town, where his wife from Karachi, who speaks fluent English, is also staying. They make a special meal of goat's head, and I smile and chew on the brains with lots of rice, reminding myself of the great honor they are doing me.

Fida and I catch up on old times. The house is nearly bare, as it was looted by rioters last year. A few neighbors had brought back stolen carpets, and one had even sheltered Fida's family. Fida, who had been visiting his brother in a remote village near the Afghan border, didn't know about the tragedy until he returned two weeks later.

I am thankful that he and his family are safe, and have lost comparatively little, though it will take him years to rebuild the hotel. He still has a job with the Aga Khan Real Estate Board, and has an income. He tells me a story that has restored his faith in humanity. Fida had left a briefcase with 10,000 rupees in it in a truck coming from Karachi to Peshawar, and the driver had returned it untouched. Now Fida is looking forward to the visit of the Aga Khan as a chance for spiritual renewal. For Ismailis, the 49th Imam is a conduit to Godhead, and *deedar,* or sitting in presence with him, is a great blessing.

Fida will send me with his family to the tiny village of Susum, far up the Chitral Valley, where we will have a chance to see the Aga Khan when he comes by helicopter. I too am excited, caught up in the collective love for this man. Is he a great spiritual leader, or simply a rich man? Or both?

Fida drives the jeep himself. The journey is rough, and takes us hours. He puts us in the care of one of his friends, and returns to his duties in Chitral. We stay in his friend's house, where fourteen of us sleep crowded onto an eight by eight foot platform. The next morning, all change their clothes except me. It had never occurred to me to bring a change on a rough trip like this. Fida's wife is worried, because of the symbolic purity of clean clothes. But his Afghan mother tells me in Farsi, "Your heart is pure. That is all that is important."

We make our way to the field where the Aga Khan will land. The crowd begins to assemble soon after dawn. The faithful have come from villages many miles away over rugged jeep and foot tracks. It is a beautiful scene–the first green blush of early spring upon the land, a few wildflowers under the alpine snow above us. A gold and maroon velvet throne awaits the Aga Khan, near a special house which was built several years ago for a visit he never made.

I am the only non-Ismaili. But I don't feel out of place, I feel a part of this loving group. Everyone thinks I am an Afghan from Badakhshan, as I am with Fida's mother and speaking Farsi. The people around us welcome me, and together we sit for eight hours in the hot sun without food or water, waiting and hoping. Every flutter of breeze sounds like a helicopter, but no helicopter comes, and there is no news. No one knows what has gone wrong, but at sunset the disappointed crowd begins to disperse.

I am disappointed too, but mostly for these faithful villagers waiting for a once in a lifetime glimpse of their spiritual king. They feel unworthy, as if they are being punished. "What did we do to deserve this?" asks Fida's wife. But his mother, bent with the years, remains stoic, full of prayer and compassion.

After missing the Aga Khan, I arrive back in Rumbur too late for Zhoshi. I return to Peshawar in disappointment, feeling caught out of synchronicity. My dreams are full of troubling, anxious images. Am I supposed to be in Pakistan at all? I don't want to leave, but why is everything so difficult?

For a long time, I think the film of Kunar I had sent to my parents via a U.S. Consular official who was going to the States on a private visit is lost. After six weeks, my parents phone and tell me that the photos are all great, but the film had arrived in a torn brown packet marked "State Department," rewrapped in plastic by the post office. I wonder what happened to the jiffy bag I'd packed it in, and why my cassette tape of war sounds had been partially played.

All my articles about Kunar, written from various angles—focusing on women, on Dr. Farid, on life in a war zone—begin to boomerang back from U.S. publications. The rejections are the same old lines: "Although this is a well-written piece...it is not breaking news...we did a piece on Afghanistan last year...it is not for us...Afghanistan is not news..." I read these and weep, feeling ashamed at my ineffectiveness. I wonder what Ishaq and Fatana think of the journalist who can't get anything published.

But I keep trying. I visit hospitals, and track down projects I consider worthwhile, like the International Committee of the Red Cross prosthetics project. I am interested in these self-help projects, where Afghans learn skills to help their countrymen. At the prosthetics project, a few men are learning to work with wood and metal to make limbs that are not as fancy and aesthetically pleasing as foreign ones, but much lighter and easier to maneuver. The legless men who are waiting to be fitted are full of bravado. Most vow to go back to Afghanistan and fight, once they are used to their new legs. These legs are like old-fashioned wooden peg legs, but the men don't care. They spurn the more expensive, heavier legs from Lahore, even though they look like human legs.

I write stories about ordinary human beings forced by circumstances to become heroes. These are not just stories of torture and imprisonment, but the stories of people I know through Fatana and Ishaq. Fauzia, who is from the prominent Mojadidi family, keeps a picture of her handsome husband on a shelf in her unfurnished flat, which she shares with her brother and children. She believes her husband is still alive, after years of imprisonment in Kabul's notorious Pul-e-Charkhi, though everyone else whispers that surely he is dead.

One day, about 150 Afghan soldiers surrender to the Mujahedeen. A few of them are killed, and a number wounded when they are shot at from behind by Soviet soldiers trying to prevent their defection. Ishaq alerts me first, hoping that I can get the story before anyone else does, even though I don't have the telex, the overnight mail, or the expense account that people working for big magazines do. But "breaking news" is not my forte. I choose to do an in-depth, human interest feature that I feel will have a more lasting value than another dry account of casualties.

The deserters are mostly young men, some still teenagers, like the Mujahedeen themselves. There are a few *grey*beards among them, and they all alike look miserable. They are scared, and don't know what will happen to them. An official from Ishaq's party tells me that the wounded have been taken to the hospital. The rest of the men will be questioned, taken in groups to sign up with the Mujahedeen party of their choice, and then allowed to choose whether to stay with the Mujahedeen here, or go back to their home districts to join the local Mujahedeen.

Among them is a bewildered young man fluent in English. "I was a student at Santa Monica City College," he informs me when I tell him I am from L.A.

After a few questions, we establish that I know his uncle, a university professor. He tells me how he went to Kabul in 1980 to see his aunts, uncles, and cousins, and was conscripted. He swears that he never fought until now, that he was an accountant in a field office. I don't know whether to believe him, but I feel sorry for him.

"My parents haven't heard from me in two years," he says softly. "Maybe you can let them know you have met me."

Peter Jouvenal, a fine British journalist who is with me, asks the Mujahedeen leaders if the boy can write a letter to his parents for us to send. Permission is granted, and Peter films the boy writing the letter, hope glowing on his face. Peter promises to send the letter air freight from Islamabad with his film. He tells me to throw in my film and story if I can write it up by tomorrow, and promises to send it to a contact of his.

We later find out that Peter's film arrived safely, but my story and film arrived much later, and the young POW's letter not at all. Six months later I will receive a letter, postmarked in July and delivered in November, from the boy's uncle who heard about his nephew through the grapevine.

My visa is expiring, but I don't really want to leave Pakistan. I feel drawn to stay here, amongst those I consider family. I apply to renew my visa so I can stay another month, for the beginning of Ramazan. The police at the Special Branch greet me with suspicion, then give me tea.

"Mulk-e-mast mulk-e-khodast," quotes one erudite fellow. "My country is God's country."

"Exactly my point," I tell him. "I don't believe in borders or nations. So please just give me my visa."

My visa is renewed, but people begin to spy on me. "Your own embassy has made a report against you," confides one official, "but you have been declared white." My own embassy denies all knowledge of such a thing, but I begin to wonder.

The police send four people to Ishaq's house to see if I really live there. Ishaq gives them cold drinks in the garden, and sends in a servant for my passport. He tells them that we practice *purdah* in the house, and they must respect that. When he comes in, Fatana and I are waiting anxiously.

"What happened?"

"They said you have to leave."

"When?"

"Within 24 hours."

"What!?" I burst into tears, and Ishaq begins laughing.

"No, no, I am only joking. They said everything is fine."

My tears turn into laughter of relief, and I begin to understand some of what foreigners in America go through. We Americans are so spoiled, naively thinking we are welcome in most countries. It is an interesting experience to be prejudged by my passport and my nationality, and blamed for policies I often do not support, and for elected officials I didn't vote for.

Ramazan is a blessed time, the month in which the Holy Quran was first revealed to Prophet Mohammed. Muslims fast from dawn till dusk, remembering what it is to be hungry, and to be humble before God, who gives us all our sustenance. If anyone cannot fast, he or she is allowed to pay a ransom by feeding a hungry person.

As a new Muslim, I join my Afghan family in fasting. The first day is not too hard, though it is very hot, and my throat is dry. I know it is a tradition not even to drink water, but I begin to think God never meant to be so harsh. I dream that I break the fast accidentally by swallowing water while brushing my teeth. Then in the afternoon I fall asleep and dream that I eat too soon, before the evening call to prayer.

The Gailanis are strict with themselves, but not with others. For guests who are travelers, they cook meals. The scent of food permeates the whole house and makes my mouth water. I wonder how Fatana and the cook restrain themselves.

Iftar, the breaking of the fast each evening, is a joyous, communal event. We first pray the brief sunset prayer, and then quench our thirst with cooling drinks. Our dinners are light, often a delicious soup before the main meal of rice, vegetables, and a little meat. After a few days I find my stomach has shrunk.

The hardest part is eating before dawn. The first two nights, we get up at about 3 a.m. Ishaq sits silently, Fatana rubs her eyes, and I stare stupidly. After that, we stay up late and eat breakfast around 1 a.m., then sleep as late as we can–except for Ishaq, who always has work to do. He tells me not to fast everyday, but I try anyway, until I get a migraine on the third day.

"You are not used to it from the age of fourteen or fifteen, like we are. You will make yourself sick and weak. God understands. Just fast every other day, if you can."

I do my best. Fatana prides herself on her discipline, but one very hot day, she gets sick as soon as she has broken her fast. Ishaq tells her not to fast the next day, but she is stubborn, and does so anyway.

I hate to leave, but my extended visa is running out. I must go to India, to Kashmir, where I intend to write a novel about the war in Afghanistan. In a novel I can reach more people, and give them depth and understanding in a way that no news article can.

The last days before I leave are sad. Mujahedeen of Ishaq's uncle's party and another party have been fighting, and have beaten each other severely. One man is in the hospital. For the first time, I see Ishaq angry. "I want to go to the front," he tells me. "This Peshawar is dirty and corrupt. I want to go to fight Jehad."

The morning that I leave, Ishaq rushes out of the house. The man in the hospital has died, and Ishaq fears there may be revenge killings. I leave with sorrow, vowing to do all I can to communicate the heroism and the greatness of heart, mixed with the pettiness and in-fighting that makes up an all too human comi-tragedy.

23 Kashmir Unveiled

Srinagar, Kashmir
Summer, 1983

The full moon hangs high in the silken black sky over the Dal Lake, shooting the dark water through with silvery light. On the surface of the lake, the moon shatters and rejoins a thousand times, with each stroke of the boatman's paddle.

In this transcendent moment, I wish I were with my Beloved, whoever he will be. But I am instead with two young German travellers, with whom I have hired this *shikara* to take us to the fabled Shalimar Gardens and back to our houseboat.

The boatman parts the thick reeds with heavy sighs, and finally lets the boat drift for awhile. At last he hands the heart-shaped wooden paddle to me, and I sit in the pointed prow like an Egyptian priestess, quietly paddling first one side, then the other. I am entranced by the broken moonlight on the surface of the still, black water, as I voyage alone on dark Niles of memory.

"You come to my house for tea," says the boatman.

It is somewhere between an invitation and a command.

"No, thank you," says one of the German fellows quickly. "It is too late and we are tired."

The boatman unceremoniously takes the oar back from me and begins to paddle. He is obviously a little offended. But as he turns the boat amongst trees and leaves and softly shining lotuses, it soon becomes apparent that we are to be his guests anyway.

In the middle of this lake are islands in the country of night that surely do not exist by day. We clamber sleepily out of the boat, as if we have dozed off in a field of poppies and been spirited off to fairyland. We climb up wooden steps to a house and sit on woven straw mats on the floor while the boatman's wife serves us a strange pink beverage out of a long-spouted copper samovar. I taste it cautiously, and find that it is salted tea, a Kashmiri tradition. We are also given small round pieces of hard Kashmiri bread to soak in the tea.

It is Ramazan, the month of fasting, and this is the continuation of *iftar,* the daily breaking of the fast after sundown. Our boatman, who had to break his fast alone while he waited for us in Shalimar Gardens, obviously wants to make up for it by celebrating with his family late into the night.

Another man, dark and handsome as the devil himself, strums on a rebab and sings religious hymns. The Germans take out a little of their precious hashish and share it with the boatman, who is delighted. As he smokes, he grows ecstastic, and grabs a terracotta jug and begins wildly playing drumbeats to accompany the soaring music of the rebab and the singer's voice. It is almost frightening as he bends to the ground and then violently throws his head back, writhing and dancing until he is one with some spirit which only he sees.

When the music finishes, he falls exhausted, sweat and tears mingled on his face and in his moustache. The women, somber in the tied headscarves which hang down their backs, again pour a round of tea and pass out bread. The boatman's wife is a handsome, strong woman with a dark beauty and lively eyes. She is kind and solicitous to us, though we exchange no words but the ubiquitous greeting and farewell, *"Salaam aleikum."*

Outside, the moon no longer hangs at the zenith. It is closer, less remote, and shines on worlds of ordinary reality and alternate reality. I know I can never find this island again, beyond the black veil of night which has moved aside for a few brief moments of time.

Kashmir is indeed a seductive land, veiled in mist and mystery, in darkness and in golden sunlight. The Emperor Jehangir built the Shalimar Gardens for his beloved wife, Noor Jehan, light of the world. During the reign of the Moghuls, Srinagar, capital of this mountain land, was also the summer capital of the Emperor.

I have been here before, and have seen its magic and sorcery, and its tawdry tourism. But still it casts a romantic spell woven of the delicate gossamer of sheer beauty reflected in the mirror of the Dal Lake, the glass-green mountain streams, and the open sky itself.

This year, I have come to write a novel about the war in Afghanistan, and to heal the psychic wounds I have sustained in covering the war and the wounded. Kashmir in 1983 is a calm land, a land where I can walk in beauty, without fear of helicopters and land mines. At least this summer it is calm, in between savage conflicts, some religious and some political, which have rent the fine silk of harmony time and again and stained the fabric of this land with blood.

An idea is being born to me in this quiet clearing amongst the pines where the fimiliar Aksa Lodge lies. Afghanistan is no longer "news," and it is extremely difficult to publish feature stories about it. But to write a novel, to create Afghan characters that Americans can identify with, to make the war real and personal to them, to make them cry and feel angry and swell with admiration of simple heroes–that would indeed be a worthwhile task.

The genesis of this story was in the cave in Kunar. There I invented a character whom I could easily fall in love with. At a moment I wanted to be rescued, I fell back on my own creativity and invoked the character of Yusuf, an Afghan doctor who has lived in America for many years. He is a synthesis of the best and worst of Eastern and Western values, a handsome and mercurial Sufi poet who jokingly calls himself a "born-again Muslim." After his divorce from his American wife, he has decided to return to his country and do service in the war zone with the Resistance. But his brother Ayub is a collaborator with the Communists. Ayub was an idealistic and sincere child, who has become a cynical opportunist. He is now governor of the brothers' ancestral province. I set the story in Kunar, because it is familiar.

The female character, Elizabeth, is a journalist. I know I'll put a lot of me in her, but she will take on her own existence as well. I think of other women photographers and journalists I have admired, and Elizabeth begins to come to life in my notes. She is impetuous, impulsive, and yet professional. After the break-up of a long and unhappy relationship, she decides to risk everything by going to Afghanistan to make or break her career.

As I take notes, the characters become living spirits, and scenes play out before my eyes. I see the scene where Elizabeth and Yusuf meet, in a cave in Kunar. I watch how the sparks fly and how they spar, both of them denying love for the longest time. Yes, it is a love story. But not just a love story.

As the theme of the conflict between the brothers becomes more central to the book, I find a title, *War in the Land of Cain.* And I am ready to begin.

Mohammed Yasin, proprietor of the Aksa Lodge, welcomes me warmly upon my return to Pahalgam. He shows me where he has posted my article from the *Los Angeles Times* travel section, which mentions the Aksa favorably and prominently.

He has maintained the childlike enthusiasm which makes him so endearing. He helps me choose a room, bargains with me, and provides me with a small wicker table and chair so I can type comfortably.

The first chapter of my novel flows well, which I take as a good omen. I soon find that a break and a walk in the garden, or amongst the pines, leaves me ever more inspired to return to writing, and I fall into a routine of self-discipline mixed with pleasure. I wake up early and have a delicious breakfast sitting in the garden of roses, zinnias, and marigolds. I talk to other guests, some of them delightful people. I walk down to the village post office, or up the mountain to the nomads, and then return in the late morning to work on the book.

My dreams are strange, and often troubled. Often I am in an Afghan city, sometimes living openly but in fear, and sometimes in elaborate disguise. At other times I am in a war zone, climbing a very high mountain, or being purified by fire. One night I dream that power, heat, and healing energy are coming from the palms of my hands. I awaken suddenly and expect to see rays of light streaming from them. I see nothing, but I know that in some sense the power is really there.

In a few days, a few hours of conversation, I connect with treasured souls I hope I will know the rest of my life. Travelling makes life more intense, time more compressed. In daily life at home, I can meet someone and get to know him or her slowly, with the luxury of time. It is rare in that world to feel an intense and lasting connection at first sight or word. But here some who stay for weeks never touch me, and others who stay a night or two form lasting and deep attachments.

The Aksa's guests and their dramas would make a fascinating novel or play in their own right. I meet a quiet Iranian student who turns out to be a member of the Bahai community, which is cruelly persecuted in Iran. Iran is his home, but he can never go back while the Islamic clerics are in power. Another Iranian student comes, his eyes burning with passion for the Jehad against Iraq. He is proud that he fought for six months; but he has survived, and is married now to a sweet woman who always wears a plain grey dress with a *burqa* over it, and rarely smiles.

Louisa has come from Holland to study yoga in an intensive program. She is full of life and love, and often walks in with a handful of wildflowers, a bounce to her footstep, and the sky reflected in her laughing eyes. She is always happy, and always ready to be of comfort to everyone else.

When Erik, a gentle and spiritual Swede, arrives, Louisa and I stay up late at night talking with him. He is a solitary traveller, a quiet hermit at this time in his life, preferring to trek alone through the Himalaya, to travel on silent pilgrimages to holy men of Muslim and Hindu faiths. He has studied Sufism, as has Louisa, and we talk about poets and dervishes. Erik tells stories about the *jinn,* spirits who live somewhere in the Dal Lake, and I wonder if the man who took us to the mysterious island was one. The boatman on Erik's houseboat had told him many tales of haunted boats and *jinn.* The Kashmir Valley, the man had said, is divided into light and dark sides. Pahalgam, I am glad to know, is on the side of light. Gulmarg, another popular tourist destination, is on the dark side. An Englishwoman who is listening frowns thoughtfully and admits that she had not felt happy in Gulmarg, for no particular reason.

Kashmir, we find, affects both the conscious and unconscious senses. In the summer, there are frequent rains from the ragged northern edge of the monsoon that never crosses these green south-facing slopes to the rainshadows of Ladakh and Baltistan, beyond the great massif. The rains, mist, and clouds hide whatever goes on beneath the surface. Underneath is both the ugliness and the brighter beauties that the casual visitor never perceives.

In the future, the enchantment laid upon me will allow me to recall only the beauties and the harmony. It is only with an effort that I will remember the tourist touts in Srinagar, the dirty lake and brown river, the bad food and the stench of sewers, the cheating, hustling, and theft. I think of Pahalgam as paradise, especially compared with Srinagar, which is much lower in altitude and thus hotter and muggier in the summer. But Pahalgam was also at times my place of agony and fear, of noisy tourists and frustration. I remember the scented pines dripping with fresh sparkling raindrops, not the letters rejecting my articles about Afghanistan, faithfully forwarded to me by my parents, all the way from California.

Each rejection throws me into agonies of self-doubt. One editor thinks he is doing me a favor by writing a five-page critique of my three-page article. I shake with rage, but secretly wonder if he is right. Other editors say I can write, but Afghanistan is no longer newsworthy. I wonder how they would feel if their families were suffering, and some editor decided it wasn't newsworthy.

Two months pass with no good news, and it becomes clear that none of my articles about Kunar will be published. My satisfaction lies in my character, Elizabeth, publishing in the *New York Times.* I pour my energy and my will into this story with the magical power to change reality, sure of its effect. I almost hesitate to write the ugly scenes of destruction, bombing, and firefights. In the end it becomes clear that there will be a ceasefire, that the Soviets will withdraw though civil war will likely follow.

I don't know why the book is writing itself this way. I know few people believe the Soviets will leave Afghanistan. But I have seen the faith of the men and women of Kunar, and this quality is not easily quantified and plugged into political and military calculations.

Although I love Kashmir, I am in exile here. My heart longs for Afghanistan, and for my friends in Pakistan. I feel lonely at *Eid,* the festival celebrating the end of Ramazan, and miss Fatana, Ishaq, and the whole family. I give the Aksa servants little gifts, and order a whole chicken to be roasted. I share some with Louisa, and give the rest to the servants.

For the first time in my life, I am learning to wait. "Patience is bitter, but bears a sweet fruit," runs the old Persian saying. I write and rewrite this phrase, practicing my Persian calligraphy. I wait for the mail, wait for good news. "Good news is coming any day," Yasin says cheerfully each day. But days go by, and nothing changes, except that my manuscript grows like rich crops in the field.

After Louisa leaves, and long after Erik, my brother in spirit, has left for Ladakh, a Canadian woman named Anne Demko comes to stay. Like Louisa, she is always cheerful, and has a deep faith in the generosity and bounty of the universe. We exchange stories of our travels late into the night. We two night owls enjoy each other's company as the stars blaze overhead and the moon swings slowly through the summer sky.

I tell Anne about my novel, and also about my frustration over not getting my articles published. "Let me tell you a way of praying that has worked for me," she says. She tells me to write lists, first of my immediate needs, then of future goals, then of personal goals like better posture or perfect health. "Think it and it's done," she says. "Each night, concentrate on your list, and pray for each thing you want. Visualize it as if you are there, in detail. Do it more than once a day, whenever you have some quiet time. You can manifest anything you want in your life. But it's important to believe in your heart that it is done, and to be thankful to God for each thing that you are given."

Hearing this from anyone else, I might have been skeptical. But Anne's voice and manner are so certain and positive that I cannot believe this wouldn't work. I write out my lists. "Don't worry how many things you ask for," she says, "My first list had more than thirty things." So does mine. I wonder if I am greedy. But I am resolute. Many of my wants are connected with ego, it is true, but many others are connected with service. I decide I need about $1,000; I want to write an article on Afghanistan for *National Geographic;* and I want to make a documentary on the Afghan refugees.

None of these seems very likely to occur, but I pray fervently, before or after the Muslim *namaz* I am learning from a tape. I visualize a check with my name on it; I visualize a copy of *National Geographic* with an article on Afghanistan, and my name under it; I go ahead and visualize an Afghan on the cover, for good measure; finally I see a documentary on the refugees with "Produced by Debra Denker" in the credits.

Nothing happens immediately. I don't write any letters to *National Geographic,* and I don't know where to start getting the tens of thousands of dollars it would take to make a documentary. But Anne encourages me. "The universe is generous. Let God do it His own way. You just see the final outcome, and let God figure out how to bring it about. Don't tell God how you want it done. Just be thankful. Think it and it's done."

After two months of daily work, on a day of pouring rain which matches my tears, I finish the first draft of the novel. I am sobbing with the effort of this birth, proud, knowing that I must let it sit awhile now. But it is done.

Althea Maddrell, an Englishwoman travelling with her boyfriend Richard Lanchester, is the first person to read my draft. She and Richard have been camping in the garden, revelling in these beautiful surroundings, the privacy of their tent, good food, and the luxury of access to hot water for showers. They are a delightful couple. Althea is a fine writer in her own right, eloquent and learned in literature, which she studied at York University as a "mature student" who had married and had children before beginning her education. Richard is a musician, and a wonderful artist as well. He shows me beautiful pen and ink sketches he has done during their treks, of mountains, shrines, and whistling marmots. He has a few tapes of local folk music he has made while travelling throughout India with Althea. We spend many hours comparing folk music in various regions, while Althea reads my manuscript.

Althea is quiet, but sometimes she smiles and makes a comment about my characters, and there is excitement in her blue eyes. I wait nervously for her verdict, repeating over and over to her that this is only a first draft, and sometimes wishing I hadn't let anyone see it.

The two are welcoming, not isolated like so many travelling couples. The circle of their love opens to include others as friends, brothers, and sisters. They invite me to trek with them on the pilgrimage to the ice lingam cave at Amarnath, but I decline. I don't like crowds, I explain, but plan to go at least partway before the official pilgrimage starts.

I start out early one morning, sauntering up the trail with a light pack, wearing my usual *shalwar kameez*, my hair tied into a long printed cotton scarf in the fashion of Kashmiri women. The first part of the walk is pleasant and easy. I practice some of the Urdu I have been assiduously studying, and find many friendly faces. I reach Chandanwari, the first stop on the pilgrimage, before noon. Since it is so early, I decide to continue after stopping for a cold Limca, a couple of chapaties, and some dal.

When I head up the trail, I fall into conversation with a middle-aged shepherd and his young nephew. They live in Shesh Nag, by the green lake which is the second stop on the piigrimage, and they are going there today. If they can make it, I think, so can I. The man offers to porter my bag, but I smile and refuse.

They go on ahead, and I am lost in thought and the stupendous scenery. Snow bridges arch across fierce streams, pure springs seep from sheer rock walls, and green hillsides turn to rock and high meadows. Beyond, in the distance, are craggy peaks. On the road is a trickle of early pilgrims, some on foot, some on tiny Kashmiri ponies dangerously overloaded with the prosperous and portly. Some of the wealthy sit in sedan chairs carried on the shoulders of Kashmiri peasants.

The day grows hotter as the path continues to rise. I catch up with the shepherd and his nephew, who are resting. Now I ask if they can help me carry my bag. I almost want to give up, but I know my choice is either to go back to Chandanwari and regain the altitude tomorrow, or to continue on to Shesh Nag. Ghulam Hassan, the older man, is cheerful. "Just one high pass," he tells me. "Just two more hours."

My experience with the Mujahedeen should have told me what "two more hours" meant. By the time I labor up the steep switchbacks of the pass, weeping and terrified as dusk is falling, I recognize my own folly. I am out of breath and have ascended too high, too quickly. Ghulam Hassan and his nephew are far ahead, carrying my pack and sleeping bag, and I can only pray that they are trustworthy.

The two are waiting for me at the top of the pass, just as the sun sinks below the horizon. "Just a little further," says Ghulam Hassan encouragingly, then sets a pace as fast as the Mujahedeen along a gently rising path which fades into the night. By the light of a gibbous moon, I am dimly aware of tiny irises alongside the narrow path, and a gleaming body of water in the distance.

Ghulam Hassan leads me to a tiny hut. The crude walls are made of piled up fieldstone, and the roof of corrugated metal sheeting held down with more stones. I am glad to see two women inside. One is Ghulam Hassan's wife, the other his brother's. The kindly, giggling women fix me salt tea and spinach, and give me a little cold leftover rice.

Grateful for their hospitality, I feel ready to fall into a deep sleep. I curl up in my sleeping bag, but babies are crying, and small children restlessly kick my back and stumble over my feet. And I feel as if something is sitting on my chest. I can't seem to get enough air, and my heart is beating very quickly. In a panic, I realize I have altitude sickness. I have come too far too fast, from 7,000 feet to 12,500. But I have none of the serious symptoms, at least not yet.

I finally doze off, but sleep fitfully. Every time I awaken, Ghulam Hassan and his brother, both dressed in strange peaked caps and heavy woolen cloaks against the damp cold, seem to be staring at me. They move outside to sleep, but I hear the murmur of their words. I don't understand Kashmiri, but a few words are common to Urdu and Farsi. Was that "camera" or *kamra,* the word for room? I strain to hear, and my eye falls on a sharp-bladed ax hung over the doorway. My stomach turns cold. No one knows where I am. They could murder me in cold blood, and throw my body in the lake, and steal my camera. They don't know that the camera doesn't work right, and that the wide angle lens actually fell apart in my hands yesterday. Breathless and fearful, I doze and wake, doze and wake.

But at last dawn breaks. I am alive, and breathing is a little easier. I recognize my panic as probably another symptom of altitude sickness. I go outside the hut to see the sun falling on a jade green lake, cutting through the mist. All around me are hundreds of sheep and thousands of wildflowers. I know that to be safe, I must descend today and return from this strange and impatient journey—but this moment alone is worth the agony.

My life in Kashmir is measured by full moons. I remember again the full moon upon the waters of the Dal Lake, and the number of times it has sailed across the sky on invisible winds of gravity. The novel is finished, and it is time to move on. The nomads I have visited throughout the summer have left their rough shelter of fragrant pine boughs, and are on the move. Whole caravans of Gujar nomads are walking slowly downhill to warmer pastures, their buffalo before them, and a few ponies loaded with colorful bundles behind. Their lives, like the cicadas which whir more frantically each day in these northern woods, are guided by seasons and lunar tides with which we in the West have long since lost touch.

But inside, beyond the clocks which stop and speed up, I feel some ancient rhythm, which tells me too it is time to go. When Althea and Richard invite me to accompany them on the bus to Ladakh, the region two days east of Srinagar which was once a part of Western Tibet, I accept, glad for the company, glad to be on the road again.

24 Fragile Seeds of Hope

Ladakh, India
Summer, 1983

The piercing light of the crystal morning gives way to a somnolent afternoon as I sit with two elderly Buddhist nuns, quietly splitting ripe apricots and leaving them out in the sun to dry. Most of the younger *chomos,* as Buddhist nuns are called in Ladakh, are off in the fields, while the elders are left to this work.

Splitting apricots is a meditative task. Its repetitiousness lulls the verbal mind, which becomes occupied by the variety of form, color, and texture of apricots. Some come apart easily, splitting into perfect halves; others squish into saffron pulp, which we lick off our hands; the occasional hard, tricky one refuses to split.

I shoo away the flies wich buzz greedily around our golden pile, and throw a handful of hard kernels into another pile. These will later be husked for their delicious almond-like nut, as they are in Chitral, Hunza, and the Kalash Valleys, and apricot oil will be made from some of them.

Julichan is the only nunnery in Ladakh. It is attached to Ridzong Monastery, which perches imposingly, the color of bleached bones, on the side of the sere, monotone mountain at the head of this rocky valley. The nuns are of all ages, from young women to very old, bent crones. Their heads are shaved, and they wear maroon robes the same color as monks wear. They are vowed to celibacy and given to contemplation, but retain the ready smile and spontaneous laughter of all Ladakhis.

We don't speak while we work, but when we take a break I shyly practice my Ladakhi, referring frequently to my typed list of vocabulary words and phrases which I had compiled with the help of a friend in Leh, the capital of Ladakh. I answer a few curious questions about my family, and show pictures of family, friends, and cats to everyone.

One old woman, so bent that she must walk with two canes as she scuttles across the dusty courtyard, is delighted with the cat pictures. This gentle woman likes cats and feeds a scrawny silver tiger kitten from her own supply of butter tea and tsampa, roast barley flour. Like her, the kitten is unsteady on its feet, but it mews vociferously for food and gratefully laps up the buttery tea.

We resume our work, sitting under the shade of an overhanging roof, but are invaded by a horde of German tourists, blond, overweight, and excited, who enter the courtyard without asking permission and start snapping pictures. I look up in surprise as a beefy man snaps my picture and hands me a cheap silk scarf as thanks.

"Where are you from?" I ask.

"You speak English!" he cries.

"Yes, I am from America."

"I thought you were Ladakhi."

I hand him back the scarf, smiling. "Sorry to disappoint you. I am just visiting. Maybe one of the nuns would like this."

The Germans talk among themselves, then leave as suddenly as they have come, having presented a tea-strainer to the matriarch of the nunnery. The nuns pass it around, with quizzical looks on their round, open faces, until I demonstrate how it is used. They laugh, the Ladakhi answer to everything.

I puzzle over the German mistaking me for a Ladakhi. My features are not in the least Ladakhi or Tibetan, but the fact that my dark hair is in a braid and I happen to be wearing maroon, albeit a *shalwar kameez* rather than nun's robes, perhaps has fooled them.

The air is still and stifling during the day, but the golden afternoons cool quickly at this altitude, well over 10,000 feet. More apricots hang in heavy, sensuous saffron clusters against deep green leaves. The nuns begin to return as the narrow cobalt sky above the valley fades to palest blue, then luminescent white before darkening again to the blackness of the earth's shadow.

Sonam Tsang-mo, one of the younger nuns, speaks some Urdu so we converse in a mixture of Urdu and Ladakhi, and she helps me with my pronunciation. She has been a *chomo* for three years, she tells me. It is the custom for the fifth daughter to become a nun, just as younger sons generally became monks. Sonam is content to follow the custom, and is happy with her life. In the falling dusk, she lights an oil lamp and proudly shows me a book that an American woman who had stayed for a month in the nunnery had sent her from Seattle. It is a beautiful book, full of color-saturated photos of urban beauty, night views and waterfront scenes, strangely alien in this timeless setting.

"A letter came with it," says Sonam. She pulls out a thin sheet of air mail paper, which looks so fragile in this vast landscape. "Can you tell me what it says?"

The letter is full of simple, elegant thanks in English. The sender wants to share what her home looks like. I translate this into Urdu as best I can, and Sonam's beautiful face, her cheekbones emphasized by her close-cropped hair, begins to glow with delight.

When it is full dark, she leads me inside one of the adobe rooms around the courtyard, to the kitchen where a nun is churning the butter tea which is a staple in Tibetan cultures. The liquid is in a wooden pail, churned with a stick attached to a pillar. A stout thong is wrapped around the churning stick several times. Each time the nun pulls it with her strong arms, she is propelled back by its rebound. She sings as she works, pausing occasionally to put her head down for a moment of rest. I watch in fascination, thinking of the generations which have drunk yak butter tea. Then she reaches for a packet I haven't noticed before—Amul butter, one of the best known brands of pre-packaged butter in India.

We sleep outside under the stars in the dusty courtyard. I am awakened at dawn by the sound of the nuns chanting their prayers. The old nun assumes her accustomed place, and softly chants as she spins a prayer wheel made of a discarded tin of cooking oil pasted over with pictures of pink lotuses. It tinkles softly as it hits small bells with each revolution, and the grey kitten mews impatiently for its breakfast. Inside the battered tin are the same prayers that stuff elaborate, hand-held silver and turquoise prayer wheels, and the huge prayer wheels found in many *gompas*. *"Om mani padme hum,"* translated as "Oh jewel in the lotus," will fly to heaven from this humble wheel as effectively as it will from wheels of precious metals encrusted with jewels.

We breakfast on butter tea with tsampa. The nuns survey my silver-lined wooden cup, which I have bought in the bazaar in Leh, approvingly. It is good etiquette for the traveller to carry his or her own tea-bowl, which is kept in the robes and produced whenever tea is served. A handful of tsampa is tossed into my cup, and I carefully imitate the nuns as they sip the steaming tea, then knead the tsampa into lumps which they eat with their hands.

I am glad that I like butter tea, the bane of most Western travellers to Tibetan cultures. The secret seems to be to drink it while it's hot, and think of it in terms of consome rather than tea. Many travellers have been unpleasantly surprised by the brown, milky-looking tea, expecting oversweetened Indian milk tea and receiving a shock from which their taste buds never quite recover. The tea is strong, oily, slightly salty, and very fortifying in the cold season. Tsampa I find rather tasteless, but reasonably nutritious.

After breakfast, I rinse out my tea-bowl and head up the valley to Ridzong Gompa, as the monastery is known, before the blasting midday heat sets in. The *gompa* is not old as *gompas* go, only a little over a hundred years old, but it is built in traditional Tibetan style. The monastery consists of a stack of whitewashed cubes with dramatically sloping walls, few openings in the lower floors, larger windows and balconies on the upper floors, and faded valances waving softly in the breeze. Brick red trim beneath the roof lines indicates that this is a monastery, and cobalt blue trim around the windows echoes the sky.

From a distance, there is not a sign of life. The blinding white of the buildings contrasts alarmingly with the intense sky, several shades bluer than it ever gets at sea level. Spindly poles extend from the corners of some of the buildings, and something golden gleams in the harsh sun. Only when I get closer and stop to take a picture with a telephoto lens do I realize that they are grinning skulls. I am chilled for a moment, then remember that Buddhist iconography reminds us that all life is transient.

I pass through a rectangular opening that leads under a *chorten,* as stupas are known in Tibet, and continue, still panting with exertion at this unaccustomed altitude, up the steep, uneven steps that lead to the temple portion of the *gompa.* I hear the basso profundo chanting of monks, punctuated by the clash of cymbals, the shriek of horns, the ringing of bells and the beating of drums that will frighten away all unwelcome spirits.

I approach quietly, and with reverence. A monk gestures for me to sit in a corner, where a local man is already sitting. I find a place on the worn piliows, and put my cup on the low table in front of me, knowing that I will be given butter tea when the monks are served.

The *puja,* or worship, goes on for hours. A couple of the younger monks get bored and fidget restlessly in the heat. One looks at his wristwatch frequently; a devastatingly handsome one gazes at me now and then. I have plenty of time to examine the painted silk *thankas* hanging from the ceiling, and the wall frescoes of deities and demons sitting on wispy clouds, their countenances benign or fierce. Tibetan bookshelves, actually a series of nooks, line the walls. In these are kept the flat, looseleaf books of Tibetan script bound between wooden boards and wrapped in siik brocade. I wonder what treasures reside here and in other monasteries in Ladakh and in Nepal; in Tibet, so much material culture has been lost in the years of Chinese occupation that much of what is valuable has been preserved outside the country.

When the *puja* is over, I reverentiy lay my *kata,* a filmy white cheesecloth prayer scarf, before the golden Buddha. The monks are happy that I respect their faith, and turn curious eyes toward me. I am learning that one of the most appealing things about Ladakh is its religious harmony. The population includes a large percentage of Muslims, and a few hundred Moravian Christians. All the major religious holidays are celebrated by everyone. At Losar, the Tibetan Buddhist New Year, Muslims and Christians take *kata*-wrapped gifts to their Buddhist neighbors, and the Buddhists do the same on Christmas, and the Muslim festival of Eid-e-Ramazan.

Lunch is being served in the dining hall nearby, and I am invited with a gesture to remain. The fare is better here than at the nunnery. We dine on rice and shredded carrots, bread, tsampa, soup, yogurt, juicy apricots, and a sweet mixture of sugar, flour, and oil. In between the courses, which are served by young monks, the monks chant. I wait until everyone else starts eating, and notice that they eat in silence. The boy monks struggle with huge brass and copper kettles almost as big as themselves. They pour out steaming tea, trying to be serious, but always on the edge of a smile.

After lunch, most of the monks disappear to their individual cells until the afternoon *puja.* A middle-aged monk with an inquisitive face, who speaks a few words of Urdu, shows me around the temple. He pulls back the curtains of a tent to reveal an exquisite mandala, a complicated form based on the circle which Tibetan Buddhists use for meditation. It is made of colored powders, ground-up minerals in brilliant blues, yellows, reds, and oranges. I remember, several years ago, watching for hours as monks painstakingly created a similar mandala, ever so gently tapping a metal tube to get just the right amount of orange powder to make the tiger's stripes. It took four monks twelve days to make this one, this monk tells me, and they will keep it for nine months. Then it will be destroyed, as all things must be destroyed in time.

Leh seems like a major metropolitan center after the peace of Ridzong and Julichan. It is indeed a boomtown, a city newly ugly, with concrete block and tin-roofed complexes arising outside the old town in a blight of military suburbia and tattered billboards. Gaudy Hindi film-hoardings in dayglow colors plaster adobe walls in narrow alleys, and diesel-belching buses and trucks lurch down the main road, churning up dust.

The central bazaar is festooned with what I at first take to be turquoise prayer flags, gaily strung across the road. But my heart sinks when I see that the paper pennants are imprinted with the name of Amul butter, and all the shops are eagerly offering discount coupons with a picture of a Jersey cow in a green English field.

I am relieved to get out of the town to Sonam Tashi's guesthouse in an outlying village. I thread my way through the irrigation channels and the wandering paths until I come to the walled garden full of bright yellow sunflowers and green herbs. Thubstan, the daughter of the house, greets me as I climb the stairs into the kitchen. The young nun laughs a little as she shyly speaks a few words of English. Her mother, whom everyone calls *Ama-le,* comes in from outside and offers me butter tea and bread that was baked that morning, along with apricot jam. The grandmother of the house comes up the stairs, bobbing the youngest baby of the house, and grinning to see me.

"Julay, julay," they each call as they come in, and I return their greeting.

Angchuk, *Ama-le's* grown son, comes in a little later. He speaks good English, and tells me that Althea and Richard are still in Leh, and that my friend Helena Norberg-Hodge who founded the Ladakh Ecological Development Group, LEDeG, is back from Kathmandu. Angchuk works with the group, and is learning how to make ram pumps that use the force of flowing water to pump water uphill. He promises to take me to Helena's house, in another village still further out of Leh, the next morning.

I am overjoyed to be reunited with Althea and Richard that evening. After travelling up to Ladakh on the bus, we had spent some time together in Leh before setting off on our separate journeys. We had all ended up based at Sonam Tashi's, which has the family atmosphere we love. Guests are accepted as family members, whether we are from America, England, France, or New Zealand. Sonam and his wife easily share tasks. They bake bread together in the morning, or one peels carrots while the other begins the meal. Sonam is as likely to pick up the baby if she's crying as *Ama-le* is.

The food, too, is delicious. Althea and Richard love butter tea as much as Ladakhis and Tibetans do, and will drink it at all hours. *Ama-le* obliges them, making a thermos-full in the morning. Guests are left on their own for lunch, but we've solved that by making yogurt and vegetable salads, or yogurt and fruit salads, and occasionally stopping by the Tibetan Corner, a tiny cafe in Leh run by a cheerful Tibetan refugee woman, for rice pudding with cinnamon.

Dinners are fairly traditional–*thukpa*, a noodle soup, or vegetables delicately spiced and seasoned with fresh coriander. We help Angchuk with his advanced English, and Thubstan with her simple English. We sit by lanternlight, and drink tea into the night. There is always lots of laughter, and the guests join in, whether we understand the joke or not.

Angchuk shows me the way to Sankar village, where Helena and her partner John Page have rented spacious quarters on the upper level of a Ladakhi house. I have met Helena once before, at UCLA when we were both lecturing as part of the "Silk Road and the Diamond Path" exhibition, I on Afghanistan and she on appropriate technology in Ladakh. I had been impressed by her project and had promised to visit her in Ladakh.

"I told you I'd make it here," I greet her.

"I'm glad you did. I heard from some of the volunteers that you were around."

Over tea, Helena brings me up to date on her project. She is a remarkable woman, single-minded in her dedication to preventing her adopted homeland from being over-run by conventional development, while at the same time demonstrating a viable alternative for developing societies in the Third World. Her heritage is multi-lingual–Swedish, German, and English–and she speaks several other languages, including fluent Ladakhi. She and a Ladakhi colleague have completed the first Ladakhi-English dictionary. She moves easily between languages, chatting in German, Swedish, or French to visitors, explaining something to me in English, and suddenly breaking off to call to the *Ama-le* of her household in Ladakhi. When she speaks Ladakhi, the timbre of her voice changes, and her face takes on a different appearance. She is too tall for a Ladakhi, too fair-skinned and round-faced, and her eyes are blue, but in her *pumet,* as the wraparound sleeveless Tibetan dresses are called in Ladakh, with her long straight hair, she is often mistaken by Ladakhis who don't know her for an educated Ladakhi returned from Kashmir or India.

"People never felt they were poor before," Helena explains to me. "When I first came here nine years ago, as a linguist for a German film crew, there weren't tourists here, and there wasn't much of an army presence. Now, since they started allowing tourism, some 13,000 tourists a year pass through Leh, which only has a population of 6,000. The average tourist, the well-off Americans and Europeans on tours, spends what in the Ladakhi economy is the equivalent of $200,000 a day. It would be as if a visitor from Mars came to New York and spent that much. How would people feel?

"People here always felt they were rich if they had enough to eat. The population was small, partly because about 25% of the people became celibate nuns and monks. Also, polyandry used to be more common. A woman might marry more than one man, usually brothers. Ladakhis are incredibly tolerant, and polyandry, polygamy, and monogamy used to exist side by side. It was the individual's choice.

"But things are changing now. The population is going up, kerosene and coal are being imported from India, and the Ladakhi economy is being changed from an independent economy to one that is more and more linked to the outside world. *Ama-le* doesn't have time to make butter for the butter tea any more; now she goes to the bazaar and sells vegetables to the Army so she can buy Amul butter."

But Helena has a passionate vision. She knows there is no way to return to the perfectly balanced past where everything was recycled, and nothing was ever thrown away. But she believes Ladakh can skip the stage of industrial pollution, conspicuous consumption, and waste, and move on to the post-industrial era.

"We want to show the Ladakhis that the most modern way of thinking in the West is not to over-consume, but to build a sustainable society. They have beautiful architecture, with thick walls that provide insulation, and rooftops to use in summer, and big windows to catch the winter sun. But now the well-off want to live in concrete block houses. That's why one of our members, a monk named Gelong Thubstan Paldan, has written a play called 'Ladakh: Look Before You Leap' to demonstrate these ideas.

"It's about a young man whose family sends him to college in Kashmir. He comes back to Ladakh smoking cigarettes, and wanting to eat only white bread and have flush toilets. When his grandfather gets ill, he of course doesn't want him to go to the *amchi,* the traditional doctor. So he takes him to a Western-educated Ladakhi doctor. But this doctor, who was educated in America, tells the young man that in America only the poor people eat white bread, live in concrete houses, and wear polyester. The rich people want big adobe houses, eat whole wheat bread and organic vegetables, and wear natural fabrics!"

Helena has transformed her grim observations of change into

action. She and LEDeG have been able to offer some real alternatives, such as the ram pump Angchuk has learned to build, and the Trombe wall, an elegantly simple solution to the problem of winter heating.

Helena admits that she has spent only one winter in her adopted land. "My Ladakhi friends often tease me," she says. "They always beg me to stay for the winter. But it gets so cold that the tea freezes in the cup ten feet away from the fire." She now spends her winters lecturing and raising funds for LEDeG in Europe and America.

But that one miserable winter gave her fodder for thought. Traditional Ladakhi life was indeed harmonious, and pleasant and peaceful for much of the year. But in the winter people suffered from the cold, and the smoke from cooking fires gave them eye and respiratory ailments. People didn't wash much in the cold season, so hygiene standards also dropped, breeding illness.

The Trombe wall uses the sun to heat a room. An existing south-facing wall is painted black, and vents are cut into it. Double-glazing in a frame is installed over the wall. The principle is simple—during the day, the sun's rays shining on the black wall are absorbed, and trapped heat rises and enters the house through the upper vents. As it cools, it sinks and recirculates through the lower vents to be heated again. At night, the Trombe wall radiates heat steadily into the room. The entire cost is about the same as a *dzo,* a yak-cow hybrid used as a draft animal in Ladakh. Savings on heating fuel will make up the homeowner's investment in just two years.

In the following days, I accompany Helena on her rounds, and learn more about her work. Trombe walls, I find, do alter the traditional architecture, but the owners are thrilled with them. During the winter, they keep the room temperature well within the comfort range for Ladakhis, with no supplementary heating.

Ladakh, explains Helena, is one of the best places in the world for solar energy. It has an average of 300 sunny days each year, and gets less rainfall than the Sahara. Near the junction of the Karakoram and Himalayan ranges, it is a high altitude desert in the rainshadow of the high mountains.

The former Deputy Commissioner, a Ladakhi supporter of LEDeG, has just offered the group land in a prime section of Leh. The volunteers are building a structure which will demonstrate several types of appropriate technology, and serve as a library, gathering place, and restaurant.

Under Helena's tutelage, I learn much about the richness of Ladakhi culture. She helps me with the language, and though I still have a limited vocabulary, I get the right intonation down well. As I accompany her, she sadly points out jarring technological anachronisms, like the monks at the Sankar festival who use a PA system that doesn't even work properly, just because it is "modern," or the boys in the bazaar who are perfectly capable of adding in their heads, but use a calculator to impress their friends.

In few societies, perhaps, is change so apparent, and in yet fewer are the choices so clear. As the years go by, the billboards and tourists, ugly buildings and Amul butter will increase; but at the same time the Ladakhi philosophy of living in harmony with nature will transform and grow with the times, and the Trombe walls and solar cookers will quietly, unostentatiously grow in number.

Helena and her friends and supporters, Ladakhi and foreign, are idealists, but not Don Quixotes. They don't tilt at windmills, but create alternatives. It hasn't been easy, she confides. There are times when she has despaired. But her friend Tashi Rabgyas, Ladakh's most distinguished scholar, once said to her, with characteristic Buddhist equanimity, "Let your work grow slowly, like a tree, a little from year to year. Not like some machine which starts up with a big bang."

The days are growing shorter, and the harvest is underway. In the fields, men and women dressed in long-sleeved, wraparound garments tied with magenta sashes work together, singing in rising and falling antiphonies, calling the rhythms of scythes and hands. The golden barley that has been waving in the breeze is now cut down to feed another season. It is bundled in stacks that echo the mounds of *chortens,* and beyond, the shapes of the high purple and ochre mountains. It is threshed by teams of *dzo,* and winnowed in the morning breeze, producing showers of golden chaff.

There is a chill in the morning, but the days are warm, and the harvesters take breaks, inviting passers-by to join them for butter tea, tsampa, and the Tibetan barley beer known as *chang.*

Winter is not far off. Clouds climb the sky like angels on a ladder, and one morning I wake up to find the nearby mountains dusted with snow, which whispers elegant threats.

There are no more winter festivals. Now they are held in autumn, before all the tourists are gone. The Ladakhis are left to get through the long nights and short, dark days of frost and paralyzing cold by telling stories before the fires in their black cast iron stoves studded with turquoise and coral.

The Thiksey Festival is one of the biggest and most elaborate of the former winter festivals. I go with Marie-Claude Bonnet, a charming Frenchwoman who is as constantly cheerful as a Ladakhi. The bus stand is chaotic—people are crammed inside the bus and on the roof. The Ladakhis are taking it all good-naturedly. The men wear fine new purple brocade tophats with half-brims that turn up at the sides. The women wear long earrings made of seed pearls, and necklaces of coral and turquoise. A few wealthy ones sport heirloom headdresses covered with valuable turquoise, and gold relic boxes around their necks.

It is the foreign tourists who are rude and angry. The Ladakhis are pilgrims, but we foreigners just want to get there and see a spectacle. Marie-Claude steps onto the bus and pulls me up, just as a German shoves me and starts screaming at me to get off the steps and into the bus. There is nowhere for me to go, and anger rises from the pit of my stomach. I have a momentary desire to push him to the depths of hell, and hiss curses in English and Farsi. But Marie-Claude merely squeezes in further against someone else, and pulls me up after her.

"I think I won't go," I tell her. "I don't know if I can take this."

"No, you are going to go," she says firmly. "Don't worry. Just a little while in the bus, and then we will be there and you will have a wonderful time."

She is right, as usual. Once again I have been *shon,* "easy to anger," which is the greatest insult one Ladakhi can say to another. It is said that even if someone's spouse has an affair, it is considered bad form for the wronged spouse to react with anger, which is much worse behavior than merely having an affair.

The ride is claustrophobic, but not long. The German glares at me occasionally, but some Ladakhis squeeze closer together so Marie-Claude and I can have seats. When we reach Thiksey Gompa, a line of pilgrims winds up the steep path like ants. We join them and finally reach a crowded courtyard. Marie-Claude, full of *joie de vivre,* scampers up a set of stone steps and finds spaces for us on an earthen rooftop. We don't know if it's a good space or not, but soon we are so packed in with men, women, and children of all ages that we couldn't move if we wanted to.

Somewhere in the depths of the *gompa,* a deep-throated drum beats in a slow, even rhythm. It has been going since before we arrived, and will go on after we leave, the beat of the heart of time itself. The sky is white-grey, and chill winds whip up stinging dust. The crowd presses us forward, and I am glad for the thick ledge which stops me from pitching forward.

I see Althea and Richard, who have come here from their trip to a *gompa* far up a side valley off the Indus, and Helena with her Ladakhi family and LEDeG colleagues, and *Ama-le* and Thubstan. We wave to all of them, but we can't get to them through the thick crowd.

The dances begin suddenly, and the visual spectacle takes over all else in a richness of color, form, and movement, counterpointed by the beat of drums and the reedy wail of surnai and shaums. Marie-Claude's intuition has chosen well, as the dancers enter from a door immediately to our right, and a huge painted *thanka* is unfurled on the wall above and behind us.

The monks playing the sacred instruments wear helmet-like caps, fringed with yellow on top. The masked dancers of the sacred *cham* dance appear, in groups, in singles. There are deities and demons, horrific masks with many eyes and fearsome teeth, or benign and gentle faces. One group of playful demons in black has many white skulls on the ends of their masks. This is a mystery play, whose origins are more ancient than Buddhism in this part of the world, dating from the shamanic traditions of the indigenous Bon religion of Tibet, incorporated into the Vajrayana, the Diamond Path of Tibetan Buddhism.

For two days they will dance, with swords and bells and drums, and the ten-foot long *gyaling* trumpets booming into the thin air and out over the upper Indus Valley. These sounds will echo over the thin river, whose course is lined with dark green poplars turning golden, the only color in that monochromatic landscape except for the brilliant saffron, crimson, orange, and ultramarine of the dancers' masks and silken costumes. At the end, a dancer will slice a human figure made out of bread dough, symbolically killing the ego.

Listening to the drums, and feeling the energy of this eager and reverent crowd, I see the seeds of hope scattered to the four winds. Some will fall on stony desert ground, some will fly far, and yet others will fall in the fertile fields irrigated with the wisdom of generations, and grow to bear fruit even as the apricots bud, bloom, and ripen each season to provide sustenance for the future.

25 Fighting with God?

India and Pakistan
Fall, 1983

"Think it and it's done," my Canadian friend Anne had encouraged me. So each night I visualize the things I want and pray for them to happen. I thank God fervently as my mind's eye sees each one come to pass, even the things my common sense tells me are absolutely impossible.

The practice breaks long-held patterns of negativity and fear of failure. I am cheerful and optimistic the day I go to the Pakistan Embassy in New Delhi to get a visa to return to Pakistan. I decide to follow the advice of my friend Hugh, who told me how he was treated with great courtesy when he showed his trekking book at the Embassy. He was given tea and a visa with no delay, while impressed officials gushed over the book. I smile charmingly as I present the consular official with a copy of my *National Geographic* article on the Kalash.

The thin young gentleman smiles back and looks at the article politely. "You are a journalist?"

At the sound of the word which so many governments find so nasty, I instantly realize my mistake "No, not really. This is a travel article."

"One moment please."

The official returns a few minutes later, his smile faded. "Please come this way."

''Is there a problem?"

"No problem. Our Press Minister will speak with you."

I am ushered into a plush office. The Press Minister greets me politely, then asks, "Which newspaper do you work for?"

I explain that I am freelance.

"Then it will be extremely difficult to get you clearance."

My Kafkaesque nightmare has begun. The Pakistani officials say I need a journalist's visa, but no journalist's visas are currently being granted because of demonstrations by the Movement for the Restoration of Democracy, which the Zia-ul-Haq government would prefer to conceal. But now I'm in a double bind. I can't get a tourist visa because they know I am a journalist. In a moment of passionate frustration, I show my photo of the planet Earth from the moon's surface to the Press Minister. "See, no borders!"

My photographic display does not impress him, and I am sent back to my hotel, to wait, and wait, living in the uncertainty which the East honors and the West denies.

The Western part of me is impatient. I phone the embassy at least once a day. I phone my parents to ask them to phone influential friends in Pakistan, as it is not possible to phone directiy from India.

After a few days, I am befriended by an elderly Indian Muslim couple who are temporarily living at the "Y." They offer their help: "My brother works at the Pakistan Embassy," says Mrs. Masud. "Most of my family went to Pakistan during Partition, and so they are Pakistani." I grasp eagerly at their proffered help, but to my everlasting mortification, I discover that her brother is the Press Minister. After Mrs. Masud's kind intervention, he is less annoyed with me, but still can do nothing to help me.

New Delhi begins to feel like a prison. My Indian visa is about to expire, and I can't get back to Pakistan, where I have left luggage. I feel compassion for every alien in every country, every Third World taxi driver dreaming of an American green card, every Guatemalan seeking political asylum, every Vietnamese and Haitian leaving on a leaky boat, whether fleeing persecution or longing for a better life.

After ten days, the Press Minister leans over his desk and says confidentially, "If you fly to Pakistan, you can get a 30-day visa. Normally this cannot be renewed, but you have friends. Use your influence. Good luck."

I am relieved to be in Pakistan, and glad to see Fatana, though she is in a constant state of worry because Ishaq is in Afghanistan again. One night a few weeks ago, when she was alone in the house, Kabul Radio reported falsely that Ishaq had been captured by the Communists. For two days, she tells me, she had prayed, waiting until a messenger came with word from her husband. She shows a cheerful face for her daughter, for friends and extended family, for the servants. But I see signs of stress in her usually vivacious face.

My visa remains a problem. I make a trip to Islamabad, and finally decide to play my trump card. Long ago, a flamboyant American actor and film-maker had given me a personal card to General Mujibur Rahman Khan, the Minister of Information. I had never tried to look him up, preferring to avoid too close a connection to the regime. But now I am desperate to renew my visa.

It takes many tries to get through to the General's private secretary. My hands shaking, my voice choking, I try to sound casual, confident, and sophisticated. "Yes, my friend Charles Fawcett suggested that I contact General Mujib to say hello."

To my surprise, the secretary's voice gushes, "By all means. The General will be pleased to see you. Please come at 9 a.m. tomorrow morning."

I am nervous when I walk into the office. The man behind the enormous desk is gracious, smiling, and to my great relief, unimposing.

After the usual *Salaams,* I hand him the card on which Charles had scrawled his introduction so long ago.

"Ah, you are a friend of Charles'. He is like a brother to me. We consider him a citizen of Pakistan. Where is he now?"

"The last I heard he was in London. He's been very involved in fund-raising for Afghanistan in America."

So it was all true! Charles, whom I had met in L.A. when he was editing his documentary on Afghanistan, told such amazing stories that I never quite knew what to believe. I knew that he had worked with Pakistan Television on his film, but I had never realized the high esteem in which he was held in Pakistan.

"Why didn't you come before?" asks General Mujib.

"I didn't want to bother you. Well, actually, I'd never met a general before."

"We're just like other people," he says, surprised into disarmament.

The General has a genuine kindness and desire to help. He also has the power to do so. A little matter of a visa that under normal circumstances can never be renewed is nothing to him. We drink the sweet milky tea which lubricates the Pakistani bureaucracy, and he tells me to contact his private secretary tomorrow about expediting my visa. Then we chat for awhile about Afghanistan, Charles' film, and my novel.

"Did you go in?" he asks, with a twinkle in his eye.

I laugh, knowing Pakistan's official policy of discouraging cross-border visits. "Ask me no questions, I'll tell you no lies."

"You are a brave girl," he says admiringly. "You know our official policy. But unofficially, we are glad when journalists tell the world the truth about what is happening in Afghanistan."

I continue to worry, despite the General's assurances. But magically, I am directed to return to Peshawar and work through the office of a Mr. Azim Afridi, who sits in a dim green semi-basement office from which he directs the increasing traffic of journalists come to cover the refugees officially and the war unofficially.

Mr. Azim is a thin, middle-aged Pathan who laughs a lot, drinks copious quantities of green tea, and peers over his glasses, sizing people up. He seems mischievous, and I watch as he gives some foreign journalists a hard time, and others immediate help. When I practice a few words of Pashtu on him, he warms up, and takes some time out from his work to lecture me from his considerable knowledge of Pathan culture, history, and language.

Finally he says, "I want to help you." He has decided I am sincere, and knows I don't have the financial resources that journalists and photographers working for international magazines have. "Don't worry about your visa," he says. "You are under the protection of this office. Your visa will come through us, *inshallah.* Meanwhile, I will see what we can do for you."

Azim's brainstorm is to introduce me to a newly arrived American video crew. Their government liaison will take me in a rickshaw to Green's Hotel to meet them. "We are providing transport out to the camps for them," Azim says. "We'll tell them to let you ride with them, and you can do your work."

The producer, Theonie Gilmore, is an energetic whirlwind of a woman from Oregon. She is recently widowed, and on her first visit to a Third World country. She is excited and irrepressible, with the outgoing friendliness many Americans carry abroad. She is not in the least phased by my Pakistani dress and the black *chador* I wear in public in Peshawar, but keeps chattering away—"Sure you can ride with us. What do you do? How long have you been in Pakistan?"—in a string of breathless questions which do not await answers.

One of the two camera operators is a woman. Judy Mann is quiet, watchful, and calm even as she takes in the overwhelming data of this alien culture.

"I would be glad to translate for you," I offer her. "We could probably get some good footage of women if you are interested, since you can get in where a man can't."

Theonie and Judy eagerly take up my offer, and we arrange to meet the next day.

My eye casually glances down the back page of *The Muslim,* an English-language newspaper I occasionally buy. An item catches my eye. "Two Americans Held in Rawalpindi."

Shock settles in as I recognize the names of two frlends, one of whom I know quite well. It is simply not possible. Don would never try to smuggle a kilo of heroin.

Thoughts race through my head and collide as I read and reread the short item. Impossible! I've known Don for years, first by his American name, then by his Muslim name, Noor Mohammed. I think back to his Afghan craft and clothing shop in L.A. A front for smuggling? Impossible. Noor is eccentric, yes, but no more so than I am. He wears Afghan clothes and a turban, hangs out in the old bazaar with Afghan silver merchants, and plays the stringed rebab with the sweetness of a master. But he's an innocent. He would never use heroin, let alone sell it.

I am outraged at the police. This is an obvious frameup. They are just looking for a scapegoat. In righteous anger, I want to storm the jail. But on the way home, fear and doubt begin to set in. How well do I know his friend? Noor might not do it, but his friend? But why? Nothing adds up. Even if they were going to do it, wouldn't they be smarter than to keep it in a suitcase in a cheap hotel room?

I tell Fatana about it when I get home. At first she says, "God has struck them," but when I tell her that Noor has been a friend for several years, she feels sorry for them. Everyone knows that the police are not above setting up people.

I also tell her I'm scared. I gave Noor some letters to mail to friends in India, and a photocopy of my novel. My name, and my novel, may be in the hands of the police.

Fatana is concerned, and I can see her thinking. In the evening, she comes to talk to me in my room.

"Do you think they would come to search me?" I ask.

She shrugs. "You have nothing to hide."

But we both know that as long as I am staying here, her household could be in danger. I don't want to leave, and she doesn't want me to leave. But Ishaq, who with a few phone calls to influential Pakistani friends could probably straighten everything out, is far away beyond the border.

I tell Fatana I will leave. She goes to her room to pray, and I begin to pack. I am feeling cast out, even though I know she doesn't really want me to go. I'm scared, and have no idea where to go. What hotel that I can afford will be safe? I've felt so safe with a family all this time, and I don't want to go out into the dangerous, intrigue-filled world of this frontier town full of spies, immoral narcs, drug dealers, and Communist-sponsored terrorists who plant bombs in cinemas, hotels, and restaurants.

I can't keep back my sobs anymore. I am furious at the situation, furious at the injustice, terrified that I too am about to be framed, or that Fatana will turn against me as an immoral American and I will be left to fend for myself. I am not blood family, I will never be Afghan, no matter how many years I spend here, no matter how well I speak the language, even if I someday marry an Afghan. And what Fatana doesn't know is that I've changed too much to ever again be truly American either.

She hears me crying and opens the door. As I hit the bed in fury, she grabs my fist. "Who are you fighting with? Are you fighting with God?" Her words stun me into numb calmness.

"No, no, I don't mean to fight with God," I say quietly.

"Then you must have faith. Everything will be better. I do not want you to leave. Stay until you find a safe place. I will ask the Mujahedeen to help you. Wherever you go, you will be safe, you are under our protection. I will loan you money if you need it. And you will come to visit us every night for dinner, any time. As soon as Ishaq comes home, *inshallah,* then we will see what to do."

It is my first day of work with the video crew, and I feel honorbound to tell them about my friends' arrest, in case I might somehow taint their work. No one seems very worried, least of all Theonie. She sits me down, and in a calm voice, gives me a lesson in "focusing" that leaves me even more confused.

Judy takes me under her wing, quietly, gently. She is a real professional, though new to this part of the world. She is compassionate toward the Afghans and interested in the Pakistanis. She enjoys the view of hordes of handsome men in silk turbans and luxuriant moustaches, and has a good sense of humor. In the car on the way to the camp, someone in the crew asks about prostitution in Pakistan.

"Well, Peshawar is pretty conservative," I reply, "but in Lahore..."

Judy bursts into a laugh, I get the pun, and I know I've got an ally. By the end of the day, Judy has convinced Theonie to pay my room and board at Green's Hotel while they are in town for the next ten days. I will work with them everyday, taking continuity notes and translating in the women's quarters, where their Americanized Afghan male director cannot go.

Fatana is sad to see me leave the house, but I sense she is also relieved. I take only one small bag, as I want to leave a presence in her house. I grow more paranoid everyday, and check the drawers and closets of my hotel room as soon as I come in, and keep my bag locked. I wonder what I would do if I did find a packet of some white powdery substance?

The long working days and the anxious nights blend into one another. I am glad to be working hard as a translator, though I have the feeling that the director is not always pleased to have me around. Despite his Afghan background, he seems uncomfortable in this culture—he wears a *shalwar kameez* for one day, then switches back to jeans and a flannel shirt. Judy adapts well, opting for a loose earth-toned man's *shalwar kameez,* but topping her blond hair with a shocking pink *dupata,* leaving no doubt that she is a woman.

We go to many camps, and the squalor of even the showplace camps is more widespread than I had realized. Wherever we go, the refugees are friendly, and follow us in crowds of mostly men and children. When I speak Farsi, I am often asked if I am Afghan. I tell them I am American, and one man says ingenuously, "Yes, there is another American here who speaks Farsi. That man in the jeans over there." I don't tell our director that they think he is American, but share the joke with Judy.

Two brash teen-age girls take Judy, Theonie, and me by the hand and pull us into their mud-walled compound. We are surrounded by a sea of women from the extended family and the neighborhood. They clear a place of honor for us on a string bed, and immediately bring us tea and sweet yellow cakes. While the two ringleaders stroke our hair and jewelry, Theonie speaks to them in English, and I translate as quickly as I can.

Most in the group are Pashtu-speaking, but the two teenage girls and a few others speak some Dari. We ask them if they will agree to be videotaped, but at first they are scared. "We are afraid of the mullahs," says one middle-aged woman in a strident voice. "In Afghanistan it was not like this. Here they tell us what to do, because the Pakistani goverment has made them powerful."

Many of the group filter away, afraid of the consequences if the mullahs discover that cameras are here, even cameras wielded by women. But a few stay, and the two teen-age girls decide that the fun of being taped is worth the risk.

Theonie's goal is to find out how and if Afghan culture is being preserved in the camps. She is a new convert to this cause, having only recently heard that this is the largest refugee situation in the world today. The fact haunted her, and shortly afterwards she dreamed of Mahatma Gandhi, who told her to make a documentary on Afghan refugees. Theonie gave way to her impulses. She refinanced her house, found a director and two camera operators, Judy and a young Englishman named Chris Thomerson, and headed for Pakistan.

I ask the questions Theonie wants to ask, about music, weddings, and songs. One girl becomes angry—the weddings were good in Afghanistan, she says, but here in the camps they are nothing. No one dances, there are not many songs. When we ask the girls to sing, they sing a song of the Jehad, sad but defiant. This is a generation growing up in anger, cut from their roots. Judy will later give the documentary its fitting title, *A Nation Uprooted.*

One day, we are taken to the Widows Camp at Nasir Bagh outside Peshawar, where a thin, elderly, henna-haired woman agrees to talk to us. It is arranged for several men, relatives of some of the widows and orphans, to carry in our heavy equipment, since our director and cameraman can't enter the compound.

The camp's *de facto* spokeswoman is named Noor Jehan. Her name means "Light of the World," and was also the name of the empress for whom Shalimar Gardens were built. This Noor Jehan is no beauty, but she is a flame. She has a riveting presence in front of the camera. I stand behind Judy and ask Noor Jehan questions. She looks me straight in the eye and answers, breaking off to fiercely hush an interrupting child. Her story grows in passion as she tells it; her figure seems to grow as her eyes gaze off into a distant vision of future freedom, not only for Afghanistan, but for the women of the country.

"We had houses, farms, good things..." she tells us, "...and now we have nothing. We came barefoot, through bombings. Our homes were destroyed, our husbands killed, and here we are in this desert."

My throat is beginning to choke with tears, and Theonie is already quietly crying, even though she doesn't understand a word.

I ask Noor Jehan if she knows any songs. She tosses her head and says, "I will sing a song I made up myself, from the burning pain of my heart, the burning pain of widows and martyrs."

She launches into a Pashtu song, and tears begin to course down her face as she sings. By the end, all the surrounding women and children are crying along with us.

Noor Jehan leads the compound in a prayer for freedom. "If God wills," she begins, "the moment we hear that our country is free, we will run barefoot to our homes."

And then we pray together, for victory, for freedom.

When we finish and put away our equipment, the women cling to us. A small girl gives Judy a silver-colored bracelet engraved with verses from the Quran, and Judy spontaneously takes off her silver earrings and gives them to the girl. Noor Jehan cannot stop embracing me, kissing me, calling me her daughter. I ask if there is anything we can do for her. She refuses proudly, then whispers, "The next time you come, please, if you could bring me a sewing machine so I can make clothes for the children."

In the midst of this daily push and pull of passionate emotion, Althea and Richard arrive from India. I am overjoyed to see "old friends," forgetting that I have known them but a short time. I am eager to show them my city, and immediately take Althea to the bazaar to buy a proper *shalwar kameez.*

I am beginning to feel at home in Green's Hotel, though the crew will be leaving soon, and then I don't know where I will go. There has been no fallout from the arrest of my two American friends, no questions asked at the Gailani house. But at the American Consulate, officials have discouraged me from visiting my friends, and strongly implied that they think the two are guilty. I am more confused than ever, ashamed of my cowardice, but truly afraid.

The day the crew is leaving, an American professor introduces us to an Afghan musician, a flute-player. It is arranged that he will meet us in the lobby of Green's. What does he look like? "You'll know him. He has presence," the professor says.

A tall, dignified man with shoulder length black hair, intense eyes, a hawk nose, and a Rasputin beard stands in the lobby. There is no question that this is Azim, the legendary flute-player. We videotape him in a hotel room, as he plays his heart out on the homemade wooden flute in cheerful Afghan folk tunes that sing of love, bubbling brooks, and the skirts of the mountains. Azim is gentle, passionate, and deferential. He is delighted that I speak Farsi, and calls me his countrywoman and his sister. Like Noor Jehan, he has great charisma, and I know that he will add vision to our documentary. In him lives the music of Afghanistan, the wildness of the mountains, and the pride of the Afghan people. As long as Azim lives and plays his magic flute, no one can ever destroy the culture of Afghanistan.

I am sad that the crew is leaving. I've come to think of this documentary as "ours," but now I have to let it go into other hands. But when I hug Judy good-bye, she says, "I have a feeling you and I are going to end up finishing this tape."

"Inshallah," I answer, remembering to honor uncertainty.

With the crew gone, my meal ticket has expired. I move out of Green's Hotel, down the bazaar to the International Hotel. It is much cheaper, with good reason. I become obsessive about checking my luggage to make sure no one has planted any drugs. The hotel, though it has hot water and an attached bathroom, is decidedly sleazy. The manager, a slick, imitation-leather jacketed young man, spends all his time smoking cigarettes with his cronies and listening to cassettes of Hindi film music, which echo up the stairs till the early hours of the morning.

My visa extension remains unconfirmed, but Mr. Azim at the Press Information office is unworried. I call on him from time to time, and he seems to enjoy our chats about traditional Pashtun culture, Afghan politics, and Islam.

I also spend time with Althea and Richard, who are recovering from bad colds they got in India. I take Althea to lunch at Fatana's one day and another day Althea, Richard, and I go to Kachagari Camp to visit a family from Mazare Sharif whom I had met while we were making the documentary. Althea comes inside with me to meet my young friend Nadia and her mother Hanifa, while Richard is relegated to the guest house at the entrance to the mud-walled compound. Always a good sport, Richard spends his time communicating in sign language to the mystified men of the house, who don't speak a word of English. We are all treated to a lavish feast by Qazi Aminullah, who had been a judge in his native land, and now lives behind simple mud walls like any other refugee.

Hanifa, a beautiful and chaste woman who is much younger than her husband, was a teacher in Afghanistan. She speaks just a little English, shyly, and relies on me to translate the rest of the conversation to Althea. Aithea has brought gifts—peach-colored yarn for Nadia, who loves to knit, and crayons, pencils, and papers for her four younger brothers. We've also brought a bag of oranges and bananas, a real treat in a refugee camp. Nadia fondly caresses the yarn, talking of the clothes she will make for her baby sister, now in Hanifa's arms. She is thirteen, and goes to the

Naheed Shaheed School for girls, run by the more moderate Mujahedeen alliance, which supports education for women. But it is only a matter of time before she will have to quit school and stay at home to help care for the baby.

Qazi is frustrated with his lack of employment. He wants a job, he tells us, but he wants it to be of service to the Afghan people. And Hanifa wants to teach. If Nadia has to quit school, still she will be able to learn at home from Hanifa. But he is an educated man, and an educated man should be working for his people. Is there any way we can help?

Sometimes it seems there is so little we can do. A bag of fruit, a few books and pencils, is like giving a meal to a homeless man or woman in an American city, just a temporary Band-Aid. It doesn't change anyone's lives, but allows them to survive another day in the hopes that maybe circumstances will change, or they themselves can change their circumstances. I ache to tell the world the story of these refugees, and the story of the heroic Afghans in Kunar, but up till now I still have not been able to get anything published. I comfort myself with the thought that Judy will finish the documentary, with or without my help.

In the evening, I go back to Althea's and Richard's hotel, which is even worse than mine. It is now called the Green Star, but I remember it as the Old Green's, where I had stayed the first time I was in Peshawar. It is now four years dirtier and more decayed.

We are having tea when there is a knock at the door. I open it, expecting the hotel servant come to pick up the tea tray. A nervous young man, handsome in a sleazy sort of way, pushes his way into the room.

"Hello, I am a student of Khyber Medical College. I am heroin addicted, and I was wondering where I can buy some heroin."

Richard is articulately outraged in the polite way only the British can be outraged. "We don't use the stuff, and we don't know where to get it. We didn't ask you in here, so please get out."

The man doesn't move, but repeats his speech.

"I told you we don't use the stuff. Now get out of here!" Richard shouts, drawing himself up to his full imposing height.

The "student" retreats at once, slamming the door hard behind him. I immediately bolt it.

Althea is inclined to ignore the incident, but Richard is fuming. "I'm going to speak to the manager. They should keep people like that out."

There is a commotion outside, shouting in Pashtu, the sound of footsteps running down the stairs. Richard flings open the door to find the besieged manager trying to assuage two other foreigners, while excitedly talking to two tall, thin, sour-faced Pakistanis.

The sour-faced men stride off on what appears to be a purposeful investigation of some sort. The manager turns to us and whispers, "They are from Special Branch. They live upstairs. No one is supposed to know. They are looking for people selling heroin. That man was bothering a foreigner, a German, at the bus station today. He is a well-known heroin addict, and they have gone after him. I am very, very sorry for your trouble."

Richard accompanies me downstairs. My hotel is not far away, but I am now afraid to walk alone. Richard is not too well, so I decide to take a rickshaw. The only one we find wants such an outrageous fare that I refuse. I am still cursing at the driver when the two narcs arrive, screeching to a halt on a motorcycle.

"We have pursued the culprit, but were unable to find him," the leader announces. Then, "What is the problem?"

"I can't find an honest rickshaw driver. Will you please accompany me to my hotel, as my friend is too ill to be out in the night air?"

The two men offer me a ride on the back of the motorcycle, but I point out that it would be most improper.

Disarmed by my Pakistani dress and my covered head, they agree to accompany me on foot. On the way, I ask them a few questions. "What is your work?"

"I am a student at Khyber University," one volunteers.

Knowing he is lying, I decide to play a little more. "Oh really? What department?"

"Uh, literature."

"Oh, I have many friends who teach there. Who is your professor?"

He changes the subject quickly, and I smile inwardly, bidding them a cheerful and short good-bye as soon as we reach the hotel.

After this incident, I am even more frightened of being framed. On a trip to Islamabad, I have been told by a consular official that I should not visit Noor in prison. The official is decidedly snappish and rude, ready to tar me with the same brush that has already smeared my friends. He half listens to me explain that they have a copy of my novel, and I am worried about what the police will think of a story about going into Afghanistan. "All I can say is that if they are guilty, they certainly aren't really any kind of Muslim," he says, by way of dismissing me.

I hand him an English-language copy of the Quran and a *tasbeh,* a

Muslim rosary. "Please tell them Rabia sent these," I say, hoping to let them know I have not forgotten them. Only months later, after Noor and his friend have been released with a government apology, will I find out that instead of conveying my concern, this official had said I accused them of trying to publish my novel!

I feel a little safer knowing that I have the patronage of people like General Mujib, but I also know that he doesn't know me well. Just when I feel I can't stand this situation any more, a few miracles happen. My visa is extended, I am invited to visit friends in Hong Kong, and Abid Zareef Khan, an old friend of mine, rescues me from the International Hotel.

Abid is also an old family friend of Ishaq's and Fatana's. He and Ishaq have been comrades in arms in Afghanistan, and have written in the Quran that they are brothers. Abid has been into Afghanistan a number of times, unbeknownst to his protective and loving mother, as a Mujaheed, a medic, and a journalist. Now he is working for the UN High Commission for Refugees.

"Pack your bags," he says, "My parents have invited you to stay with us. I just finished my exams, and went to see if Ishaq was back from Paktia. Fatana told me you are in some trouble, and asked me to help you."

My tall bearded friend is suddenly a white knight. I am warmly welcomed by his father, an elderly doctor who still practices at the age of 80-odd, and his kind and solicitous mother. I am so relieved to be in a home again, safe from overzealous narcotics agents, that I don't even notice the din of traffic outside the walled compound of the rambling house.

I tell Abid all about the documentary, ending with the story of Azim the flute-player.

"Ah, Azim is a good friend of mine. He's a great guy. I used to go with Ishaq's brother Ismail and another friend, Aziz, to listen to Azim. Azim is living with Aziz now. Aziz is the one they used to call Aziz International because he lived in the International Hotel and used to forge passports and visas for Afghans."

I suddenly realize that the famous "Aziz International" is Parwez's good friend, whom I had known in Kabul in what seems another lifetime.

Abid immediately takes me to meet Aziz, whom he has just seen at another friend's. Aziz zooms up on a motorcycle, looking much older than the few years that have passed would warrant. I know that he was in the Kabul underground before he turned his artistic talents to forgery, and that he was briefly in prison. It is evident that he is far from the carefree student I had met.

Aziz cannot believe his eyes, or ears, for when I knew him in Kabul I was just learning a few words of Farsi . He is eager to entertain us, and proposes to set up a musical evening with Azim that night. Abid and I pick up Althea and Richard, who are thrilled to be invited, and drive out towards the Khyber Pass. The dark and silent streets, virtually deserted at 9 p.m. though there is no official curfew, remind me that we are still in a country ruled by martial law. Abid turns off the main road into a narrow alley leading between high-walled compounds. A servant who recognizes him opens a steel gate, and we are admitted into the home of a wealthy businessman, probably a smuggler of some sort.

Azim is glad to see me. He is at the same time shy and full of laughter, charm, and charisma. He teases, but respectfully calls me "sister." Aziz has told him the story of how we met in Kabul years before.

I am glad to see Azim in his element, as he had looked so awkward when I had last seen him, at a party of wealthy Pakistanis where he was the hired flute. During the dinner, he had been uneasy, uncertainly fiddling with a knife and fork. Though he was the son of a general, he came from a traditional family and was uncomfortable with the formal manners of elite Pakistanis, who eat their buffet dinners standing up, balancing their plates and utensils.

We dine on kebab wrapped in *nan,* just as I had so many times in Kabul. We wash our meal down with light aromatic tea. Aziz and I reminisce. I recall every detail of the day we had spent with Annick and Parwez at Paghman. Aziz marvels as I describe the purple and yellow garlands, and the *ashak* lunch we had had back at the restaurant.

"You have such a memory! I had one, but it has been destroyed by the war."

I ask him about Chukria, the beautiful girlfriend he had hoped to marry.

He shakes his head sadly. "Her family were Communists. They took her to Moscow, and wouldn't let her write to me. I didn't know where she was. I got one letter, then I never heard again. She was a good Muslim girl, but her father was a Communist."

It is another story to add to the annals of this tragic war that goes on and on. The heavy mood is broken when Azim picks up his magic flute, touches it to his lips, and begins to play a sweet, cheerful tune that invokes images of mountain meadows filled with wildflowers. The tabla player quietly begins to tap his drums, and together they move through a repetoire of tunes, shamelessly manipulating our emotions between light-heartedness, joy, and aching sadness as the notes of his flute fly up and down the scale of the heart.

But this talented and handsome young man is a *charassi,* a hash-smoker. In between songs, he rolls cigarettes and smokes them through his hand, but he soon notices that I will not look him in the eye while he is doing it.

"Oh, sister, you don't like me to smoke this *charass.*"

"It is not good for your health. You are such a wonderful musician, I worry for you, my brother."

He looks abashed, but it does not stop him. "All my life I have smoked it. I can't play unless I smoke."

"That's what musicians say in America too. But I know you could play anyway."

He begins to spout spontaneous Pashtu poetry, which Althea, Richard, and I don't understand. But we enjoy the raucous laughter the poems engender, and we laugh too, enjoying a respite from fear, from war, from stories of grief and tragedy.

26 Year of the White Hyacinths

"If you have only one coin, take half and buy bread;
with the other half buy white hyacinths."
–Saadi

American Interlude
Summer, 1984

"Deb! It's *National Geographic* on the phone!" my mother shouts.

I hurry to the phone, heart pounding. Good news always comes to writers in a phone call; if it's a letter, you know it's either a form letter or a polite but firm rejection.

"Hello, Debra, this is Charles McCarry," booms the voice of the editor who deals with free lance writers.

After minimal pleasantries, he gets to the point: "How would you like to go to Afghanistan for us?"

Without hesitation, I say yes to a trip to Nuristan and Panjsher. Steve McCurry will again be my photographer. It is settled that we will leave in April, and I rush out to buy a new pair of hiking boots.

By now I am accustomed to secrecy. To friends I casually mention another trip to Pakistan. To Judy Mann, who has indeed become my partner in producing the documentary we worked on in Peshawar last winter, I tell the truth. We have done all our pre-editing, we have a script, but we don't yet have the money to finish the project, so my absence will not hold up the process.

A week later the magazine calls again. "You'll have to put off your trip. McCurry just got a visa to go to Baghdad with one of our staff writers, and no American journalist has been there for years."

We reschedule the trip for the fall. At first I feel disappointed and depressed, and wonder if more obstacles will crop up to this incredible dream of being able to reach millions of people throughout the world. But Judy tells me a wonderful story about a time of disappointment in her life, when as a single parent her financial outlook seemed quite bleak. A friend reminded her of the Sufi saying: "If you have only one coin, take half and buy bread; with the other half, buy white hyacinths." The next morning, as the spring sun rose, she saw that three white hyacinths, which she had not known were there, were blooming in her garden. With her change in attitude, her luck had likewise changed, almost immediately.

I find, after all, there are good reasons for me to remain in California. Donated money and editing facilities make it possible for Judy and I to do more work on the documentary. Interest in Afghanistan is growing, and I find myself a frequent lecturer to groups that vary from church congregations to women's clubs to a retired officer's club.

In the middle of all this activity, I accept the invitation of a friend to go to a Native American festival at the Morongo Reservation near Palm Springs. Harry Lawton, who teaches creative writing at U.C. Riverside, has been a longtime friend and mentor, whom I met through another writer, my friend Susan Baker. When Harry was a cub reporter in the 1950's, he used to write for the Banning newspaper about the deplorable conditions on the nearby reservation, a subject that was not yet in vogue. As a result of his efforts on behalf of this poorer branch of the Cahuilla (another branch of the tribe owns much of the land in and around Palm Springs), he has been accepted as a friend by many of the Cahuilla. He is a member of the Board of Trustees of the tribe's Malki Museum, and is an ardent supporter of the yearly Malki Fiesta, held each Memorial Day weekend.

On a typical L.A. summer day, suffocating with a grey stinging breath-stealing haze, my old high school friend Diane Church and I head out toward Banning. We look forward to a weekend without smog, but are disappointed when we get out to Morongo and find out that it's one of those weekends when the smog extends a hundred miles east into the desert.

But the warmth of our welcome compensates. Harry takes us to meet some of his Cahuilla friends, and I realize that despite the fact that I grew up in California and have a bloodsister in a distant tribe in the Hindu Kush, I really know very little about the Native peoples of this continent, and have never spoken at length to a Native American. Kathy and her husband are pretty much like lots of people I've met travelling around the world. Kathy's face is round, coppery-bronze, lined with smiles and emotions. She looks rather like a Ladakhi or a Tibetan to my eyes.

Soon we are standing behind the thatched ramadas where the festival will be held tomorrow, shucking corn into huge tubs. Harry disappears, and Diane, Kathy's husband, and I keep on shucking corn in endless rhythm until the purple twilight settles into night. There are more stars out here than in the city, but still, this is not the desert night I had dreamed of.

Diane and I share a suite with Harry at a rundown hotel by the freeway in Banning. All night long, cockroaches skitter across old linoleum floors, and someone keeps pounding on our door, drunkenly calling out love epithets to a prostitute. Every time someone starts up a car and screeches out of the lot, one of us gets up to make sure it's not one of ours.

The next morning we visit some of Harry's friends on the reservation, and I begin to see why Native America is often referred to as the Fourth World. The Cahuilla have electricity, he explains, but they haven't had it all that long. The houses are mostly poor clapboard houses or trailers on broken land, the cars rusted and scraped. There is a bingo parlor at the entrance to the reservation, and it's a lot richer than it used to be, but it's hard for a Cahuilla who stays on the reservation to have a decent life.

I look out at the canyons and wonder what they were like before our white ancestors came. I wonder how the ancestors of these people lived in harmony with the land and with other tribes, what songs they sang beneath desert stars, what houses they built out of thatch and earth, and how they honored the Earth which the now dominant mono-culture of the world desecrates on such a regular basis.

"You ever heard of the Iranian architect Nader Khalili?" asks Harry, pronouncing the name like an American.

"No, who is he?"

"He builds domes out of adobe and fires them, like a big kiln. He gave a talk at Riverside, and we wanted him to come out and take a look at the site here, to see if he and his students would like to build a round building for the new museum. You should see his students! They follow him around and will do anything he asks them to do," says Harry, with a gleam of envy in his eye.

"Anyway," he continues, "you speak Farsi, don't you?"

"Yes, but..."

"Good, you can keep him busy."

Harry keeps me and Diane busy selling books at the museum bookstall once the crowd begins to arrive for the fiesta. The ramadas are soon full of Indians from various tribes, selling turquoise, beaded jewelry, fry bread, and silver. By nine in the morning it is already stifling hot and dusty. When the dancers, some from Indian schools and some professional troupes, arrive at mid-morning, the courtyard is full of swirling dust and hot whirlwinds, and has to be wet down in between numbers.

Business is brisk in our stall, and I don't have much time to sit down and rest. Finally Harry grabs my arm and introduces me to the architect, an unmistakably Iranian man with strong features and the fire of enthusiasm for ideals in his black eyes. I speak a few words in Farsi, and he is delighted. He explains, slowly, clearly, in eloquent and simple Persian, this strange process of building and firing a structure, which he calls *geltaftan,* or Ceramic Houses. I am riveted by the idea, fascinated by his method of "firing clay," as the word translates literally.

Nader introduces me to his students, two Iranian women, a white American woman who specializes in Native American studies, and Tsosie Tsinhnahjinnie, a lanky, reserved Navajo-Seminole architecture student who wears his hair long, in traditional fashion.

Whenever Harry gives me a break from book-selling, I join Nader and his students in watching the dancers and taking pictures, all the while feeling the drum beats in my heart and stomach. Nader is curious and friendly, and asks lots of questions. Tsosie sticks close, listening intently but rarely commenting, while the three women students wander around the stalls.

"What's the name of your book?" I ask Nader.

"*Racing Alone.* It's about the time I went across the deserts of Iran for five years on a motorcycle. I wanted to look at the traditional architecture of the villages and then to find ways to improve on it while keeping the architecture simple and beautiful. Well, the book got good reviews, but I am not really a writer.

"But what about you?" he asks. "Harry said you were writing a novel. What is it about?"

"It's about an Afghan doctor who has been trained in this country. After his divorce from his American wife, he returns to Afghanistan to serve the people by working in the war zone. It's also sort of a romance. There is an American woman journalist who has gone there to cover the war..."

I'm not sure whether I am rambling, but he listens patiently.

"What ever made you want to go to Afghanistan?" he asks.

So many times I am asked this question, and still don't have a satisfactory answer. "I felt drawn there," I say carefully, avoiding talk of reincarnation and karma. "Ever since I was a child I wanted to go. I always read about it in *National Geographic.* And for the last few years I have been studying Sufism."

His eyes light up with interest. "You should read *Conference of the Birds,"* he says.

"I have. But only in English."

"Then you should improve your Persian until you can read it in the original."

I don't question either his suggestion, or my ability to follow through. This man obviously has great faith in his students, and goes out of his way to encourage them. I look at him and nod in agreement, knowing I have found a teacher.

All summer long, as I wait for the autumn to come so I can go on my assignment for *National Geographic,* I work on draft after draft of my novel. I also take one day a week off and go to meet Nader and his students at the Southern California Institute of Architecture. Each week he hosts a gathering of idealistic minds and souls including both his architecture students and people from many walks of life who are inspired by his book and attracted to his work.

Over the weeks, shy Tsosie gradually opens up to me. The day I bring Tarot cards to do a reading for him, he presents me with a graceful, elongated wood-carving he has done of a Navajo *yei.* He says it is a rainbow. I am moved by this special gift, and begin to think of him as a brother.

I look at the students Nader has attracted, and find a varied group. The architecture students are from many nations and cultures–Navajo, Argentina, Israel, Iran, Lebanon, Mexico, America. This concept of building a house out of adobe, with your own hands, and then firing it like a kiln, from the inside out and glazing it to turn it to a Ceramic House, like a giant bowl or seashell, is electrifying to many. A Filipina woman psychiatrist comes to visit, and a Polish artist. The psychiatrist wants to use the healing power of working with clay-earth for her clients, many of whom are Southeast Asian refugees whose psyches were wounded by years of war and terror.

I don't know how I will integrate architecture into my life, as I've never been particularly interested in it before. But I am interested in appropriate technology, especially since visiting Ladakh last summer, and I have always loved the simplicity of domes, arches, courtyards, and wind-catchers which funnel cool breezes down into the interior of the house. Many of these forms are familiar to me from my travels, and the idea of firing and ceramic glazing them adds an exciting new dimension.

Nader is a natural teacher, and one who transcends his subject. "You will look at many things differently when you look at them the way architects do. Just wait till you go on your next trip. Who knows, maybe someday you will become an architect," he teases.

I still think of architects as mostly males with expensive clothes and arrogant attitudes who work in high-rises in Beverly Hills and drive conspicuous cars to the pristine sites they are over-developing with oversized luxury houses. But Nader and his students break my rigid ideas about the profession, and I become their whole-hearted supporters.

On another level, Nader speaks of the mystic poet Rumi, of Sufism, and of the Four Universal Elements–Earth, Water, Air, and Fire. Throughout history, he says, Earth Architecture has used only the first three elements. Bricks were made of earth, mixed with water, dried in the air. It was fire that was missing. By firing a house, we restore the structure and the material to physical and spiritual equilibrium, a true Unity of the Elements. At the same time, we are engaged in a subtle internal alchemy of process and spirit.

All of this is inspiring to my quest to complete my novel, finish our documentary, and be ready to go to Afghanistan in September. Carried on the crest of this fire of inspiration, and having finally accepted the advantages of computers, I finish four drafts of the novel between June and August, and plunge full-force into almost-final editing of the documentary.

My dreams and prayers are coming true, but I am in turmoil. My life is changing, expanding its scope. Already I have begun to look at my surroundings in Los Angeles a little differently, with a critical eye to the built environment and the urban landscape which I had before ignored except for noting flowers, trees, and necessary landmarks.

A thousand "ifs" float around me like a plague of flies in the twilight. "If you had gone to Afghanistan in spring, as you so stubbornly wanted to, would you have met this teacher, these students?" "If you had gone, would you have finished your novel?" "If you had gone, would the documentary be nearly finished?"

I wonder about the fabric of time, shimmering and uncertain in its pattern. Always nagging are the questions, is this delay protecting me? Is it keeping me safe, or taking me into further danger? Am I really meant to do this story and reach millions of people, after such a long struggle? Are the Afghan people meant to win their fight? And is there such a thing as fate, or is it all merely shifting fortune?

But there is such a thing as faith, and such a thing as life metaphorically acting out the myth of faith. Just before I am to leave on my trip to Afghanistan, I take a short vacation and drive north with my English friend Toni Hertenstein, who has long been like an elder sister to me. On the way back, driving through the empty high deserts of the Owens Valley, on the eastern side of the Sierra Nevada range, we run into a terrific storm. The sky is a roiling black inverted pit, its hidden gods and demons hurling spears of lightning toward the earth, which is accepting this attack with the equanimity of greatness. I am exhilarated, loving this vastness of desert, mountain, and sky which characterizes the lands which I have loved the most–California, Afghanistan, Ladakh, and the lands I dream of, Tibet and Iran. Toni, born and raised on an island of fog, mist, and quiet thunder, is unnerved, especially when a bolt of lightning strikes a hundred yards off to our right, and a pillar of smoke and dust rises up to meet the sky.

I keep driving, knowing there is nothing else we can do, and that probably the rubber tires will ground any strikes. Time compresses, and expands, and compresses again. Ahead in the road, a black eagle lands and snatches a black writhing snake from the surface of the rain-soaked road. The sun, golden, breaks through the charcoal-smudged veil of cloud, and shines a rainbow behind, to the left, over a turquoise lake. Strangely, we can see only one half of the rainbow. A golden eagle, gilded by the sun, flies under the rainbow, toward the lake, and all at once we see the other half of the rainbow.

And at that moment, I am certain in my faith. I am certain that I will again "fight with God" and fall into the sin of black despair, and equally certain that my faith will be renewed, each time at a higher level on the upward spiral journey of the soul.

27 Rich Meals and Turnips

"I pitied myself because I had no shoes,
until I saw a man who had no feet;
To a rich man, the richest meal means nothing,
but to a poor man turnips are the finest meal."
–Saadi

Peshawar, Pakistan
Fall, 1984

It is a very different Pakistan to which I return in the autumn of 1984. In just nine months, while my life has gone on on the other side of the world, life for three million refugees has gotten worse. Eighty-three million Pakistanis are beginning to get tired of what seems to be an endless burden of refugees, and a never-ending war that is beginning to spill over their borders. In the last year there have been incidents of incursions into air space, aerial bombings of Paksitani territory, and terrorist bombs hidden in cinemas, restaurants and hotels frequented by Afghan refugees and Mujahedeen.

The suspicion in the air is palpable in the chaotic atmosphere of Peshawar, smokey and heavy in this autumn dusk. All the Mujahedeen offices have been moved outside the city limits, and male refugees are not allowed to spend the night in the city's hotels, or even in their own shops in the bazaars. Everyone is watchful–this handsome young Pathan with the huge turban might not be a refugee, but an agent of Khad, the Afghan equivalent of the KGB, with hidden explosives ready to be planted amongst unsuspecting victims.

For the time being, I have decided to stay with Abid's kind family, as they are Pakistani, and unlikely to have trouble because of a foreigner in the house. And this time, instead of begging for a visa extension, I have been given a visa without a time limit, treated to tea and the poetry of Iqbal in the Pakistan Embassy in Washington, and given thousands of dollars in expense account money from *National Geographic.*

I am treated with deference by the same officials who had previously preferred to ignore me. My first class air ticket ensures all kinds of privileges and politesse. My first night in Islamabad I spend at the Holiday Inn, where I am to meet Steve McCurry. I toss and turn in jet-lagged dreams, feeling strange to be in such opulence in a Third World country. The printed notice, "Temporary telephone disorder," reminds me that I am in Pakistan.

Abid meets me at the airport in Peshawar, glad to see me again so soon after his Summer Olympics visit to Los Angeles just two months before. He speaks excitedly of his work with the UN High Commission for Refugees, detailing with military precision what projects I "should" take a look at. His parents, younger brother, and a plethora of cousins greet me at the rambling family homestead in Peshawar. Everyone is talking at once in English, Urdu, and Pashtu, as I piece together bits of each language. I am given strong Pakistani tea as servants whisk my luggage into a cavernous suite in the back of the old house, and photo albums of Abid's trip to America are thrust into my lap.

In the evening we go to Fatana's and Ishaq's house for dinner. Fatana and I can't stop hugging each other, and Wana is practically jumping up and down. Ishaq is as usual more reserved, but even he has a delighted smile. Everyone is proud that at last I have come back with a real assignment.

My friends all love the gifts I have brought them, and Fatana in turn presents me with a gift of honor, a bright pink silk traditional Afghan dress, richly embroidered and beaded. Wana teases me that I've forgotten some of my Farsi, but by the end of the evening, Fatana and I are whispering women-talk in the corner, giggling like teen-agers. Fatana is at first upset that I am staying with Abid instead of accepting her and Ishaq's hospitality, but she admits that she's not sure where she'd put me, as all the rooms are taken up by relatives. One is leaving in a month, and she makes me promise to come and stay with them then.

It is wonderful to be in one of the many homes of my heart again, knowing I am welcome. Before I go to sleep in the big, chilly room at Abid's house, I pray that I will really be able to pull this assignment off, that this opportunity will not somehow slip from my grasp. But all of the sudden, in a moment of peaceful insight, I realize that this assignment is exactly what I had prayed for and visualized, just like the documentary was.

Neither Steve nor I allow much time for jet-lag. We are both workaholics, though we have different styles. Steve's passion is for his story, whatever it is, and mine is to tell the story of the people of Afghanistan. Early on, I have an insight which hadn't occurred to me in the Kalash Valleys: Steve is simply not verbal; he perceives and communicates visually. He has compassion for the victims of war, but he can only communicate it by shooting pictures which will later profoundly move millions. Often he stops midway through a sentence, gazing at something and processing visual bits of information. When I ask a question, there are long lags, like an early generation computer, before his often-vague reply.

Despite our different viewpoints, we make a pact to cooperate to get the best story possible, both verbally and visually, and to integrate the two to the best of our ability. It rapidly becomes apparent that this is going to be our biggest challenge. Our original assignment had been to go to Nuristan and Panjsher and cover both the war and the surviving cultures. Then suddenly, when we visited Washington for a story conference on the way to Pakistan, everything changed. Editor Bill Garrett decided that the real story was the Pakistan border, and we were not to go into Afghanistan unless we were awfully sure we could do it safely.

That directive makes the story a lot harder. It is less focused, and there is more territory to cover. But both Steve and I are experienced in Pakistan, and have many contacts amongst Afghans and Pakistanis. Steve has been "inside" many times, and is respected for his tough, no-nonsense attitude, even though many Afghans don't understand his lack of social graces when accepting hospitality conflicts with shooting pictures in the right light.

Steve and I hire a driver to make our work easier. It is a refreshing change from the rupee-pinching days of 1983 when I had to beg rides, take over-crowded buses, or as an occasional luxury, flag down a rickshaw. We get our various permits from various agencies, and begin to visit refugee camps. But the stories I need to write about are not always the most visually exciting I ones, and at the time of day that I can meet certain people, the light is often too harsh for photography.

I introduce Steve to my friends in the refugee camps, like Qazi Aminullah and his family. But while I chatter eagerly and tearfully in Farsi, catching up, exchanging gifts, and leisurely sipping tea, Steve gulps his tea down and begins to fidget restlessly, looking up at the sun and gauging light. He is bored and frustrated by this language he has no inclination to understand, as all of his clues are visual.

We soon begin to go our separate ways, checking in with each other daily, and agreeing on general subject areas to cover. This frees us both, though the lack of control over the unfolding story is difficult for me. I have my own problems, however, looking, feeling, and listening to the vast sea of information, emotion, and images that surrounds me, and wondering how I am to weave a meaningful story out of all this, what narrative thread might possibly bring it all together in a way that the American people and the magazine's international readership can understand.

Ishaq will do anything to help me, because I am his wife's *khwahar khandah,* a good friend who is like a sister. But he complains bitterly about all the journalists who have come through in the past few years. "What good has it done for the people of Afghanistan? They have come, written their stories, taken their pictures, and gone back home to publish. But what difference has it made for us?"

But I notice that Ishaq will still help nearly any journalist. I feel sympathy for the scruffy free-lancers, as I was in their ranks not so long ago, and will be again in the future. Ishaq has a soft heart underneath the sometimes distant and austere exterior. His hospitality does not spring out of Pashtun duty, but out of love for his fellow humans. He easily recognizes the fragility of individuals, and is much less likely than I to rail bitterly about this or that journalist or official.

Like most Afghans, though, Ishaq is frustrated and discouraged about the prospects of getting anti-aircraft guns. By late 1984, most of Afghanistan has experienced severe carpet-bombing. Three million refugees have been driven into Pakistan, about one and a half million into Iran, and another million have become internal refugees in cities or in the mountains. Many areas never were planted in the spring, and the infrastructure has been devastated. An unknown number of people have been killed.

So far, the American government has not been all that responsive, Ishaq says. They send arms, but not anti-aircraft guns. What they do send is routed to Gulbuddin Hikmatyar's extreme fundamentalist Hisbi Islami party, a policy that will later prolong the civil war long after the Soviets have gone. These are folks with posters extolling Imam Khomeini (though most Afghans are Sunni rather than Shiah), and the glories of the Islamic Revolution. Women are shown only as faceless black-silhouetted shapes defined by *chadors,* and are utterly absent from the offices, clinics, and schools run by this party. There are also dark rumors of Hisbi groups attacking Mujahedeen from other parties, and occasional accusations that Gulbuddin is really a KGB agent. Soviet POW's are always held by other Mujahedeen groups who follow the Geneva Conventions. Hisbi usually doesn't take prisoners, considering them too expensive to feed.

Ishaq is beginning to wonder where the Americans get some of their information, and who makes decisions. "The American Consul-General, after talking to me for 15 minutes, asked whether I was Afghan or Pakistani," he says ruefully.

It's been a hard year for Ishaq. His real love is to be at the front with the Mujahedeen, despite the danger, despite his wife's and daughter's fears for him. But his uncle, the leader of the party and the family clan, has not paid heed to Ishaq's entreaties to be allowed to go to the front. To defy him would be unthinkable in this family-oriented culture, so for the time being Ishaq chafes in Peshawar, helping journalists get their stories.

Every day, people with stories of war and tragedy find their way to Ishaq's house. Most of the women come to Fatana. They are refugees who want help, an educated family who wants to send their daughters to school, widows, orphans, injured men. Fatana and Ishaq do all they can to give comfort and material help to their countryfellows, and yet stay afloat in this vast sea of sadness. One day Abid and I visit the Gailanis after an exhausting day in refugee camps and official offices, and find Fatana in a dark, shaken mood.

"A girl came to Ishaq today for help. She is half Afghan, half German, and had been living in America. She came here to try to help the refugees, though she doesn't know what she can do. She said she had cancer and had gotten better, but she is so thin, I think she is dying. She is such a wonderful girl, so intelligent and beautiful and she really wants to do service, but my heart tells me she is dying."

"What is her name?" asks Abid. "I met a girl like that in Karachi last year."

"Kamillah Mansury."

"That's the same girl! She was visiting my friends in Karachi, the same ones you visited, Debra."

Ishaq too is worried for this fragile 25-year-old woman. He joins us for tea with a frown on his handsome face.

"What does she want to do?" I ask.

He shakes his head. "I don't know. She was shy at first. She didn't want to speak Farsi, because she has an accent from living in America. But I told her she must speak Farsi. She said she couldn't say what was in her heart, but I told her to try. She spoke well. She really is a good girl, and has a great desire to do service, so I sent her to Naheed Shaheed School. Maybe she can teach English, as the girls there need a good English teacher. But Fatana is right, Kamillah is not well."

All evening long, Fatana is troubled. Usually she is unflappable through all the stories of war, bombings, wounded Mujahedeen, and refugees strafed on their way to the border. But this woman has shaken her foundations. Kamillah, who was diagnosed with cancer at 20, is not one of the expected casualties of war, and this is somehow more frightening and more random.

"You must come to meet her tomorrow," Fatana tells me. "I've told her all about you. She's a wonderful girl, but..." she sighs, "She says she has cured the cancer by diet, but I don't know. Five years ago the doctors told her she would die, but she fought with them. Maybe she will get better, *inshallah.* But she is so thin."

The next day, I come to afternoon tea to meet Kamillah. Her green, cat-like eyes are vivacious and laughing, full of the fire of life. She seems full of vitality, though she is indeed very thin.

We speak mostly in Farsi, slipping into English when Fatana is out of the room, or in a joke, or when Fatana demands that we teach her more English.

"Kamillah has been reading my face," Fatana says, impressed. "She knows all about medicine and is prescribing a diet for me."

"What kind of diet?"

Kamillah falls easily into English. "A macrobiotic diet." Back into Farsi. "Six years ago I was diagnosed with Hodgkin's disease," she says. "The doctors told me I had six months to live, but I fought with them. 'You're not God,' I said, 'You don't know.' So after they removed my spleen I was very angry, and I went to find alternatives. I found a macrobiotic center in Boston and studied there, and now I am just fine."

Fatana gives me a sidelong glance, which I ignore.

"What do you eat now?" I ask. "Are you still on the diet?"

"It's harder here," she admits. "But I bought lots of seaweed in Japan, and I can get brown rice here. In fact, it's cheaper than the white rice they like so much. But it's hard when I visit someone–I love Afghan food like *bolani,* and *qabli pilau.* I try to eat just yogurt and bread and a little meat, but I can't always."

Kamillah puts Fatana on a diet of brown rice, with no dairy products, eggs, meat, or salt. Fatana takes this all very seriously, despite Ishaq's jokes that she, Kamillah, and I are very cheap to feed if we eat brown rice. The cook dutifully makes two separate meals, one for Ishaq,

Wana, and guests, and one for Fatana, which I share when I am there.

Kamillah gets the job at Naheed Shaheed School. Every morning she gets up from the mattress on the floor of her Pakistani friends' house, rolls up her bedding, and takes the bus through the foggy haze of woodsmoke out to the school, where she teaches all morning. In the afternoons, she teaches English to my friend Zarghuna, one of the teachers we had videotaped in the refugee camp last year, and her sisters.

Fatana, Kamillah, and I become fast friends. After a month has passed, I move into Fatana's house, as one of the relatives has left, vacating a room. Kamillah sometimes stays overnight, and the three of us talk, laugh, and study languages together, acting like teen-agers at a slumber party.

Ishaq introduces Kamillah and me to visitors as "daughters of the house," and tells people all about the service we are doing for the Afghan people and the Jehad. Both of us get a little embarrassed. At the dinner table, Kamillah often slips into English. As a girl, she had gone to Kabul International School, where she had studied in English, then had lived in America, so many concepts are much easier for her in English. But Ishaq reprimands both of us with mock severity: "Speak only Farsi at the table."

One day, I go to visit Kamillah at the Naheed Shaheed Girls School. The school is in a vast, cold, echoing cement building. It is named after a high school girl who was killed in a demonstration against the Soviet invasion in early 1980. Naheed Shaheed means "Naheed the Martyr," and I soon see that sacrifice and martyrdom for Islam is stressed in this school, just like in the refugee camp schools.

The children here are a mixed group. Some are urban refugees, the children of middle class people who are almost invariably waiting for visas to America, Germany, or France. This is their first chance to continue their education since their families left Kabul, usually sneaking out by night dressed as villagers, praying their accents and their soft hands won't betray them if they are questioned.

The rest of the girls are from the camps. In the lower grades, boys and girls study together, but the upper grades have only girls, wispy adolescents who shyly pull their white veils over their faces and giggle when a visitor walks in.

My friend Hanifa, Qazi Aminullah's wife, is now teaching one of the lower grades. She is proud of her job, and has asked the children to decorate the room for the visitor. Paper streamers and gaudy golden garlands hang from the ceiling. Tiny tots stand up and charmingly recite the beginning of the Muslim prayers; then, as a group, they shout slogans like *"Marg ba Shuravi*–Death to the Russians." These are interspersed with "God is great!" shouted with great fervor and intensity. One small boy's veins stand out on his forehead as he shouts, and a tiny, tiny girl in a red triangular scarf leads another round, her chubby fist punching at the air.

In another classroom, the teacher shows the children off in much the same way. One boy, about six years old, is silent and unresponsive. The teacher, a plump, motherly woman in her mid-30's, coos to him. "Your father is off fighting the Soviets, fighting for Islam, and he will come back and bring you sweets."

But she whispers to me, "His father died two years ago, and they haven't told him. What is the use of telling him? He hardly speaks as it is."

Turning back to the child, she continues, "His father is a brave Mujaheed fighting the Jehad, and he'll be coming back soon." She turns to me, "Won't he?"

I nod, my heart breaking from this deception regarded as so necessary.

Kamillah, I find out, is as caught between East and West as I am, though she approached this bridge from a different direction. "I hate it when they lie to that child," she says later. "But that's the way Afghans are. They'll never tell a child the truth about bad news. I wonder what it does to them psychologically when they do find out?"

Kamillah understands the psychology of the West, and the spirit of the East. She longs to do service, perhaps because she burns like a thin, hot flame, knowing that she is living on time that is a gift of grace. She understands what Steve and I are trying to do with *National Geographic,* and helps as much as she can.

But sometimes Kamillah surprises me, acting more Afghan than a lot of Afghans I know. "I've asked Fatana to look for a husband for me," she announces one day. "And I think you also should consider getting married."

"But I want to marry someone I love," I protest.

"Islam is very practical about marriage. If you married the right man, someone who is interested in service, then you would fall in love after some time "

I appreciate Kamillah's thoughts, and I am even touched when she and Fatana plot to introduce me to a well-respected intellectual poet. But

I realize that the part of me that will probably always be Western is the part that wants romantic love.

Kamillah was once married to an American, I find out. It was brief and emotionally disastrous. I never ask her whether her illness came before or after the marriage. Now she is an independent woman who travels all over the world by herself, studies macrobiotics at the Kushi Institute in Boston, and recommends dietary changes for the Afghan and Pakistani society women of Peshawar, who are ever eager for some new novelty to ease their tedium.

Kamillah has joy in her life, but I also sense an echoing emptiness. Like me, she doesn't quite belong. Her face is just a little too broad and Germanic to be Afghan, and her Dari is a little bit accented. Ironically, on some occasions people think I am Afghan and she is the foreigner, which brings a pang to both our hearts. She does her best to be as Islamic as possible, but she eats sheets of seaweed which she has brought from Japan, endeavoring to stay on the diet which has prolonged her life.

We are at Ibn Sina Balkhi hospital one day, visiting some wounded Mujahedeen, when she runs into a handsome young man with an American accent.

"Kaye Mansury! Is that you, after all these years?"

Zia, too, has returned from years of schooling in America, sharing the culture of his Afghan father and American mother, to find a way to serve his people in a time of tribulation. Kamillah and Zia talk animatedly, recalling simpler, happier times together at Kabul International School, more than ten years ago.

I watch these two "bridge people," as I call those caught between East and West, and wonder if they could ever be together, work together, love together. Instead of seeing those from the East who have embraced some of the West, and those from the West who have embraced some of the East as "caught" between East and West, I see them as bridge builders. And yet this is not an easy task, for it requires the risk of stretching to what seems an impossible limit of mind, body, heart, and spirit, to reach those on the other side who may not always want to be reached.

Still, watching these two young people chatting in the American slang which is so natural to them, the one a young woman wearing Pakistani dress and a white eyelet veil, the other a young man getting used to a *shalwar kameez*, I have hope for the future of Afghanistan, America, and the world.

The better I get to know Ishaq, the more I understand his longing to be "inside," leading a group of Mujahedeen. "Oh, to hold a Kalashnikov I my hands again," he laments one day. "You feel like you have the whole world in your hands."

Ishaq is a warrior in innocence. I know that he doesn't like killing for killing's sake. Nor is he afraid to kill for a greater good. He is a warrior in the sense that the Lakota Medicine Wheel conceives of a warrior, one who responds to a threat and kills, if necessary, in innocence and without joy, certainly without revenge. He is also what they call a "Dog Soldier"—one who protects the "children and the children's children."

In Ishaq, I see a gentle hero, a man of truly fine character, an aristocrat who might have been a lawyer or a legislator, or even a professor of literature. He had studied Political Science at Tehran University, but had had to leave and take up his post in the Gailani family's political party while still a very young man. In the last year, his black hair has become dusted with silver, which glitters in the sun. He has barely turned 30.

Ishaq makes my way easy. He waits for me to ask, but arranges every meeting I need. Unlike most of the Afghans, who are wedded to sectarian party politics, he urges me to go to the other parties and find out for myself what their politics are. He has good relations with nearly everyone, even many of the fundamentalist leaders. As I meet more and more Afghans in the camps and bazaars, I find that virtually everyone has a good word for him, from the fiercely loyal *murids* of the Qadiriya Sufi sect to Mujahedeen who support the fundamentalism of Gulbuddin Hekmatyar.

In my view, Ishaq is well deserving of such admiration. What touches me most deeply is the sight of him on the verge of tears at the news of the riots in India after Indira Gandhi's assassination, which comes as a shock to all of us.

Munshi, the kind Punjabi driver I have hired during the duration of my stay, tells me the news when I emerge from the Widow's Camp. He stands numb, his slim feet kicking at the dirt, his thin shadow falling on the barren land. He shakes his head angrily. "This is very bad news, even though Pakistan and India have not been the best of friends."

Ishaq is troubled. "She was a great leader, a stateswoman for her people," he said. "I didn't like her policies on Afghanistan, of course, but she was a great leader for India."

Then when the news comes in on the radio, later in the evening, of hundreds, maybe thousands of Sikh deaths in the mad vengeful riots that followed the assassination, Ishaq's eyes fill with tears. "A thousand dead in Delhi!" he exclaims, translating the Urdu news for me. "For what?"

All at once, in a vivid moment, I realize how much he really hates war and killing. I remember the time when he came home and dropped the holstered pistol he always wore onto the fine red Bukhara carpet. "I will be glad when this is all over," he had said tiredly.

To our surprise, some of our Pakistani friends rejoice at the news. "The women at the sewing course offered me sweets," said Fatana. "I told them in Islam we should not rejoice at the death of another."

Wana is listening to all of this very seriously. She asks me quietly, "Why is everyone sad that Indira Gandhi has died?"

"Because she was a good woman, a strong leader for her people. I also didn't agree with her policies about Afghanistan, and felt she was too close to the Soviets. But she was a good leader."

The next morning at breakfast, Wana is quiet and pensive. When Fatana asks her what's wrong, she says, "I'm sad that Indira Gandhi was killed. Even though she was too much of a friend to the Russians, she was a good leader. And now all the Sikh people are being killed, all for nothing."

The pain of war and loss gives people a keen sense of the pain of others, if they can avoid the numbness of trauma. A lot of people I meet, in hospitals and camps, can think only of expelling the Russians from their country. Many have lost whole families, and are lost in their own grief. But others feel deeply the losses of others, and find themselves relatively blessed, even in their misfortunes; they are the ones who adopt the orphaned children of their extended family or clan, and go to great lengths to maintain the customs of hospitality and generosity to guests.

Mundah camp in 1984 is a camp for new arrivals, those who can't get registered and don't have ration cards. It is on "marginal land," which means that sometimes, in some years, the locals might get a crop off of it. It is bleak and pale brown-green, a camp full of weathered tents bought or traded for, and a few bright yellow tents which four families crowd into in the chill November nights.

These refugees are most generous with their time, and their words. Men, women, and children are eager to talk into my tape recorder, filling it with their experiences. They are generous with their images too, and I capture an unforgettable portrait of a young man holding three beautiful orphaned children whom he and his family had adopted, not worrying whether or not there were enough rations for them.

They pour us endless rounds of tea, and they bring sweet yellow corn cakes, dry pastries, and hard candies. An elder with a long white beard announces that he is going to kill a sheep for Steve, me, and our escort. It is a delicate moment. I don't want them to kill the sheep, yet I don't want to reject their hospitality. "Oh, we are late," I say in dismay. "I'm sorry, but we have been invited to dine with Syed Ishaq today."

The white lie seems to satisfy them; their honor and their sheep are saved. But Ishaq later reprimands me. "It is hospitality. You should have said yes. They really wanted to kill the sheep for you."

As long as I have been here, as much of the language as I speak, I still sometimes find myself disoriented in my attempts to balance. Morality is so culturally defined, I am no longer clear what views are mine and what comes from the cultural mind-field that surrounds my own mind while I am here.

Sometimes, I envy Steve his clarity. He has no confusion about these issues. He knows that his job is to be the best photographer he can be, to get the shots no matter what it takes, to travel where he needs to, offend if he must, and run to cover the breaking news. He's happy staying at Dean's Hotel, and having dinners and bourbon with the macho foreign journalists. The few times I stumble upon him and his colleagues having drinks in his room, I feel confused and out of place; more often than not, my dress and my *chador* confuse them too, and they do a double take when what they think is an Afghan or Pakistani woman starts speaking English to Steve.

Abid, too, lives between worlds. He now has a very responsible job with the UN High Commission for Refugees, and is even forming a professional association of Pakistani employees. He has just been promoted to international work, and will soon be sent to Sudan and achieve his long-held dream of seeing Africa.

But at home, he is very Pakistani, very Pashtun. He is completely devoted to his elderly mother and father, and feels responsible for them. His elder brother lives in Karachi, his younger brother is still in college, and the other siblings are all married sisters, so what choice does he have? The offer to go to Africa throws him into deep conflict, but his parents urge him to take it.

Before he leaves, we go to a party held by two of his UN colleages. The high compound walls screen out the rest of the world in University Town, where all the foreigners live now. Inside is a world of fairy lights on the trees, spreading, well-trimmed lawns, servants, kebabs, opulence, and imported beer. Everyone mistakes me for a sister of Abid's, and I decide to enjoy the masquerade. But in the crisp air is a hint of the British

Raj—or Reagan's America. I cannot get it out of my head that a few miles away, in refugee camps and in poor houses and mean urban flats, Afghan and Pakistani children cry and cough, women weep and toss in fever, and families share grief and joy and a plate of rice and a pot of sugarless, weak tea. A few miles further, over the border, men die in nighttime firefights, boys writhe in pain, and terrified refugees walk by night, praying with each step to arrive safely beyond the cold, stoney ridges of snow-covered mountains that mark the border.

Abid's family gives him a big farewell party on the eve of his departure. The house is full of people, extended family members, and a few close friends. Ishaq drives me, Fatana, Kamillah, and Wana to the house, but he is preoccupied with news from Afghanistan, and spends much of the evening in the living room listening to the BBC Farsi service. Wana, dressed up in new clothes, is excited by the crowd, the music, and the tasty lamb kebabs with lumps of fat roasted just right. Fatana, Kamillah, and I enjoy a rare night out, wearing our new glittery dupatas. Fatana has talked me into wearing the rose silk Afghan dress which she had presented to me.

As a special treat, Abid has asked Azim Zarbakhsh, our favorite flute player, to play. Fatana hangs back, as a proper Afghan woman should, but she and Kamillah push me forward to dance. I am reluctant at first, but the music captures me in its spiral, and I swirl and spin, my hands weaving the sounds into pictures and feelings for me to always remember.

But this is a sad autumn. The excitement of a war which the Afghans, in their bravado, were sure they would win, has long since faded and been replaced by the grim realization that they are in for a long haul. Quiet faith, and the willingness to be martyred, have grown in place of the fervor of certainty. The Afghans are beginning to realize that only an infusion of American arms can save them, and only anti-aircraft missiles can tip the balance in their favor.

The Pakistanis are divided; some are beginning to question the Islamic brotherhood that has brought nearly three million refugees across the border; others, fervent supporters of Islam and of General Zia's military government, believe in helping the Afghans to continue the war at any cost. Still others are simply waiting and worrying; "the real Mujahedeen," says one Pakistani friend, a high official, "are very much admired here. But people are tired of seeing fake refugees getting lots of money and owning buses and rickshaws."

Lots of people are making fortunes, no question of it. Some

unscrupulous Afghans do double register; sad old women con artists do tell amazing stories of grief that move some of the softer-hearted Pakistani administrators. Some administrators and camp commanders are said to be building fine villas, even though they were younger sons of their families. Where did this sudden wealth come from? And where did the truckloads of tennis shoes, pencils, schoolbooks, or wheat, really go? Ishaq mentions that even some of the Americans who had helped Afghans over the years are now quite successful. One woman, he says, has moved from a small apartment in Washington to a large country farm with horses in Virginia. Lots of people are making money off the misery of others.

When Steve and I go to the Widow's Camp the first time, we find ourselves face to face with official corruption. The Camp Commander gives us a hard time about meeting my friend Noor Jehan. Judy and I had promised her last year that we would buy her a sewing machine in thanks for her appearance in our documentary, which is one of our strongest segments. I want to make sure she's still here, and I'm sure she won't mind if Steve takes a few pictures of her and her family.

Noor Jehan indeed does not mind if we take some pictures. But the Camp Commander does. A tall mud *purdah* wall is being built around the camp, in response to the complaints of Pakistani religious officials that these widowed women are being allowed to roam about much too freely. No way will they bend the rules to let Steve in, even with a sworn promise to photograph only Noor Jehan and her family.

I am allowed to visit her, and discover that her adult daughter has been widowed in the past year, and has found her way to her mother's humble tent. A few things are better; some of the widows, including Noor Jehan's family, now have small, dark, windowless, concrete rooms, which, as bad as they are, are better than a tent. Now sixteen people crowd into the room and the tent, and live off of rations for seven.

The Camp Commander and two women guards are very unhappy that I speak Farsi and I can understand Noor Jehan's laments. Noor Jehan cleverly takes pains to flatter the Commander and his staff. The staff, however, are used to journalists for whom they can translate or not translate, as the mood strikes them, and resent someone they cannot effectively control.

Steve, meanwhile, is getting anxious, and wanders off to the school, where he is allowed to photograph. Here he takes a picture that will later become our cover photo. She is a beautiful 13-year-old girl with green-violet eyes, the poster child of a generation of refugees.

Finally, we are told to come back tomorrow, after getting permission for photography from the Commissionerate in town. I know one of the officials, and I'm not too worried, though we've taken a long drive for nothing.

We get our permission and come back a couple of days later, but this time the Camp Commander has decided to wield his power. He doesn't like the fact that I've brought a sewing machine, which Abid helped me pick out in the bazaar. "Give me the machine," he says impassively, "and I will give it to Noor Jehan. I'm not letting you go in there today."

"But we have permission."

"There must be some mistake. I was just told not to let you go in there. You can go to the field station and call."

His delaying tactic works, as of course the phone does not work, and we are miles outside of Peshawar. I try being nice, but he is not swayed.

"All the rich Arabs come and when they give money, they give it to me and I give it to the widows," he says. "So just give me the sewing machine and anything else you want to give to this trouble-maker Noor Jehan. All she does is complain to the foreigners anyway."

I finally lose my temper, and fling all my money, thousands of rupees, on the ground in front of the Camp Commander. "Here, if you are so greedy, then take this! If you want to take everything from the refugees who have nothing, then take this too."

He is dumbfounded, and merely stares at me. The men gathered around the room to petition him fall silent, and I feel their energy cheering me on. They watch, and a few men whisper. A young guard finally picks the money up, and puts it on the chair next to me. I continue staring at the Camp Commander.

"You can give her the sewing machine yourself," he finally says. "I will send someone for her. Then, please go. "

It is a small victory. Noor Jehan has tears in her eyes, tears of gratitude, but also a look of fear.

Three days later, I find out why. As I come out of an office in Peshawar, a small knot of women shout at me. Noor Jehan grabs my hand, a little angry. "Because of that sewing machine, they threw us out of the camp. The Camp Commander came to us and said we were making trouble with foreigners, and we had to go. He took away our ration cards and our house, and told us to leave the camp. We have been sleeping under the bridge for three nights."

I am incensed, at the Camp Commander and at myself. I take Noor Jehan's hand and sweep past the protesting guards, right into the District

Administrator's office. My friend Arbab Dost is not there, but his assistant, Mr. Roghani, sits in his chair. I tell the story to a surprised and compassionate Roghani as men look on in shocked silence. Before I can finish, the Camp Commander himself, whom I had not noticed, springs up from his chair and says in English, "Don't worry, it was all a mistake. Here, I will make good for her. I will make sure they can return to the camp and that they all have rations." He hands her a written chit, and she practically falls to her knees, a dramatic and desperate woman trying to keep her family together however she can.

The next time I visit the camp, I am not allowed to see her at all, despite written permission from Arbab Dost Mohammed, my sympathetic friend. Every camp, it seems, is a feudal fiefdom, and papers don't mean any more than the power to enforce them. I go to the school, and the teachers tell me that Noor Jehan is fine, she loves her sewing machine, they are all back in the same house–and now all sixteen of them have rations.

Later, Mr. Roghani tells me the rest of the story. "We know that man is corrupt," he says resignedly. "But his father was a provincial minister and he comes from a powerful family. We know we have good men and bad men, and we just do the best we can with them."

Roghani is one of the best. One day he takes me to Mundah. When I recognize people I had met before, he just smiles, knowing that I had gone illegally. He looks at each face before him, searching for clues as to whether that man or woman is telling the truth. He grants some requests that the local officials insist are bogus. And then, when we are walking, we come upon a young Uzbek who is in great pain. A friend of his calls us into the tent where the young man lies. The sick man shows us huge tubercular abcesses, not knowing what they are, only that they are sapping his strength. Roghani looks at the man's eyes, and I can see the compassion in his heart.

"Put him in our jeep," he says. "We will take him to Peshawar. Find a man to come with him, a friend or a brother or cousin who can stay with him in the hospital."

An Afghan doctor who works at a nearby tent clinic shows up, and decides to take the man himself. Roghani gives the doctor his card, and asks to be kept informed of the man's progress.

I am confused by this magic lantern pattern of good and bad, brilliant light and deepest darkness, heroism and pettiness, sacrifice and evil. I have travelled the camps, the cities, the bazaars, the sparsely-furnished rooms rented by the middle class refugees, the offices of Pakistanis, foreigners, and Mujahedeen, the deserts of Baluchistan and the mountains of Chitral. And now, if I want to understand what is really happening in 1984, and to tell the world about the state of Afghanistan in the mid-80's, I know I must go "inside."

To my surprise, Steve has beaten me to the punch. He is not at the hotel, and has left no message. A cousin of Ishaq's comes to dinner, and casually mentions that he had sent Steve into Afghanistan yesterday.

I see our story unravelling before my eyes. How can we produce an integrated story when we have rarely been together? Tears of frustration brim in my eyes, and I try to hide them in my napkin. Ishaq looks at me sympathetically, and jokingly offers to have Steve ambushed. The thought momentarily appeals to me, but I instead take up his offer to arrange my own trip inside I soon as possible.

We talk details after dinner. I look at the calendar, and remember a dream about a friend having a heart attack on a certain day. The calendar was clear, and the dates fell on the same days of the week as this month. I feel an eerie premonition of disaster if I go in this week and tell Ishaq my concerns.

This is a culture which pays attention to dreams. He does not question my reading of the omen, but simply says, "Then you must go on Friday, for it is the beginning of a new week. I will arrange it."

28 A Nation of Builders and Poets

Jaji, Paktia Province, Afghanistan
Fall, 1984

"They have bombed here every day for four months. Today it is snowing, and the planes will not come." The woman's face is calm, resigned, almost saint-like in her gentleness. She rests in the certainty that she is where she is supposed to be, beside her husband here in the war zone in Paktia province, preparing food for Mujahedeen who stop on the way to or from war.

I will never know her name, for the custom amongst these Pashtun villagers is to address a woman as "mother of so-and-so" or "wife of so-and-so." Strange to think how intimately one can come to know a person, and yet never know her secret name.

She's heavily pregnant, but very active. Her long, shiny black braids escape from the thick veil over her head, and swing as she bustles about the room, making tea, boiling turnips. Sometime in the darkness and snows of deep December, around the fifth anniversary of the Soviet invasion, she will give birth to her tenth child.

"When the planes come, I can't run very fast to the bomb shelter any more. What can I do? I don't want more children, but husbands are hungry for sons. I would take medicine not to have more children, but I can't get it here."

I am the first foreign woman she has ever spoken to. She has seen a few women journalists, as her home is on a main route and is near the border, but none of them had been able to speak Farsi or Pashtu. She speaks to me in a lilting Farsi, learned when she had lived with her husband in Kabul, with the cadence of the Paktia dialect of Pashtu.

In Kabul, her husband had worked as a driver, and life had been good. "Now our life is hard," she tells me. "We have many guests all the time, but by the grace of God, we have a cow, some chickens, a little flour, and some turnips. I am happy to be able to feed the Mujahedeen and do service to the Jehad."

Two brothers and their wives and children live in this small house, built out of mudbrick in the traditional style. It is tidy, and the painted geometric and floral designs in red ochre on the walls are new, belying the war. The family seems for a moment like prosperous farmers, until my friend's husband mentions that the house had been destroyed and rebuilt.

He rolls up the sleeve of his long shirt and shows me a deep, puckered hole in his upper arm, and a long jagged scar on the forearm. "I was wounded two years ago, and was three months in the hospital in Peshawar. By the grace of God I recovered, and now my brother and I take turns going to fight.

"This area is free, up to the Communist post at Ali Khel, but the planes come and bomb the villages nearly every day. They are trying to drive us all to Pakistan, so no one is left to feed the Mujahedeen. Today you are lucky. Because it is snowing, no planes will come. Tomorrow, only God knows. *Inshallah,* you will be safe."

I turn the conversation away from war, to daily life, to children and family. The late autumn darkness descends early on this benighted land under a thin, ragged coverlet of snow, and the men retreat to another room as the women face Mecca. I join them in their evening prayer, and then watch as the children play with a fluffy grey kitten, who knows that the warmest spot in the house is right beneath the cast iron stove. When the children lose interest, it curls up and falls asleep under the stove, with the trusting innocence of kittens everywhere, and for a moment, I forget that we are in a land of war.

Except for the snow, which is a welcome protector from planes and helicopters, this has been a much easier trip than Kunar. The journey from Ishaq's house down to the town of Parachinar in the tribal areas was uneventful. The *chadori* which I had to wear to pass the police checkpoints is no longer a novelty to me, and I am much more confident of my abiity to talk my way out of an awkward situation in Farsi. I have heard guns and mortars fired before, and though I don't relish the thought of being in a war zone, at least this time I know the story I write will be published in a major magazine.

The night before I left for Afghanistan, *Ustad* Khalilullah Khalili, the *de facto* poet laureate of Afghanistan, came by Ishaq's house with his son Massoud, a prominent Mujahedeen leader. To be sent off by a master is indeed a good omen for my trip, and some of my anxiety evaporates.

The elder Khalili is a venerable man, though small in stature. His body is frail at 80, and I wonder if he will ever see his homeland again. But his mind and tongue are sharp. He alternates between jokes, political pronouncements, and poetry which always contains a Sufi lesson.

Last year, Judy Mann and the original director of our documentary had interviewed Khalili in New York. I tell him that I have seen many hours of him on videotape since I met him in Peshawar in spring of '83. He is honored that his statements and poetry have become the narrative thread of the documentary.

"I came from exile in America to exile in Pakistan, to work for the Jehad," he says. "I wanted to be at the foot of Khyber, for the winds of Afghanistan blow through there. Because I am 80 years old and can't ride a horse anymore, I can't go into Afghanistan myself.

"I am like a wounded bird fallen from a tree, who looks up and sees that his nest is on fire, and his children are burning. I sit here wounded, crying and writing poetry, but my voice is heard by the Mujahedeen in all their places of battle, where they repeat my words."

Ustad Sahib, the master, is pleased that I have learned better Farsi since our last meeting. I listen entranced to his words. This is a man who saw his own father executed by Amanullah Shah, the king of Afghanistan in the early years of the century, and subsequently grew up a vagabond. But he went on to become an internationally recognized poet and literary scholar, deeply respected in all Persian-speaking lands. An *ustad* is not only a poet, but must have memorized 10,000 verses of Persian poetry, a rich body of literature with which we in the West are little familiar. *Ustad* Khalili thus has a poem for nearly every occasion, either one of his own, or one from the great poets Hafez, Rumi, or Saadi.

I listen to him with fervor and attention, frustrated when my Farsi is not up to understanding one of his poems or remarks. But I simply enjoy being in his presence, learning something of his peaceful way of being.

I quote to him a couplet I have written:

"Dunya watan-e-man ast
Wale Afghanistan khanah-e-dialm ast."
"The world is my homeland,
but Afghanistan is the home of my heart."

He is deeply touched by my attempt at rhyme from the heart. He shakes his head back and forth, and scratches his fingers on the carpet, vigorously feline in his enjoyment of the power of words.

Ustad Sahib approves of my choice of the name Rabia. He asks me what I know of the Arab Sufi poet Rabia Basri, who lived in what is now Iraq in the 8th century. I admit that I know very little.

"Rabia Basri once walked in the desert with fire in one hand, and water in the other. She said she would guench the fires of hell, and set fire to paradise, so that humans would love God neither from fear of hell nor from hope of Paradise, but only from pure love."

As he is leaving that night, *Ustad Sahib* gives me a blessing on my journey into Afghanistan. "You are a brave girl and a great soul," he says. I blink back tears, feeling I can never live up to his words. "Go with God, and come back and tell the story of the Afghan people."

My first morning in Afghanistan, I awake just before dawn to a crystalline silence, which is soon shattered by gunfire. It is a frosty morning, and a thin snow still lies on the hard ground. My six Mujahedeen companions are all in the guest house on the other side of the compound, but I have slept with the women and children in this warm room, covered by quilts and blankets which are soon stacked against the walls by practiced hands.

No one reacts to the sounds of war, not even the grey kitten. It goes on playing, stopping to nibble a crust of bread one of the little girls has given it. One of the boys, who is about eleven, picks up a piece of chalk and begins drawing on the black stove. Like all children of war, his spontaneous drawings are of planes and guns, bombs falling, missiles hitting planes–and the occasional flower. My friend stirs a pot of boiled sugar beets and turnips, all that remains in the garden. The turnips remind me of lines from the Persian poet Saadi: "I pitied myself because I had no shoes, until I saw a man who had no feet; to a man with a full stomach, a rich meal is like a raw turnip, to a hungry man, even a raw turnip is the richest meal."

My friend hugs and kisses me affectionately in farewell. She says the traditional things: "Go with God; this house is your house," but I know the words are from her heart, not mechanical phrases of politeness. "Next time you come to Jaji, come straight to us."

I silently pray that her child will come on a snowy day, when no planes can fly, and she will not be trapped in the damp underground bomb shelter, or worse, stuck in a house from which she cannot run.

The day is bright and rain-washed, but the land is sere. The pale blue sky suddenly looms threatening, and I look and listen for the scars of jets.

The Mujahedeen decide it is safe to cross this open valley by day, instead of waiting for night. Either way, we would be sitting ducks in this open land with not a proper ditch in sight, and only bare-branched trees.

My stomach is a tight knot as we march quickly down the dirt road. I look for cover, trying to imagine where I would run. Large bomb craters pock fields which this year bore no harvest, for there was no one to plant them. Most of the villages lie deserted, a few undamaged houses standing forlornly amongst piles of rubble like surviving orphans.

As we fall into the rhythm of the day, my fear lessens. We stop at a tea house in the middle of nowhere, near where an Afghan government post used to be. The Mujahedeen pose on a disabled tank, but when I step back to compose the picture, they shout at me, "There are mines there!" Gingerly, I step back to the path, step by step in the outlines of my footprints in the soft earth.

The bullets, the bombs, the wounds, physical and psychological, are the same whether in Beirut or El Salvador, Afghanistan or Nicaragua, Angola or Northern Ireland. I don't care for pictures of dead bodies and destroyed villages, armies, brave guerrilla fighters, captured POW's. My quest is to write large the story of a people's struggle for survival, a metaphor for a brave human spirit beyond all borders and confusions of culture. This spirit will grow, nurture, build and beautify, even as the village family had built their home again after losing it to bombs.

This walk under the pale autumn sky feels like a bad dream of a deserted land. We reach the remains of the village of Ali Sangi, which before the war was a thriving village of a couple of hundred families. The place is eerie and full of ghosts. We walk over random piles of rubble, bricks and shattered boards, flotsam and jetsam of simple lives. A small black and white cat prowls delicately on the rough edge of a ruined wall, and runs away when we approach, wanting nothing more to do with human madness.

Roofless and naked to the open sky, a floor lies askew, as if after an earthquake, and a beautifully carved wooden chest tilts down onto the second floor. Beneath my feet lie bedposts, crushed cans of cooking oil, scattered seeds of grain, and a single child's shoe, very small.

On the other side of the road, a mosque still stands, though much of its floor has fallen away due to the impact of bombs But it is still a sacred space, and someone has strewn fresh straw on the part of the floor which is intact. Mustafa and Bahram Jan, the two men who have escorted me all the way from Peshawar, lay down their Kalashnikovs and face away from destruction, towards the holy city of Mecca, where all good

Muslims hope to pay pilgrimage one day. They pray amongst the lovingly carved columns, perching on the wide stone wall which is the only safe place in the building.

As we continue walking on into the afternoon, we relax a little. If the planes have not come by now, they are off destroying other villages today. We pass the gaping, fly-encrusted carcass of a dead camel in the middle of the road, and nearby see a dead cow and a dead donkey in the field. A mangey yellow dog cowers and runs away when Bahram Jan throws a stone. It hangs back, watchfully, looking from dead cow to dead donkey, to the small party of humans which will soon leave it to its feast.

"Tell the world they kill even the animals, anything that moves," says Mustafa angrily. "Anything that can feed the Mujahedeen or carry supplies for us. No one and nothing is safe in this war."

In another village, a man stands on a high brick wall, stoically evening out the jagged edges with a shovel. He is salvaging bricks so he can repair his home. Half the village is ruined, but the other half stands intact, though every wall is cracked from the impact of explosions.

In a field of brown stubble, Mustafa finds the remains of the only crop these fields have produced this year. The broken green wings of butterfly bombs stand out against the dark earth. They are designed to maim, not kill, and thus demoralize. I have seen innumerable children, and some men and women, who have stepped on these bombs or picked them up in curiosity, and have lost a hand or foot. This is the source of the stories of "toy bombs." There never were trucks, dolls, or pens—but to a village child, these aerodynamically-designed devices look like a bright plastic bauble, a bird or a butterfly, begging to be touched. Regardless of intention, they are effective instruments of evil.

The veil of dusk is falling swiftly when our small party reaches a deserted farmhouse. A couple of local men walk by, glancing suspiciously at the woman in the midst of the Mujahedeen, and ask a question.

"I told them you are from Kabul," says Mustafa softly in Farsi. "They are from another party. The parties work together in the daytime, but at night we only trust our own."

Bahram Jan and another man have gone ahead to a safehouse virtually in the shadow of the government post at Ali Khel. We shelter from the stiff, chill breeze of sunset behind a mud wall, and the Mujahedeen hide their rifles under their warm, camel-colored *pattu* blankets, and I hide my camera under mine.

Mustafa points to the post. "There are Afghan soldiers there, and some Soviet officers. Every night the Mujahedeen attack the post. Do you want to go with us? You will be in a rain of bullets."

Despite the fact that these men have been praising me all day for my bravery and strength, I find the prospect unappealing, and decline. "I am here to tell your story, and I have to return safely to tell it," I explain.

Under cover of darkness, we make our way to the house of a *malik*, a village headman, who is loyal to Ishaq's party. A few hours later, the battle begins in earnest. Bahram Jan and the *malik* lead me up the steep stairs to the square tower of the fortified compound, which has a picture window view of the war. This is a sound-and-light show unlike any I have ever seen. As I watch, firey parabolae of tracer bullets arc from the mountainsides toward the Communist-held posts, like pretty Fourth of July fireworks.

Watching a war again brings on that strange shift of perspective, away from reality and into some alternate time. It does not make any sense for people to be shooting at each other with the intention to kill, no matter how right the cause of one or the other. The Afghan conflict at least has the advantage of having one side that most people in the world, except for a few leftist diehards and opportunists, can clearly feel is right. Not too many people blame the Afghans for fighting against an invading force, and against those in their own government who have supported the invaders, imprisoned countless people, violated human rights as a matter of course, and killed, by 1984, about half a milllon people.

As a former pacifist, I sometimes feel odd arguing for supplying arms to the Afghans—but I also feel I have no choice. The Mujahedeen have no chance to win this war outright. They can only wage a stern and steely war of nerves, hanging on with tenacious faith until some miracle happens and they are given the missiles they need to shoot down enough hardware to make the war costiy. The Soviet government may not care about Private Ivan Ivanovich any more than Uncle Sam cared about Private John Doe in Vietnam, but losing expensive high-tech hardware makes governments think twice.

Bahram Jan interrupts my cynical thoughts with a more human story. He tells me of young Commander Mohammed Naim, a man from this very village, who one week ago led an attack on the fort which had resulted in the capture of fifty government soliders, as well as the loss of one of his own legs. Naim belongs to Gulbuddin Hekmatyar's fundamentalist party, the Hisbi Islami, but everyone here in Jaji District loves the lengendary young hero who began fighting six years ago, when he didn't even have a beard. "In Jaji," Bahram Jan concludes, "we don't worry about one party or the other. We love good commanders like Syed Ishaq or Naim, whatever party they are from."

In the midst of this strange visual spectacle of destruction hidden in the night, in the midst of the cacaphony of battle which violates the senses, a single white star falls quietly from the black satin sky, and I make a wish for peace.

After the battle of Ali Khel, we rise hours before dawn and march into the black and frigid night. We must be well into the hills before dawn, Mustafa tells me, out of the line of mortar fire from the post. It is hard to walk over this rough, frozen ground in the darkness, lit only by a thin crescent moon. I stumble with exhaustion, emotional overwhelm, and fear as I listen to the unabated sound of gunfire not far behind us.

But at dawn the gunfire pauses. The Mujahedeen lay down their blankets and face towards Mecca, and I sense that many of the soldiers in the fort are doing the same. On a day that one might die, it only makes sense to reaffirm belief in Deity.

Not long after dawn, when we are making our way up the narrow valley towards the ridges that mark the border, the roar of the first jet violates the innocent blue sky and overwhelms the land beneath. Though it is high overhead, and its course lies above the main valley far below us, we instinctively scatter, each hiding under a scrawny pine tree, covering our heads and bodies with our *pattus.* The violent concussions of bombs echo through the earth-brown and snow white hills, and helicopters ride in sinister formation, shooting off rockets in bursts of yellow-orange flame.

Mustafa is closest to me. I want to ask him what will happen to Abdul Wahed's family, to my friend who is with child. But I do not speak, and his face remains grim and set, his poor arms helpless against the power of possession of the skies, and the thunder that does not stop.

And if I had a rocket launcher, I think, I too would use it now, to protect the children and the future. I too would blindly fling a technological implement of destruction against someone whom I will never know, but could kill from a distance.

I return to Pakistan, my psyche, my soul, changed and scarred. My body, unlike so many others', is healthy and intact. My heart, mind, and soul, like those of so many others in the more than forty countries which are now at war, is damaged, wounded. The only hope is to turn it into a sacred wound, and become a healer who works for peace.

Steve too, has returned safely, and I know we have a story. Only a few loose ends remain to be tied up.

Far from the snows of the Afghan border, in the sticky air of Pakistan's Punjab Province, Commander Mohammed Naim lies shivering in a hospital bed. The severely wounded young man, only twenty-two, sweats and trembles with his body's effort to fight off the violation done to it when an artillery shell ripped off his left leg and broke his right leg and left arm.

Naim's voice is weak and halting as he tells me the story of the night he was wounded. I want to reach out to him, to comfort him, but I know that he would be deeply shocked at the touch of a woman not his sister, mother, or wife, so I restrain myself and touch him only with compassion.

Naim's elder brother watches protectively, and whenever the young commander's voice grows weak, supplies the narrative to the story he has heard so many times in the last days.

"I did not even have a beard when I started fighting," says Naim ruefully. He makes a visible effort to speak clearly, and halts often. He is a good-looking man, his features straight and strong, but now one side of his face is wounded, battered, part of a nostril gone. He and five other men were carried on a Mujahedeen ambulance—on horseback, all the way to the hospital in Parachinar. "By the grace of God, I had no pain at all during the journey. God made it easy for me, because I was wounded in his service."

I tell Naim that everyone in Jaji, from every party, admires what he has done. His dark, frank eyes meet mine. It is perhaps one of the few times he has looked at a woman directly. "Everything I have done, I have done for our faith."

The faith of this young warrior echoes the faith of another warrior I have met, Mother Teresa of Calcutta, the relentless warrior against poverty. I reflect on the certainty of these two, and wonder if they would understand each other and allow the differences of dogma to be submerged in a sea of faith.

After I visit Commander Naim in Lahore, I go to see his family in a camp in Kohat. Naim's father, Khan Mohammed, rushes in from the camp school where he teaches, overjoyed to have news of his son. He puts on his narrow spectacles and eagerly reads the letter from his elder son, then folds it neatly and thanks me. "If you had not come I would have asked leave from my job to go to Lahore to see Naim. Now I am less worried."

We listen to a cassette of my interview with Naim, while more and more men and children gather in the narrow, oblong room. Naim's grandmother brings in a pot of green tea and a bowl of walnuts. When it is time to go, Khan Mohammed presses a sack of walnuts on me. "These are from our own trees, in the homeland. My sons picked as many as they could this year. When we taste these, we remember our home."

At another camp not too far away, the survivors of Ali Sangi are not all so lucky. Against the counterpoint of a nearby wedding, where women chant and bang handdrums in a semblance of joy and normalcy, a middle-aged widow named Hazrat Bibi sobs out her story. She is probably in her forties, but her face is thin and worn with the grief of her husband's recent death in a bombing, and the trauma of her journey with six children into exile.

As the men of the village gather, her sobs lessen, and she turns away towards the wall, hiding her face, but always watching me. Akbar Khan, a middle-aged man who used to be a farmer, speaks for the village. "We came here about a month ago. Now there is not a single family living in Ali Sangi. Everything was destroyed, our clothes and possessions buried under the earth, our children buried under the earth.

"Our future is to keep fighting. Until the time when Islam triumphs, we will never give up, never. Until our chidren are grown, as long as our women are alive, we will not give up. The Communists are turning our country to dust, but the people of Afghanistan will never allow the Communists to stay, even after a hundred years."

The two Soviet POW's in this Mujahedeen training camp near the Afghan border are about the same age as most of the Mujahedeen, but they didn't know what they were fighting for when they were conscripted at nineteen. I don't at first recognize the two as Soviet defectors, as they are in Afghan dress, and their features are not so different from those of many Afghans. One has light skin, blue eyes, and a dark beard; the other has sandy brown hair, high cheek bones, and broader features. I can tell by their faces that they do not want this interview. They have been paraded before one too many journalists. They speak reasonable Farsi, but prefer to speak Russian through Commander Rahmatullah Khan, the Mujahedeen commander.

I turn on the tape recorder, as I don't quite trust the bombastic Commander's translation. I soon catch on that he summarizes whole paragraphs in a few words, and I remember just enough Russian from my college days to question his accuracy.

Garik Moradovich Dzamalbekov, the light-skinned, bearded man, is a Tajik from Doshambe in Soviet Tajikistan; Nikolai Vasilovich Balabonov is half-Kazakh, half-Russian, from Alma-Ata in Soviet Kazakhstan. Both men chain smoke, looking down during the interview, only looking up to cast an occasional resentful glance at me as they narrate how they were conscripted into the Red Army and sent to Afghanistan.

"We didn't know anything at all," says Garik. "When we arrived, they said we would fight Americans, Chinese, and Pakistanis," adds Nikolai.

The two met in Afghanistan, where they served as truck drivers, in late 1980. They soon become convinced of the immorality of the Soviet presence in Afghanistan, and began giving and selling weapons to the Mujahedeen. The two were caught and jailed, and were due to be shipped back to the Soviet Union to be court-martialed and probably executed. Desperate, they concocted a ruse of illness, knocked out their drunken guard, and escaped to the Mujahedeen.

Their future is bleak and uncertain. Their families don't know where they are, and their only hope is for asylum in some Western country. They are not like some of the soldiers who have actually converted to Islam and joined the Mujahedeen. In fact, Commander Rahmatullah makes fun of them, telling a story in Persian about another Soviet defector who has become a brave fighter for Islam. "He is a very smart man," he says, "and these men are stupid."

Everybody else laughs, but I can't bring myself to laugh at these hapless young men. We all eat an incongruous picnic lunch under the shade of willow trees by a clear stream. When the commander leaves to lead the men through training exercises for Steve McCurry's camera, we are left alone, and the two relax and speak to me in Persian.

Their hostility melts away, and we are no longer journalist and defectors but three human beings talking about our lives and hopes. "I can't say what is in my heart in Persian," says Garik, "Because all my studies were in Russian and I'm used to speaking Russian." But the three of us range over many subjects, from the American election, about which they know a great deal (and in fact disagree with my choice), to Sufism.

They ask me about life in America, and I ask them what it was like growing up in the Soviet Union. They are impressed that I visited their country three times, and have even been to Alma-Ata. "We were happy as children," says Garik, "but then we grew up." We decide between us that it is not the ordinary people of nations who are to blame for wars, but their leaders.

I think deeply about war, Jehad, "holy war" as it is translated in the West. Various friends have told me its real meaning is "the struggle for the right"; the Ismailis interpret it as the constant struggle against the darkness in the self. But some times it must truly be war against others.

While watching the Mujahedeen pray after a hard day of guerrilla training at a camp in the Tribal Areas, I ask Ishaq, "Why is your party's flag black?"

He glances first at the uneven row of men, from teen-age boys to greybeards, who are prostrated in prayer. Then he turns back to me and says, "When the Prophet and his companions used to go to Jehad, they carried black flags, because war is not a good thing, but something forced on good Muslims from time to time. Our flag is black because when we go to Jehad today, it is not because we love to fight, but because we are compelled to fight a war for the sake of Islam and for the freedom of Afghanistan, until our country is free and we can again live in peace."

29 Epilogue—Not-Ending

Los Angeles
December, 1992

In real life, stories have no ending. Follow a happy ending, and it will sink into despair, become mired in everyday mundanity, or suddenly take a tragic turn. And likewise, the sequel to a tragedy is often the triumph of the human spirit, a dazzling leap of faith from turmoil to inner peace.

It is now thirteen years since the Christmas-time invasion of Afghanistan by about 100,000 Soviet troops. In the dark years in which the travels recounted in this book took place, few "foreign experts" believed that the Soviets would ever leave Afghanistan. The Afghans, however, despite moments of despair and wracking grief, never really doubted that their struggle would succeed in the end.

My own dream, to tell a slice of the story of Afghanistan in a way that would deeply touch people and move them to action, came true in June, 1985, when Steve McCurry's photos and my story became the cover story of *National Geographic.* At the time, there were fourteen million subscribers, and millions more in additional readership. Many people called and wrote the magazine, asking how they could help the refugees and the Afghan civilians inside Afghanistan.

A few years later, the U.S. government finally gave the Mujahedeen the Stinger missiles they had asked for. The Soviets promptly started losing helicopters and aircraft, and the war became more costly. Meanwhile, Mr. Gorbachev had come to power and had begun to institute *Glasnost* and *Perestroika*. The Geneva peace talks dragged on, as the Vietnam peace talks had, and many more people died, many more were wounded, and more villages were destroyed. The Mujahedeen never were represented in the talks, but the Soviet Union, the U.S., Pakistan, and Iran apparently agreed that it was time to defuse this war. Unfortunately, the Soviets left the Kabul government well-armed when they withdrew in February, 1989, so the war became a civil war, with the Americans and their allies continuing to arm the Mujahedeen. Finally, in the spring of 1992, the Mujahedeen recaptured Kabul, with the cooperation of the militia of the former government, which had more or less disavowed communism. Elections are scheduled for mid-1994.

Though the Soviets are gone, their empire vanished, Afghanistan does not yet know true peace or democracy. The situation changes daily, but it is an astounding miracle just that an interim government headed by the Mujahedeen now sits in Kabul. Upon its establishment, the new government was threatened by fundamentalists from Gulbuddin Hekmatyar's Hisbi Islami party. As I write, a fragile truce, occasionally broken by bloody rocket attacks, has now descended upon the land, and people are cautiously hoping they can rebuild their lives, though over a million landmines must be removed to make the land tillable, and most of the country's infrastructure must be rebuilt.

Many of my friends and acquaintances are playing important parts in the embryonic post-war reconstruction. Syed Ishaq Gailani has returned to his beloved Kabul and now plays a key role in food distribution, a skill he had learned in the last years of the war. His wife Fatana has become an international spokesperson for women and children refugees, after spending two years administrating a clinic in Peshawar. During the last chaotic years of the war, this work became very dangerous, as fundamentalists threatened, attacked, and even "disappeared" Afghan women who were working for their people. Ishaq took Fatana and their daughter Wana to safety in Switzerlarld, which became Fatana's base for her international work. The International Rescue Committee's Women's Commission for Refugee Women and Children invited her to visit the U.S., where she gave interviews and spoke to members of Congress about the specific needs of women and children. Now she and Wana, who at age fifteen speaks seven languages, are preparing to return to Pakistan, and eventually to Afghanistan.

Throughout the world, many people who for many years have not dared to hope are entering 1993 with hope reborn. I fervently want to believe that Afghanistan's movement towards peace and democracy is part of a worldwide paradigm shift, away from the old ways of thinking that led to war, destructive economic competition, and environmental degradation. I believe that, despite bitter nationalist conflicts, there is an overall shift towards an attitude of cooperation in staving off military conflict in favor of jointly fighting hunger, overpopulation, and the ecological disasters that stalk our whole planet like hungry wolves waiting for the fires of consciousness to die down.

Humanity's greatest hope is in the rebirth of spirit. The great Russian Soul, so long under domination, may yet meet a renewed American Spirit, and together work with the ancient religions and spiritual systems of India, China, the Middle East, Africa, Australia, Latin America, and Europe.

The 90's must be the decade of Healing the Planet. We really have no other choice, for we are a global community–what we do affects our neighbors at every point of our imperfect sphere.

Personally, I am far richer for the cultures, customs, and, most of all, the people I have known. I've come to know a whole group of what I call "Bridge People." These are people who have either been born in the West and have learned many of the ways of the East, or who were born in the East and came to the West for their education. Many of us are at home both in the East and in the West, and yet in neither place. We travel by intercontinental jet, and arrive disoriented and culture shocked on both ends. Interestingly, it is going home, in whatever direction, that is the most disorienting.

It was my friend and teacher, architect Nader Khalili, who first used the bridge image. He wrote of feeling pulled in tension between his native Persian, Muslim culture, and the Western culture with its differing values. Yet he was a bridge between the two.

I resonated with his words. Yes, I thought, nearly everyone in this book, in this first five years of my travels and in the years beyond which have taken me to Tibet, Nepal, and China, is a Bridge Person. Sometimes we are stretched beyond our limits–we reach to understand and to help others understand, and we feel trampled upon, our feet slipping from the earth behind us, our clutching fingers unable to quite grasp the firm rocks on the other side, and a great chasm below with a violent river that threatens to sweep us away. At other times, the reach is comfortable. We write books, we give lectures, we simply live our lives in a healing way, enriching our social lives with the spices of many different cultures, languages, and customs.

Ultimately, this is a very human story. Some of my Bridge friends have passed beyond this Earth, and if you've come to care about them by reading this book, you will want to know what happened to them.

The poet *Ustad* Khalilullah Khalili never saw the freedom of his country, never smelled the sweet orange blossoms of Jalalabad or the lilacs of Kabul again. He died in exile in Pakistan in 1988. But I believe that where he is now, since there is no time, he knows that Afghanistan is already free and at peace.

The vibrant flute-player Azim Zarbakhsh died in Afghanistan in 1988. For a couple of years he had worked for the Red Cross in Peshawar, but something made him go back to war, and he never returned. Strangely, in all these years, he is my only personal friend who was martyred. All of my Mujahedeen escorts were still alive and well as of the last time I asked Ishaq.

Anthropologist Louis Dupree, a good friend and a longtime expert on and lover of Afghanistan, died of cancer in 1989. His timing was impeccable—he passed away just at the time of the Afghan New Year. His wife Nancy Dupree, a brilliant woman and an Afghan expert in her own right, is continuing their unfinished work.

Our dear friend Kamillah Mansury, she of the irrepressible energy, died of cancer at age twenty-six in Hong Kong in 1985. Our lives were made brighter by the time we knew her, and many Afghans in Peshawar mourned her and prayed for her soul.

A large part of the living history of Hunza disappeared with the passing of the venerable elder Haji Qudratullah Beg a few years ago. His sons and daughters carry his memory with honor, but live lives their father could only begin to comprehend.

Marie-Claude Bonnet, my traveling companion in Ladakh, disappeared on a small boat in the Philippines on December 27th, 1986, on her way to one of the paradisiacal islands she loved so much, the kind with palm-fringed beaches, lots of sun, and no electricity or phones. She was a world traveller who lived a rich, exciting life and brought joy and humor to all whom she touched; now her spirit journeys in other realms.

Another friend disappeared without a trace when a small plane was lost on the way from Gilgit to Islamabad. The tragedy was covered in the L.A. newspapers because a young woman from the area was on the missing plane. I wrote to Ghulam Mohammed Beg the next day. A letter from him arrived the day after, saying he was on his way to China. But about three weeks later, a letter arrived from his son, Inam, saying that indeed his beloved father was on the missing plane.

Probably the most ironic loss was the death of my friend Hugh Swift, one of the "Himalayan nuts" who had circumambulated the sacred Mt. Kailash three times and had led trekkers some 25 times around Annapurna. Hugh had faced many dangers since his first trip across Asia in 1967. When most young Americans and Europeans were traveling from West to East, he began in Vietnam, where the young conscientious objector taught English, and headed East to Europe. The ever-eccentric Hugh left his body after an accidental fall on a street in Oakland in February, 1991, leaving the rest of us to ponder the ancient and unanswerable questions about life, death, and karma, and to taste the sweet and bitter intensities of our own lives.

I hike into the canyon behind my family's house. The perennial stream in Fryman Canyon has survived years of drought, always carrying enough water for the racoons, rabbits, bobcats, possums, deer, squirrels, owls, hawks, and insects of this lovely urban wildlife sanctuary.

This fragile stream, the well of life for countless animals, birds, and insects, and the well of the soul for hikers who come here seeking solace and healing, is part of the great cycle of life of the planet, of the elements. I run my fingers through the smooth water, and follow it on its journey. Even though it goes underground, this water eventually flows to the sea, and my mind can go with it, and on across the wide Pacific, to the shores of the Orient, of India, to the deltas where the great rivers of Asia meet the Mother Sea. I can journey up the great rivers, all the way up the Indus through the mountains of Pakistan, Baltistan, Ladakh, and into Tibet to the sacred mountain of Kailash. Or anywhere I can choose to branch aside to a tributary, into the high glacial valleys of Hunza, or up the rivers into Kabul, or into the fertile Kunar Valley, and from there, the boulder-strewn mountain streams of the Kalash Valleys, right to the river that runs by the house of Saifullah and my bloodsister Washlim Gul.

I can be with any of my loved ones at any moment. If I touch this earth, covered with oak leaves, I can smell the hollyoak of the Rumbur Valley in December, and I can likewise follow the Earth element across the planet, knowing it is the same earth in infinite variation. The Air too, as thick, heavy, and poisoned as it often is, I can follow on the winds to the high plateaus of Tibet and Afghanistan, to the narrow valleys of the Hindu Kush, to the lush forests of Kashmir and the tropics of India.

But it is the Fire which is the clearest beacon, and the hardest to reach. Nader Khalili has taught me to honor and work with fire, to harden small pots and human-scale domes into ceramic chambers, empty and waiting to be filled. My healing teacher, Rosalyn Bruyere, has taught me to honor the sacred fire of life within us, the power of healing and regeneration. The fire of the sun, and the sparkling, tantalizing fires of the stars, are far beyond our reach right now, but their light is a symbol. While the sun shines on me, and the moon on my beloved friends on the other side of the world, I know that the same sun will rise for them in a few hours, and I will soon see the same phase of the moon they have seen.

The Teaching of the Elements is that each element connects us all, all elements connect us. It is one of the things the five billion souls on the planet now have in common. I love our differences, as long as we don't start thinking there is only one right way to worship, one right way to live, be, or speak. It is time to stop seeing the differences first, to look beyond to what unites us, and delight in the fascination of the rainbow facets of diversity. Freedom of religion, I've heard Rosalyn say, is the right to worship "how we want, when we want, with whom we want." It means a Christmas service with a minorah, the sound of "Om," and a Native American drum; and maybe going home to pray the Muslim prayers at dawn, followed by some Buddhist meditation and a Bon-po chant.

If, after much travel, I have attained a little ripeness, it is because of my many companions upon this endless road, those who nurtured me and taught me with love, and the "good enemies" who taught me by mistake. I am grateful for the lessons, and I ask only to share the experiences, the knowledge, and the light of wisdom that has been imparted to me by my beloved friends and teachers.

These stories have no endings—even death does not end them. I have dreamed of Ghulam Mohammed, sitting in his bookshop, laughing, sipping tea, wearing his trademark Jinnah cap. Hugh has walked a step ahead of me on a wind-chilled Himalayan pass, encouraging me with his brotherly strength. And I have seen Marie-Claude, wrapped in a green-flowered *lungi,* standing by the palm-trees, looking out thoughtfully over the tropical waters. And Kamillah in her winter-wool *chador,* playing with children at a wedding in the tents, while Azim plays his wooden flute for the dance of spirits.

They live in my memories, and in those of all who have known them. And now in yours.